Frances P. Cobbe

Darwinism in Morals and Other Essays

Frances P. Cobbe

Darwinism in Morals and Other Essays

ISBN/EAN: 9783337250423

Printed in Europe, USA, Canada, Australia, Japan

Cover: Foto ©Lupo / pixelio.de

More available books at **www.hansebooks.com**

DARWINISM IN MORALS.

MISS FRANCES POWER COBBE'S WORKS.

1. RELIGIOUS DUTY. 8vo. Cloth. Published at 7s. 6d.   5s.

2. BROKEN LIGHTS. An Inquiry into the Present Condition and Future Prospects of Religious Faith. New Edition. 8vo. Cloth.   5s.

3. DAWNING LIGHTS. An Inquiry concerning the Secular Results of the New Reformation. 8vo. Cloth.   5s.

4. THANKSGIVING. A Chapter of Religious Duty. 12mo. Cloth.   1s.
   Twelve copies for 6s.

5. ALONE TO THE ALONE. Prayers for Theists, by several Contributors. Crown 8vo. Cloth, gilt edges. 5s.

6. STUDIES, NEW AND OLD, OF ETHICAL AND SOCIAL SUBJECTS. 8vo. Cloth. Published at 10s. 6d.   5s.

7. ITALICS. Brief Notes on Politics, People, and Places in Italy in 1864. 8vo. Cloth. Published at 12s. 6d.   5s.

8. HOURS OF WORK AND PLAY. 8vo. Cloth.   5s.

May be had from her present Publishers,

WILLIAMS AND NORGATE,
14, HENRIETTA STREET, COVENT GARDEN, LONDON;
AND 20, SOUTH FREDERICK STREET, EDINBURGH.

DARWINISM IN MORALS,

AND OTHER ESSAYS.

Reprinted from the THEOLOGICAL and FORTNIGHTLY REVIEWS, FRASER'S and MACMILLAN'S MAGAZINES, and the MANCHESTER FRIEND.)

BY

FRANCES POWER COBBE.

WILLIAMS AND NORGATE,
14, HENRIETTA STREET, COVENT GARDEN, LONDON;
AND 20, SOUTH FREDERICK STREET, EDINBURGH.
1872.

HERTFORD:
PRINTED BY STEPHEN AUSTIN AND SONS.

CONTENTS.

ESSAY		PAGE
1.	DARWINISM IN MORALS. (*Theological Review*, April, 1871.)	1
2.	HEREDITARY PIETY. (*Theological Review*, April, 1870.) ...	35
3.	THE RELIGION OF CHILDHOOD. (*Theological Review*, July, 1866.)	65
4.	AN ENGLISH BROAD CHURCHMAN. (*Theological Review*, January, 1866.)	95
5.	A FRENCH THEIST. (*Theological Review*, May, 1865.) ...	129
6.	THE DEVIL. (*Fortnightly Review*, August, 1871.)	147
7.	A PRE-HISTORIC RELIGION. (*Fraser's Magazine*, April, 1869.)	175
8.	THE RELIGIONS OF THE WORLD. (*Fraser's Magazine*, June, 1868.)	203
9.	THE RELIGIONS OF THE EAST. (*Fraser's Magazine*, February, 1868.)	235
10.	THE RELIGION AND LITERATURE OF INDIA. (*Fraser's Magazine*, March, 1870.)	269
11.	UNCONSCIOUS CEREBRATION. (*Macmillan's Magazine*, November, 1870.)	305
12.	DREAMS, AS ILLUSTRATIONS OF INVOLUNTARY CEREBRATION. (*Macmillan's Magazine*, April, 1871.)	335
13.	AURICULAR CONFESSION IN THE CHURCH OF ENGLAND. (*Theological Review*, January, 1872.)	363
14.	THE EVOLUTION OF MORALS AND RELIGION. (*Manchester Friend*, January 15, 1872.)	391

DARWINISM IN MORALS,

AND OTHER ESSAYS.

ESSAY I.

DARWINISM IN MORALS.[1]

It is a singular fact that whenever we find out how anything is done, our first conclusion seems to be that God did not do it. No matter how wonderful, how beautiful, how infinitely complex and delicate, has been the machinery which has worked, perhaps for centuries, perhaps for millions of ages, to bring about some beneficent result—if we can but catch a glimpse of the wheels, its divine character disappears. The machinery did it all. It would be altogether superfluous to look further.

The olive has been commonly called the Phœnix of trees, because when it is cut down it springs to life again. The notion that God is only discernible in the miraculous and the inexplicable, may likewise be called the Phœnix of ideas; for again and again it has been exploded, and yet it re-appears with the utmost regularity whenever a new step is made in the march of Science. The explanation of each phenomenon is still first angrily disputed and then mournfully accepted by the majority of pious people, just

[1] *The Descent of Man.* By Charles Darwin, M.A., F.R.S. Two vols. 8vo. London: Murray. 1871.

as if finding out the ways of God were not necessarily bringing ourselves nearer to the knowledge of Him, and the highest bound of the human intellect were not to be able to say, like Kepler, "O God, I think Thy thoughts after Thee."

That the doctrine of the descent of man from the lower animals, of which Mr. Darwin has been the great teacher, should be looked on as well nigh impious by men not mentally chained to the Hebrew cosmogony, has always appeared to me surprising. Of course, in so far as it disturbs the roots of the old theology and dispels the golden haze which hung in poetic fancy over the morning garden of the world, it may prove a rude and painful innovation. A Calvin, a Milton, and a Fra Angelico, may be excused if they recalcitrate against it. [Doubtless, also, the special Semitic contempt for the brutes which has unhappily passed with our religion into so many of our graver views, adds its quota to the common sentiment of repugnance; and we stupidly imagine that to trace Man to the Ape is to degrade the progeny, and not (as a Chinese would justly hold) to ennoble the ancestry. But that, beyond all these prejudices, there should lurk in any free mind a dislike to Darwinism on *religious* grounds, is wholly beyond comprehension. Surely, were any one to come to us now in these days for the first time with the story that the eternal God produced all His greatest works by fits and starts; that just 6000 years ago He suddenly brought out of nothing the sun, moon, and stars; and finally as the climax of six days of such labour, "made man of the dust of the ground," we should be inclined to say that *this* was the derogatory and insufferable doctrine of creation; and that when we compared it with that of the slow evolution of order, beauty, life, joy, and intelligence, from the immeasurable past of the primal nebula's "fiery cloud," we had no language to express how infinitely more religious is the story of modern science than·that of ancient tradition?

Nor are we alarmed or disturbed because the same hand which has opened for us these grand vistas of physical development has now touched the phenomena of the moral world, and sought to apply the same method of investigation to its most sacred mysteries. The only question we can ask is, whether the method has been as successful in the one case as (we learn from competent judges) it may be accounted in the other, and whether the proffered explanation of moral facts really suffices to explain them. Should it prove so successful and sufficient, we can but accept it, even as we welcomed the discovery of the physical laws of evolution as a step towards a more just conception than we had hitherto possessed of the order of things; and *therefore*—if God be their Orderer—a step towards a better knowledge of Him.

The book before us is doubtless one whose issue will make an era in the history of modern thought. Of its wealth of classified anecdotes of animal peculiarities and instincts, and its wide sweep of cumulative argument in favour of the author's various deductions, it would be almost useless to speak, seeing that before these pages are printed the reading public of England will have spent many happy hours over these "fairy tales of science." Of the inexpressible charm of the author's manner, the straightforwardness of every argument he employs, and the simplicity of every sketch and recital, it is still less needful to write, when years have elapsed since Mr. Darwin took his place in the literature of England and the philosophy of the world. Very soon that delightful pen will have made familiar to thousands the pictures of which the book is a gallery. Every one will know that our first human parents, far from resembling Milton's glorious couple, were hideous beings covered with hair, with pointed and movable ears, beards, tusks, and tails,—the very Devils of mediæval fancy. And behind these we shall dimly behold yet earlier and lower ancestors, receding through the ages till we reach a period before even the vertebrate rank was attained, and when the creature whose descendants were to be heroes and sages swam about in the waters in likeness between an eel and a worm. At every dinner-table will be told the story of the brave ape which came down amid its dreaded human foes to redeem a young one of its species; and of the sagacious baboon which, Bismarck-like, finding itself scratched by a cat, deliberately bit off its enemy's claws. Satirists will note the description of the seals which, in wooing, bow to the females and coax them gently till they get them fairly landed; then, "with a changed manner and a harsh growl," drive the poor wedded creatures home to their holes. The suggestion that animals love beauty of colour and of song, and even (in the case of the bower-bird) build halls of pleasure distinct from their nests for purposes of amusement only, will be commented on, and afford suggestive talk wherever books of such a class are read in England. Few students, we think, will pass over without respectful pause the passage[1] where Mr. Darwin with so much candour explains that he "now admits that in the earlier editions of his Origin of Species he probably attributed too much to the action of natural selection," nor that[2] where he calls attention to Sir J. Lubbock's "most just remark," that "Mr. Wallace, with characteristic unselfishness, ascribes the idea of natural selection unreservedly to Mr. Darwin, although, as is well known, he struck out the idea independently, and published it, though not with the same elaboration, at the same time." Whatever doubt any reader may entertain of the philosophy of Evolution, it is quite

[1] Vol. i., page 152. [2] Page 137, *note*.

impossible that, after perusing such pages, he can have any hesitation about the philosophic spirit of its author.

But we must turn from these topics, which properly concern the journals of physical science, to the one whose treatment by Mr. Darwin gives to a Theological Review the right to criticize the present volume. Mr. Darwin's theories have hitherto chiefly invaded the precincts of traditional Theology. We have now to regard him as crowning the edifice of Utilitarian ethics by certain doctrines respecting the nature and origin of the Moral Sense, which, if permanently allowed to rest upon it, will, we fear, go far to crush the idea of Duty level with the least hallowed of natural instincts. It is needless to say that Mr. Darwin puts forth his views on this, as on all other topics, with perfect moderation and simplicity, and that the reader of his book has no difficulty whatever in comprehending the full bearing of the facts he cites and the conclusions he draws from them.

In the present volume he has followed out to their results certain hints given in his "Origin of Species" and "Animals under Domestication," and has, as it seems, given Mr. Herbert Spencer's abstract view of the origin of the moral sense its concrete application. Mr. Spencer broached the doctrine that our moral sense is nothing but the "experiences of utility organized and consolidated through all past generations." Mr. Darwin has afforded a sketch of how such experiences of utility, beginning in the ape, might (as he thinks) consolidate into the virtue of a saint; and adds some important and quite harmonious remarks, tending to show that the Virtue so learned is somewhat accidental, and might perhaps have been what we now call Vice. To mark his position fairly, it will be necessary to glance at the recent history of ethical philosophy.

Independent or Intuitive Morality has of course always taught that there is a supreme and necessary moral law common to all free agents in the universe, and known to man by means of a transcendental reason or divine voice of conscience. Dependent or Utilitarian Morality has equally steadily rejected the idea of a law other than the law of utility; but its teachers have differed exceedingly amongst themselves as to the existence or non-existence of a specific sense in man, requiring him to perform actions whose utility constitutes them duties; and among those who have admitted that such a sense exists, there still appear wide variations in the explanations they offer of the nature and origin of such a sense. The older English Utilitarians, such as Mandeville, Hobbes, Paley and Waterland, denied vigorously that man had any spring of action but self-interest. Hume, Hartley, and Bentham advanced a step further; Hartley thinking it just possible to love virtue "as a form of happiness," and Bentham being kind enough elaborately to explain that we may truly sympathize with the woes of our friends. Finally, when the coldest of philosophies passed into one of the loftiest of minds and warmest of hearts, Utilitarianism in the school of Mr. Mill underwent a sort of divine travesty. Starting from the principle that "actions are only virtuous because they promote another end than virtue," he attained the conclusion, that sooner than flatter a cruel Almighty Being he would go to hell. As Mr. Mill thinks such a decision morally right, he would of course desire that all men should follow his example; and thus we should behold the apostle of Utility conducting the whole human race to eternal perdition for the sake of—shall we say—" the Greatest Happiness of the Greatest Number"?

At this stage, the motive-power on which Utilitarianism must rely for the support of virtue is obviously complex, if not rather unstable. So long as the old teachers appealed simply to the interest of the individual, here or hereafter, the argument was clear enough, however absurd a misuse of language it seems to make Virtue and Vice the names respectively of a systematized and an unsystematized rule of selfishness. But when we begin to speak of the happiness of *others* as our aim, we necessarily shift our ground, and appeal to sympathy, to social instincts, or to the disinterested pleasures of benevolence, till finally, when we are bid to relinquish self altogether in behalf of the Greatest Happiness of the Greatest Number, we have left the Utilitarian ground so far away, that we find ourselves on the proper territories of the Intuitionist, and he turns round with the question, " Why should I sacrifice myself for the happiness of mankind, if I have no intuitions of duty compelling me to do so ? " The result has practically been, that the Social Instincts to which Utilitarians in such straits were forced to appeal, as the springs of action in lieu of the Intuitions of duty, have been gradually raised by them to the rank of a distinct element of our nature, to be treated now (as self-interest was treated by their predecessors) as the admitted motives of virtue. They agree with Intuitionists that man has a Conscience; they only differ from them on the two points of how he comes by it; and whether its office be supreme and legislative, or merely subsidiary and supplemental.

[It is the problem of, How we come by a conscience, which Mr. Darwin applies himself to solve, and with which we shall be now concerned.] Needless to say that the Kantian doctrine of a Pure Reason, giving us transcendental knowledge of necessary truths, is not entertained by the school of thinkers to which he belongs; and that as for the notion of all the old teachers of the world, that the voice of Conscience is the voice of God,—the doctrine of Job and Zoroaster, Menu and Pythagoras, Plato and Antoninus, Chrysostom and Gregory, Fénélon and Jeremy Taylor,—it can have no place in their science. As Comte would say, we have passed the theologic stage, and must not think of running to a First Cause to explain phenomena. After all (they seem to say), cannot we easily suggest how man might acquire a conscience from causes obviously at work around him? (Education, fear of penalties, sympathy, desire of approval, with imaginary religious sanctions, would altogether, well mixed and supporting one another, afford sufficient explanation of feelings, acquired, as Mr. Bain thinks, by each individual in his lifetime, and, as Mr. Mill justly says, not the less natural for being acquired and not innate.

[At this point of the history, the gradual extension of the Darwinian theory of Evolution brought it into contact with the speculations of moralists, and the result was a new hypothesis, which has greatly altered the character of the whole controversy. The doctrine of the transmission by hereditary descent of all mental and moral qualities, of which Mr. Galton's book is the chief exponent,[1] received, in 1868, from Mr. Herbert Spencer the following definition, as applied to the moral sentiments :[2] "I believe that the experiences of utility, organized and consolidated through all past generations of the human race, have been producing corresponding modifications, which by continued transmission and accumulation have become in us certain faculties

---

[1] Reviewed in the next essay.

[2] Letter to Mr. Mill, in Bain's "Mental and Moral Science," p. 722 ; quoted in "Descent of Man," p. 101. On the day of the original publication of this essay there appeared in the *Fortnightly Review* an article by Mr. Spencer, designed to rectify the misapprehension of his doctrine into which Mr. Hutton, Sir John Lubbock, Mr. Mivart, Sir Alexander Grant, and, as it proved, my humble self, had all fallen regarding the point in question. "If," says Mr. Spencer very pertinently, "a general doctrine concerning a highly involved class of phenomena could be adequately presented in a single paragraph of a letter, the writing of books would be superfluous." I may add that as it would be equally impossible for me adequately to present Mr. Spencer's rectifications and modifications in a single paragraph of an essay, I must, while apologizing to him for my involuntary errors, refer the reader to his own article (*Fortnightly Review*, April 1, 1871) for better comprehension of the subject.

of moral intuition, certain emotions responding to right and wrong conduct, which have no apparent basis in the individual experiences of utility." This doctrine (which received a very remarkable answer in an article by Mr. R. H. Hutton, *Macmillan's Magazine*, July, 1869) may be considered as the basis on which Mr. Darwin proceeds, approaching the subject, as he modestly says, "exclusively from the side of natural history," and "attempting to see how far the study of the lower animals can throw light on one of the highest psychical faculties of man." His results, as fairly as I can state them, are as follows :

If we assume an animal to possess social instincts (such, I suppose, as those of rooks, for example), and also to acquire some degree of intelligence corresponding to that of man, it would inevitably acquire contemporaneously a moral sense of a certain kind. In the first place, its social instincts would cause it to take pleasure in the society of its fellows, to feel a certain amount of sympathy with them, and to perform various services for them. After this, the next step in mental advance would cause certain phenomena of regretful sentiments (hereafter to be more fully analyzed) to ensue on the commission of anti-social acts, which obey a transient impulse at the cost of a permanent social instinct. Thirdly, the approval expressed by the members of the community for acts tending to the general welfare, and disapproval for those of a contrary nature, would greatly strengthen and guide the original instincts as Language came into full play. Lastly, habit in each individual would gradually perform an important part in the regulation of conduct. If these positions be all granted, the problem of the origin of the moral sense seems to be solved. It is found to be an instinct in favour of the social virtues which has grown up in mankind, and would have grown up in any animal similarly endowed and situated ; and it does not involve any higher agency for its production than that of the play of common human life, nor indicate any higher nature for its seat than the further developed intelligence of any gregarious brute. So far, Mr. Darwin's view seems only to give to those he has quoted from Mr. Spencer their full expansion. The points on which he appears to break fresh ground from this starting-place are these two: 1st, his theory of the nature of conscientious Repentance, which represents it as solely the triumph of a permanent over a transient impulse ; 2nd, his frank admission, that though another animal, if it became intelligent, would acquire *a* moral sense, yet that he sees no reason why its moral sense should be the same as ours, or lead it to attach the idea of right or wrong to the same actions. In extreme cases (such as that of bees), the moral sense, developed under the conditions of the hive, would, he thinks, impress it as a duty on sisters to murder their brothers.

It must be admitted that these two doctrines between them effectively revolutionize Morals, as they have been hitherto commonly understood. The first dethrones the moral sense from that place of mysterious supremacy which Butler considered its grand characteristic. Mr. Darwin's Moral Sense is simply an instinct originated, like a dozen others, by the conditions under which we live, but which happens, in the struggle for existence among all our instincts, to resume the upper hand when no other chances to be in the ascendant. And the second theory aims a still more deadly blow at ethics, by affirming that, not only has our moral sense come to us from a source commanding no special respect, but that it answers to no external or durable, not to say universal or eternal, reality, and is merely tentative and provisional, the provincial prejudice, as we may describe it, of this little world and its temporary inhabitants, which would be looked on with a smile of derision by better-informed people now residing in Mars, or hereafter to be developed on earth, and who in their turn may be considered as walking in a vain shadow by other races. Instead of Montesquieu's grand aphorism, "La justice est un rapport de convenance qui se trouve réellement entre deux choses ; ce rapport est toujours le même quelque être qui le considère, soit que ce soit Dieu, soit que ce soit un homme," Mr. Darwin will leave us only the sad assurance that our idea of Justice is all our own, and may mean nothing to any other intelligent being in the universe. It is not even, as Dean Mansel has told us, given us by our Creator as a representative truth, intended at least to indicate some actual transcendent verity behind it. We have now neither Veil nor Revelation, but only an earth-born instinct, carrying with it no authority whatever beyond the limits of our race and special social state, nor within them further than we choose to permit it to weigh on our minds.

Let me say it at once. These doctrines appear to me simply the most dangerous which have ever been set forth since the days of Mandeville. Of course, if science can really show good cause for accepting them, their consequences must be frankly faced. But it is at least fitting to come to the examination of them, conscious that it is no ordinary problems we are criticizing, but theories whose validity must involve the *in*validity of all the sanctions which morality has hitherto received from powers beyond those of the penal laws. As a matter of practice, no doubt men act in nine cases out of ten with very small regard to their theories of ethics, even when they are thoughtful enough to have grasped any theory at all; and generations might elapse after the universal acceptance of these new views by philosophers, before they would sensibly influence the conduct of the masses of mankind. But however slowly they might work, I cannot but believe that in the hour of their triumph would be sounded the knell of the virtue of mankind. It has been hard enough for tempted men and women heretofore to be honest, true, unselfish, chaste, or sober, while passion was clamouring for gratification, or want pining for relief. The strength of the fulcrum on which has rested the virtue of many a martyr and saint, must have been vast as the Law of the Universe could make it. But where will that fulcrum be found hereafter, if men consciously recognize that what they have dreamed to be

> "The unwritten law divine,
> Immutable, eternal, not like those of yesterday,
> But made ere Time began,"[1] —

the law by which "the most ancient heavens are fresh and strong,"—is, in truth, after all, neither durable nor even general among intelligent beings, but simply consists of those rules of conduct which, among many that might have been adopted, have proved themselves on experiment to be most convenient; and which, in the lapse of ages, through hereditary transmission, legislation, education, and such methods, have got woven into the texture of our brains? What will be the power of such a law as this to enable it to contend for mastery in the soul with any passion capable of rousing the most languid impulse? Hitherto good men have looked on Repentance as the most sacred of all sentiments, and have measured the nearness of the soul to God by the depth of its sense of the shame and heinousness of sin. The boldest of criminals have betrayed at intervals their terror of the Erinnyes of Remorse, against whose scourges all religions have presented themselves as protectors, with their devices of expiations, sacrifices, penances, and atonements. From Orestes at the foot of the

[1] Sophoc. Antig. 454.

altar of Phœbus, to the Anglican in his new confessional to-day; from the Aztec eating the heart of the victim slain in propitiation for sin, to the Hindoo obeying the law of Menu, and voluntarily starving himself to death as an expiation of his offences, history bears testimony again and again to the power of this tremendous sentiment; and if it have driven mankind into numberless superstitions, it has, beyond a doubt, also served as a threat more effective against crime than all the penalties ever enacted by legislators. But where is Repentance to find place hereafter, if Mr. Darwin's view of its nature be received? Will any man allow himself to attend to the reproaches of Conscience, and bow his head to her rebukes, when he clearly understands that it is only his more durable Social Instinct which is re-asserting itself, because the more variable instinct which has caused him to disregard it is temporarily asleep? Such a Physiology of Repentance reduces its claims on our attention to the level of those of our bodily wants; and our grief for a past crime assumes the same aspect as our regret that we yesterday unadvisedly preferred the temporary enjoyment of conversation to the permanent benefit of a long night's rest, or the flavour of an indigestible dish to the wholesomeness of our habitual food. We may regret our *imprudence;* but it is quite impossible we should ever again feel penitence for a *sin.*

But is this all true? Can such a view of the moral nature of man be sustained? Mr. Darwin says that he has arrived at it by approaching the subject from the side of natural history; and we may therefore, without disrespect, accept it as the best which the study of man simply as a highly developed animal can afford. That glimmering of something resembling our moral sense often observable in brutes, which Mr. Darwin has admirably described, may (we will assume) be so accounted for. But viewing human nature from other sides besides that of its animal origin, studying the mind from within rather than from without, and taking into consideration the whole phenomenon presented by such a department of creation as the Human Race, must we not hold that this Simious Theory of Morals is wholly inadequate and unsatisfactory? Probably Mr. Darwin himself would say that he does not pretend to claim for it the power to explain exhaustively all the mysteries of our moral nature, but only to afford such a clue to them as ought to satisfy us that, if pursued further, they might be so revealed; and to render, by its obvious simplicity, other and more transcendent theories superfluous. The matter to be decided (and it is almost impossible, I think, to overrate its importance) is: *Does* it give such an explanation of the facts as to justify us in accepting it, provisionally, as an hypothesis of the origin of Morals?

It is hard to know how to approach properly the later developments of a doctrine like that of Utilitarian Morality, which we conceive to be founded on a radically false basis. If we begin at the beginning, and dispute its primary positions, we shift the controversy in hand to the interminable wastes of metaphysical discussion, where few readers will follow, and where the wanderer may truly say that *doubts*,

"immeasurably spread,
Seem lengthening as I go."

All the time which is wanted to argue the last link of the system, is lost in seeking some common ground to stand upon with our opponent, who probably will end by disputing the firmness of whatever islet of granite we have chosen in the bog; and will tell us that the greatest modern thinkers are doubtful whether twice two will make four in all worlds, or whether Space may not have more than three dimensions. Yet to grant the premisses of Utilitarian ethics, and then attempt to dispute one by one the chain of doctrines which has been unrolling from them during the last century, and which has now reached, as it would seem, its ultimate, and perhaps logical, development, is to place our arguments at an unfair disadvantage. To treat scientifically the theories of Mr. Darwin, we ought to commence by an inquiry into the validity of the human consciousness; into the respective value of our various faculties, the senses, the intellect, the moral, religious and æsthetic sentiments, as witnesses of external truths; and, finally, into the justice or fallacy of attaching belief exclusively to facts of which we have cognizance through one faculty—let us say the intellect; and denying those which we observe by another—say the æsthetic taste or the religious or moral sentiments. He who will concede that the intellect is not the organ through which we appreciate a song or a picture, and that it would be absurd to test songs and pictures by inductive reasoning and not by the specific sense of the beautiful, is obviously bound to show cause why, if—after making such admission in the case of our æsthetic faculties—he refuse to concede to the religious and moral faculties the same right to have their testimony admitted in their own domain.

Proceeding to our next step, if we are to do justice to our cause, we must dispute the Utilitarian's first assumption on his proper ground. We must question whether the Right and the Useful are really synonymous, and whether Self-interest and Virtue can be made convertible terms even by such stringent methods as those of extending the meaning of "Self-interest" to signify a devotion to the "Greatest Happiness of the Greatest Number" (always inclusive of Number One), and of curtailing that of Virtue to signify the fulfilment of Social, irrespective of Personal and Religious obligations. That the common sentiment of mankind looks to something different from Utility in the actions to which it pays the tribute of its highest reverence, and to something different from noxiousness in those which it most profoundly abhors, is a fact so obvious, that modern Utilitarians have recognized the impossibility of ignoring it after the manner of their predecessors; and Mr. Herbert Spencer has fully admitted that the ideas of the Right and the Useful are now entirely different, although they had once, he thinks, the same origin. But that the idea of the Right was ever potentially enwrapped or latent in the idea of the Useful, we entirely deny, seeing that it not only *overlaps* it altogether, and goes far beyond it in the direction of the Noble and the Holy, but that it is continually in direct antithesis to it; and acts of generosity and courage (such as Mr. Mill's resolution to go to hell rather than say an untruth) command from us admiration, not only apart from their utility, but *because* they set at defiance every principle of utility, and make us feel that to such men there are things dearer than eternal joy. As Mr. Mivart says well, the sentiment of all ages which has found expression in the cry, "Fiat Justitia ruat cœlum," could never have sprung from the same root as our sense of Utility.

Proceeding a step farther downwards to the point wherewith alone Mr. Darwin concerns himself—the origin of such moral sense as recent Utilitarians grant that we possess—we come again on a huge field of controversy. Are our intuitions of all kinds, those, for instance, regarding space, numbers and moral distinctions, ultimate data of our mental constitution, ideas obtained by the *à-priori* action of the normally developed mind; or are they merely, as Mr. Hutton has paraphrased Mr. Spencer's theory, "a special susceptibility in our nerves produced by a vast number of homogeneous ancestral experiences agglutinated into a single intellectual tendency"? Is our sense of the necessity and universality of a truth (*e.g.*, that the three sides of all triangles in the universe are equal to two right angles), and the unhesitating certainty with which we affirm such universality, over and above any possible experience of generality, —is this sense we say, the expression of pure Reason, or is it nothing but a blind incapacity for imagining as altered that which we have never seen or heard of as changed? Volumes deep and long as Kant's Kritik or Mr. Spencer's "Principles" are needed, if this question is to receive any justice at our hands. All that it is possible to do in passing onward to our remarks on Mr. Darwin's views, is to enter our protest against the admission of any such parentage either for mathematical or moral intuitions. No event in a man's mental development is, I think, more startling than his first clear apprehension of the nature of a geometrical demonstration, and of the immutable nature of the truth he has acquired, against which a thousand miracles would not avail to shake his faith. The hypothesis of the inheritance of space-intuitions through numberless ancestral experiments, leaves this marvellous sense of certainty absolutely inexplicable. And when we apply the same hypothesis of inheritance to moral intuitions, it appears to me to break down still more completely; supplying us at the utmost with a plausible theory for the explanation of our preference for some acts as more useful than others, but utterly failing to suggest a reason for that which is the real phenomenon to be accounted for, namely, our sense of the sacred obligation of Rightfulness, over and above or apart from Utility. Nay, what Mr. Mill calls the "mystical extension" of the idea of Utility into the idea of Right is not only left wholly unexplained, but the explanation offered points, not to any such mystical extension, but quite the other way. The waters of our moral life cannot possibly rise above their source; and if Utility be that source, they ought by this time to have settled into a dead pond of plain and acknowledged self-interestedness. As Mr. Hutton observes: "Mr. Spencer's theory appears to find the feeling of moral obligation at its maximum, when the perception of the quality which ultimately produces that feeling is at its minimum."

But we must now do Mr. Darwin the justice to let him speak for himself, and for the only part of the Utilitarian theory for which he has made himself directly responsible; though his whole argument is so obviously founded solely on an Utilitarian basis, that we are tempted to doubt whether a mind so large, so just and so candid, can have ever added to its treasures of physical science the thorough mastery of any of the great works in which the opposite system of ethics have been set forth.

Animals display affection, fidelity and sympathy. Man when he first rose above the Ape was probably of a social disposition, and lived in herds. Mr. Darwin adds that he would probably inherit a tendency to be faithful to his comrades, and have also some capacity for self-command, and a readiness to aid and defend his fellow-men.[1] These latter qualities, we must observe, do not agree very well with what Mr. Galton recently told us[2] of the result of his interesting studies of the cattle of South Africa, and at all events need that we should suppose the forefathers of our race to have united all the best moral as well as physical qualities of other animals. But assuming that so it may have been, Mr. Darwin says, Man's next motive, acquired by sympathy, would be the love of praise and horror of infamy. After this, as such feelings became clearer and reason advanced, he would "feel himself impelled, independently of any pleasure or pain felt at the moment, to certain lines of

---

[1] Page 85.   [2] *Macmillan's Magazine*, February, 1871.

conduct. He may then say: I am the supreme judge of my own conduct; and in the words of Kant, I will not in my own person violate the dignity of humanity."[1] That any savage or half-civilized man ever felt anything like this, or that the "dignity of humanity" could come in sight for endless generations of progress, conducted only in such ways as Mr. Darwin has suggested, nay, that it could ever occur at all to a creature who had not some higher conception of the nature of that Virtue in which man's only "dignity" consists, than Mr. Darwin has hinted,—is a matter, I venture to think, of gravest doubt.

But again passing onward, we reach the first of our author's special theories; his doctrine of the nature of Repentance. Earnestly I wish to do it justice; for upon it hinges our theory of the nature of the moral sense. As our bodily sense of feeling can best be studied when we touch hard objects or shrink from a burn or a blow, so our spiritual sense of feeling becomes most evident when it comes in contact with wrong, or recoils in the agony of remorse from a crime.

"Why"—it is Mr. Darwin who asks the question—"why should a man feel that he ought to obey one instinctive feeling rather than another? Why does he bitterly regret if he has yielded to the strong sense of self-preservation, and has not risked his life to save that of a fellow-creature?" The answer is, that in some cases the social or maternal instincts will always spur generous natures to unselfish deeds. But where such social instincts are less strong than the instincts of self-preservation, hunger, vengeance, etc., then these last are naturally paramount, and the question is pressed, "Why does man regret, even though he may endeavour to banish any such regret, that he has followed the one natural impulse rather than the other? and why

[1] Page 86.

does he further feel that he ought to regret his conduct?" Man in this respect differs, Mr. Darwin admits, profoundly from the lower animals, but he thinks he sees the reason of the difference. It is this: Man has reflection. From the activity of his mental qualities, he cannot help past impressions incessantly passing through his mind. The animals have no need to reflect; for those who have social instincts never quit the herd, and never fail to obey their kindly impulses. But man, though he has the same or stronger social impulses, has other, though more, temporary passions, such as hunger, vengeance, and the like, which obtain transient indulgence often at the expense of his kind. These, however, are all temporary in their nature. When hunger, vengeance, covetousness, or the desire for preservation, has been satisfied, such feelings not only fade, but it is impossible to recall their full vividness by an act of memory.

"Thus as man cannot prevent old impressions from passing through his mind, he will be compelled to compare the weaker impression of, for instance, past hunger, or of vengeance satisfied, with the instinct of sympathy and goodwill to his fellows which is still present, and ever in some degree active in his mind. He will then feel in his imagination that a stronger instinct has yielded to one which now seems comparatively weak, and then that sense of dissatisfaction will inevitably be felt with which man is endowed, like every other animal, in order that his instincts may be obeyed."[1]

Leaving out for the present the last singular clause of this paragraph, which appears to point to a Cause altogether outside of the range of phenomena we are considering,—a Cause which, if it (or HE?) exist at all, may well "endow" human hearts more directly than through such dim animal instincts as are in question,—leaving out of view this hint of a Creator, we ask: Is this physiology of Repentance true to fact? It would be hard, I venture to think, to describe one more at variance with it. The reader might be excused

[1] Page 90.

who should figure to himself the author as a man who has never in his lifetime had cause seriously to regret a single unkindly or ignoble deed, and who has unconsciously attributed his own abnormally generous and placable nature to the rest of his species, and then theorized as if the world were made of Darwins. Where (we ask in bewilderment), where are the people to be found in whom "sympathy and goodwill" to all their neighbours exist in the state of permanent instincts, and whose resentful feelings, as a matter of course, die out after every little temporary exhibition, and leave them in charity with their enemies, *not* as the result of repentance, but as its preliminary? Where, O where may we find the population for whom the precept, "Love your enemies," is altogether superfluous, and who always revert to affection as soon as they have gratified any transient sentiment of an opposite tendency? Hitherto we have been accustomed to believe that (as Buddhists are wont to insist) a kind action done to a foe is the surest way to enable ourselves to return to charitable feelings, and that, in like manner, doing him an ill-turn is calculated to exasperate our own rancour. We have held it as axiomatic that "revenge and wrong bring forth their kind;" and that we hate those whom we have injured with an ever-growing spite and cruelty as we continue to give our malice headway. But instead of agreeing with Tacitus that "*Humani generis proprium est odisse quem læseris*," Mr. Darwin actually supposes that as soon as ever we have delivered our blow it is customary for us immediately to wish to wipe it off with a kiss! In what Island of the Blessed do people love all the way round their social circles, the mean and the vulgar, the disgusting, and the tiresome, not excepted? If such beings are entirely exceptional now, when the careful husbandry of Christianity has been employed for eighteen centuries in cultivating that virtue of mansuetude, of which the ancient world produced so limited a crop, how is it to be supposed that our hirsute and tusky progenitors of the Palæolithic or yet remoter age, were thoroughly imbued with such gentle sentiments? Let it be borne in mind that, unless the great majority of men, after injuring their neighbours, spontaneously turned to sympathize with them, there could not possibly be a chance for the foundation of a *general* sentiment such as Mr. Darwin supposes to grow up in the community.

The natural history (so to speak) of Repentance seems to indicate almost a converse process to that assumed by Mr. Darwin. Having done a wrong in word or deed to our neighbour, the first sentiment we distinguish afterwards is usually, I conceive, an accession of dislike towards him. Then after a time we become conscious of uneasiness, but rather in the way of feeling that we have broken the law in our own breasts and are ashamed of it, than that we pity the person we have injured or are sorry for him. On the contrary, if I am not mistaken, we are very apt to comfort ourselves at this stage of the proceedings by reflecting that he is a very odious person, who well deserves all he has got and worse; and we are even tempted to add to our offence a little further evil speaking. Then comes the sense that we have really done wrong in the sight of God; and last of all (as it seems to me), as the final climax, not the first step of repentance, we first undo or apologize for our wrong act, and then, and only then, return to the feeling of love and charity.

This whole theory, then, of the origin of Repentance, namely, that it is the "innings" of our permanent social instincts when the transient selfish ones have played out their game, seems to be without basis on any known condition of human nature. Ostensibly raised on induction, it lacks the primary facts from which its inductions profess to be drawn; and Mr. Darwin, in offering it to us as the result of his studies in Natural History, seems to have betrayed that he has observed other species of animals more accurately than his own; and that he has overlooked the vast class of intelligences which lie between baboons and philosophers.

The theory of the nature of Repentance which we have been considering, is a characteristic improvement on the current Utilitarian doctrine, in so far that it suggests a cause for the *human tenderness*, if I may so describe it, which forms one element in true repentance. If it were true of mankind in general (as it may be true of the most gentle individuals) that a return to sympathy and goodwill spontaneously follows, sooner or later, every unkind act, then Mr. Darwin's account of the case would supply us with an explanation of that side of the sentiment of repentance which is turned towards the person injured. It would still, I think, fail altogether to render an account of the mysterious awe and horror which the greater crimes have in all ages left on the minds of their perpetrators, far beyond any feelings of pity for the sufferers, and quite irrespective of fear of human justice or retaliation. This tremendous sentiment of Remorse, though it allies itself with religious fears, seems to me not so much to be derived from religious considerations as to be in itself one of the roots of religion. The typical Orestes does not feel horror because he fears the Erinnyes, but he has called up the phantoms of the Erinnyes in the nightmare of his horror. Nothing which Mr. Darwin, or any other writer on his side, so far as I am aware, has ever suggested as the origin of the moral sense, has supplied us with a plausible explanation of either such Remorse or of ordinary Repentance. In the former case, we have soul-shaking terrors to be accounted for, either (according to Mr. Darwin) by mere pity and sympathy, or (according to the old Utilitarians) by fear of retaliation or disgrace, such as the sufferer often notoriously defies or even courts. In the case of ordinary Repentance, we have a feeling infinitely sacred and tender, capable of transforming our whole nature as by an enchanter's wand, softening and refreshing our hearts as the dry and dusty earth is quickened by an April shower, but yet (we are asked to believe) caused by no higher sorcery, fallen from no loftier sky, than our own every-day instincts, one hour selfish and the next social, asserting themselves in wearisome alternation! What is the right of one of these instincts as against the other, that its resumption of its temporary supremacy should be accompanied by such portents of solemn augury? Why, when we return to love our neighbour, do we at the same time hate ourselves, and *wish* to do so still more?· Why, instead of shrinking from punishment, do men, under such impressions, always desire to expiate their offences so fervently, that with the smallest sanction from their religious teachers they rush to the cloister or seize the scourge? Why, above all, do we look inevitably beyond the fellow-creature whom we have injured up to God, and repeat the cry which has burst from every penitent heart for millenniums back, "Against Thee, Thee only, have I sinned!"

Putting aside the obvious fact that the alleged cause of repentance could, at the utmost, only explain repentance for social wrong-doing, and leave inexplicable the equally bitter grief for personal offences, we find, then, that it fails even on its own ground. To make it meet approximately the facts of the case, we want something altogether different. We want to be told, not only why we feel sorry for our neighbour when we have wronged him, but how we come by the profound sense of a Justice which our wrong has infringed, and which we yet revere so humbly, that we often prefer to suffer that it may be vindicated. Of all this, the

Utilitarian scheme, with Mr. Darwin's additions, affords not the vaguest indication.

I cannot but think that, had any professed psychologist dealt thus with the mental phenomena which it was his business to explain, had he first assumed that we returned spontaneously to benevolent feelings after injuring our neighbours, and then presented such relenting as the essence of repentance, few readers would have failed to notice the disproportion between the unquestionable facts and their alleged cause. But when a great natural philosopher weaves mental phenomena into his general theory of physical development, it is to be feared that many a student will hastily accept a doctrine which seems to fit neatly enough into the system which he adopts as a whole; even though it could find on its own merits no admission into a scheme of psychology. The theory of Morals which alone ought to command our adhesion must surely be one, not like this harmonizing only with one side of our philosophy, but equally true to all the facts of the case, whether we regard them from without or from within, whether we study Man, *ab extra*, as one animal amongst all the tribes of zoology, or from within by the experience of our own hearts. From the outside, it is obvious that the two human sentiments of Regret and Repentance may very easily be confounded. A theory which should account for Regret might be supposed to cover the facts of Repentance, did no inward experience of the difference forbid us to accept it. But since Coleridge pointed out this loose link in the chain of Utilitarian argument, no disciple of the school has been able to mend it; and even Mr. Darwin's theory only supplies an hypothesis for the origin of relenting Pity, not one for Penitence. Let us suppose two simple cases: first, that in an accident at sea, while striving eagerly to help a friend, we had unfortunately caused his death;

second, that in the same contingency, an impulse of jealousy or anger had induced us purposely to withhold from him the means of safety. What would be our feelings in the two cases? In the first, we should feel Regret which, however deep and poignant, would never be anything else than simple Regret, and which, if it assumed the slightest tinge of self-reproach, would be instantly rebuked by every sound-minded spectator as morbid and unhealthy. In the second case (assuming that we had perfect security against discovery of our crime), we should feel, perhaps, very little Regret, but we should endure Remorse to the end of our days; we should carry about in our inner hearts a shadow of fear and misery and self-reproach which would make us evermore alone amid our fellows. Now, will Mr. Darwin, or any other thinker who traces the origin of the Moral Sense to the "agglutinated" experience of utility of a hundred generations, point out to us how that experience can possibly have bequeathed to us the latter sentiment of Remorse for a crime, as contra-distinguished from that of Regret for having unintentionally caused a misfortune?

But if the origin of repentance, in the case of obvious capital injuries to our neighbour, cannot be accounted for merely as the result of ancestral experience, it appears still more impossible to account in the same way for the moral shame which attaches to many lesser offences, whose noxiousness is by no means self-evident, which no legislation has ever made penal, and which few religions have condemned. Mr. Wallace, in his Contributions to the Theory of Natural Selection, appears to me to sum up this argument admirably.[1] After explaining how very inadequate are the Utilitarian sanctions for Truthfulness, and observing how many savages yet make veracity a point

[1] Page 355.

of honour, he says, "It is difficult to conceive that such an intense and mystical feeling of right and wrong (so intense as to overcome all ideas of personal advantage or utility) could have been developed out of accumulated ancestral experiences of utility; but still more difficult to understand how feelings developed by one set of utilities could be transferred to acts of which the utility was partial, imaginary or absent,"—or (as he might justly have added) so remote as to be quite beyond the ken of uncivilized or semi-civilized man. It is no doubt a fact that, in the long run, Truthfulness contributes more than Lying to the Greatest Happiness of the Greatest Number. But to discover that fact needs a philosopher, not a savage. Other virtues, such as that of care for the weak and aged, seem still less capable, as Mr. Mivart has admirably shown,[1] of being evolved out of a sense of utility, seeing that savages and animals find it much the most useful practice to kill and devour such sufferers, and by the law of the Survival of the Fittest, all nature below civilized man is arranged on the plan of so doing. Mr. W. R. Greg's very clever paper in *Fraser's Magazine*, pointing out how Natural Selection fails in the case of Man in consequence of our feelings of pity for the weak, affords incidentally the best possible proof that human society is based on an element which has no counterpart in the utility which rules the animal world.

It would be doing Mr. Darwin injustice if we were to quit the consideration of his observations on the nature of Repentance, leaving on the reader's mind the impression that he has put them forward formally as delineating an exhaustive theory of the matter, or that he has denied, otherwise than by implication, the doctrine that higher and more spiritual influences enter into the phenomena of the moral

[1] Genesis of Species, page 192.

life. The absence of the slightest allusion to any such higher sources of moral sentiment leaves, however, on the reader's mind a very strong impression that here we are supposed to rest. The developed Ape has acquired a moral sense by adaptive changes of mental structure precisely analogous to those adaptive changes of bodily structure which have altered his foot and rolled up his ear. To seek for a more recondite source for the one class of changes than for the other would be arbitrary and unphilosophical.

But now we come to the last, and, as it seems to me, the saddest doctrine of all. Our moral sense, however acquired, does not, it is asserted, correspond to anything real outside of itself, to any law which must be the same for all Intelligences, mundane or supernal. It merely affords us a sort of Ready Reckoner for our particular wages, a Rule of Thumb for our special work, in the position in which we find ourselves just at present. That I may do Mr. Darwin no injustice, I shall quote his observations on this point in his own words :

"It may be well first to premise that I do not wish to maintain that any strictly social animal, if its intellectual faculties were to become as active and as highly developed as in man, would acquire exactly the same moral sense as ours. . . . If, for instance, to take an extreme case, men were reared precisely under the same conditions as hive-bees, there can hardly be a doubt that our unmarried females would, like the worker-bees, think it a sacred duty to kill their brothers, and mothers would strive to kill their fertile daughters, and no one would think of interfering. Nevertheless, the bee, or any other social animal, would in our supposed case gain, as it appears to me, some feeling of right and wrong, or a conscience. For each individual would have an inward sense of possessing certain stronger or more enduring instincts, and others less strong or enduring ; so that there would often be a struggle which impulse should be followed, and satisfaction or dissatisfaction would be felt as past impressions were compared during their incessant passage through the mind. In this case, an inward monitor would tell the animal that it would have been better to have followed the one impulse rather than the other. The one course ought to have been followed. The one would have been right and the other wrong."[1]

Now it is a little difficult to clear our minds on this subject of the mutable or immutable in morals. No believer in the immutability of morality holds that it is any *physical* act itself which is immutably right, but only the *principles* of Benevolence, Truth, and so on, by which such acts must be judged. The parallel between Ethics and Geometry here holds strictly true. The axioms of both sciences are necessary truths known to us as facts of consciousness. The subordinate propositions are deduced from such axioms by reflection. The application of the propositions to the actual circumstances of life is effected by a process (sometimes called "traduction") by which all applied sciences become practically available. For example, Geometry teaches us that a triangle is equal to half a rectangle upon the same base and with the same altitude, but no geometry can teach us whether a certain field be a triangle with equal base and altitude to the adjoining rectangle. To know this we must measure both, and then we shall know that if such be their proportions, the one will contain half as much space as the other. Similarly in morals, Intuition teaches us to "Love our Neighbour," and reflection will thence deduce that we ought to relieve the wants of the suffering. But no ethics can teach A what are the special wants of B, or how they can best be supplied. According, then, to the doctrines of Intuitive Morality, considerations of Utility have a most important, though altogether subordinate, place in ethics. It is the office of experience to show us *how* to put the mandates of intuition into execution, though not to originate our moral code,—*how* to fulfil the duty of conferring Happiness, though not to set up Happiness as the sole end and aim of Morality.

[1] Descent of Man, pp. 33, 34.

Now if Mr. Darwin had simply said that under totally different conditions of life many of the existing human duties would have been altered, we could have no possible fault to find with his remarks. In a world where nobody needed food there could be no duty of feeding the hungry; in a world of immortals there could be no such crime as murder. Every alteration in circumstance produces a certain variation in moral obligation, for the plain reason (as above stated) that Morals only supply abstract principles, and, according to the circumstances of each case, their application must necessarily vary. If the triangular field have a rood cut off it, or a rood added on, it will no longer be the half of the rectangle beside it. It would not be difficult to imagine a state of existence in which the immutable principles of Benevolence would require quite a different set of actions from those which they now demand; in fact, no one supposes that among the Blessed, where they will rule all hearts, they will inspire the same manifestations which they call for on earth.

But Mr. Darwin's doctrine seems to imply something very different indeed from this. He thinks (if I do not mistake him) that, under altered circumstances, human beings would have acquired consciences in which not only the *acts* of social duty would have been different, but its *principles* would have been transformed or reversed. It is obviously impossible to stretch our conception of the principle of Benevolence far enough to enable us to include under its possible manifestations the conduct of the worker bees to the drones; and I suppose few of us have hitherto reflected on this and similar strange phenomena of natural history, without falling back with relief on the reflection that the animal, devoid of moral sense, does its destructive work as guiltlessly as the storm or the flood.

On Mr. Darwin's system, the developed bee would have

an "inward monitor" actually prompting the murderous sting, and telling her that such a course "*ought* to have been followed." The Danaïdes of the hive, instead of the eternal nightmare to which Greek imagination consigned them, would thus receive the reward of their assassinations in the delights of the *mens conscia recti;* or, as Mr. Darwin expresses it, by the satisfaction of "the stronger and more enduring instinct." Hitherto we have believed that the human moral sense, though of slow and gradual development and liable to sad oscillations under the influence of false religion and education, yet points normally to one true Pole. Now we are called on to think there is no pole at all, and that it may swing all round the circle of crimes and virtues, and be equally trustworthy whether it point north, south, east or west. In brief, there are no such things really as Right and Wrong; and our idea that they have existence outside of our own poor little minds is pure delusion.

The bearings of this doctrine on Morality and on Religion seem to be equally fatal. The all-embracing Law which alone could command our reverence has disappeared from the universe; and God, if He exist, may, for aught we can surmise, have for Himself a code of Right in which every cruelty and every injustice may form a part, quite as probably as the opposite principles.

Does such an hypothesis actually fit any of the known facts of human consciousness? Is there anywhere to be found an indication of the supposed possibility of acquiring a conscience in which the *principles* of Right and Wrong should be transformed, as well as their application altered? It would seem (as already mentioned) that, as a matter of fact, the utility of destroying old people and female infants has actually appeared so great to many savage and semi-civilized people, as to have caused them to practise such murders in a systematic way for thousands of years. But we have never been told that the Fuegians made it more than a matter of good sense to eat their grandfathers, or that the Chinese, when they deposited their drowned babies in the public receptacles labelled "For Toothless Infants," did so with the proud consciousness of fulfilling one of those time-hallowed Rites of which they are so fond. The transition from a sense of Utility to a sense of Moral Obligation seems to be one which has never yet been observed in human history. Mr. Darwin himself, with his unvarying candour, remarks that no instance is known of an arbitrary or superstitious practice, though pursued for ages, leaving hereditary tendencies of the nature of a moral sense. Of course where a religious sanction is believed to elevate any special act (such as Sabbath-keeping) into an express tribute of homage to God, it justly assumes in the conscience precisely the place such homage should occupy. But even here the world-old distinction between offences against such arbitrary laws, *mala prohibita*, and those against the eternal laws of morals, *mala in se*, has never been wholly overlooked.

I think, then, we are justified in concluding that the moral history of mankind, so far as we know it, gives no countenance to the hypothesis that Conscience is the result of certain contingencies in our development, and that it might at an earlier stage have been moulded into quite another form, causing Good to appear to us Evil, and Evil Good. I think we have a right to say that the suggestions offered by the highest scientific intellects of our time, to account for its existence on principles which shall leave it on the level of other instincts, have failed to approve themselves as true to the facts of the case. And I think, therefore, that we are called on to believe still in the validity of our own moral consciousness, even as we believe in the validity of our other faculties, and to rest in the faith (well-nigh universal) of the human race, in a fixed and supreme Law of which the will of God is the embodiment, and Conscience the Divine transcript. I think that we may still repeat the hymn of Cleanthes :

> "That our wills blended into Thine,
> Concurrent in the Law divine,
> Eternal, universal, just and good,
> Honouring and honoured in our servitude,
> Creation's Pæan march may swell,
> The march of Law immutable,
> Wherein, as to its noblest end,
> All being doth for ever tend."

ESSAY II.

HEREDITARY PIETY.[1]

THE history of Public Opinion during the last half century may be not inaptly compared to that of a well-fed, steady-going old roadster, long cherished by a respectable elderly squire, but unluckily transferred at his demise to his wild young heir. Accustomed to all the neighbouring highways, and trained to jog along them at five miles an hour, the poor beast suddenly found itself lashed by "the discipline of facts" and sundry new and cruel spurs, to get over the ground at double its wonted pace, and at last to leave the beaten tracks altogether and cut across country, over walls and hedges which it never so much as peeped over before. Under this altered régime it would appear that Public Opinion at first behaved with the restiveness which was to be expected. On some occasions he stood stock-still like a donkey, with his feet stretched out, refusing to budge an inch; and anon he bolted and shied and took buck leaps into the air, rather than go the way which stern destiny ordained. But as time went on, such resistance naturally grew less violent. The plungings and rearings subsided by degrees, and anybody who now pays attention to the animal will probably be only led to observe that he is a little hard in the mouth and apt to refuse his fences till he has been brought

[1] Hereditary Genius. An Inquiry into its Laws and Consequences. By Francis Galton, F.R.S. 1 vol. 8vo. pp. 390. Macmillan. 1869.
Psychologie Naturelle. Etude sur les Facultés Intellectuelles et Morales. Par Prosper Despine. 3 vols. 8vo. Paris: F. Savy. 1868.

up to them two or three times. In his equine way he finds each new discovery first "false" and then "against religion;" but at last he always makes a spring over it and knocks off the top stone with his hind feet: "Everybody knew it before!"

Had not this process of accustoming Public Opinion to a sharp pace and difficult leaps been going on for some time, it is to be believed that Mr. Galton's book would have produced considerably more dismay and called forth more virtuous indignation than under present training has actually greeted it. We have had to modify our ideas of all things in heaven and earth so fast, that another shock even to our conceptions of the nature of our own individual minds and faculties, is not so terrible as it would once have been. We used first to think (or our fathers and grandfathers thought for us) that each of us, so far as our mental and moral parts were concerned, were wholly fresh, isolated specimens of creative Power, "trailing clouds of glory," straight out of heaven. Then came the generation which believed in the omnipotence of education. Its creed was, that you had only to "catch your hare," or your child, and were he or she born bright or dull-witted, the offspring of two drunken tramps, or of a philosopher married to a poetess, it was all the same. It depended only on the care with which you trained it and crammed it with "useful knowledge" to make it a Cato and a Plato rolled into one. Grapes were to be had off thorns and figs off thistles with the utmost facility in the forcing-houses of Edgeworthian schools. It had, of course, been a hard matter to bring Public Opinion up to this point. The worthy old beast recalcitrated long, and when London University reared its head, the trophy of the First Educational Crusade, all the waggery left in England was thought to be displayed by dubbing it "Stinkomalee." But university in town, and schools all over the country were overleaped at last, and nobody for years afterwards so much as whispered a doubt that the Three Learned R's were signposts on the high road to Utopia.

Then arose the brothers Combe to put in some wise words about physical, over and above mental, education. And somehow talking of physical education led to discussing hereditary physical qualities, and the "Constitution of Man" was admitted to be influenced in a certain measure by the heritage of his bodily organization. Children born of diseased and vicious parents, the philosopher insisted, ran a double chance of being themselves diseased and vicious, or even idiotic; and sound conditions in father, mother, and nurse, had much to do, he thought, with similar good conditions in their offspring and nursling. Strange to remember! Ideas obvious and undeniable, as these appear to us, seemed nothing short of revolutionary when they first were published; and Public Opinion put back its ears and plunged and snorted at a terrible rate, ere, as usual, it went over them and "knew it all before." Nevertheless the inalienable right of diseased, deformed, and semi-idiotic married people to bring as many miserable children into the world as they please, is yet an article of national faith, which to question is the most direful of all heresies.

But these three doctrines of mental and moral development,—the doctrines, namely, 1st, that we came straight down from heaven; 2nd, that we could be educated into anything; 3rd, that some of our physical peculiarities might be traced to inheritance,—were all three kept pretty clear of meddlings with the Religious part of man. Experience, no doubt, showed sufficiently decisively that Piety was not a thing to be made to order, and that (at all events under the existing dispensation) there was no bespeaking little Samuels. The mysterious proclivity of children intended for such a vocation to turn out pickles, luckily coincided with—or possibly had a share in originating—the Calvinistic views of Arbitrary Election; while even the Arminians of those days would have vehemently repudiated either the notion that a man might inherit a pious disposition just as well as a tendency to the gout, or that he would be likely to find the true route to Paradise among other items of Useful Knowledge in the *Penny Magazine.*

Now it seems we are trotting up to another fence, videlicet, the doctrine that *all* man's faculties and qualities, physical, mental, moral and religious, have a certain given relation to the conditions of his birth. The hereditary element in him,—that element of which we have hitherto entertained the vaguest ideas, admitting it in his features and diseases, and ignoring it in his genius and his passions; recognizing it in noble races as a source of pride, and forgetting it as the extenuation of the faults of degraded ones,—this mysterious element must, we are told, henceforth challenge a place in all our calculations. We must learn to trace it equally in every department of our nature; and no analysis of character can be held valid which has not weighed it with such accuracy as may be attainable. Our gauge of moral responsibility must make large allowance for the good or evil tendencies inherited by saint or sinner, and our whole theory of the meaning and scope of Education must rise from the crude delusion that it is in our power wholly to transform any individual child, to embrace the vaster but remoter possibilities of gradually training successive generations into higher intelligence and more complete self-control, till the tendencies towards brute vice grow weaker and expire, and "the heir of all the ages" shall be born with only healthful instincts and lofty aspirations.

As always happens when a new truth is to be discovered, there have been foreshadowings of this doctrine for some years back. The hereditary qualities of Races of men have occupied large room in our discussions. The awful phenomena of inherited criminal propensities have interested not only physicians (like the writer of the second book at the head of our paper), but philosophic novelists like the author of "Elsie Venner." Under the enormous impetus given to all speculations concerning descent by Mr. Darwin, some applications of the doctrine of development to the mind as well as body of man became inevitable, and a most remarkable article in *Fraser's Magazine*, Oct. 1868, brought to light a variety of unobserved facts regarding the "Failure of Natural Selection in the case of Man," due to the special tendencies of our civilization. Mr. Galton himself, five or six years ago, published in *Macmillan's Magazine* the results of his preliminary inquiries as to inherited ability in the legal profession; and Professor Tyndall perhaps gave the most remarkable hint of all, by ascribing the "baby-love" of women to the "set of the molecules of the brain" through a thousand generations of mothers exercised in the same functions.

But the work which has finally afforded fixed ground to these floating speculations, and, in the humble judgment of the present writer, inaugurated a new science with a great future before it, is Mr. Galton's "Essay on Hereditary Genius." The few errors of detail into which the author has fallen in the wide and untrodden field he has attempted to map out, and his easily explicable tendency to give undue weight to disputable indications, and to treat a man's attainment of high office as equivalent to proof of his fitness for it,—these weak points, on which the reviewers have fastened with their usual bull-dog tenacity, cannot eventually influence the acceptance of the immense mass of evidence adduced to prove the main theses of the work, or bar our admiration of its great originality. I do not propose in the ensuing pages to give a general notice of the work, or to mark either all the principles which I conceive Mr. Galton has established, nor those others on which I should venture to differ from him. His main doctrine he has, I believe, demonstrated with mathematical certainty, viz., that all mental faculties, from the most ordinary to the highest and apparently most erratic forms of genius, the various gifts of the statesman, soldier, artist and man of letters, are distributed according to conditions among which inheritance by descent of blood occupies the foremost place; and that there is no such thing in the order of nature as a mighty genius who should be an intellectual Melchisedek.

The further deductions which Mr. Galton draws appear to me curious and suggestive in the extreme; as, for example, the calculation of the proportion now obtaining in Europe of Eminent Men to the general population; and, again, of the far rarer Illustrious Men to those of ordinary eminence. Based on this calculation, the number of both illustrious and eminent men who flourished among the 135,000 free citizens of Attica during the age of Pericles, is so nearly miraculous, that we find it hard to picture such an intellectual feast as life must then have offered. Society at Athens in those days must have surpassed that of the choicest circles of Paris and London now, as these are superior to the ale-house gossipings of George Eliot's rustics. *That* populace for whose eye Phidias chiselled, *those* play-goers for whose taste Sophocles and Aristophanes provided entertainment, *that* "jeunesse dorée" whose daily lounge involved an argument with Socrates— what were they all? What rain of heaven had watered the human tree when it bore such fruit in such profusion? And what hope may remain that it will ever bring them forth in such clusters once more?

Again, a flood of light is poured on the degeneracy of mediæval Europe by Mr. Galton's observations concerning the celibacy of the clergy and the monastic orders. The moment when, as Mr. Lecky shows, chastity (understood to mean celibacy) was elevated into the sublimest of Christian virtues, that moment the chance that any man should perpetuate his race became calculable in the inverse ratio of his piety and goodness. Archbishop Whately long ago exposed the absurdity of the common boast of Catholics concerning the learning and virtue hidden in the monasteries during the Dark Ages. It would be equally reasonable to take the lamps and candles out of every room in a house and deposit them in the coal-cellar, and then call the passers-by to remark how gloomy were the library and drawing-room, how beautifully illuminated the coal-hole! But Mr. Galton points out that the evil of the ascetic system was immeasurably wider and more enduring in its results even than the subtraction for generation after generation of the brightest minds and gentlest hearts from the world which so grievously needed them. According to the laws of hereditary descent, it was the whole future human race which was being cruelly spoiled of its fairest hopes, its best chances of enjoying the services of genius and of true saintship. Some of those who read these pages may remember in the first Great Exhibition a set of samples of what was called "Pedigree Wheat." The gigantic ears, loaded with double-sized seeds, were simply the result of ten years' successive selection of the finest ears, and again the finest in each crop. The process which Romanism effected for the human race was precisely and accurately the converse of that by which this Pedigree Wheat was obtained. It simply *cut off* each stem which rose above the average in mental or moral gifts. The moment a man or a woman showed signs of being something better than a clod, a little more disposed for learning, a little more gentle-natured, more pious or more charitable, instantly he or she was induced to take the vow never to become a parent; and only by the infraction of such vows was there a chance for the world of an heir to his or her virtues. The best-born man among us now living, if he could trace out the million or so of his ancestors contemporary twenty generations ago, would hardly find among them a single person mentally distinguished in any way. We are all the descendants of the caterans and hunters, the serfs and boors of a thousand years. The better and greater men born in the same ages hid their light under a bushel while they lived, and took care that it should not be rekindled after their death. When the Reformation came, the case was even worse; for then the ablest, the bravest and the truest-hearted, were picked out for slaughter. The human tares were left to flourish and reproduce their kind abundantly, but the wheat was gathered in bundles to be burnt. To this hour France feels the loss of Huguenot blood (so strangely vigorous wherever it has been scattered!), and Spain halts for ever under the paralysis of half her motor nerves, cut off by the Inquisition.

Besides these discussions, Mr. Galton's book is full of suggestive and original ideas concerning the results of marriages with heiresses,—concerning the influence of able mothers on their sons,—concerning the choice of wives by gifted men,—and, finally, concerning the application of Mr. Darwin's hypothesis of Pangenesis to human inheritance of special qualities. Of these topics nothing can here be said, though against some of them I would fain enter my expression of dissent. There remains not more than space enough to discuss the branch of Mr. Galton's subject which properly falls under the notice of a Theological Review, viz., the statistics he has collected concerning Divines.

It was not a little mischievous of Mr. Galton to preface his investigations about the families of pious men, by quoting Psalms cxxviii. 3, cxiii. 9, xxv. 13, and then innocently asking whether the wives of Christian divines have any special resemblance to "fruitful vines," or their children to "olive-branches;" and whether, on the whole, their seed does "inherit the land" in any noticeable manner. Certainly, on the one hand, almost every one of us would be ready to assure the inquirer that, to the best of our persuasion, curates with small salaries have larger families than men of any other profession; and that "Mrs. Quiverfull" was, and could only be, according to the natural fitness of things, a poor clergyman's wife. But then, per contra, our author is evidently unprepared to admit that the unbeneficed clergy of the National Church have a monopoly of piety, or that we ought to look among them especially for the fruits of the first part of the patriarchal benediction; while it is manifest that the second blessing, namely, the "inheriting of the land," falls much more richly on the profane generation of the squirearchy.

Mr. Galton says he finds two conflicting theories afloat on this matter. The first is, that there is a special good providence for the children of the godly. The second is, that the sons of religious persons mostly turn out exceptionally ill. He proceeds to inquire carefully what light statistics can throw on these views, and whether both of them must not yield to the ordinary law of heredity as ruling in other spheres of human activity.

It was not an easy matter to settle at starting what qualification should entitle a man to be reckoned among the eminently pious. Obviously Roman Catholic saints were out of the running, owing to the fatal law of celibacy, whereby fruitful vines and numerous olive-branches are allowed only to decorate the houses of persons who followed not "counsels of perfection." Protestants, on the other hand, have rarely been able to see all the merits of men of different opinions from their own. The name of Laud has not a sweet savour in Evangelical nostrils; while the Ritualist Dr. Littledale talks unconcernedly of those "scoundrels," the martyrs Hooper and Latimer. Nevertheless, Mr. Galton has happily got over his difficulty through an excellent collection—" Middleton's Biographia Evangelica," published in 4 vols. in 1786, and containing 196 picked lives of Protestant saints, from the Reformation downwards. Our author subjects these biographies to sharp analysis, and the following are the conclusions which he deduces from them.

These 196 Protestant saints were no canting humbugs. They were for the greater part men of exceedingly noble characters. Twenty-two of them were martyrs. They had considerable intellectual gifts. None of them are reported to have had sinful parents; and out of the last 100 (whose relations alone are traceable), 41 had pious fathers or mothers. Their social condition was of every rank, from the highest to the lowest. Only one-half were married men, and of these the wives were mostly very pious. The number of their children was a trifle below the average. No families of importance in England are traceable to divines as founders, except those of Lord Sandys and of the Hookers, the famous botanists, who are the lineal descendants of the author of the *Ecclesiastical Polity*. As regards health, the constitution of most of the divines was remarkably bad. Sickly lads are apt to be more studious than robust ones, and the weakly students who arrived at manhood chiefly recruited the band of divines. Among these semi-invalids were Calvin, Melancthon, George Herbert, Baxter, and Philip Henry. Reading the lives of eminent lawyers and statesmen, one is struck by the number of them who have had constitutions of iron; but out of all Middleton's 196 divines, he only speaks of 12 or 13 as vigorous. Out of these, 5 or 6 were wild in their youth and reformed in later years; while only 3 or 4 of the other divines were ever addicted to dissipated habits. Seventeen out of the 196 were inter-related, and 8 more had other pious connexions. The influence of inheritance of character through the female line is much greater in the case of divines than in that of any other eminent men; an influence Mr. Galton attributes to the utility, in their case, of a " blind conviction which can best be obtained through maternal teaching in childhood."

These results, as Mr. Galton would no doubt readily admit, might be liable to considerable modification, could we extend our field of operations over double or treble the number of instances of piety, and especially if we could include types of piety from other creeds and a greater variety of nations. Taken as it is, however, as the outcome of an inquiry based on freely gathered specimens of Protestant religious eminence, it appears to convey one of the most curious morals ever presented by an historical investigation. A true Christian has been often defined as " the highest kind of man," and Mr. Galton himself avows that these subjects of his anatomy were " exceedingly noble characters." And yet he is forced to pronounce with equal decision from the evidence before him, that they were mostly a tribe of valetudinarians; that there must exist "a correlation between an unusually devout disposition and a weak constitution;" that "a gently complaining and fatigued spirit is that in which Evangelical divines are apt to pass their days;" and, finally, that " we are compelled to conclude that robustness of constitution is antagonistic in a very marked degree to an extremely pious disposition"!

There are no doubt still surviving in the world a good many people who will find in these conclusions of Mr. Galton's nothing to shock their conceptions of what ought to be the causes, tenor and temper of a religious life. There are those who still repeat, with Cowper, that this world is, and ought to be, a Vale of Tears, and that a very proper way to view our position therein is to liken ourselves to "crowded forest ·trees, marked to fall." To such persons, no doubt, it is natural to pass through the varied joys and interests of youth, manhood and old age, plaintively observing to all whom it may concern, that they

> Drag the dull remains of life
> Along the tiresome road.

But these worthy people have certainly been in a minority for the last twenty years, since the Psalm of Life took definitively the place of the lugubrious "Stanzas subjoined to the Bills of Mortality." And to us in our day it is undoubtedly somewhat of a blow to be told that Religion, instead of being (as the old Hebrews believed) the correlative of health and cheerfulness and length of years, is, on the contrary, near akin to disease; and that he among men whom the Creator has blessed with the soundest body and coolest brain, is, by some fiendish fatality, the least likely of all to give his heart to God or devote his manly strength to His cause. The Glorious Company of the Apostles is reduced to a band of invalids, and the Noble Army of Martyrs is all on the sick list!

Is this true? Shall we sit down quietly under this dictum of Mr. Galton's, and agree for the future to consider health and piety as mutually antagonistic? For my own part, I must confess that if facts really drove me to such a conclusion, I should be inclined to say, with the French philosopher contradicted in his theories, "Eh bien, messieurs! tant pis pour les faits!" No statistics should lash my (private) opinion over that six-barred gate. But are we really driven to such straits at all? It seems to me that Mr. Galton's own words give us the key to the whole mystery, and to a very important truth beside. He tells us at starting that though Middleton assures the reader that no bigoted partiality rules his selection of divines, yet that "it is easy to see his leaning is strongly towards the Calvinists." His 196 picked men are chosen (honestly enough, no doubt) from the churches in which more or less closely the Evangelical type of piety was adhered to as the standard of holiness. No Unitarian or Latitudinarian, no Deist or Freethinker, had a chance of admission into his lists. We have thus 196 specimens of the plants reared in the peculiar hot-beds of the dominant Protestantism of the seventeenth and eighteenth centuries. Let us take them, then, by all means, and reason on them as excellent examples, 1st, of the persons on whom that creed was calculated to fasten; and, 2ndly, of what really fine characters it was able to form. But do not let us be misled for a moment into the use of generalizations implying that it is "piety" *pur et simple*, piety as it must always be, or always ought to be, which is intrinsically "unsuited to a robust constitution," and specially calculated to take root in a sickly one. Do not let us rest content with the picture of "the gently complaining and fatigued spirit," as if it were the normal spirit of any other pious folk than those of the orthodox persuasion.

And, again, does not this remarkable fact discovered by Mr. Galton, namely, the physical sickliness attendant on the prevalent forms of Christian piety, let in some light on the fact which has been so often noticed, but so little explained, namely, the lack of manliness among clergymen, bishops and "professors" at large? If the phenomenon were not so familiar, it would surely be the most astonishing in the world, that the preachers of religion and morality should be as a body less straightforward, less simple, less brave, than other men. When a clergyman twaddles and cants and equivocates; or when one Bishop "chalks up Free

Thought and runs away;" or another talks blasphemously of "The Voice" guiding him to exchange a poor and provincial See for a rich one with a good town-house; or, finally, when "eminent saints" prove dishonest bankers,—how is it that we do not all wring our hands and cry that the heavens are falling? Why do we only nod our heads lugubriously and observe, "What a different sort of man is the Rev. A. B.'s brother, Captain C. D., of the Navy, or Colonel E. F., of the —th Dragoons!" or, "How the episcopal apron transforms a man into an old woman!" or, "How very dangerous it is to have dealings with the saints!"[1]

Things like these ought to strike us dumb with amazement and horror, had not experience hardened us to a vague anticipation of a correlation between an extraordinary display of Christian sentiment and a proportionate lack of the element of manly honesty and courage. Without formularizing our ideas on the matter, there are few of us who, if we were attacked by robbers in a house with a saintly clergyman upstairs and a profane man of the world below, would not rush first to seek our defender in the lower story. Again, in matters of veracity, to whose recommendation of a servant or a teacher do we attach most value—that of the pious vicar of the parish, or that of the fox-hunting squire? Not to pursue these illustrations further, I think my position will be hardly gainsaid if I assert that, while the theological virtues, faith, hope, charity, purity, and resignation, flourish abundantly in the vineyard of the Church, the merely moral virtues, courage, fortitude, honesty, generosity and veracity, are found to grow more vigorously elsewhere. It is not of course maintained that either side of the wall

---

[1] We have heard an authentic story of a clergyman who, being present at a prayer-meeting at which Sir John Dean Paul engaged in devotion, immediately afterwards rushed up to town and drew all his money out of the too pious banker's hands!

has a monopoly of either class of virtues; but that the priestly or evangelical character has a tendency to form a distinct type of its own; and that in that type there is a preponderance of the more fragile and feeble virtues, and a corresponding deficiency in those which are healthy, robust and masculine. "Muscular Christianity" is a modern innovation, a hazardous and not over-successful attempt to combine physical vigour and spiritual devotion; and the very convulsiveness of the efforts of its apostles to achieve such a harmony affords the best possible proof of how widely apart to all our apprehensions had previously been "Muscularity" and "Christianity."

But all these remarks apply to what has hitherto passed muster as the received type of piety, and not by any means to Piety in the abstract apart from its orthodox colouring. The unmanliness belongs wholly to the mould, and not to the thing moulded. No man has ever yet felt himself, or been felt by others to be, less manly because in public or in private he has professed his faith in God and his allegiance towards Him. The noblest line perhaps in all French poetry is that which Racine puts into the mouth of the Jewish High-priest,

" Je crains Dieu, cher Abner, et n'ai point d'autre crainte."

It must be admitted that the same cannot be said of the profession of belief in sundry doctrines of orthodoxy. The urgency of a man's dread of hell-fire, his anxiety to obtain the benefits of the Atonement, and his undisguised rejoicing that "Christ his Passover is slain for him," are none of them sentiments to which we attach the character of manliness or generosity.

Perhaps there is no point on which the religion of the future is so certain to differ from that of the past, as in its comparative healthfulness of spirit. And just as a sickly creed, full of dreadful threats and mystic ways of expiation, appealed to minds more or less morbidly constituted, so it is to be believed that a thoroughly healthy and manly creed will harmonize no less distinctly with natures happy, healthful and normally developed.

From this branch of the subject we pass to a most curious and original analysis which Mr. Galton has made of what he considers the typical religious character. It must be premised that in another part of his book he has broached the doctrine, that the sense of incompleteness and imperfection which theologians define to be the sense of Original Sin, is probably only our vague sense that we are as yet not thoroughly trained to the conditions of civilized life in which we find ourselves, and that there yet remains in us too much of the wild beast, or at least of the hunter and the nomad, to accommodate ourselves perfectly with the polished forms of life in our age and country. "The sense of original sin," he says,[1] "would show, according to my theory, not that man was fallen from a high estate, but that he was rising in moral culture with more rapidity than the nature of his race could follow." Generations hence, when civilization has thoroughly done its work, and the instincts of sudden passion and unreasoning selfishness and impatience of law and rule have died out of the whole human family, then we may expect the vague sense of imperfection and guilt to die out too. We are, if I may venture to suggest the simile to Mr. Galton, at the present day much in the condition of that unhappy bird, the Apteryx. Through long ages of gradual disuse of flying, our wings have grown smaller and weaker, so that if we desired to return to the habits of our remote progenitors, we should infallibly come to the ground. But the vestiges of the pinions are still there, more or less hidden under our

[1] Page 350.

plumage, and so long as they are to be felt, we cannot help flapping them sometimes and pining for a flight. The discovery that we can neither be happy flying or walking, barbarous or civilized, constitutes the grand discontent of life. The sense that we are always inclined to make flaps and flights and fall on our beaks in the dust, is the natural element in Original Sin.

On this very singular idea Mr. Galton evidently proceeds, in the part of his book under present consideration, to define what he deems to be the typical Religious Character. He holds that its chief feature is its *conscious moral instability*. It is the conjunction of warm affections and high aspirations with frequent failures and downfalls, which makes a man alike sensible of his own frailty and inclined to rely on the serene Strength which he believes rules above him. The religious man is "liable to extremes; now swinging forwards into regions of enthusiasm, now backwards into those of sensuality and selfishness." David, in fact, the David who both slew Uriah and wrote the penitential psalms, is the eternal type of the godly man; and it is much more easy to find Davids among semi-civilized Judæan shepherds or Negroes or Celts than among long civilized races such as the Chinese.

With this religious type Mr. Galton contrasts the ideal Sceptic, and concludes that the differences of character which in the one case make a man happy in the belief in a Divine Guide and Father, and in the other, content in a mental state tantamount to Atheism, must needs lie in this, that while the Religious man is conscious of his infirmity of will and instability of resolution, insomuch that he needs the thought of God for his support, the Sceptic, on the contrary, is sufficiently sure of himself and confident in his own self-guidance to feel comparatively no such need for external aid, and to be able without pain to stifle any instinctive longings for a Divine Protector which may arise in his heart. In other words, as Religion had been previously found to be correlated with a feeble physical constitution, so here it is identified with a moral constitution feverish, vacillating and incapable of self-reliance. The sceptic, on the contrary, is no longer to be looked on, as we had pictured him, as a man in whom the moral nature never rises to the spring-tide where its waves break at the feet of God. He is the exalted being whose whole moral and intellectual economy is in such perfect balance and harmony, that he can say with Heine, "I am no longer a child. I do not need any more a Heavenly Father."

These views, which Mr. Galton has by no means illustrated in the above manner, but which I think I do him no injustice in so translating, are, in my humble judgment, among the most original and striking of any of the theories propounded on these subjects for many a day. That there is a considerable element of truth in them, I must heartily acknowledge, albeit I would read it in a somewhat different sense from Mr. Galton. The impulsive temperament is beyond question by far the most genuinely religious temperament. The calm, cold, prudential nature, when it adopts religion, does so as an additional precaution of prudence, and is "other-worldly" neither more nor less than it is worldly. Real, spontaneous, self-forgetful religion, springs and flourishes in the heart which is swayed by feeling, not by interest. Nay, more: the sense of Sin, which is the deepest part of all true piety is (we cannot doubt) far more vivid in natures wherein much of the wild, untamed human being still survives, which are swayed alternately by opposite motives, and are yet far from having been so disciplined and moulded in the school of the world as to be mere civilized machines. Probably it has happened to all of us at some time or other to wish that we could see some self-satisfied paragon of steadiness and respectability fall for once into some disgraceful fault, get drunk, or swear, or do something which should shake him out of his self-conceit, and give him a chance to learn that Religion and Pharisaism are not convertible terms. Many of us also must have watched the deplorable delusion of some originally good and always well-balanced character, in which, as there seems no need for self-restraint, no self-restraint is ever tried, and amiability lapses into self-indulgence, and self-indulgence into selfishness, and selfishness into hypocrisy and hardness of heart.

On the other hand, the permanent Sceptic is probably equally fairly described as a man who has not only made up his mind to the intellectual conclusion that there is nothing to be known about God, but also has reconciled his heart to the lack of religious supports and consolations through the help of a sturdy self-reliance. Either he is a sinner without any particular shame or hatred for his sin; or, as oftener happens, he is of so passionless a temperament, so prudent and well-balanced a constitution, that he recognizes few sins to repent of in the past, and knows that no serious temptation is likely to overmaster him in the future. In every case, the double sense of self-abasement and self-mistrust are absent. He has no need to be reconciled with himself, so he feels no need of being reconciled with God. He walks firmly along a certain broad and beaten path of ordinary honesty, justice, and sobriety, without toiling up celestial heights in the pursuit of love and faith and purity; and for his own road, and so far as he means to travel, he calls for no angels to bear him on their wings.

Lastly, it is easy to verify the fact, that these temperaments correspond in their main outlines to the races and sexes in which religion and scepticism are each most frequently developed. The impulsive races of mankind, the

Southern nations of Europe, are more inclined to religion and less to incredulity than those of the North. The unstable Celt is more pious, whether he be Catholic in Ireland or Methodist in Wales, than the steady-going, law-abiding Saxon of any denomination. And, finally, women are more religious than men, while displaying usually more vacillation of the will and (probably in most cases) higher aspirations after ideal holiness and purity.

What is now to be our conclusion respecting Mr. Galton's theory of the Origin of Piety? We have seen, in the first instance, that he identifies it with a sickly physical constitution, and I ventured so far to correct this result as to substitute for Piety in general, Piety in the particular form of Evangelical Christianity. I pointed out that it was only from among Evangelical Divines that the premisses of his argument had been taken, and that there was a very strong presumption that Piety equally deep and true, but of an opposite type, would, on experience, be found to show a no less marked affinity for those " robust constitutions " wherein the orthodox seed finds an ungenial soil.

In the present case, we have to decide whether we can admit Mr. Galton's second correlation of Piety with moral instability of purpose. In my opinion, we may rightly trace in this case a relation between all true types of piety and such instability, provided that we interpret the instability to consist, *not* in an unusual degree of frailty in acting up to a mediocre standard of virtue, *not* in having merely, as he avers, a greater " amplitude of moral oscillations than other men of equal average position," but in a necessarily imperfect attempt to act up to a standard higher than that commonly received, and for which the man (to apply Mr. Galton's system) has not been sufficiently highly *bred*.

What, then, is the bearing of our admission as regards this matter? It is tantamount only to this: that the temperament which contains the noblest elements and aspires highest, even if it fall lowest, is also the nature on which the crowning glory of the love of God most often descends. Just as Longinus decides that the greatest poem is not the one which longest sustains an even flight, but the one which ever and anon soars into the highest empyrean, even so the man who *in his highest moments rises highest* is truly the greatest man. It is he who, though his nature be a very chaos of passions—a den of wild beasts, as many of the saints have spoken of their own souls—yet has in him longings and strivings and yearnings after the Holy and the Perfect; it is he who is not only naturally predisposed to piety, but worthy to know the joy of religion. Out of such stuff demi-gods are made. Out of well-ordered, prudent, self-reliant sceptics, men of the world are made, and nothing more.

It is, I apprehend, a definite and very valuable acquisition to psychology, to recognize that it is not by accident, but natural law, that the characters wherein flesh and spirit do hardest battle, and Apollyon not seldom gains temporary advantage, are yet precisely those who are "bound for the Celestial City." Mr. Worldly-Wiseman never descends into the Valley of Humiliation; but neither does he ever climb the Delectable Mountains nor push through the Golden Gates.

With regard to the hereditary descent of religious as well as other qualities, Mr. Galton developes his theory in the following manner. Starting on the assumption that the typical religious man is one who combines high moral gifts with instability of character, it is obvious that if one of the two elements whose *combination* makes the parent's piety is *separately* inherited by the son, an opposite result will appear. If the son's heritage "consist of the moral gifts without the instability, he will not feel the need of extreme piety," and may become Mr. Galton's ideal sceptic. "If he inherit great instability without morality, he may very probably disgrace his name." Only in the third contingency, namely, that of the son inheriting both the father's qualities, is there any security for his following in the parental steps.

Thus we have an explanation more or less satisfactory of the double phenomenon, that there is such a thing as hereditary piety, and that there is also an occasional (though I hardly think a very common) tendency for the sons of a really religious man to turn out either sceptics or reprobates. So far as my judgment goes, I should say that the common disposition of children is to share in a very marked manner the emotional religious constitutions of their parents, and that this is only counteracted when piety is presented to them in so repulsive a shape, as to provoke the over-lectured "little Samuels" into rebellion. There are two facts connected with such heritage which must have forced themselves on the attention of all my readers. One of them falls in with Mr. Galton's theories of heredity, but the other must needs be explained by reference to post-natal influences. The first is the tendency of strong religious feeling to pervade whole families. The second is the equally strong tendency of the different members of such religious families to adopt different creeds and types of piety from one another, insomuch that the sympathy which ought to have united them in closer bonds than other households is too often converted into a source of dissensions.

These two facts will, I think, be disputed by few observers. All of us are acquainted with families in which no vehement warmth of religion has ever shown itself, and in which, according to Evangelical language, "conversions" never take place. Again, we all know, personally, a few, and by report a great many families, where for successive generations there are men and women of either saintly piety or fanatic zeal.

As Hindoos would say, there are Brahmin races in which twice-born men are found, and Kshatriyas and Soodras in which the phenomenon of regeneration never occurs.

This remarkable fact may, of course, be explained doubly. There is the hereditary tendency to the religious constitution; and there are all the thousand circumstances of youthful impression likely to bring that tendency into action. Family traditions of deeds and words, family pictures, and of course family habits of devotion, where these are maintained, are incentives of incalculable weight. It would be hard for the present writer to define how much of her own earlier feelings on such matters were due to a handful of books of the Fénélon school of devotion, left by chance in an old library, the property of a long dead ancestress.

But if the fact of hereditary piety be easily explicable, who is to explain to us the mystery of the radiation in opposite directions of the theological compass, so frequently witnessed in the sons and daughters of these particular homes? Do we see in an Evangelical family one son become a Roman Catholic? Then, ten to one, another will ere long avow himself an Unitarian. Does sister A enter an Anglican convent? Then brother B will probably become a Plymouth brother; while C, having gone through a dozen phases of faith, will settle finally in Theism.

It seems to be a law, that though the *predisposition* to piety may be conveyed by our parents both by blood and education, yet the awakening to strong spiritual life rarely or never happens under their influence, or that of any one altogether familiar with us. The spark must be kindled by a more distant torch, the pollen brought from a remoter flower. When the mysterious process does not take place wholly spontaneously, it comes from some person who adds a fresh impetus and keener sympathy to elements hitherto dormant in our souls. Then happens the marvellous "palingenesia;"

and whether he who has helped to work it be of one creed or another, he colours the spiritual world for us at that decisive hour and evermore. We do not "adopt his opinions;" we seize by sympathy on his faith, and make our own both its strength and its limitations.

If we admit, on the whole, Mr. Galton's views with these modifications, the serious questions arise: What must be their general bearing on our theories of the Order of Providence; and on our anticipations respecting the probable future of Religion? Is it not, in the first place (as our fathers would certainly have held), injurious to the Divine character to suppose that men are in this new sense "elected" to piety by the accident of birth, or, conversely, left so poorly endowed with the religious sentiment, that their attainment of a high grade of devotion is extremely improbable? And in the second place, if the impulsive character be the most genuinely religious, and the tendency of civilization be to reduce all impulse to a minimum, is there not reason to apprehend that in the course of centuries Religion, no longer finding its fitting soil in human characters, will dwindle and continually lessen its influence? I shall do my best to answer both these questions honestly in succession.

The blasphemy of the Calvinistic doctrines of Predestination and Election does not lie in their representing God as dealing differently with His creatures A and B, but in representing Him as inflicting on B an infinite penalty for no fault of his own, or, as we should say in common parlance, for his ill-luck in having been born B and not A. Repudiating all ideas of such penalties, and of any final evil for a creature of God, insisting, as the first article of our faith,

"that somehow good,
Shall be the final goal of ill,
To pangs of nature, sins of will,
Defects of doubt and *taints of blood*,"

the doctrine of Election is reduced to dimensions which it would be hard for one who has cast an eye over history or society altogether to deny. The inequalities of moral advantages in education and the circumstances of life are as obvious as the inequalities of height, weight, ability, fortune, or any other of the conditions allotted to us by Providence. If we mortals would fain have constructed the world on the plan of the Spartan commonwealth, and given each man an equal share of the good things thereof, it is quite certain that God entertains no such scheme, and that the principle of infinite Variety which prevails over every leaf and blade of grass, approves itself to His supreme judgment no less perfectly, applied to the gifts and conditions of His rational creatures. Is there anything in this to hurt our sense of justice? It is to be trusted that there is not, seeing that, if it were so, religious reverence must be at an end, since no argument can possibly overthrow the omnipresent fact before our eyes. The uneasiness we feel in contemplating it arises, I believe, from causes all destined to vanish with the progress of a nobler theology. Beside the idea of the final perdition of the sinful which it is so difficult ever thoroughly to root out of our minds, we are hampered with a dozen false conceptions all allied thereto. We think that all acts which we call sins, and which would be sins for us who recognize them as such and have no urgent temptations to commit them, are necessarily the same sins to the ignorant, the helpless, and besotted; and we dream that Divine Justice must somehow vindicate itself against them in the next life. We make no sufficient allowance for the immeasurable difference of the standard by which the Pharisee and the Publican must be weighed. We forget how, when the poor bodily frames, so often disgraced, fall away at last into the dust, the souls which wore them, released from all their contaminations, may arise, purer than we can think, cleaner than we can know, to the higher worlds above. Least of all do we take count of the comparative responsibility which must belong to what must be called the comparative *sanity* of human beings. In the very remarkable and exhaustive treatise whose title I have placed second at the head of this article, there is to be found a most elaborate analysis of scores of cases of heinous crime committed of late years in France. Making allowance for the author's zeal leading him to push his conclusions somewhat beyond what his premisses warrant, the multitude of these crimes, which he gives us good reasons to believe were committed either under temporary aberration of mind or congenital moral idiotcy, are perfectly appalling. Little doubt can remain on any reader's mind that multitudes of men and women are so constituted as to have but an infinitesimal share of moral responsibility. The most atrocious crimes are often precisely those which, on learning the utter insensibility displayed from first to last by the perpetrators, we are obliged most distinctly to class with such maniacal homicides as that of poor Lamb's sister, or with the ravages of a man-eating tiger in an Indian village.

Again, the inequalities of moral endowment become salient to our apprehension when we contemplate the different races of mankind. Who can imagine for a moment that the same measure will be meted to a Malay or a Kaffir assassin as to an English Pritchard or a French La Pommerais?

But (it may be said) we are not now concerned about the righteous judgments of God on human transgressions. We are content to believe they will be meted out with absolute impartiality at last. What is painful in the theory of Hereditary Piety is the idea that, through such material instrumentality as natural birth, the most divine of all gifts should be bestowed or denied, and that, in fact, a pious man owes his piety not so much (as we had ever believed) to the direct action of the Holy Ghost on his soul, blowing like the wind where it listeth, but rather to his earthly father's physical bequest of a constitution adapted to the religious emotions.

It does not seem to me that the two views, that of the need for the free inspiration of God's Spirit, and that of the heritage of what we will call the religious constitution, are in themselves incompatible. The one is the seed which must needs be sown; the other is the ground, more or less rich and well prepared, into which it must be cast. That among those natural laws which are simply the permanent mode of Divine action, should be found the law that the ground-work of piety may be laid through generations, and that the godly man may bequeath to his child not only a body free from the diseases entailed by vice, but also a mind specially qualified for all high and pure emotions,—this, I think, ought to be no great stumbling-block. That there is something else necessary beside a constitutional *receptivity* towards pious emotions, and that there remains as much as ever for God to do for man's soul after we have supposed he has inherited such receptivity, is, I think, sufficiently clear.

But how of those who inherit no such character, but rather the opposite tendency towards absorption in purely secular interests, towards incredulity, or towards that evenly-balanced nature which Mr. Galton attributes to the typical sceptic, and is alike without penitence and without "ambition sainte"? Surely we have only to admit that here is one more of the thousand cases in which this world's tuitions are extended only to the elementary parts of that moral education which is to go on for eternity? That God teaches a few of us some lessons here, which others must wait to learn hereafter, is as certain as that infants, idolators, idiots and boors, are not on the intellectual level of Plato or the moral level of Christ. That it is all the *more* (and not the *less*) certain that an immortality of knowledge and love awaits these disinherited ones of earth and "trims the balance of eternity," appears to me the most direct of all deductions from the justice and goodness of God.

The truth seems to be that every human soul has its special task and its special help. Some of us have to toil against merely gross sensual passion. Others are raised a step higher, and fight with less ignoble irascible feelings and selfish ambitions. Yet, again, others rise above all these. But is their work therefore at an end? Not so. Metaphysical doubts, moral despondencies, spiritual vanities, meet them and buffet them in the higher air to which they have ascended; and who may say that their battle is not hardest of all? To help us to contend against these difficulties, one of us is blessed with happy circumstances, another has a sunny and loving disposition, a third is gifted with a stern moral sense, and a fourth with a fervent love for God. He who sees all these springs and wheels moving with or against one another, can alone judge which is the noblest victor among all the combatants.

Lastly, we have to touch the question, whether the tendency of Civilization to check the impulsive temperament and foster the more balanced prudential character, will in future time re-act upon Religion by suppressing the development of those natures in which it now takes easiest root.

At first sight, it would undoubtedly appear that such might be the case. Yet, as it is certain that in our day, while civilization increases more rapidly than ever and the power of mere creeds is evaporating into thin air, the religious feelings of mankind are by no means dying out, but are perhaps higher pitched than ever before, so we may fairly conclude that some other law comes into play to compensate for the rude zeal of semi-barbarism. One thing is obvious. The moral conception which men entertain of

God rises constantly with their own moral progress. When the nations shall have reached a pinnacle of ethical excellence far beyond our present standard, when the wild and fierce instincts now rampant shall have died out of the human race, and the ever-fostered social affections wreathe the earth with garlands of grace and fragrance,—even when that far-off millennium comes, God will assuredly seem just as far above man as He seems now. His holiness will transcend human virtue, as the Chaldæan sky overarched the Tower which was built to reach it.

Another point must not be forgotten in this connexion. The conscious instability of a nature capable alike of great good and great evil, is indeed often, as Mr. Galton teaches us, the first motive which makes a man religious. But *having* become religious, he does not normally remain in a continual tempest of contending principle and passion. That Supreme Guidance which he looks for from on high, and which he believes himself to obtain, leads him onward, as the years go by, out of the wilderness with its fiery scorpions of remorse, into a land of green pastures, beside still waters. The calm of a really religious old age, is a peace compared to which the equipoise of the sceptic is as the stillness of a mill-pond to that of the ocean on whose breast all the host of stars is reflected.

It must needs be the same as regards the race. *Now* it is ever those,

> "Who rowing hard against the stream,
> See distant gates of Eden gleam,
> And do not dream it is a dream."

But hereafter, in the far-off future, when the wilder impulses are dead, mankind may not need to strive always so violently to "take the kingdom of Heaven by force;" but glide on softly and surely, borne by the ever-swelling currents of Faith and Love.

ESSAY III.

THE RELIGION OF CHILDHOOD.

In his great work, "Les Apôtres," M. Renan prophesies that a hundred years to come the ostensible boundaries of Judaism, Catholicism and Protestantism, will not have undergone essential alteration. Each church, however, will then consist of two distinct classes of adherents—those who honestly believe in its doctrines, and those who disbelieve them altogether, but continue to pay them outward homage, and to conform to established rites, from motives of public policy, tenderness for the weak, romantic sentiment, or, perchance, indifference. Dogma will, in those happy times, be treated as a sacred ark, never to be opened, and therefore harmless even if empty.

I must beg leave to doubt that this millennium is so near as M. Renan supposes; nay, that it will ever arrive. The pure love of theoretic truth, which he justly lays down as the one proper motive for those historical researches which are undermining the popular creed, will hardly conduct men generally to lives of practical falsehood. To study with the simple desire of obtaining facts, regardless of the bearing such facts may have upon our most cherished prejudices, can scarcely be a good preparatory training for acting ever afterwards as if there were no such things as facts in the most solemn concerns of human existence. To arrive at the conclusion that the Divine mercy is withheld from no honest seeker, however many mental errors he may have ignorantly imbibed, is not precisely the same conclusion (albeit M. Renan would have it so) as that religious belief is of no consequence to the soul which entertains it, and that it is just as possible to be noble with a base faith as with the purest—to love God when He is represented as a cruel and capricious Despot, as when He is revealed as the holy and blessed Father of all.

Rather do I believe that a very different future is before the world. The reaction has come from the belief of Christendom for eighteen centuries, that "everlasting fire" might be the penalty of even unwitting error concerning Trinities and Unities, Incarnations and Processions; and the first result of that reaction is very obviously and naturally to lead men to depreciate for a time the real value which must for ever belong to the possession of such religious truth as each soul may be permitted to grasp. Because an artificial extrinsic penalty upon error is no longer feared, the intrinsic and unchangeable value of truth is for a moment forgotten. But ere long a juster estimate will be made. That calm, earnest, fearless spirit of search, which distinguishes so strangely the great thinkers of pre-Christian times from the feverish and terror-haunted anxiety of those who followed them, will return to the world, and will become the habitual temper of all the wise and good. Men will no longer seek the waters of life, as in a tale of enchantment, because they can save the drinker from some fiend's spell of torture or transport him to a fairy paradise. But they will seek them as when, after long, weary days of desert march, the traveller, dust-soiled and parched with thirst, sees Jordan eddying between its willowy banks, and flings himself on the grass and drinks its sweet waters and bends in its waves till they go over, even over his soul.

Religious errors imbibed in youth are like those constitutional maladies which may lie latent for years and perhaps never produce acute evil of any kind, but which also may at any time burst into painful and sharp disease. Human nature possesses sometimes such a tendency to all things healthy, bright and beautiful, that the most gloomy creeds fail to depress its natural buoyancy of hope and trustfulness, and the most immoral ones to soil its purity. We all know, and rejoice to know, many men, many more women, who are among the excellent of the earth, but who if they did but succeed (as they profess to aim to do) in likening themselves to the Deity they have imagined, would needs be transformed from the most gentle and pitiful to the most cruel and relentless. The non-operative dogmas in such creeds as theirs would terrify them, could they but recognize them. But because of these blessed inconsistencies, numerous as they are, we must not suppose that such seeds of unmeasured evil as religious falsehoods, are always, or even oftenest, innoxious. Like the man with hereditary disease, the mischief may long lie unperceived, while the course of his life does not tend to bring it into action. But an accident of most trivial kind, a blow to body or mind, a change of climate or of habits, may suddenly develope what has been hidden so long, and the man may sink under a calamity which with healthier constitution he would have surmounted in safety.

On the other hand, no words can adequately describe the value of a religious faith which supplies the soul, I will not say with absolute and final truth, but with such measure of truth as is its sufficient bread of life, its pure and healthful sustenance. We may not always see that this is so. As error may lie long innoxious, so truth may remain latent in the mind, and, as it would seem, useless and unprofitable. He who has been blessed with the priceless boon may go his way, and the "cares of the world and deceitfulness of riches," the thousand joys and sorrows, pursuits and interests, faults and follies of life, may carry him on year after year heeding but little the treasure he carries in his breast. Yet, even in his worst hours, that truth is a talisman to ennoble what might else be wholly base, to warm what might be all selfish, to purify and to cheer by half-understood influence over all thoughts and feelings. But it is in the supreme moments of life, the hours of agony or danger or temptation to mortal sin, the hours when it is given to us either to step down into a gulf whose bottom we may not find before the grave, or to spring back out of falsehood or bitterness or self-indulgence upon the higher level of truth and love and holiness—it is in *these* hours that true religious faith shows itself as the power of God unto salvation. *With* it, there is nothing man may not bear and do. Without it, he is in danger immeasurable. With a false creed—a creed false to the instincts of the soul, incapable of supplying its needs of reverence and love, such as they have been constituted by the Creator—a man's joys may cover the whole surface of his life; but underneath there is a cold, dark abyss of doubt and fear. He passes hastily on in the bright sunshine, but under his feet he knows the ice may at any time give way and crash beneath him. Happiness is to him the exception in the world of existence. The rule is sorrow and pain; endless sorrow, eternal pain. But he whose creed tells him of a God whom he can wholly love, entirely trust, even though his outward life may be full of gloom and toil, has for ever the consciousness of a great deep joy underlying all care and grief; a joy he pauses not always to contemplate, but which he knows is there, waiting for him whenever he turns to it; and his sorrows and all the sorrows of the world are in his sight but passing shadows which shall give place at last to everlasting bliss. His plot of earth may be barren and flowerless, and he may till it often in weariness and pain, but he would not exchange it for a paradise, for within it there is the well of water springing up into everlasting life.

The time will come, I am persuaded, when men will be more than ever awake to these facts of the value of true religious faith and the danger and misery of error. When this happens, so far from becoming indifferentists and treating all creeds as alike, they will necessarily seek more earnestly than ever for truth, not under the scourge of the terrors of hell, but with a calm, deep appreciation of the intrinsic importance of such faith for its own sake. Will they then be content, as M. Renan supposes, to go on paying outward adhesion to churches whose office it is to teach the very errors from which they have escaped? Will they endure to perform solemn rites before God which have become to them solemn mockeries? Will they by their countenance and example maintain for the young and uneducated the delusions from which every hour they thank God they have been themselves delivered? Will they act *lies* such as the saints of old went to the stake and the rack rather than be guilty of, because they have found higher, nobler, more heart-encouraging truths than it was given to those saints to know? I believe it not! The day will yet come when the consciences of mankind will recognize that it was for no delusion those martyrs died, no fictitious virtue of honesty of lips and brain, which our greater enlightenment has discovered to be but a fanaticism and a prejudice. It will be recognized that to *live* a lie is more base even than to speak a lie; and that a religious lie is the basest, because the cowardliest, of lies. It will be recognized that to mislead others by our example or teaching, is to do them a wrong and injury only to be measured by the tremendous realities of the spiritual and moral life into which we dare to interpose our falsehoods to serve, or frustrate, God's designs. It will be recognized that as religious truth is the greatest of treasures, so every word and deed by which we tamper therewith involves a dishonesty which, when all the cheats and thefts of this world's goods are forgotten and pardoned, the offender may need to weep over and repent.

If these views have in them any justice, the question so often asked in our day, "What religion shall we teach our children?" assumes new significance. That all-precious religious truth which year by year men will learn better to value and more simply to follow, how are the young to be taught to seek and aided to find it? How are we to guard them against that fatal pseudo-liberal indifferentism which would make of Christendom another China, with each man lauding his neighbour's religion and depreciating with mock humility his own? These are large questions, which for the general public correspond to the anxious private inquiry of so many parents: What shall we teach our children concerning God and Christ and the Bible? In what position ought we to place them as regards the popular theology, and the Churches wherein we were ourselves brought up, and whereto we now hold more or less loosely? In a word, what is the Religion for Childhood in our age and phase of thought?

With much distrust of my own power to deal with so great a theme or offer counsel to those who alone have practical knowledge of the training of children, I shall venture to attempt some answer to these questions in the following pages. It must happen to all who have striven to urge the claims of a creed founded upon consciousness rather than authority, to be frequently challenged by the inquiry, "How would your faith suit children and ignorant persons? It may be all very well for educated men and women, but how would it apply to the poor? How could you bring up a child under its simple doctrines?" The faith which shrinks from such a challenge stands self-condemned. To prove that the most liberal theology need not do so, but has its blessed work to accomplish for the child no less than for the man, will be my present task.

It might be thought at first sight and prior to experience of the fact, that in this latest Reformation, as in all preceding ones, it would be a matter of course for parents not only freely to transmit their religious ideas to their sons and daughters, but to take peculiar care to guard them against the errors they have renounced, and to instruct them in the truths they have gained. The children of the early Christians, Moslems, Protestants, were no doubt imbued to the uttermost of their parents' skill with the doctrines of their religion. The idea of teaching a young Huguenot to believe in the Real Presence or to worship the Virgin, or even of sending him to a school where he might learn to do so, would have been held scarcely less than a crime in the eyes of his father and mother. Nay, to let him grow up with the notion that the question was an open one, and that his parents were as ready to see him choose a religion as a secular profession, and become a Romanist or a Jew as he might become a soldier or a physician,—this also would have seemed to them monstrous, and even impious.

How far we are from such a view of parental duty, it is startling to reflect. Professed Unitarians, indeed, habitually train their children in Unitarian principles, and lead them to the public services of their church.[1] But even they continually allow motives of convenience or economy to induce them to send them to schools where they know that the young minds and hearts will be subjected to the fullest influences of orthodoxy. The whole tenor of their guidance is calculated, hardly so much to secure their children's intelligent adherence to the creed they themselves profess, as to afford them a fair option to accept it if they see fit. Of course there are many exceptions, but I venture to

[1] This Essay was first published in the Theological (Unitarian) Review.

think this description may be taken as a true one as regards the majority of Unitarian families, and that the result may be traced in the innumerable lapses of the sons and daughters of Unitarians into the ranks of churches from whose errors a very moderate share of parental care and warning ought to have protected them. That worldly interest has some part in all this must perhaps be conceded. The social and (let it be added, shameful as it is) the matrimonial disadvantages of membership in a small sect, may make some Unitarian parents less unwilling than they ought to be to sacrifice their sons' and daughters' spiritual for temporal benefit. I am persuaded, however, that far more often the motives of Unitarian parents, even of those who act most unguardedly, are higher than these. Many of them doubtless imagine that what is so clear to their minds will needs be clear to those of their children. Others suppose that even if their son receive false instruction at school, they will be able in a few weeks of holidays to supply an antidote of rational argument which shall neutralize the poison which month after month has been slowly infiltered and taken up into the child's system of thought and feeling. Many more, having been themselves educated in the older and stricter Unitarian training, have never experienced and have formed no adequate idea of the evil, and of the tenacity of the darker doctrines of the popular creed. They think them *silly* rather than deadly. They have never known what it is to believe in Eternal Hell. They have never knelt to thank God when that horror of horrors was lifted from their souls. Nay, even their own boasted doctrine of the Divine Unity has been always to them a mere negation of Trinitarian error. They have never known the power of that flood-tide of reverence and love when all the religious emotions, long divided, confused, and scattered, are turned at last into the one channel, and the same Lord is recognized as

Creating, Redeeming, and Sanctifying God. All these experiences, which belong to those who have been brought up in the old creed and through struggle and difficulty have reached to the new, are unknown to Unitarians born and educated in the church of Channing or Priestley. They almost marvel at the ardour of converts for truths valuable indeed, they admit, in the highest degree, but still, so obvious! the very alphabet, to them, of religious knowledge. They as little expect their children to renounce these elementary truths and go back to the creeds which their grandfathers renounced, as they expect them to give up modern geology and astronomy for those of the dark ages; and they take as little precaution to guard them against one mistake as the other. When the catastrophe arrives, and the entail of Unitarianism is broken, as usual, at the third generation, they are grieved and wounded; but perhaps even then they hardly realize all their child has lost of an inheritance which they were bound to transmit to him securely.

The case of those who are not members of the Unitarian Church, but who entertain Unitarian or Theistic opinions while nominally ranked with the orthodox, is of course still worse than the others. For them to bring up their children to believe as they do themselves is a real difficulty, and one they very rarely even try to surmount. Those who have not such definite views as to make them wish to break with the Church in which they were born, or who, while having them, lack courage to do it, are not very likely to train their children in clearer light or greater sincerity. The extreme latitude of opinion which the laity enjoy in the National Church, makes it appear a needless and ungrateful effort to release ourselves from the arms which received us in baptism, and will (whatever be our offences) drop us gently and tenderly into the grave, but which, in all the interval between, will never exercise over us any forceful interference. How many thus remain in the Church because they are never called on by any test, or even inquiry, to renew or renounce their adherence to it; how many more remain with the idea of Colenso and *Presbyter Anglicanus*, that they have a right as members of the nation to be members of the National Church, whatever their views may be of its doctrine—how many of all these there are now in England, it is not easy to tell. Such as they are, while young men and women, their position perhaps entails little difficulty of a moral sort. But when they become parents the case is altered. Shall they have their children baptized? Shall they teach them to read the Bible, and repeat the usual hymns and collects? Above all, shall they take them to church and make them learn prayers and listen to sermons all and each saturated with doctrines the parent disbelieves? On the other hand, shall they omit all these traditional processes and bring up the children, as their friends will assuredly say, like little heathens? The question is making many a father anxious, and giving many a mother the heart-ache, in England at this moment.

It must be owned that the case is beset with difficulties. Putting aside special family difficulties—difference of opinion between the two parents, interference of other relatives, and last, not least, the forbidden efforts of orthodox servants to impress children with their crude and cruel theology—putting all these aside, there remain gravest difficulties common to all. I cannot presume to offer counsel as to these difficulties in detail, but I venture to urge the consideration of a few general principles which, if approved, may serve as guides to decide the outline of conduct to be filled by each parent according to special circumstances.

In the first place, a critical spirit can never be rightly fostered in a child. It is not for one who has all the evidence yet to learn, and even the process by which evidence must be weighed, to mount any seat of judgment and pronounce sentence. To lead a child to do so, even in matters tenfold less solemn than those which pertain to religion, must needs distort the natural order and development of his faculties. Nay, more: the critical faculty, even when exercised in the plenitude of the powers of middle life, is always somewhat opposed to the instincts of reverence and humility, and only becomes good and noble when used under the spur of pure love of truth, and with all the caution and self-distrust which facts may warrant. Often must it have happened to all of us to feel how violent a revulsion is created when a sermon appealing to criticism, and demanding of us to revise arguments of history, philology, metaphysics, has followed suddenly upon prayers which for the time had restored us to a more humble, childlike attitude of mind. To be brought to realize somewhat of the distance between ourselves and the Divine Holiness, to feel some of the deeper emotions of penitence and aspiration, perhaps to pray in the true sense of prayer, and then, a moment afterwards, instead of having fresh moral life poured into us, with high thoughts of God and duty and immortality, instead of being lifted by our stronger brother into nearer gaze at the Supreme Goodness, to be suddenly called on to revise our intellectual stores, recall this detail of history and that fact of science, and then balance the validity of the arguments by which the preacher has appealed to us for a verdict of "Proven" or "Not proven," —this is the weariness of preaching, this is the feast where the rich Intellect may be fed, but the hungry Soul goes empty away. There is no harm in it all. Perhaps it is very necessary that congregations should have such facts and arguments often placed before them; and if they are to be placed at all, they must needs be placed for critical free judgment. Only the religious sentiment and the religious intellect are brought into painful and jarring proximity, the attitude of the soul is altered too rudely.

But if this be so with us all in middle life, how much more incongruous must be anything like such critical judgment in a child ! The most fatal and hopeless lack in any child's character is that of the feeling of reverence; and it would almost seem that when from any cause it is deficient, it is well-nigh impossible to create it afresh. But if a mode were to be devised expressly for the extinction of reverence, it would manifestly be to set a child to pass its wretched little judgments on the opinions of those who constitute for it the world. Thus, whatever else a child ought to be taught about the popular religion, it is quite clear it must not be taught to set itself up to decide that such and such doctrines are foolish or absurd.

Secondly : We have been all a good deal misled by the vaunt of our ancestors, that a Christian child knows more about God than Socrates or Plato. We have a latent idea that it is our business to verify the boast, and stock a baby's mind with formulæ about that Ineffable Existence, whose relations to us we may indeed learn, but whose awful Nature not all the wisdom of the immortal life may fully reveal to His creatures. Thus there is a constant effort to give a child notions about what could only be fitly treated as too solemn a mystery to pretend to have notions of at all; and the natural inquisitive questions of the pupil are not met by the grave warning which best would instil reverence and awe, but by efforts to give or correct ideas where no ideas may be. We have all been so accustomed to "Bodies of Divinity," Catechisms and Creeds, that we find it hard to imagine religion despoiled of such paraphernalia, and mothers ask, with an alarm which would be ludicrous were the subject less solemn : "What am I to teach my child if I am not to make him learn the Church

Catechism, or the Shorter Catechism, or Watts' Catechism, or tell him the story of Adam and Eve and the apple, and Noah's ark, or the history of Elisha and the naughty boys, or the fate of Ananias and Sapphira? If all these things are to be left out, and the child is not even to know what each Person of the Trinity does for him, and what his godfathers and god-mothers have promised he shall believe, what remains for me to teach him of religion?"

It is a startling idea to such good mothers to reflect that all these lessons are not religion at all, but instructions which much oftener turn their children from religion than engage them to love it, and that the utter cessation of such tasks would leave them open to far more devout feelings. "*No religious teaching?*" But can a mother, herself penetrated with religious feeling, teach *anything* to her child which shall not also teach him religion? Can she direct his mind to the objects around him, sun and star and bird and bee, can she lead him to check his little selfishnesses and angry passions, and be kind to his brothers and sisters and obedient to herself, can she read with him a single story or poem or book of infant science, in which the thought of God the Maker, God the Observer, God the Lord of all things beautiful and good, shall not shine over all her teachings? Religion entering in this its natural way is full of interest and delight to the child. Behind the dry facts, which have for him perhaps little value, he finds that meaning which elevates Fact into Truth. All things have a personal sense and purpose, since he is made to see a Personal Will directing them all; and by degrees the vast unity of the world, the unity of order, beauty and beneficence, dawns upon his soul.

Again: There is need to bear in mind that a child's faculties of love are given *data* in his nature. We have not got to create them, and we can in very small degree warp and alter them from what they have been created. They are so constituted as spontaneously to open to an object of one kind, and to shrink from an object of another. The task of him who believes children's hearts to be God's handiwork and not that of a Devil, is to *educate* (draw out) what God has put there, and to present to those faculties, as they grow, that idea of God and duty which they are *made* to fasten upon with honour and love. Divines talk of children being wholly corrupt, and poets tell us they " trail clouds of glory"; but parents neither find the corruption nor see much of the clouds of glory. It is a germ of a soul, rather than a soul either burdened with sin or "trailing" any foreknown light, which lies covered up in a little child's cradle. But assuredly it is a germ in which God has folded potentially all the blossoms of holy feelings man can know on earth. Surely it is always proof that the teaching is wrong, when those sentiments which God has intended should turn to Himself do not turn to Him as spontaneously as the young plant to the light? It must always be because it is not God, the true God, whom we have presented to the soul of the child, but some grim idol whom it was never made to love, that it has failed to lift itself to Him.

Again: The sense of sin is so deeply connected with the religious sentiment, it is so profoundly true that the holiness of God is first intimately revealed to us through the sense of our own unholy deeds and thoughts, that it is of the first importance in all religious teaching to place aright this matter of "the exceeding sinfulness of sin." No human piety, even the piety of a little innocent child, can live and bloom without some tears of penitence to water it. Nay, the readiness and fulness of repentance in early youth, the April flood of pure and blessed sorrow which falls so abundantly and then leaves the sky so clear and earth so tremulously bright, is evidence enough that repentance has its inevitable work even in the religious life of the infant. But there is no part of religion which has been so cruelly perverted as this. No theological dogmas impressed on a child's intellect can be half so mischievous as the practical moral training which distorts for it the natural processes of penitence and restoration; and no efforts of religious teachers have been so persistent as those which have been directed to this fatal aim. Starting with the wholly false conception of the highest religious life as if it were one perpetual sickly anxiety and "worrying about the soul," they are uneasy if their child enjoys a healthier state, and weeps only for a real fall, instead of puling continually from over-tenderness of conscience. A child's moral life ought to go on, like its physical life, all unconsciously to itself; but just as the precocious offspring of over-anxious parents think about cold or heat or unwholesome food, the children of some religious people are made to know all about their own spiritual condition, and commence in the nursery a life of moral valetudinarianism. Of course such mistakes lie chiefly with Evangelical parents, and few others are likely to fall into them, but into opposite errors of which we shall speak presently. But the narrowness of a woman's life has undoubtedly a tendency to make mothers vastly exaggerate the lilliputian sins and miniature transgressions of their little kingdom, the nursery; and the result is too often an attempt to construct for its inhabitants a baby-house morality, wherein the true proportion of good and evil is lost, and the horrible mischief introduced of perpetual forced and untrue repentance. A wise mother once said to me—"I wish my children to know there are such things as great crimes in the world. It will teach them that their own little sins and bad feelings are not enormous offences, but are the seeds which, if unchecked, may grow to be enormous offences. I wish them to understand the *solidarity* of sin, and that all sins are allied and interactive."

The opposite error of moral laxity and indifferentism is one into which parents who have themselves escaped from the evils of Calvinistic training are naturally most prone to fall. While one child's conscience is over-stimulated to the verge of disease, another finds its own instinctive penitence treated so lightly, its real faults passed over as if so trivial and unimportant, that it is impossible but that, with a child's susceptibility to the opinion of those above it, the penitence soon dies away and the fault is repeated.

Now the parent who would hold the mean between these two errors, and neither excite a child's conscience to disease nor lull it to lethargy, has a most difficult task to perform in face of the common preaching and common juvenile religious literature of the day. Clergymen addressing audiences of grown men and women may well be excused if they consider that there is small danger of their adult hearers making too much of their sins, but much danger of their making too little. The most spirit-stirring, and probably on the whole the most useful, preachers in the orthodox churches are those who are for ever proclaiming "the wrath of God against sin," and urging their hearers to more earnest self-scrutiny and deeper penitence. But these spiritual medicines, meted out for the hard conscience of a man, are almost poison to the tender heart of the child; and the very solemnity of the place where the lesson is heard increases the power of the words to exaggerate and distort. Again: religious books for children and religious novels for the young are half of them written by women of sickly sentiment, full of that trivial, baby-house morality of which I have spoken; and the child whose mind is fed with such petty thoughts cannot possibly grow up to health and vigour of soul. The truth cannot be too often recalled that human beings have not got an infinite store of attention and reverence to bestow, insomuch that they may harmlessly lavish a great deal of either upon trifles, and then retain afterwards an equal amount ready for really important and sacred things. Waste of the spiritual emotions is the most fatal waste of which we can be guilty.

If the reader concede the principles now stated, the ground of debate regarding the religious education of a child will be found at least considerably narrowed. If the possession of religious truth be the most priceless of heritages—if a critical spirit must never be fostered in a child—if systems of theology and a store of cut-and-dried facts in divinity be no needful or desirable part of a child's religion—if a child's faculties of love and reverence be given *data*, and our task in relation to them only to present worthily their proper Object—if the due place to be assigned in moral training to sin and penitence be the most important and sacred part of education, wherein to err either on the side of exaggeration or underrating is well-nigh fatal—if all these things be so, then some of the following consequences may be fairly assumed to follow.

1st. The admission that religious truth is the most priceless of heritages must surely decide the question for each parent, what are the doctrines which he or she individually is morally bound to teach to son or daughter. Catholic and Calvinist parents, with their gloomy creeds, their gospels of evil tidings, still without hesitation feel it their duty to teach what is to them, subjectively, true. Common honesty, common regard for the welfare of their children, require it of them; and no greater causes of public and even national disturbance are found than the efforts of rulers to interfere with this duty, and teach the child of a Catholic, Calvinism, or of a Jew, Catholicism. Shall, then, those whom I am addressing in this paper, whose creed (as *they* are at least persuaded) is truest of all, and ten thousand times a happier, holier, nobler faith than that of Rome or Geneva,

—shall they alone hesitate whether they shall bring up their children in their own creed or in that of their neighbours? How deplorable is it there should even be a question in such a matter! Yet question there is; and the actual practice of liberal-minded parents at this moment is so variable and devoid of fixed principle of action, that it would be ridiculous, were it not lamentable, to describe it. Here is a mother who does not believe a syllable of the popular theology, but brings up her daughters carefully to believe it all, and pretends to them that she believes it also, guarding them from the chance of reading a book or conversing with a person who could disturb their faith. Here is a father who allows his boys to be taught the whole system, which he himself believes to be as much a delusion as the vortices of Descartes; but he thinks to remedy some of the evil by applying an antidote in the shape of a little levity. Here is one who trains his child to criticize the opinions of those around, and to set up its small judgment over the mysteries of heaven and earth. Here is another who teaches "Elegant Extracts" of Christianity, and leaves the child by and by to discover that the authority for what it was told was true and what it was told was false, was precisely one and the same. Here, again, is one who, from fear of "prejudicing" the child's mind, teaches him no religion at all, and thus loses for him for ever all the tender associations of youthful piety. Placed clearly before a parent's mind, the idea of deliberately teaching a child falsehood, or choosing for it secular advantage rather than spiritual benefit, would seem shocking and monstrous to all save the most worldly. But the falsehoods are popular falsehoods, filling the very air of English thought; the secular advantages offered by orthodoxy are tangible, considerable, every day present. The spiritual benefits of a pure creed (now we have ceased to believe in eternal penalties for error) are purely spiritual; and in the violent reaction from the old overestimate of the importance of opinion, it is a natural error of liberalism to overlook them. We see good men and women—nay, noble and saintly men and women—whose opinions are the furthest from our own; and many a parent may feel he would be content to see his son or daughter like them, and at the same time making "the best of both worlds" in the safe shelter of orthodoxy. But we forget perhaps that another generation will not stand where the last stood, and that the good fruit we admire did not indeed grow off the thorns of the Five Points of Calvinism, but off the true vine of Divine Love which wreathed itself around them. The *chance* that, if we plant only the thorns, the vine will grow over them, is one assuredly not to be counted upon.

2ndly. From the observation of the evil results of instilling a critical spirit at an age when a child cannot possibly possess either the materials or true method for forming a critical judgment, it follows that liberal parents, like others, must needs teach their religion to their children *didactically*. There lies here a great practical difficulty. On the one hand, we all know too well the evil and danger of bringing up a young mind to believe a whole mass of doctrines as certain and unquestionable, and then leaving it to find out at its entrance into independent life and when temptation is at its highest, that many of these doctrines, if not all of them, are utterly uncertain and doubtful. On the other hand, to teach a child to consider all the truths of the unseen world as matters of speculation, would be still more absurd and mischievous. To impart knowledge of them, and yet to impart at the same time that other knowledge, that parents are not infallible; that no human knowledge is infallible; that to love Truth and search for it as for hid treasure, rather than to receive it unasked and undeserved, like the rain, is the duty and the lot of man;—to impart this must needs be a task of great delicacy and difficulty. It is to be remembered, however, that a child is always naturally disposed to look on his parents' opinion as final truth so long as the parents' mind bounds its narrow horizon of all wisdom. Thus to make a child understand that any doctrine is or is not true *in its parents' opinion*, is to give it at once the prestige of truth, and yet not to incur any risk of future break-down and discovery. By and by the child will learn what is the value of its parents' opinions on all matters, and if the parent be truly good and wise, that value will be very great indeed, though of course far short of absolute authority. In any case, the parent will obtain for his religious teaching precisely the respect it deserves to obtain—that of his own personal weight in the estimation of his son or daughter. How much this view of the proper nature of instruction adds to the responsibility of *forming* the opinions which are thus to be bequeathed as the most precious heritage, there is no need to tell. In this, as in all other things, a man or woman's responsibility in thought, feeling and action, seems to become doubled and quadrupled as they assume the holy rank of a father or a mother. Doubtless, many of them must in their hearts echo poor Margaret Fuller's exclamation: "I am the parent of an immortal soul! God be merciful to me—a sinner!"

3rdly. If we abandon the idea that children should be crammed with facts connected somehow with religion, and made capable of "telling more about God than Plato and Socrates" (much more indeed than it is likely Plato and Socrates can now tell after two thousand years of heaven), there will be an end in a great measure of the difficulty which now besets liberal parents in their inquiry, "What shall we teach our children of a Sunday?" With the imaginary necessity will disappear the imaginary duty of meeting it, and small Platos of five years old and Socrates in white frocks will no longer be made to pore over catechisms or repeat the beautiful collects like so many little parrots in a row. The abolition of those "burdens grievous to be borne," the wearisome Sunday lessons of childhood, would, we believe, accomplish no small step towards making children love the religion which they heard of in other and happier ways. Can anybody fancy the result of teaching "Affection to Parents" by a regular educational battery of catechisms and texts once a week? Would it make a child love its mother better? We rather imagine the reverse. Nor can we conceive why the analogous sentiment of love to the Father in heaven should follow a different law.

The old Hebrew prophet believed that a special blessing would come to those who "called the Sabbath a *delight*." It would seem to have been the peculiar pride of our Puritan fathers to make this blessing as difficult of attainment as possible, especially to children. Those to whom this paper is addressed need not be adjured to abandon the Puritanical Sabbath-keeping, whose memory returns to some of us as the dreariest recollection of youth; Sabbaths with the hardest lessons of the week, whose imperfect acquirement somehow involved double offence; Sabbaths with wearisome litanies and incomprehensible sermons through long bright summer mornings, when we sighed to run out and gather cowslips in the sweet green grass; Sabbaths with unwholesome cold meals crowded one on another, making young and old heavy and ill-tempered; Sabbaths toyless and joyless, when all books permitted to be read had the same indescribable flavour of unreal goodness, and whose perusal was accompanied by the same sense of soreness of the elbows and weariness of the poor little dangling legs! These are not Sabbaths which the children of liberal thinkers are likely ever to recall. But there would surely be a loss incurred the other way, were the Sunday obliterated from their childish calendar or made a purely secular holiday. There is no need it should be so. Calvinism and all the forms of the old theology appeal to grown men and women, that is, to persons conscious of actual sin, and they either need to be modified to meet the requirements of innocent childhood, or else they distort childish souls to meet their darker lessons. But a true theology, whose basis shall be the spontaneous religious consciousness of our nature, is not thus unfitted for childhood, nor will its simple and natural services be otherwise than delightful to the young mind and heart to whom the sentiments of awe and love are full of joy. Parents, we believe, will be obliged rather to hold back and calm the fervent religious emotions of their children, than fictitiously to nurse them as now, when they teach them to think of God as indeed He is, and not as the creeds have represented Him. We have known a few such happy children, and in nearly every case their mothers have said, "I hardly dare to speak much of religious things, they feel too much."

Bible-reading, again, is a difficulty. An education which should omit the study of the greatest of all books—a book which, in a literary sense alone, is to other books as Shakespeare is to the puny poets of the age of Queen Anne, and which, in a religious sense, is the quarry whence men will draw praise and prayer while the world remaineth—an education which should omit the study of the Bible, would be no education at all. Even as the chief historical document of the past, and the Guide-book (we had almost said, "idol") of half Christendom at present, the Bible is a fact no more to be ignored in the instruction of a child, than the existence of the sovereign or the capital city of its native country. But how is a child to read the Bible and not acquire the orthodox theology? Let me rather ask, Would any child construct for itself the orthodox theology if it were to ponder over the Bible for years, provided it had not been previously taught to *find* that theology therein? That the idea of the Trinity and the "Plan of Salvation" would even occur to a child on reading the Gospels, I utterly disbelieve. What it would find there, beyond some beautiful stories and words of prayer and precept grandly sounding in its ears, it is hard to say. But a child's mind does not construct systems. The simple system of God's Unity and Fatherhood once presented to it, will more than suffice for its wants in this respect.

The evil which comes of Bible-reading for children surely arises from the ineradicable habit of treating the book mystically, and as differing, not in degree only, but utterly in kind, from other books. The child reads it long before any other history, and quite as a different lesson, and therefore he thinks of Adam and Eve and Noah and Balaam quite otherwise than he thinks of the characters he reads of elsewhere. The writer knew a case of a boy whose education was conducted on the opposite principle. His parents (disciples of Theodore Parker) first gave him to read some of Mr. Cox's beautiful Grecian stories, and then afterwards, without any special preparation, the book of Genesis. The little fellow, a clever child of eight or nine, was immensely delighted with it, but very manifestly had no other impression than that the Israelites believed in the One God and the Greeks in many false ones, and that the early legends of each might fitly be compared. He even found out for himself the resemblance between the story of Noah and Deucalion, of Jephtha's daughter and Iphigenia. To a child thus beginning it, the Bible would have a thousand good lessons, but no lesson of superstition. I may add that the same boy was without exception the most religious I ever knew, brave and true, and beautifully dutiful to his parents, and his early manhood bears no less excellent promise.

Finally, there is the church-going difficulty. Unitarians of course have a clear path before them; they naturally take their children to the chapels they themselves attend. The assurance that the worship in such chapels is addressed to the Supreme Father only, that the prayers are always of a pure and spiritual cast, and that the morals inculcated in the sermon are universally lofty and true,—all these are immense advantages which may well solve the question for any parent as to the desirability of bringing his child to public worship. But even Unitarians must feel how little of the service or sermon suited for intellectual men and women, *can*, by any effort of the minister, be made also suitable for little children. Some of the preaching, indeed, suggests rather the impression of the utter *unfitness* that childish ears should hear it and childish minds be called to judge in such controversies. The Evangelical teaching, over-stimulating to sickliness and burning out in brief flame of excitement the fuel of sentiment which should have warmed a life-time,—even this is hardly more injurious to a child than to be introduced in infancy to the polemics of the churches, and allowed to turn to the page of scepticism. before it has learned the lesson of faith. As well might a primrose grow in a dusty arena, as the tender piety of youth flourish in the midst of theological controversy.

Liberal parents who take their children to the services of the Church of England have perhaps not so much to fear in the way of controversy from the pulpit, though they *may* be compelled to sit by silent and helpless while their children hear their own profoundest convictions treated as criminal and abominable, and those who hold them comdemned to everlasting fire. They *may* hear these things. But what they are sure to hear are doctrines they believe to be false, and prayers which, according to their views, are mockeries as regards the things asked for, and well-nigh idolatrous as regards the Person at intervals addressed.

Is this, can this, be right? It seems as if we must have wandered far from simplicity and honesty before we can say so deliberately. Of course there are all sorts of moral expediencies in the case. The impression produced by a dignified *cultus*, by the sense of public opinion and sympathy, and by all the historical associations and æsthetic influences belonging to the great National Church—all these are excellent things to give a child. When it is added, that giving them cuts the knot of twenty petty difficulties which beset the course of keeping him at home, and that it is so much the natural order of the family that to diverge from it would require an effort, there is of course a goodly show of argument for the expediency of taking a child to church. But is there not a higher expediency which points a different way, even that expediency of simple truth and honesty which must needs be the best guide to the ultimate good of any human soul?

Among the numerous immoral stories of the Jewish Scriptures there is one which is always strangely slurred over by friends and foes; by friends because it is indefensible, by foes because in condemning it they must condemn their own conduct. In the moment of his rapturous gratitude for his miraculous cure, we are told that Naaman bargained with the prophet, that his conversion to the worship of the true God was not to prevent him from attending his sovereign and bowing to his idol in courtier fashion whenever it might be desirable. The inspired prophet is recorded to have sanctioned this stipulation, and bade the deliberate hypocrite " Go in peace." Can this wretched story have had much influence? I hardly believe it, and yet it might pass for a parable of what is done every day in England. So commonly is it done, that to speak gravely of it as moral error sounds crude and rough; the residue of the harsh prejudices and trenchant ideas of bygone times. We have been accustomed to soften down everything of this kind; to concede gracefully that every opinion is true in some sense or other, and that it is fanatical to make a stand against this phrase in a creed or that expression in a prayer, or talk as if the sin of idolatry could possibly be incurred in England in the nineteenth century. But it does not clearly appear how truth and sincerity have altered their characters, or why, because we are enabled to do better justice to our neighbour's views, we are to be less honest in following out our own. If, *to the individual concerned*, it be as clear a conviction that Christ is not the Infinite Deity as (according to the story) it was to Naaman that Rimmon was not He, it remains to be shown how bowing to the one differs essentially as a moral act from bowing to the other.

These are matters of solemn import, rising to questions beyond the subject of this paper. Let it be remarked, at all events, that the free-thinking parent who means to make his son a thoroughly upright man, hardly sets about it in the best way, when he makes the most impressive action of his childish life consist in praying for things which he believes are never granted to prayer, and in paying divine worship to a being whom he believes to have been a mortal man. When the two fallacies are discovered (as the parent who knows the current of modern thought must expect they will be) in the boy's advancing youth—when the son shall find out that the father taught him what he did not himself believe—how shall filial respect for the veracity of the parent survive, or an example of uprightness be derived from his conduct?

To conclude. The last principle laid down was this: That in teaching religion to a child, our task is *not* to distort and forcibly wrench aside the child's spontaneous sentiments, but to present to them the Object they are made expressly to love and reverence.

Let us for a moment revert to first principles to set before ourselves clearly what is the aim of religious education.

Each human love has its peculiar character. Parental love combines itself with tenderness and protection, filial love with reverence, conjugal love with passion, friendly love with esteem, brotherly and sisterly love with the sympathies and confidence of consanguinity. Love directed, not to child or parent, wife or friend, but to GOD, has also its peculiar character. It is a love of Reverence, of Admiration, of Gratitude; above all, of absolute MORAL ALLEGIANCE, as to a rightful Moral Lord. Such sentiments as may be given to an unseen Creator, which are not of this character— the sentiments to which history bears horrible testimony, of raptures of devotion felt by wicked and cruel men who believed God to be as cruel and unjust as themselves—these sentiments do not constitute Love of God. They are hideous aberrations of the soul, diseased emotions addressed to an imaginary Being.

Again: The true love of God, of which we have spoken, is not merely a part of religion, or the ultimate aim of religion. It *is* religion. The dawn of it in the heart is the aurora of the eternal day which is to shine more and more perfectly through the ages without end. Till it begins, there is no real religion, only at best the preparation for religion.

Thus it follows that to awaken in a child's heart the true love of God, is the alpha and omega of religious education. Make it feel this love, and the highest good a creature can know has been secured for it. Fail to make it feel it, and the most elaborate instructions, the largest store of theological knowledge and religious precepts, are useless and absurd. In the battle of life, children taught everything *else* except this love, go forth like those mockeries of steamships the Chinese constructed to contend with ours, fitted with all the appliances which would have been useful had there been any engine within, but without that which should have given power and motion.

These are principles to which all will agree. Even Romanists say their colossal system of priestly mediation aims *at the end* to help souls to the love of God; and Calvinists, whose dogmas make the Deity hateful, yet profess to instil them with the view of inspiring a love which can only be the reaction from fear. But the great difference between the followers of such churches and those who hold a happier faith must consist, not in the end all may contemplate as desirable, but in the means each may pursue for its attainment.

There is something very deplorable, when we reflect upon it, in the way in which mankind in all ages have sought to take by violence that kingdom of heaven whose golden gates are ever open to him who knocks thereat in filial entreaty. From lands and times when they tortured the body, to days like our own in England when they only strive to wrench the affections and distort the judgment, the same all-pervading error may be traced. Naturally, men who have thus acted in the case of their own souls, have no scruple to act so in their children's behalf; and to drill a young mind to religion is conceived of from first to last as a difficult task, to be achieved by constant coercion of the spontaneous sentiments, and the enforcement of a duty naturally distasteful. It is an immense evidence of the readiness of the human heart to love the Divine Father, that, with the training usually given in this Christian land, so many are still found to resist its natural consequences, and to love God *in spite* of their education.

If a mother wished to make her boy grow up full of affection and respect for a father in India or Australia, how would she set about it? Would she first start with the notion that it would be a very hard thing to do, and contrary to the child's nature? Would she insist on it, morning, noon and night, as his severe duty? Would she talk of the absent parent in a conventional voice, and make addressing him by letter, or doing anything for him, a sterner task than any other? Lastly, would she perpetually tell the child that when the father came home, if he had not been obedient and was not affectionate to him, the father would turn him out of the house and burn him alive? Are these the methods by which a wife and mother's instincts would lead her to act? Surely we have only to imagine the reverse of all these—the popular processes of religious instruction—to find the true method for guiding children's hearts to love their Father in heaven? A child must *not* think it a hard thing, a task of fear and awe, a notion to be dragged into its lessons and its play to make them more irksome and less joyous, that it *ought* to be feeling what it does not feel. Above all things, the idea that such a thing is possible as an ultimate and final rejection by God ought never so much as to be presented to the mind of a child. A child can very well understand punishment; nor does it at all love the less, but rather the more, those who punish it justly and for its good. But punishment extending into infinity beyond justice, punishment whose aim and result is the evil, not the good, of the sufferer, this is an idea utterly opposed to all the instincts of childhood. Of course the poor little mind takes in the shocking doctrine, presented to it like poison from its mother's hand. But the results are fatal. In one, it is indifference; in another, dislike; in another, an atrophy of the religious nature; in a fourth, a fever of terror, from which the soul escapes only by casting off all belief. Even when the most fortunate end is reached, and the man throws away in adult life the doctrine taught him in childhood, even then for long years the shadow remains over him. We return to early *fears*, as well as loves, many a time before we relinquish them for ever. The parent who would give his child a truly religious education, must make it his care to insure him (as he would insure him against listening to far lesser blasphemies) from ever even hearing of an Eternal Hell. This done, we firmly believe that, if he himself love God, he will find it the easiest of lessons to teach his child to love Him likewise. We must remember this: God's voice speaks in the heart of a child as in the heart of a man; nay, far more clearly than in the heart of a disobedient and world-encrusted man. To teach a child *Whose* voice that is, to make him identify it with the Giver of all good, the Creator of this world (so fresh and lovely in his young eyes!)—to do this is to give him religion. And the religion thus given will grow into fuller, maturer life, till it rises to the reality of prayer, the full blessedness of Divine communion.

A wise mother once told me she had taught her child a few simple prayers to repeat at morning and night, and then had given the advice to ask of God, whenever the child needed it, help to overcome her temptations, and to thank Him when she felt very happy. After some months she asked the little girl—"Tell me, my child, when you pray to God do you feel as if it were a *real* thing, as if there were some One who heard you?" The child pondered a moment, and then replied: "Not when I say my prayers morning and evening, mama, I do not think I feel anything; but whenever I do as you told me, and just say to God what I am wanting, or how happy I am, I am *quite sure* He knows what I say."

Do we need better instance of how real and holy a thing may be the Religion of Childhood?

ESSAY IV.

AN ENGLISH BROAD CHURCHMAN.[1]

THERE exist at all times in the world's history, but rather pre-eminently in our own age, minds of an order with which it is somewhat difficult to deal justly. They are those which seem to be without logical cohesion, whose ideas and opinions (often full of genius and of wisdom) seem disparate one from another, and out of whose recorded words it is impossible to construct a consistent or even intelligible system. Like so many orchids, their luxuriant flowers attract our eyes, while their sweetness touches our hearts; but when we try to find the root of faith from which such beauty has sprung,—lo! some old decaying tree, to which the delicate stem lightly adheres, is all we can discover. We always seem in the wrong as regards them. They attract us, delight us, truly aid our spiritual life by their insight and their tender piety. Then we think to make them our guides; but the magi of old might as well have followed a fire-fly! Again, we are provoked, indignant. We condemn them, and even in our impatience question their honesty: Why does not the man who says this and this, say also this and this? Why does he who avows ideas such as the

---

[1] *The Life and Letters of the Rev. Frederick W. Robertson, M.A., Incumbent of Trinity Chapel, Brighton.* Edited by Stopford A. Brooke, M.A., late Chaplain to the Embassy at Berlin. 2 vols. 8vo. London: Smith and Elder. 1865.

founders of his Church never dreamed of, or condemned bitterly if they did, stop within their fold, and profess to find green pastures where there are but swine's husks of dead symbols? Hardly have we uttered the question, but we are rebuked. "Men so good, so meek of heart, so pure of life, so full of high and holy thoughts—what are we that we should summon them before our tribunal, or judge them by the laws of our individual conscience of sincerity? Let us return and hearken to their prophesyings." The books of these men are like those districts of Wales and Ireland,

"Where sparkles of golden splendour
All over the surface shine."

Every page has its glittering thought, its grain of pure, true gold. But the "Lagenian mine" can somehow never be worked to profit. The ore is too mixed and scattered. We explore it, and of our spoils make for us a ring of remembrance, a locket, perhaps a delicate chain of linked thoughts. But we cannot mint it into coin to pass from hand to hand, enriching ourselves and the world.

These reflections have occurred to me while reading the Sermons of one of the greatest and purest of these cloudy prophets, the lamented Frederick Robertson. They are not those which his Biography (which it is now my task to review) most prominently suggests. No man of ordinary sympathies could read this book and think first of dissecting the opinions of its subject, and testing whether, as in a child's toy, one piece fitted accurately into another. Few, on the contrary, will read it, I am persuaded, without being moved to a sad and tender sympathy, that sympathy with the soul of our brother wherein his intellectual gifts and failures alike become well-nigh indifferent. Robertson's name has for some years been one of power in the religious life of England. Dating from the publication of this admirable Life and these Letters, I believe it will become henceforth a typical one, like those of Arnold and Blanco White. The personal impression which he made on those who knew him in life, and which always seems to have exceeded (in the proportion common to highly emotional characters) the impression received through his written words, will now be shared by thousands. I envy not those who can receive it without being thereby touched to the heart as by the self-disclosure of a friend who should be worthy of all our admiration, and at the same time claim from us such compassion as may yet be given to one who walked with God on earth, and is surely gone home to Him now.

The tangible facts of the Life of Robertson may be summed up in a few brief sentences. Never had a biographer less practical material to work with, scarce even an anecdote worth narrating. If the result in this book be in a literary sense somewhat monotonous, it is redeemed by great simplicity on the part of the biographer, and much discriminating analysis of character; and perhaps I may add, by an almost excessive reticence as to family and social relations, which would have filled in the background of the picture and given it more familiar reality, at the expense, perchance, of delicacy wisely respected. Few even of the letters have any names attached to them, and if they ever contained expressions of individual attachment, they have been expunged, leaving much of the true character of the letters unexplained. I cannot but think the judgment which dictated this last measure in any case, a mistake. Letters are not *the same things* addressed to persons of different ages, sexes, and characters; persons with whom the writer holds totally different relationships. Many expressions of weariness, annoyance, personal feelings of all kinds, such as these letters contain, are natural or morbid, legitimate or else unmanly and egotistical, according to the individual addressed, and his or her relationship to the writer.

In matters like these, of course we are bound to give credit to the biographer for having exercised his best judgment under circumstances unknown to us. We can but regret the fact, and do so the more unhesitatingly, since, whatever inimical and slanderous tongues may have said, these letters, to whomsoever addressed, bear with them the refutation of all calumny, save such as first goads its victim to irritation, and then points to the irritation with sanctimonious condemnation.

Again, Robertson's friendships are not only left anonymous, but his closest ties and relationships are mentioned in the briefest way. His marriage is detailed in one sentence; and, after the beginning of the work, where one beautiful letter to his brother, and a few others to his parents are inserted, there is hardly half a page of the two bulky volumes devoted to either his early or later home circle. What Renan has striven to do for us in the case of Robertson's great Master, namely, to give us a clear mental picture of the *milieu* in which his life and thoughts revolved, is precisely what Robertson's biographer seems to have carefully avoided, till in his care to protect the susceptibilities or respect the privacy of the living, he has left us rather the startling apparition of "a priest after the order of Melchisedek," than the portrait of an English clergyman who within all our memories was the popular preacher of a familiar Brighton chapel. We can resume the bare facts of his career, such as Mr. Brooke gives them, in a single page.

Frederick William Robertson was the son and grandson of soldiers, and from his boyhood was passionately desirous of entering the military profession. After a year's futile attempt to make him a solicitor, his father endeavoured to obtain for him a commission in the army. A long delay occurred before the request was granted; and during the interval, the influence of friends and his father's wishes induced Frederick Robertson to enter Oxford and prepare for the Church. In 1840 he was ordained, and acted as curate first at Winchester, subsequently at Cheltenham and Oxford. Brief journeys to Germany and the Tyrol formed his holiday recreation. On one of these occasions, as his biographer succinctly states, "he met (at Geneva), and after a short acquaintance married, Helen, third daughter of Sir G. W. Denys, Bart., of Easton Neston, Northamptonshire. Almost immediately after his marriage he returned to Cheltenham." The "only external events which marked the subsequent five years of his life," during which he was curate to the Rev. Archibald Boyd, were "the birth of three children and the death of one." In 1847 he accepted the incumbency of Trinity Chapel, Brighton, and there he laboured, becoming each year more beloved and honoured, but each year more feeble in health and weary of spirit, till in 1853 his condition became alarming, and his congregation subscribed to supply him with a curate, by whose aid his work might be lightened. Robertson chose his friend Mr. Tower for the office. The appointment was subject to the approval of Mr. Wagner, vicar of Brighton, who had previously been engaged in controversy with Mr. Tower on financial matters connected with a charitable institution. Mr. Wagner refused to ratify the nomination of Mr. Tower, and Robertson refused to appoint another curate. During the angry contention which thereupon occupied the entire population of Brighton, the last chances of recovery for Robertson's health were irretrievably lost. A disease whose seat seemed to be at the base of the brain, and which caused him intense suffering, terminated his life on the 15th of August, 1853, in his thirty-seventh year. His last words were: "I cannot bear it. Let me rest. I must die. Let God do His work."

Such is the outline of a life which was filled in by a

thousand touches of piety, genius, and goodness. The study of it is indeed purely the study of the man Robertson, not of the career of a more or less successful preacher or student or reformer. Of the world at large, nothing is to be learned from his Biography, save the old lesson, that a good man must needs find friends, and a gifted one, admirers, and an honest and bold one, enemies. The observations on books and on social and religious problems contained in the letters are interesting, but rather as affording glimpses into the feelings of the writer, than as illuminating the subjects themselves in the way a great mind generally effects by each passing gleam of notice. Of politics, we only hear that Robertson was by sentiment an aristocrat; but by force of his allegiance to the great Reformer of Galilee, who spake the parable of Dives, a democrat and an inveigher against the luxuries of the rich. Of those works of philanthropy which men of his energy usually choose whereon to centre their labours, we hear little. Neither the relief of poverty, nor the reform of crime, nor the repression of vice, no enthusiastic alliance with abolition or temperance movements, is to be traced as a thread connecting his efforts at any period of his life. One only work did he seem to undertake with peculiar zest. The Association of the Working Men of Brighton found in him their warmest friend. His Addresses to them contain some of his very finest thoughts, and he appears to have had their cause nearer to his heart than any other. If this be so, we may perhaps adjudge to Robertson the exalted praise of having been one of the very first to turn philanthropy into a new and noble channel wherein it has since run freely. Beyond his lectures and assistance to the working men, it would seem, however, as if his great tenderness of heart poured itself out rather generally than with any special purpose or object. In a word, the power of Robertson was almost unnaturally devoid of external or tangible manifestation. Even the religious doctrines he taught have singularly little definiteness of shape or substance, such as might enable us to account him the prophet of this or that truth, or precept. We insensibly describe him rather by negatives than affirmatives, and say he did not do or teach what others have done or taught, rather than that he accomplished such a work or gave to the world such a doctrine. We close his Life with the sense (oftener left on us by women than by men) that we have been impressed beyond the calculable power of the impressing spirit, and attracted rather magnetically than by any gravitation of mere mass of mind. He was the living evidence of the truth that Character is greater than Action; and that to *be* good is more effectual to benefit mankind than the *doing* of any work whatsoever.

The first and most obvious interest to the reader of the life of Robertson is the history of his religious opinions. It may be told briefly, though less briefly than that of his worldly career.

Whatever be the evils and errors of that form of Christianity which claims the name of "Evangelical," it must be admitted to leave commonly on souls which have received its influences in childhood, what we may describe as a high-strung spiritual temperament. The early initiation into the most solemn mysteries of the inner life; the perpetual strain after a repentance disproportionately meted to childish offences; the awful terrors of eternal woe made familiar even before one human sorrow has dimmed the brightness of life's morning;—all these features of Evangelical education tend to the formation of a moral constitution delicate to the verge of disease. Much that is best and holiest, much deep sense of the realities of the unseen world, much of that keener conscientiousness which never leaves a man content with merely outward performance of duty unless he also feels the dutiful sentiment, much self-distrust and self-depreciation judged by the standard of an almost superhuman purity and devotion, are the legacies of a youth spent under the influences of Evangelical Christianity. But, like a child who has been nurtured in heated rooms on too stimulating food, and whose brain has been overtaxed by his tutors, there are also inherited highly-strung feelings subject to morbid excitement and no less morbid exhaustion and deadness, for which largest allowance must be made when we would estimate the later attainments of one subjected to such discipline. Robertson received these influences with the peculiar susceptibility of his character, and with the additional force derived from his physical predisposition to disease of the brain. It would seem as if there never were a temperament of body or mind more needing the calming influence of a perfectly healthy creed; nor one which more vividly manifested the results, both for good and evil, of the faith in which he was trained, and of the different but far from perfectly joyful one in which he lived and died.

The early Evangelical impressions of Robertson, derived apparently from both parents, were full of childlike fervour. He seems to have been " good " as a school-boy, in the same degree as Channing, whose comrades said of him that it was no merit in him to be obedient and studious; he had no temptation to be otherwise. His childhood and youth appear to have been exemplary and faultless. If they were in any measure diversified by more natural traits, his biographer has erred in suppressing them, for it is to be confessed that the impression left on us by these early pages and by certain over-wise school-boy letters is not altogether a pleasant one. Robertson, indeed, seems to have been a manly boy, steady, brave, active, fond of field sports, and enthusiastic about military glory; a " muscular Christian " even in his Evangelical days. His ambition, therefore, curiously compounded of the different elements of his character, took the form of desiring to set "the example of a pure and Christian life in his corps, and becoming the Cornelius of his regiment. . . . . To two great objects he devoted himself wholly, the profession of arms and the service of Christ." When he was persuaded to give up the military career and adopt that of a clergyman, which he had often vehemently repudiated, he seems to have done it under a singular sense of constraint and self-abnegation, and, as his biographer expresses it, to have accepted "somewhat sternly his destiny." He was, however, at that time, according to his friend Mr. Davies, in the full flush of youthful spirits and energy. "At the time to which I refer, I never knew him otherwise than cheerful, and there were times when his spirits were exuberant—times when he was in the mood of thoroughly enjoying everything. He was a constant and prayerful student of his Bible. At this time he held firmly what are understood as Evangelical views. He advocated strongly the pre-millennial advent of Christ."

Beginning his residence at Brasenose in October, 1837, it was impossible that Robertson should not have been drawn into the vortex of the great Tractarian movement then in progress. The result seems to have been a speedy recoil, and an effort to counteract the tendency among his friends by the establishment of a society for prayer and religious discussion. "No change took place in his doctrinal views, which were those of the Evangelical school, with a decided leaning to moderate Calvinism." After a college course of faultless moral excellence, he was ordained, in 1840, to a curacy in Winchester. "The prevailing tone of his mind on entering the ministry was one of sadness. His spirit consumed the body. He never was content, he never thought that he had attained, rather that he was lagging far behind, the Christian life. Everywhere this is reflected in his letters. His feeling of it was so strong, that it seemed rather to belong to a woman than to a man, and at certain times the resulting depression was so great that he fell into a morbid hopelessness." His work at Winchester, however, was largely successful, his rector proved a kind and congenial friend, and his mode of life seemed the ideal of devotion. "Study all the morning; in the afternoon hard fagging at visitation of the poor in the closest and dirtiest streets of Winchester; his evenings were spent sometimes alone, but very often with his rector." His habits, indeed, here took an ascetic shape, such as by some occult law of nature it would appear every strong soul, at the outset of its higher life, spontaneously adopts. The Quarantania fast of Christ has had its unconscious copyists in every age and under every creed. Elijah, and Buddha, and Zoroaster, each earned through such means their prophet-mantles, and since their day thousands of lesser men have felt that "lusting of the spirit against the flesh," in which the spirit is ever cruel in its first victory. Robertson, we are told, "created a system of restraint in food and sleep. For nearly a year he almost altogether refrained from meat. He compelled himself to rise early. He refrained also much from society." In some private meditations and resolutions written at this time (1843–1845) there occur long strings of reasons to fortify the determination to eat with stringent self-denial and to rise early; and the "Resolves" are full of that still deeper asceticism which starts from holiest ambitions, and, alas! ends too often in the most morbid self-anatomy and self-consciousness.

"To try to feel my own insignificance. To speak less of self, and think less. To feel it degradation to speak of my own doings as a poor braggart. To perform rigorously the examen of conscience," etc.[1]

[1] Pages 99, 100.

On all this portion of Robertson's life, the biographer makes wise and pertinent remarks; how it was the natural result of the school in which he had been trained, and how he escaped from it into a manlier spirit, not without bearing away some fruit of self-knowledge and of knowledge of other men. His sermons, in later years, at Brighton, were full of protests against these mistakes of his youth, when his very genius seemed under a cloud, and the force and originality he was soon to develope were kept under by the restraints of his creed.

A threat of hereditary consumption in 1841, compelled him to give up his work at Winchester and go abroad, oppressed by a sense of despondency and failure. A pedestrian tour, extending to Geneva, soon renewed his health and spirits. He plunged into controversy with every one who would discuss with him, Catholics, Rationalists, Atheists, and "believed that there is at this time a determined attack made by Satan and his instruments to subvert that cardinal doctrine of our best hopes—justification by faith alone." A Geneva minister denying the "Deity of Christ," is told that he cannot be a Christian, and that his young monitor "trembles for him." Altogether we have a picture of the earnest, narrow, devout Evangelical clergyman, familiar enough to all of us who have seen much of the world, but who, we have rarely had reason to suppose, could in this life assume the spiritual wings of a Robertson, and fly like him into free fields of air.

In the summer of 1842, Robertson became the curate of the Rev. Archibald Boyd, then of Cheltenham, a gentleman for whom he entertained the greatest respect, and who was certainly not likely to have guided him out of the very straitest sect of the orthodox. I can remember hearing Mr. Boyd about this period preaching at Cheltenham, and denouncing Unitarians with such singular vehemence, that it induced me to institute careful inquiries concerning a body of whose tenets at that time I was in total ignorance. Robertson was at first in full harmony with Mr. Boyd's opinions, but the hour for a great revolution in his soul's history was approaching.

Calvinism has had its Heroic Age; the age of the Pilgrim Fathers, of Brainerd and of Hopkins. It has an Age of Saints still, as many a bed of agonizing disease testifies in home and hospital in England to-day. But there is a phase of the religion not heroic nor yet saintly; a phase to check the ardour and alienate the allegiance of any man true of heart like Robertson. Probably in such a place as a fashionable church at Cheltenham, that unlovely phase may be met with in its most exaggerated development.

"At first (says his biographer) he believed that all who spoke of Christ were Christ-like. But he was rudely undeceived. His truthful character, his earnestness, at first unconsciously and afterwards consciously, recoiled from all the unreality around him. He was so pained by the expressions of religious emotion which fell from those who were living a merely fashionable life, that he states himself in one of his letters that he gave up reading all books of a devotional character, lest he should be lured into the same habit of feeling without acting. His conceptions also of Christianity as the religion of just and loving tolerance made him draw back with horror from the violent and blind denunciations which the religious agitators and the religious papers of the extreme portion of the Evangelical party indulged in under the cloak of Christianity. 'They tell lies,' he said, 'in the name of God. Others tell them in the name of the Devil: that is the only difference.' It was this, and other things of the same kind, which first shook his faith in Evangelicalism."[1]

In 1843 he wrote to a friend: "As to the state of the Evangelical clergy, I think it lamentable. I see sentiment, instead of principle, and a miserable mawkish religion superseding a state which once was healthy. I stand alone, a theological Ishmael." In the following year other doubts

[1] Vol. i. p. 108.

and difficulties arose. His preaching altered in tone, and he suddenly awoke to the conviction "that the system on which he had founded his whole faith and work could never be received by him again." An outward blow—the sudden ruin of a friendship—accelerated the inward crisis; and the result was a period of spiritual agony so awful that it smote his spirit down into a profound darkness, and of all his early faiths but one remained, "It must be right to do right!" He travelled away to Germany, and there, amid the beautiful hills and vales of the Tyrol, in long lonely walks and solitary musings, he passed through the great ordeal.

> He fought his doubts and gathered strength,
>   He would not make his judgment blind,
>   He faced the spectres of the mind
> And laid them : thus he came at length
>
> To find a stronger faith his own ;
>   And power was with him in the night,
>   Which makes the darkness and the light,
> And dwells not in the light alone.

Never has that dread battle been more faithfully fought; never has the victory been more nobly won. Long years afterwards, speaking to those working men with whom perhaps of all his hearers he had closest sympathies, men from whom most of our preachers would shut out the very name of religious doubt, or, if forced to treat of it, sternly dismiss them "to the law and to the testimony"—to these men Robertson disclosed what we cannot doubt was the history of his own spiritual struggle and the triumphant peace which followed it. I must be pardoned for copying the story at length. Few words, I believe, in any book, bear in them seeds of greater usefulness for our day of doubt and troubling of the waters. Like every true prophet, Robertson was the forerunner of his brethren, and passed before them through the dark river, telling them where ground might yet be found for their feet, even in its depths, till they should reach "the new firm land of faith beyond." For all the thousands who are now passing, and must presently pass, through those dread waters, and fear lest they go over, even over their souls, and whelm them in their deeps for ever, the history of Robertson's transition of faith is a most blessed lesson. By that way he went, and by that way only, I believe, in our day, shall the Nations of the Saved pass over.

"It is an awful moment when the soul begins to find that the props on which it blindly rested so long are, many of them, rotten, and begins to suspect them all ; when it begins to feel the nothingness of many of the traditionary opinions which have been received with implicit confidence, and in that horrible insecurity begins also to doubt whether there be anything to believe at all. It is an awful hour, let him who has passed through it say how awful, when this life has lost its meaning, when the grave appears to be the end of all, human goodness nothing but a name, and the sky above this universe a dead expanse, black with the void from which God has disappeared. In that fearful loneliness of spirit, when those who should have been his friends and counsellors only frown upon his misgivings, and profanely bid him stifle doubts which, for aught he knows, may arise from the Fountain of truth itself, I know but one way in which a man may come forth from his agony scatheless ; it is by holding fast to those things which are certain still,—the grand, simple landmarks of morality. In the darkest hour through which a human soul can pass, whatever else is doubtful, this at least is certain—*If there be no God and no future state, yet, even then, it is better to be generous than selfish, better to be chaste than licentious, better to be true than false, better to be brave than to be a coward.* Blessed, beyond all earthly blessedness, is the man who in the tempestuous darkness of the soul has dared to hold fast to these venerable landmarks. Thrice blessed is he who, when all is drear and cheerless within and without, when his teachers terrify him and his friends shrink from him, has obstinately clung to moral good. Thrice blessed, because *his* night shall pass into clear bright day. I appeal to the recollection of any man who has passed through that hour of agony, and stood upon the rock at last, the surges stilled below him, and the last cloud drifted from the sky above, with a faith and hope and trust no longer traditional, but of his own—a faith which neither earth nor hell shall shake thenceforth for ever."

Here is the "Saints' Tragedy"; nay, the Saints' triumphant Drama of Victory; the "Prometheus Unchained" of the inner life for us moderns, with our perishing theologies, our science and philosophy presenting to us a daily changing phantasmagoria of the material and mental universe. Our Apollyons are not the Apollyons of our fathers; our Valley of the Shadow of Death is haunted by far direr spectres, and opens into far deeper and more fathomless abysses, than ever they beheld. But for us, too, there is a weapon to slay the dragon, a path through the realm of darkness and despair. Not any close-linked chain-mail of Evidences, any buckler of resolute Belief, shall defend us; scarce may we even find strength to send to Heaven one winged arrow of Prayer. No guiding Star shall light our way through the pitfalls of the Valley. But, fighting blow for blow, winning step for step, against every fiend-like passion, every hell-born temptation, we shall gain at last the victory; pressing God's lamp close to our breasts,

"Its radiance soon or late shall pierce the gloom;
We shall emerge some day."

One struggle to obey Conscience, when Conscience has been for the time bereft of all her insignia of royalty, when she no longer claims to be vicegerent of an Almighty Lord, nor points with outstretched sceptre to a world where her faithful servants shall be rewarded when their tasks are done; one free and loyal act of obedience to her *then*, will roll back the bars of heaven, as no giant intellectual labours can ever help us to do.

Is this mysterious? It is the most simple of all the laws of Providence. Moral goodness is the character of God.

To love goodness is to love God, in a far deeper, truer sense, than to love any intellectually-conceived idea of a Supreme Being, whether revealed or unrevealed. Man meets God when he feels godlike feelings and performs godlike acts. He gets above and behind all the secondary, third and thousandth arguments for believing in God, and finds Him at the first and fountain-head of all religious knowledge. Small marvel it is if his doubts thenceforth are banished for ever.

Robertson wrote during the fever of his struggle,

"Moral goodness and moral beauty are realities lying at the base and beneath all forms of religious expression. They are no dream, and they are not mere utilitarian conveniences. That suspicion was an agony once. It is passing away. . . . . . As to the ministry, I am in infinite perplexity. To give it up seems throwing away the only opportunity of doing good in this short life that is now available to me ; yet to continue when my whole soul is struggling with meaning that I cannot make intelligible, is very wretched."

Returning back to England after some weeks' work at Heidelberg, Robertson accepted from Bishop Wilberforce the charge of St. Ebb's Church, Oxford. How he came to seek employment in such a quarter is hardly accounted for. He was not a High Churchman. "While the Tractarians seemed to say that forms could produce life, he said that forms were necessary only to support life ; but for that they were necessary. Bread cannot create life, but life cannot be kept up without bread." Neither was he a Broad Churchman of that first school which before the era of Essays and Reviews was held to represent the widest views in the Church of England. "Though holding Mr. Maurice in veneration, he differed on many and important points both from him and Professor Kingsley. He was the child of no theological father." A few months, however, terminated his labours under the great Tractarian Bishop, and in August,

1847, Robertson accepted the charge of Trinity Chapel, Brighton, the field of his noblest work, the post at which he died.

Trinity Chapel (I speak from the recollection of some five-and-twenty years) is an ugly square building, devoid of a chancel properly so called, and with green niches on either side of the communion-table, the one of course serving as desk, the other as pulpit. It was a drowsy, dreary locality, much favoured by the schools wherewith Brighton abounds. Robertson at once took his part, and preached as he thought and as he felt, awakening many echoes. "At Oxford he was like the swimmer who has for the first time ventured into deep water; at Brighton he struck out boldly into the open sea." From this time there does not appear to have occurred any essential modifications of his opinions. He continued to speak out freely and with surpassing energy and eloquence, till after six brief years his life burnt itself out, and his place knew him no more. I need not pursue chronologically the order of the few events which diversified his career, but endeavour to put together such materials as are given us for forming a correct idea of the man—his creed and his character, his strength and his weakness.

Mr. Brooke's view of the great work of Robertson is well summed up in the following passage:

"He represented to men, not sharp, distinct outlines of doctrine, but the fulness and depth of the Spirit of Christianity. . . . He cannot be claimed especially by any one of our conflicting parties. But all thoughtful men, however divided in opinion, find in his writings a point of contact. He has been made one of God's instruments to preserve the unity of the Christian Church in this country. . . . But though his teaching was more suggestive than dogmatic, he did not shrink from meeting in the pulpit the difficulties involved in many of the doctrines of the English Church. His explanation of the Atonement, of the doctrine of the sacraments, of absolution, of imputed righteousness, of the freedom of the gospel in contrast to the bondage of the law, have solved the difficulties of many. He believed himself that they were the true solutions. But he also believed that the time might come when they would cease to be adequate solutions. Yet notwithstanding all this, he had a fixed basis for his teaching. It was the Divine-human Life of Christ. He felt that an historical Christianity was absolutely necessary, that only through a visible Life of the Divine in the flesh could God become intelligible to man. . . . . The Incarnation was to him the centre of all history."[1]

The idea which evidently underlies this defence of Robertson's theology, or rather his Christianity without dogmatic theology, seems to me partially true and partially false. It is true that mere intellectual ideas, whether connected or not with religious belief, have in them no power to produce true unity between human souls. Sentiment unites men; opinion only serves, at the best, to make partisans and fellow-sectaries. On the other hand, it is false to assume that "sharp, distinct outlines of doctrines" have in them any necessary antagonism to fervent sentiment, or that (according to a belief which seems gaining ground in our day) the more misty is a man's creed, the more warm are likely to be his affections. Our reaction from Calvinistic stiffness is carrying us too far if it persuade us that, to love God much, it is needful to be extremely uncertain regarding all His dealings and attributes. Robertson himself, we suspect, was a proof that "sharp and distinct outlines of doctrine" were no bar to the power of uniting men of various denominations; for he accomplished that end not by lacking such distinct outlines, but (among other causes) by very distinctly preaching a certain form of Christ-worship attractive to thousands. What he really seems to have lacked, was a logical and self-consistent *system*. He had sharply-defined isolated doctrines in abundance.

[1] Pp. 167, 168.

The peculiar form of Christolatry to which I have now referred, formed so prominent a feature in Robertson's life and religion, as well as in his scheme of theology, that it is needful to give it a very important place in any estimate of him, as well as being in itself a matter deserving the gravest attention of all thinkers of the present age.

Nothing is more remarkable to one who looks over the past and present of Christendom, than to observe how very variously the sentiments of professed Christians towards their common Lord have differed, apparently without the slightest relation to the doctrines they entertained concerning his person and office. The *isothermal* lines (if I may so express it) of love to Christ intersect every altitude of intellect, every latitude of opinion. Or rather we may say, that as in geological maps all artificial political frontiers and divisions disappear, and, instead of states and provinces, we have districts of granite, of sandstone, chalk or clay,—so in studying Christian Europe beneath the surface, instead of meeting again the great divisions of churches and minor subdivisions of sects, we find a wholly new chart, wherewith the superficial lines have little or no concern. Let us take any dozen great religious writers of past times, and any dozen more of different existing sectarian denominations, and let them all be accounted believers in the actual Deity of Christ—how immeasurably different is the place which He holds, not so much in their opinions as in their affections! One man's writings are, so to speak, saturated with the love of the great Teacher. Another merely pays him a brief passing homage when the exigencies of his theme seem to demand it. Yet no reader may tell that it is either a plenitude of religious life or a deficiency of it which makes an à Kempis so full of Christ, or a Fénélon or Tauler so wrapped in God as to seem well-nigh to forget him. Nay, even among those who dogmatically deny Christ's claim to worship, he assumes a position in some minds so prominent, in others so far in the background, that, to return to our metaphor, the line marking the warmest devotion to him must be made to run half through the Unitarian church, after threading the heights of Romanism and Tractarianism, and descending to the lowest vales of Evangelical and Methodistical opinion. Channing and hundreds of Channing's disciples seem to make up in personal attachment many times more than they deduct from official homage. Even Theists who differ in little else, differ, widely as the poles, when they come to express their sentiments towards him who, to them all, is only the Man of Nazareth.

Among those who have felt vividly this supreme attraction to Christ's character, Robertson stands eminent. From his first desire to devote himself, like a knight of old, to "military service and the service of Christ," Christ's name seems to have been uppermost in his mind and on his lips; and, as his biographer affirms, he endeavoured to bring *everything*, even the petty worries of Brighton scandal, in some occult way to the test of the life passed in Galilee eighteen centuries ago. He deliberately identifies his whole religion with the *worship* of Christ, rather than with the attempt to follow God according to the doctrines of Christ. Christianity in his view is not so much the religion which Christ taught to men (though of course this he would also maintain it to be), as the religion which teaches men about Christ. In one of his sermons (quoted by Mr. Brooke) he says: "In personal love and adoration of Christ the Christian religion consists, and not in a correct morality or a correct doctrine, but in a homage to a King." In another place he writes to a friend:[1] "Only a human God and none other must be adored by man." Thus it appears that his intellect ratified the tendency of his feelings. He deliberately made "the Christian religion"

[1] Vol. i., page 290.

(*i.e.*, his own religion) *consist* in "love and adoration," not of God, but of Christ; not in morality, not in true belief, not in allegiance to the Lord of conscience, but in "homage to a King," namely, to Jesus of Nazareth. How far this creed harmonized with his other ideas, how it coincided with that faith in the supremacy of moral good which he must have brought away from that grandest passage of his life, when fidelity to his own sense of Duty and Right alone saved him amid the shipwreck of all his theology, how far the "homage to Christ" could be made the substance of religion by one who had learned *that* lesson — I cannot explain. It remains one of the thousand self-contradictions of the human mind which we are called on only to notice and not to reconcile. One remark, however, I must be permitted to make ere we leave the subject. Those who, like Robertson, affirm that a "human God and none other must be adored by man," seem strangely to forget those loftier views of the origin of our knowledge of God which at other moments they earnestly maintain. Has the Divine Father, then, indeed so constituted His children, and so ordered His relation to them, that they can never love Him in His own essential Fatherhood, but only in some "hypostasis" of Sonship or Incarnation? I confess to being somewhat wearied of this doctrine, which we meet in our day from a dozen opposite quarters; a doctrine which out-herods Herod, and would have set the Fathers of the Nicean Council aghast. Men who speak of "a human God only being knowable or adorable by man," seem to have formed for themselves a conception of our mortal life as if it were spent in a dwelling close beside the sea, yet so constructed as that by no door or window, no loophole or crevice, should the inhabitants behold, or be enabled so much as to guess at, the existence of that mighty Deep beneath whose thunder the foundations of their dwelling tremble, and the voice of whose waters is ever sounding in their ears. At length—so these teachers would have it—at length a Mariner from the far-off blessed isles has landed on that desolate shore, and said, "Behold the Ocean!"

God did *not* so make for man his tenement of clay. He made therein a window opening out to seaward, a window where, ofttimes kneeling, he may gaze and wonder and adore. The great Mariner indeed has come—many mariners have come—and brought tidings of the boundless expanse, the measureless brightness, of that Ocean of all good. But their tales would be as idle words, could not each one of us for himself look forth and with his own eyes behold the Infinite Deep beside him and around.

To assert that man can only know God as a human God, is tantamount to denying that man has any direct consciousness of Deity. But, setting aside the terrible subtraction of all the deepest part of our religious feelings which *ought* (if men were but logical) to go with such denial, let us consider how such a view can be reconciled with the most familiar facts of human nature. There are in us all, various affections and sentiments, having each their proper objects and, necessarily, their proper means of knowing those objects. One of these affections cannot be substituted or exchanged for another; for if given a different object, it thereupon becomes a different affection. There is one affection for a parent, another for a child, another for a wife, another for a friend. A parent cannot give a filial affection to his son, nor a wife a parental one to her husband, nor a man a friendly one to an infant. In like manner, there are different affections for human beings and for a Being superhuman. The human affections (like those of which I have spoken) have for their objects our human relatives and friends, all known to us through our bodily senses; the religious affections have for their object a Divine Being, not known to us through the senses, but through that special organ of consciousness which I have called the Window of the soul which opens on Deity. When Comtists talk of the "Religion of Humanity," and attempt to attach the religious sentiment to such an abstraction as this idea of Humanity, or to such a concrete image thereof as a dead or living woman, we answer confidently, " Not so—*that* is not 'religion.' Call the sentiment by what name you please, it is not *religion*, any more than conjugal or parental love is religion. It is another sentiment and must have another name. Religion is a sentiment having for its object an invisible Entity, not an abstraction or a symbol." Just the same answer may be fitly given to Christians who tell us that "a human God" is to. be alone adored. A " human God " is not an object of religion at all, but of esteem, honour, human sympathy, or (if such sentiments be transgressed and real adoration offered) then of Idolatry, of the sinful transference of the sentiment due to God alone to an idol, or being having a bodily image. In sober truth, all such wild phrases are self-deceptive. Men feel such a profound love and veneration for Christ, that they seek an infinite expression for their lawful sentiment, and then call it by a name which applies only to the love of God. When they really feel *religion* to Christ, it is when they, like half the Christian world, give his beloved name to "his Father and our Father." For "*Christ*," read " *God in His attributes of Love and Redemption* "—would be the first correction of an immense portion of modern religious literature.

In the case of Robertson, some clue to the meaning of his strange words about a "human God" may perhaps be found where he says,[1] " What is it to adore Christ ? To call him God, and say, Lord, Lord ? No. Adoration is the *mightiest love the soul can give*—call it by what name you will.

[1] Vol. ii., page 171.

Many a Unitarian, as Channing, has adored, calling it only admiration, and many an orthodox Christian, calling Christ God, with most accurate theology, has given him only a cool intellectual homage." All this is true in a sense, but overlooks the fact on which I have been insisting, that the affections are not interchangeable, and that the sentiments duly given to a human being are not the sentiments duly given to God, or vice versa, any more than conjugal and filial and parental affections are interchangeable. Robertson insists only on *degree*. He forgets there is also difference in *kind*, and that to confound the kinds of love introduces into the religious life a disorder similar to that brought into social life by the misapplication of natural affections.

What Robertson's creed actually was during the later years of his life, it is (strange to say) almost impossible to discover. We meet such curious glimpses of it as these

"If you hate evil, you are on God's side, whether there be a personal evil principle or not. *I myself believe there is*, but not so unquestioningly as to be able to say, I think it a matter of clear revelation." [1]

Again:

"Mr. Robertson was not a universalist in doctrine, however he may have hoped that universalism was true. 'My only difficulty,' he once said to a friend, 'is how *not* to believe in everlasting punishment.'" [2]

Yet with this possible Devil and probable Hell, Robertson managed to attain views of God so high and devout, that there has surely never been a reader of his Sermons whose heart has not thereby been warmed to more fervent piety, and, above all, to the effort to make pious feelings lead to holy actions. His abhorrence of the indulgence of religious emotions as a *luxury* was indeed one of the most marked features of his character, and one which doubtless the popular preacher of a Brighton chapel, no less than the Cheltenham curate, had reason to feel pretty frequently. Undoubtedly, the

[1] Vol. ii., page 64.   [2] Vol. ii., page 163.

great secret of his influence lay in the *reality* of his religion. This seems a mere truism at first sight, but when we reflect how much of self-deception, not to speak of the deception of others, "lest we spoil our usefulness," mingles with the religion of all save the highest and the holiest, it will be confessed that for a man to be in his home what he is in his pulpit, in his heart what he is in his books, in his life what he is in his prayer, is to be real in a sense which few, alas! may claim to be.

The great and peculiar glory of Robertson, in my estimation, was his power to discern the living germ of truth in dogmas long wrapped in such hard husks of forms as to need genius like his to break them through and give the seed within power to fructify once more. He deliberately adopted this high task. "I always ask" (he says, in a letter dated May 17, 1851) what does that dogma mean, and how in my language can I put into form the underlying truth, in correcter form if possible, but in only approximative form after all. In this way, Purgatory, Absolution, Mariolatry, become to me fossils, not lies." Every reader of his Sermons must remember how well he fulfilled this high purpose, and how under his hand these very doctrines came forth out of the dust of ages beautiful and full of fresh spiritual life. By this means also it happened that Robertson became in so remarkable a degree the harmonizer of men of the most opposite denominations. By his profound insight he was enabled to get at the truth which lies behind Dogma. Now as Truth is one and unchangeable, and Dogma only a distorted image of Truth, refracted by the atmospheres of those human minds through which it has passed and wearing their colours—whether of one century or another, one race, or people, or church, or philosophy—so the setting forth of Truth, once more freed from the discolourations of Dogma, is the most effectual way to unite men who have been kept apart by Dogma. Each now sees that *his* truth is also his neighbour's truth; the same great fact of the religious consciousness, the same idea of God and duty, the same universal phenomenon of the inner life. He perceives that it has only been the Dogma discolouring it which made it appear different. Henceforth, now that each knows the living truth to be the same for himself and his neighbour, he not only feels reconciled to his neighbour, but *united* with him. He learns perfect indulgence for his neighbour's dogma, and much indifference for his own. The root of bitterness is extirpated.

In another manner, also, this particular work confers an immense benefit on mankind. He who can stand before us as the Interpreter of the Past, does much to strengthen all that is best in the Present. In the last century, Protestants and Deists joined in holding up to contempt as utterly valueless those older dogmas, which, once living and beautiful, had one by one become dead, and then had been embalmed by the Church of Rome and placed like so many saints in her shrines as things to be worshipped by believing and adoring crowds, not rudely uncovered and gazed upon by common mortals. Robertson was perhaps the first and greatest of those who in our age have striven to undo the mischief alike of the Romish embalming, and the contumely wherewith Protestants had torn these mummies from their tombs and made them mere objects of curiosity or derision. He has aided us to see that the men of the primitive ages were men of like passions and like thoughts with ourselves, and that it was much more the *clothing* of their thoughts, the forms wherewith the mental fashion of that bygone world naturally dressed them, than any real difference in the thoughts themselves which distinguish them from our own. To feel this thoroughly is to resume the heirlooms of our race, to feel ourselves the "heirs of all the ages," the lawful inheritors of wisdom doubly precious because tested by the currency of millenniums. The philosophy of the eighteenth century believed itself of mushroom birth, and adopted all the rude airs of an upstart. The better philosophy of the nineteenth seeks to attach itself to the noblest names in the spiritual pedigree of the human race, and speaks with somewhat of the calm dignity of one who though far surpassing his fathers, yet deems himself to come of goodly stock and worthy parentage.

On the other hand, there are not a few dangers connected with this rehabilitating of discredited dogmas; dangers, above all to candour and simplicity. From these, however, Robertson was nobly, I had almost written, splendidly, exempt. No one could tax him with "putting new wine into old bottles," in the spirit of that Janus-preaching we hear so often; one face for those who adhere to the Past, and one for those who aspire to the Future. He was beyond the suspicion of tampering with the purest simplicity of the truth, as he understood it; nay, he seemed to desire to find always to express his thoughts, not old consecrated words which remain for ever burdened with first associations, but the freshest phrases of English life of to-day wherein his meaning might be absolutely transparent. And one other great service Robertson did for us. He taught in a thousand forms the truth, best expressed in one of his Sermons, where he says, that the Vineyard is made indeed for the culture of vines, but if vines be found healthy and full of fruit *outside* the vineyard, they are none the less therefore to be accounted true vines. Perhaps the relation of the Church to the individual soul was never more happily exemplified. Brought home, as by Robertson's eloquence, to a thousand hearts, we all owe much, and shall year by year owe more, to this lesson, gradually spreading among minds whose orthodox creed would formerly have seemed to be a wall of partition forbidding them to recognize any test of

Divine Sonship in those who "followed not us"; or any fruit in the vines which grow outside the vineyard.

With pleasure we see from this Biography that practically he felt no less than preached such liberalism. We read,[1] "He revered and spoke of Dr. Channing as one of the truest and noblest Christians of America. He was deeply indebted to his writings." And again: "He read James Martineau's books with pleasure and profit. The influence of 'The Endeavours after the Christian Life' may be traced through many of his sermons. Theodore Parker he admired for his eloquence, earnestness, learning and indignation against evil, and against forms without a spirit, which mark his writings. But he deprecated the want of reverence and the rationalizing spirit of Parker."[2]

I must pass briefly over the private character of this noble man. The Biography we are reviewing, in spite of all its warm eulogiums and discriminating criticisms, will probably be felt by most readers to leave much to be desired in the filling up of the picture of Robertson's character. Those who personally and intimately knew Mr. Robertson affirm that he was a most warm-hearted man, capable of strong attachment, and I can hardly think his biographer has done wisely in eliminating so completely the traces, or at least all means of identifying the traces, of the friendships of his manhood from these volumes.

In a most vigorous defence of Tennyson from the charge of overstrained enthusiasm for Arthur Hallam, he says:

"The friendship of a school-boy is as full of tenderness and jealousy and passionateness as even love itself. I remember my own affection for G. R. M. How my heart beat at seeing him; how the consciousness that he was listening while I was reading annihilated the presence of the master; how I fought for him; how to rescue him at prisoner's

---

[1] Vol. ii., page 171.

[2] I cannot pause to answer, for the thousandth time, the imputation conveyed in the last paragraph.

base turned the effect of mere play into a ferocious determination, as if the captivity were real; how my blood crept cold with delight when he came to rescue me or when he praised me."[1]

Yet, after his boyhood, we are hardly admitted to guess even the names of those he loved best. He details continually to his anonymous correspondents little circumstances of his life which read like the pictures drawn for a friend's perusal of the life of an invalid woman, but the passages which should account for such pages are withheld. Again, we are assured, by those who knew him best, that he displayed great gentleness and magnanimity regarding the misrepresentations and slanders heaped on him. The printed fragments of letters unfortunately recall what, in such case, must have been almost his sole utterances of indignation, weariness, and complaint. These are, doubtless, unfortunate results of a system which yet it is probable the biographer was justified in following. At least his own testimony, and that of many who knew Robertson more intimately, should be generally known, to absolve him from suspicions of weakness which these severed fragments may suggest.

We are told that Robertson's eloquence became obvious from the first sermon he ever preached. He was, as I may venture to add, like his biographer, eloquent in the best sense, that is, rich in thoughts, as well as in words to clothe his thoughts. His voice was fine, his person (it is said) even unfortunately handsome. The photograph and the bust give the idea of a man too slender of make, with too narrow chest and drooping shoulders, and a head too high and defective in depth to make such storms of emotions as he habitually underwent otherwise than perilous. To use Canon Kingsley's phrase, there was a complete lack of "healthy animalism" about his head and figure. To compensate for this, however, he was soldier-like in bearing as in taste;

[1] Page 81.

"muscular" before the term became the cant name for his school of theology. Nay, he was not only a soldier, but also to the backbone a sportsman. We have all heard the remark that a man rarely enjoys a walk in the country during which he has not had the chance of *killing something*. Without discussing this supposed evidence of manliness, I confess to a little pain at finding Robertson writing, that "as he had not a gun" he could not discover what some sea-gulls were eating. Even these beautiful and harmless sea-birds, which a Turk deems it sin and pity to destroy, would, it seems, not have been safe from his slaughter. Robertson's love of sport, indeed, led him far. With his sisters one after another dying of consumption and his own constitution continually threatened, we read that "he would walk for hours after a single bird, and reluctantly leave off the pursuit of this coy grouse when night began to fall. He would sit for hours in a barrel sunk in the border of a marsh waiting for wild ducks. *These hours of delight* (says his biographer) he obtained once a year."[1] All, doubtless, very manly and "muscular," but a curious study withal! A great religious Teacher, cheered by the sublime hope of killing a fowl, sitting "for hours in a barrel sunk in a marsh," and counting the time spent in such durance as "hours of delight," is a spectacle at which the feeble feminine mind stands by in amazement.

Robertson's feelings about women form a remarkable feature in his character. In his early boyhood he seems to have had a sort of worship for them, like that of an old knight of romance. Later in life, a high and most pure tenderness of feeling marks almost all his intercourse. In one letter he remarks, "I rather agree with the view of St. Paul having taken personally a low estimate of women. It seems to me inseparable from his temperament. . . . That respectful chivalry of feeling which characterizes some men

[1] Page 198.

can only exist where that is found which St. Paul lacked."
In another letter soon afterwards, he says: " In the estimate
formed of women, I should think there cannot be a doubt
which is the truer and deeper, that which makes her a
plaything, or that which surrounds her with the sacredness
of a silent worship. A temperament like that of St. Paul's
is happier, and for the world more useful." It is rather
surprising to think that to such a man as Robertson there
was no medium between a "plaything" and a being "surrounded with the sacredness of a silent worship;" and that
while considering the latter view "truer and deeper," he
attributed the "plaything" theory to the great apostle of
the Gentiles, and considered it (though less true and
deep) "happier, and for the world more *useful!*" The
"usefulness" of making half the human race playthings
for the other half, is surely open to some discussion! Again,
this man, with his "sacred and silent worship," did not
shrink from attributing to the objects of this "worship"
a corruption and baseness which I may venture to say few
women could hear of without indignation. He writes: "I
do believe that a secret leaning towards sin, and a secret
feeling of provocation and jealousy towards those who have
enjoyed what they dare not, lies at the bottom of half the
censorious zeal for morality which we hear. I am nearly
sure it is so with women in their virulence against their
own sex; *they feel malice because they envy them.*"[1] A
virtuous woman malicious to an unchaste one *because she
envies her*, seems to me rather an unworthy object of "the
sacredness of a silent worship"; nay, even of being made
the "plaything" of an honest man. Will men never have
done with this jargon of inflated and impossible reverence;
this under-current of vilest mistrust and contempt?

When Robertson was a boy, he is recorded to have been

[1] Page 283.

full of life and gaiety, but from the time he grew up he appears to have been constantly subject to morbid depression. At first there were alternating fits of cheerfulness and gloom; but at last he seems to have deliberately justified himself in condemning mirth and adopting a fixed melancholy. In one place, after a touching description of the sufferings of a poor soul he had visited, he says, incidentally, of his general habit, "My laugh is now a ghastly, hollow, false lie of a thing." [1] In another place, detailing a meeting of men assembled to thank him for his instructions, he says, "The applause was enthusiastic, yet all seemed weary, flat, stale, and unprofitable. In the midst of the homage of a crowd, I felt alone and as if friendless." [2] Again, in 1852, he writes: "All was warm and effervescing once, now all is cold and flat. If a mouse could change into a frog, would the affections be as warm as before, albeit they might remain unalterable? I trow not; so I only say you have as much as a cold-blooded animal can give, whose pulsations are something like one per minute." Again we are told: "He also felt deep sympathy with that want of the sense of the ridiculous in Wordsworth, which made all the world, even to its meanest things, a consecrated world. *The ludicrous now rarely troubles me*, he says; all is awful." [3] It would be hard, I venture to think, to put more deplorable and distorted ideas into one sentence. That the *want* of a sense could be a subject of congratulation—a sense the source of incalculable innocent gratification, the corrector of all taste, the true correlative of the sense of the sublime, to which it bears the relationship which tenderness does to strength—to rejoice in the loss of this God-given aid to cheer us over the stony places of life, and then to sit down and say that this sense rarely *troubles* him, for "all is awful," is (in my humble thinking) to fall into some of the worst errors of Calvinism.

---

[1] Vol. ii. page 58.   [2] Vol. ii. page 107.   [3] Vol. ii. page 175.

Shall I be pardoned if I write of a contrast suggested to me by these expressions, and by those of distaste for his work, of morbid annoyance at the attacks of the *Record* newspaper, and, lastly, of continual longing to end his task and die? There was another Reformer who died soon after Robertson, worn out like him in the prime of manhood by his labours. He also was abused and vilified, and more cruelly so than Robertson, since life and limb were often in his case in peril. There was in his home-life a want Robertson never felt, which the other felt keenly: the absence of children. Taking all in all, in outward circumstances there was not much to choose as to happiness between one lot and the other. But let any one take up the Biography of Theodore Parker (not comparable as a literary work to that of Robertson), and read page after page telling of his delight in his task, his gratitude to God when his labours were blessed by helping, perchance, some poor backwoodsman, some stranger far away, his manly scorn of danger and actual *good-humour* to those who reviled and threatened him, his joyousness of spirit, revelling in innocent jest and mirthfulness to the last, let him read his letters, overflowing with friendliness and tenderness to brother, wife, teacher, friend, disciple, as if his heart were a very treasure-house of all the kindly emotions, let him watch him at last when his health failed and he left his place in sorrow, wishing yet to spend and be spent, desiring to live, for "the world was so interesting and friends so dear," and dying at last with the words on his lips, "I am not afraid to die, but I would fain have lived to finish my work; I had great powers; I have but half used them:"— let him compare these lives and these feelings on the verge of the grave, and then say *whose* was the healthier creed, the sounder thought of God and human destiny? We must not press such parallels far. There is ever injustice in doing so;

and the law by which the joyous nature chooses a joyful creed and is thereby for ever confirmed in its joyousness, and the depressed and morbid mind chooses a sad creed and is thereby made more morbid, had probably never stronger exemplification than in the case of the sturdy New-England farmer's son and the over-sensitive English gentleman. Parker had a hero's soul in a body which, till he thoroughly wore it out, fairly bore its part in the " give and take " of matter and spirit. Robertson had an angelic soul, apparently never fitted to bear this world's jars and struggles, lodged in a body where every nerve was strung to torture, and brain disease seemed to be indigenous. To ask of the two the same bearing, the same spirit, would be unjust. Yet it must remain at least as the lesson of the two Biographies, that the religious faith which animated the life of Parker and upheld him in death was pre-eminently the healthiest conceivable in all its results; and that the belief adopted by the devout and noble-hearted Robertson left him, on the other hand, to a condition of sentiment and a view of human life which must almost be qualified as morbid. It is not allowable to ask, Was not such difference, *in a measure* at least, the legitimate result of the difference of their creeds in that one supreme point whereon they separated? Were not the joyous trust, the love of his work, the delight in success, the carelessness of rebuke, the longing to live, which characterized the one—and the gloom and depression which hung, deeper and heavier year by year, over the other—both the *natural* results of their opinions? The one saw, as the central Power of the universe, a radiant Sun of Light and Love, " with whom was no darkness at all "; and the other beheld an awful vision of blackened heavens and rending graves, and over all, upon the torturing Cross, an Agonizing God.

ESSAY V.

A FRENCH THEIST.[1]

It is a fact so familiar as to be proverbial, that there are some things in which all human beings feel alike; that "one touch of nature makes the whole world kin." It is also a fact, though a less recognized one, that there are again other things in which individuals, classes, and nations feel so differently, that the display of their peculiar sensibilities, far from making others feel akin, inspires them with something very like aversion. To take our examples only from the largest instances, the various passions and sentiments of the Classic and of the Teutonic nations rather jar on one another than call out any hidden harmony; and in our own day, English reserve and German *gemüthlichkeit*, the "sentimens délicats" of a Frenchman and the "fervido cuore" of an Italian, have the least possible attraction the one for the other. Till we have lived long in each country, fed on its literature, and drank the wine of friendship with its sons and daughters, we are rather offended than won by its peculiar spirit; rather tempted to laugh at than to be softened by its tenderness. Perhaps we "insular Britons" feel this anti-social repulsion more than others; at all events,

[1] *Le Christ et la Conscience.* Par Félix Pécaut. 12mo. Paris: Cherbuliez et Cie.

De l'Avenir du Théisme Chrétien consideré comme Réligion. Par Félix Pécaut. 12mo. Paris: Cherbuliez et Cie.

we show it more candidly. How cordially most of us dislike "German sentiment," with its (wholly imaginary) tendency to lax morality, and the unlimited indulgence in smoke, metaphorical and actual! How we abhor American "bunkum" and "tall talk." Above all, how we distrust French ideas, French phrases, French turns of thought, the pitiless logic, the unattackable dialectics, the sentimental hyperboles, of a true French writer! To hear a Frenchman talk of "la femme," with mingled gallantry, fathomless pity, and acute curiosity, is enough to set John Bull, who has known Mrs. Bull by heart these twenty years, and finds her a good, comfortable wife, not in the least mysterious or pitiable, stamping with rage. To find him apostrophizing a mother, "Une mère, voyez vous c'est une chose," etc., etc., and winding up every peroration with the Divine Name as a grand rhetorical flourish, is cause enough to justify all the wars of history. We don't like to hear that Napoleon lost Waterloo because, as M. Hugo says, "il gênait Dieu." First, we don't believe in such a philosophy of history; and, secondly, we are less shocked by a man breaking the third commandment for the purpose of devoting somebody's eyes to eternal perdition, than for that of producing a rhetorical *coup de théatre*.

Very naturally, these national antipathetic feelings come out most strongly in the case of the deepest and most sacred sentiments, wherein a single jarring note is always painfully discernible. The intensity of pleasure we derive from complete religious sympathy, is only paralleled by the soreness of the mental ear to which approximate, but imperfect, harmonies are presented. The nearer the approximation may be, if the harmony is *not* achieved, the worse is the jar. Thus when we read the religious writings of Pagans or Moslems, we feel no annoyance at the wide divergence between their expressions of piety and our own. But the habitual variations from our tone of sentiment of another and intimately known Christian nation, by whom the same order of ideas is discussed with similar power, is a stone of stumbling we cannot easily overpass. I believe I shall not misrepresent our countrymen if I say, that to nineteen out of twenty English readers of the most thoughtful classes, the rich religious literature of France is almost unknown, not from any inability to appreciate it, or, in the main, from any great difference of opinion with its authors, but because of a certain latent objection to see sacred sentiments in the dress in which French taste habitually clothes them, and from a dislike even to the terminology of Gallic religion.

Nor is this antipathy (doubtless just as reasonably reciprocated by French readers towards English writers) concerned specially with differences of opinion, such as those which render the peculiar phrases of our own High-church and Low-church, orthodox and liberal parties, mutually so distasteful. English Catholics are not particularly fond of Bossuet and Massillon, and I believe that few English evangelical Protestants would read without disgust the exhortations of M. Adolphe Monod to regard the awful Creator as *débonnaire,* and to address Him in prayer always with confidence in this astounding attribute of the "debonnaireté de Dieu." Nay, to English liberals of even the least reverential section, by whom Strauss's opinions are fully accepted, the *Vie de Jésus* of M. Renan, with all its poetry and even tenderness of feeling towards Christ, is invariably somewhat shocking; and while they can coolly read a grave German debate as to whether imposture mingled in his performance of miracles, they turn with a sense of indignation from hearing him styled " ce charmant docteur," who was "jaloux pour la gloire de son Père," in the beauty of Magdalenes, and proffered "délicieuses paraboles" of the Prodigal Son to the *pétit société* of fishermen and *doùaniers*.[1]

It is a circumstance worthy of very joyful recognition that there is a school of theological writers now arising in France between whom and our English sensibilities no such barrier as that I have described has any existence, and with whom, whether we coincide with them or not in matters of opinion, the most reverent of us are sure to sympathize profoundly in sentiment. Perhaps here also may be found one proof the more of the truth, that the nearer any mind approaches to a strictly monotheistic faith, so much will it gain in spontaneous reverence of spirit; so much the further will it be from the hateful familiarity of cant on one side, and the rude defiance of atheism on the other.

I do not design in this article to give any general account of French liberal Protestantism, of which M. Bost has lately issued so able a defence,[2] and which numbers among its teachers such able and excellent men as M. Albert Réville of Rotterdam, MM. Coquerel and Martin Paschoud of Paris, M. Gaufrés President of the Institution Duplessis-Mornay, M. Fontanés of Havre, M. Zaalberg of the Hague, and MM. Colani and Leblois of Strasbourg. My object is to introduce to better acquaintance one writer of the school whose works seem pre-eminently qualified to interest Eng-

---

[1] So completely has this English repulsion to Renan's tone been recognized by the most clever of our ecclesiastical parties, that something very like an instigation to read the *Vie de Jésus* may be traced in all allusions to the work in the High-church organs. It is, of course, "fearfully blasphemous;" still it is so original, poetical, learned, attractive in all ways, that strong minds, well rooted in the faith, may be tempted to read it, and (as the reviewers know very well) induced to confound it and all books of liberal theology in common disgust. On the other hand, such works as Jowett's, Colenso's, and Martineau's, have (if we may believe these critics) nothing in them in the slightest degree novel or interesting. *They* are the dangerous books from which orthodoxy in earnest strives to deter all readers.

[2] "Le Protestantisme Libéral. Par M. le Pasteur Th. Bost." 1 vol. 12mo. Paris: Germer Baillière.

lish readers. There are, I believe, few liberal thinkers amongst us who will not rejoice to come into contact with a mind at once so lofty, so wide and so profoundly devout, as that of M. Félix Pécaut.

The first of M. Pécaut's books known to us is an essay of considerable length, *Christ and the Religious Consciousness.* The second is a shorter work, *On the Future of Christian Theism considered as a Religion*[1] (1864).

When Strauss and Renan and the other great critics of our time afford us their lights to judge what was and was not true of the recorded words and deeds of the historical Christ, and construct for us images more or less vivid of what they suppose him to have actually seemed as a living person upon earth, they do but accomplish a portion of the task which lies before the theologian who shall effectually rectify the errors of the past and map out the creed of the future. They show us what Christ (probably) *was;* and this step being (approximately) ascertained, they leave us to estimate the place he ought to hold in the religion of mankind. But why he has occupied for eighteen centuries a very different place from that to which their theories would thus consign him, why he now holds such supreme dominion over countless thousands of hearts, what is the value of their alleged spiritual experience of his power, in a word, *what is the basis of fact in human consciousness which underlies popular Christianity*—this the mere historical critic cannot help us to learn. We want the philosopher, the religious man, nay, the man of *double* religious experience, who has felt all the great phenomena of the inner life under the two dispensations of supernaturalism and natu-

---

[1] Both published by Cherbuliez et Cie., Paris, and to be had of Messrs. Williams and Norgate, Henrietta-street. Beside these, M. Pécaut has since published Four Conferences on *Liberal Christianity and Miracles,* and several minor pieces.

ralism, to tell us this. And it is the real crux of the problem. Historical truth *ought* logically, no doubt, to harmonize absolutely with consciousness, and must do so when men have fully received and digested it. But as a matter of common every-day life, it is our own consciousness of how an historical fact affects us which inclines us to adjust its records to our political or social bias; and as a matter of religious experience we may safely affirm that every argument in Strauss's arsenal must inevitably fall dead on the mind of a man who imagines he recognizes in his own soul the positive experience of Christian phenomena disproving them all. If Christ's atonement has saved *him*, it is quite clear that Christ was not what Strauss asserts him to have been. It is the real, actual relation of Christ to the consciousness of humanity, the question of "Le Christ et la Conscience," which we must decide, if we want not only to open the way to fresh light, but to shut the door on the perpetual and eternal recurrence of error.

This task it is which M. Pécaut undertakes, namely, a very careful examination of the actual facts of the inner consciousness of devout persons as regards their supposed relation to Christ, and an inquiry as to how far these facts testify to the reality of such relation. In conducting this most solemn investigation into the *penetralia'* of the soul, M. Pécaut proceeds by the simple process of discussion between a Theist and a man of the very widest and most enlightened type of what we in England should designate as Broad Church views; and I can only say that as regards the fairness of the representation of these views, few books written by professed adherents have seemed to me to give so noble and beautiful an exposition of them. Even were the result of the discussion a matter of indifference, it would be a great gain merely to read such a delineation of deep spiritual experience. But the conclusion towards which the long argument winds itself bears in truth the highest value. It is, that the supposed experience of any action on the soul by Christ as an Incarnate Deity (*i.e.* as distinct from the historical Teacher and Exemplar) cannot be maintained; and that the One God and Father in His own person fills the whole circle of the soul's heaven; in Himself alone Creating, Redeeming, and Sanctifying God.

Few things are more needed to amend our current philosophy than the adoption of sounder ideas concerning the proper scope and domain of what is called "consciousness." It is small marvel that materialists should make light of arguments founded on this basis, while those who use them indulge in the wildest licence in setting down to the credit of consciousness notions which, from the constitution of the human mind, cannot possibly be derived from such a source. Every day we may behold historical events, ecclesiastical dogmas and metaphysical theories, thus treated as "first principles" and "facts of consciousness," till the jest of the German Professor, "constructing the idea of the camel out of his moral consciousness," appears a plain statement of the actual method which our divines and philosophers are in the habit of adopting when they "evolve" a scheme of theology or ethics. Till we have corrected this absurd error, and confined the use of the word "consciousness" to things of which it is possible for a man to have moral or spiritual perception, we shall but waste words in arguing, and at the same time bring undeserved discredit on the source—fallible, indeed, yet still the ultimate and highest source—of our knowledge.

Probably, as regards religious consciousness in particular, a considerable amount of lucidity would be gained were we to relinquish the vague term "sentiment," and adopt the plain phrase the RELIGIOUS SENSE. To those who believe in the sacred mysteries of Divine communion, in the reality of those events of the inner life which constitute the history of every regenerated soul, the words "a religious sense" scarcely can appear metaphorical. They express, perhaps, as simply as may be, the fact acknowledged by all such believers, that there is in man an Eye of the spirit which truly beholds God, an Ear which hears His voice, a Feeling which perceives His ineffable presence in the high hour of visitation. Of course the phrase is unfit for the use of those who deem these things uncertain or illusive, but all the more is it suitable for those who steadfastly hold to their reality.

Supposing such a term to be generally adopted, it is clear that the result would follow, that a misapplication of the organ in question would be more easily detected than while the vaguer phrases of Sentiment or Consciousness were employed. To say, for instance, that a man's religious sense assures him of an *historical* fact (such as the life of Christ), would speedily be recognized as no less absurd than to say that a man's moral sense supplied him with the *zoological* fact of the camel's conformation. In either case, once we are compelled to define the faculty we speak of, we inevitably perceive the absurdity of transferring to it the office of another and wholly different faculty—namely, the intellect, as informed either by testimony or the bodily senses.

Again, in the case of another error, favoured by some of the leading minds of our day, the phrase "religious sense" serves to dissipate the obscurity of the language usually employed on the argument, and to reveal the untenability of their position. It is alleged by some excellent men, attached by strong affection to Christianity, yet unable to find in either Church or infallible Bible firm anchorage for their faith, that they know *by direct consciousness* that there is an Incarnate Deity, and that He acts immediately upon their souls. Now that the religious sense may and does inform us of the action (and consequently of the existence) of *a* divine, invisible Lord and Guide, is what we most heartily believe. But that it can inform us further that the Being whose awful monitions or blessed consolations or sanctifying influences it receives, is *not* God the Father and *is* God the Son, is what cannot in any way be proved in accordance with the known laws and nature of the sense in question. Nothing but a special revelation to the individual soul that such was the case (a revelation of which, so far as we are aware, no claim has ever been made), could enable a man to assert that he had made such a discovery. Nay, it is probable that none of those who hold by this peculiar form of Christian evidence would actually lay claim to the power of making such a distinction between the divine agents whose influences they experience, on any other ground than that, the common voice of Christendom having assured them that the work of God on the soul was triformous, they have always classified their experiences on such an hypothesis, and referred them accordingly to the Creator, the Redeemer, or the Sanctifier. Such a process would be most natural and blameless under the circumstances; and the consequent conviction that there were really three Divine influences perceived by the soul, would follow of course. Yet by no means can the calm inquirer admit such testimony to prove the existence of three Divine Persons, any more than the similar testimony of Romanists can be admitted to prove the invisible influence of Mary and the Saints. The religious sense cannot be held competent to witness such multiplicity of Divine Persons, for by no means conceivable could it discern the difference between one and another, save under the contingency of a *moral* difference in their monitions perceptible to the moral sense. If there were a Devil, a man might perfectly distinguish his influence from that of God. But every inward sanctifying influence is the same as God's influence. How, then, can it be distinguished therefrom?

Surely the truth which underlies all our differences, all the mystery of prayer, heard, and *felt* to be heard, even by those who have offered it under the most cloudy conceptions of God, is simply this. There is a voice which calls to us all through the thick darkness of our mortal night. We hear it, and give it many different names; but it is the *same* voice always. And we answer that voice, philosopher or peasant, saint or sinner, all alike,

> "Infants crying in the night,
> Infants crying for the light,
> And with no language but a cry."

And the Great Parent who is "about our bed" hears us all; hears His poor helpless children none the less if sometimes they call in their ignorance on other than any of His thousand names. Even an earthly mother leaves not her babe untended because it cries to nurse or brother rather than to herself, who loves it better than any beside may love.

It is on the whole subject of these inner evidences of what we may term Broad-church Christianity, as opposed to strictly Unitarian Theism, that M. Pécaut writes; and with a depth of insight, a tenderness of feeling even towards the opinions from which he most widely differs, which make his book in itself a lesson of piety and charity. It would seem as if he had laboured to represent the interlocutor who takes the more orthodox side of the argument as the most able and the most devout of the two. Certainly fairness towards an antagonist can no further go; and if the argument in favour of a real Christian consciousness as distinguished from a simple consciousness of God be found to fail, the conclusion can hardly be avoided, that no true handling of the subject would have resulted differently. It is obviously vain in the compass of a review to give any fair abstract of such a work, whose value lies in the cumulation of details of sentiment, all needing tender and reverent treatment. I shall, therefore, in the remaining pages of this article attempt to give an account of M. Pécaut's second and smaller, but by no means less interesting book, *L'Avenir du Théisme Chrétien.* The questions of which it treats are thus stated in the Preface:

"Will France dispense with a religion and a cultus? Will she be Catholic? Will she be Protestant? Will she cease to be Christian? Is a national religion henceforth incompatible with the free exercise of criticism and the principles of science? Can a people found public and private morals, support liberty, explore the highways of intellectual activity, and keep alive in its breast those noble ambitions whose aim is the True, the Good and the Beautiful—in a word, can it deserve to live, without the aid of a religion conformed to its degree of civilization?"

To those who are interested in these questions the author addresses himself. He begins by asserting that, for all so much is said of the universal decay and disruption of ancient creeds and ecclesiastical institutions,—

"— these creeds and institutions have never been appreciated with more impartiality and even sympathy than at present. Never have their doctrines, their martyrs, their merits of all kinds, obtained more complete justice. Never have they on their part displayed a zeal more pure and active, whether for the propagation of dogma or for the foundation of works of charity. Yet public feeling recedes from them. The religious reaction of the beginning of our century, which seemed calculated to stop for ever the philosophic undertaking of the age of Voltaire and Rousseau, was not long in changing to a serious movement in a different direction. We still continue to condemn the Encyclopædists for their lack of comprehension of antiquity, their profane levity in sacred studies, their want of moral depth; but, on the other hand, we have understood that their errors and excesses must not make us close our eyes to the justice of their intellectual insurrection. .... Their criticism in its broad results is found as true in the nineteenth as in the eighteenth century."

M. Pécaut then sketches briefly, but with the hand of one intimately acquainted with the various phases of social life in France, the actual condition of religion in the country.

"The educated classes, when they do not follow the caprice of a fashion, generally belong only by name to the churches from which they have received baptism ; and from the upper ranks incredulity has descended, passing through the artisans of the towns even to the agricultural labourers, especially in the Departments of the North. Young men who receive a liberal education detach themselves soon from the creed of their mothers, simply in consequence of the discord between such creeds and the whole method of their studies. A small number among them, willing at any price to satisfy the imperative need of a religion, return in later life to the same faith, while others as they advance in years find themselves from a thousand causes—the pressure of custom, the influence of women, the necessity of educating their children (for which they have no sufficient guidance or institutions in harmony with their secret principles)—above all, the lack of definite ideas and principles to resist the incessant ecclesiastical action armed at all points for good and evil—from all these causes together, we say, they find themselves all their lives long divided between an apparent adhesion to the Church and a concealed hostility thereto. Further, how many are there who in our time remain outside of all the sects because they can find no church ready to receive them, such as they really are, with their religious aspirations more or less ardent, but in any case sincere, and with their intellectual uncertainty regarding all doctrines ! The greater number of these accustom themselves to live in a vague scepticism, or in a state of indifference regarding their highest interests, only falling into the forms of the dominant Church on occasions of family or state ceremonies. Others, again, and they are among the best, abstain on principle from participation in any religious association. They refuse to carry into it a mutilated conscience ; but they would enter it to-morrow, if they might do so, with their heads raised and without denying their true position or subscribing to degrading conditions. . . . It is for these last that I write ; I who in many ways belong to the same class. I confess I cannot resign myself without pain to the condition of religious isolation in which we find ourselves."

My space will not permit me to follow M. Pécaut at length

through the deeply philosophic discussion which follows regarding the prospects of obtaining what we may call a new term of religious life for such men as he has described. Perhaps the spirit of the constructive part of his book cannot be better illustrated than in the passage (p. 211) where, after tracing how the elder Deism and all merely moral systems fail to attract or to retain the souls of men, he shows what he trusts will be the faith of the future and whence it will be derived.

"This it is which has been wanting in the experiments of which we have spoken—the gift of prayer—the supremacy of the religious idea —a deeper alliance between human nature and the drama of the moral life. And this it is which we demand of Christian tradition, not as an artificial loan which we should rejoice not to owe to it, but as the most precious part of our patrimony which it transmits to us from God, having preserved it through the ages." . . . "What (he elsewhere says[1]) is Christian Theism? Is it a system of philosophy or theology? No. Is it one particular tradition among all those which have ploughed their furrow in the history of Christianity? No. Is it a confused eclecticism, an incoherent assemblage of divers traditions? No. Is it then perhaps a simple critical residuum, obtained by means of elimination? Not so. What is it then? It is the Christian spirit itself, the spirit of the Church, the spirit of Jesus, which by its own proper virtue and by the experience of ages has disengaged itself of the mythological elements, the errors, and perishable forms with which the disciples, and in some respects even the Master himself, had clothed it."

And this religion, this *Christian Theism*, he believes will eventually prevail.[2]

" Traditional Protestantism and Catholicism, the refuges of so many pious souls, the provisional shelter of so many uncertain ones, cannot satisfy us ; for their dogmatic tradition and the principle of supernatural authority contradict alike the testimony of history and the religious needs of the human soul, once it has attained self-guidance. But I see no reason to doubt that man being essentially religious, a

[1] Chapter i.   [2] Introduction, page xii.

religious society is a natural fact, no less inevitable than civil society; and if this be so, it must be open to us to found it on the basis of ideas which our reason recognizes as true."

M. Pécaut's volume, of which I have now given so brief a sketch, has a peculiar interest, as affording to the English reader both a view of the actual state of religion in France and an insight into the aims of its most spiritual reformers. Much that he says, however, is quite equally apposite to the condition of things in our own country; and to us, no less than to him, the questions are paramount: As the old creeds are losing their hold, which are the creeds acquiring strength? Is it any one of the existing churches which bears in its bosom the precious seed hereafter to make the harvests of the world? Or is it the yet scarcely sown "Christian Theism" of such men as Félix Pécaut which is to give to us all the bread of life? Or, yet again, shall every form, alike of Christianity and of Theism, dwindle away and disappear, even as Comte foretells, and some vague "Religion of Humanity" like his, some yet more material belief in a *Fluid* or mere recognition of a Protean *Force*, henceforward fill up in human existence that stupendous vacuum to be left by the disappearance of God?

It has been frequently remarked that each of our present churches seems to have its *raison d'être*, not so much in a claim to intrinsic and eternal truth or the possession of any complete and consistent scheme of theology, but in its extrinsic and temporary antagonism to some other church. Admitting this to be true, we are driven to conclude that none of these churches can be the prototype of the Church of the Future. A sect which exists mainly as a protest against another sect can have nothing to support it when the antagonism dies with its object. Protestant and Catholic, Churchman and Dissenter, High Churchman and Evangelical, Calvinist and Unitarian, can hardly live the one without the other, more than so many Hegelian contraries. At best, like the old orders of soldier-monks, when the Crusades are over, if they be not extinguished, like the Templars, they must change their character, like the Knights of St. John. A man beginning to study theology *ab initio*, without knowledge of any of the present churches which crowd the arena of Christendom, would hardly, we conceive, deduce from either the Bible or the Book of Nature the doctrines of any one of them. And, sooner or later, according to the immutable principles of things, as one after another of these little systems "have their day and cease to be," its antagonist sect or Protestantism must cease also, and only such a creed survive as a spiritual worshipper might arrive at in a world empty of sects. This last only can be an immortal church; this only can be the type of religion which will perpetuate itself in perennial vigour. The rest are but a crop of annuals doomed ere long to die; nay, rather fungi growing each on its decaying stem, and destined, with it, at last to perish.

But to enable ourselves to discover the creed which has its right of existence not in such mere antagonism to error, but in the possession of positive truth, it is needful that we ascend into a region of speculation very far above the debates of sects and jostlings of religious parties. We need to explore the secrets of human nature itself, and deduce from the ever-repeated characteristics of past generations the facts of our common wants and ineradicable propensities. We require to learn which are the things whose hold on our hearts no time can loosen while those hearts remain what they are; and which again are those whose tenure may be as transitory as the beliefs and dreams of infancy. Above all, we need to assure ourselves whether Religion be indeed an integral part of human nature, even as the love of kindred, of justice, of truth, of beauty, are parts thereof; or if it be, on the contrary, an accident of the world's youth; a mist of the morning, dissipating even now in the glare of the noontide sun. The analogies of the past, the testimony of science respecting the existing religious sentiments of all the races of men upon earth, the deepest consciousness of our individual souls—what evidence do they bring to aid us to decide this question? Let us face the matter resolutely.

Will the time ever arrive when the historian will write words like these:

"In these remote ages, namely, from unrecorded antiquity till the third millennium after Christ, there existed among all nations of whom we possess any records an extraordinary affection, or sentiment, called RELIGION. They experienced this singular feeling very variously, and applied it sometimes to one supposed invisible Being, sometimes to many; but they generally agreed in displaying a mixture of fear, reverence, allegiance and love to some unseen Master or Protector whom they held to be present at all times and cognizant of their invocations and thanksgivings, and who was also understood to be the supreme Guardian of morality. This 'Religious Sentiment,' as they called it, caused men to establish the largest institutions and spiritual corporations, called churches and priesthoods, and to build the greatest edifices in a profusion which amazes the archæologist, who discovers their foundations, we had almost said, over every mile of the habitable globe,—edifices whose sole purpose was the imaginary service of an imaginary Being. More remarkable than all other facts, however, connected with this long-passed-away 'Religion,' is the unquestionable one that it raised those who experienced it strongly to heights of self-devotion, ascending even to positive, painful martyrdoms most difficult for us to picture under the present sounder views of social duty. The books also which have descended to us from those ages, filled as they are with idle fables, appear to reveal an intensity of aspiration after goodness, and traces of laborious striving after inward holiness and perfection, which, while we can only ascribe them to this delusive idea of an invisible Spectator of the secrets of the heart, we are forced to regard with somewhat of admiration as well as astonishment."

It is certain that either the time will come when some such words as these will be used, or else that Religion will never die out of humanity. If German Materialists and French Positivists be right, then that time, however remote, is surely approaching. Let us not deceive ourselves. The substitutes which the best of them, such as Comte, offer us *as* Religion, is not what *we call* Religion at all, nor therefore by the laws of language properly to be called by the name. It is a mere verbal trick, a shuffle of words, to call it "Religion," to worship, *not* (as all the religions of the past have done) an Invisible Person, but instead thereof the Abstraction of our Race, or a Visible Woman conventionally elevated to the representation of such an Abstraction of Humanity. It is *another thing*, whether it be a better or a worse; and he who speaks of the religious sentiment being thus given the change by the intellect as to the object of its emotions, talks as idly as he who should say that filial, parental, conjugal and fraternal love could be counterchanged at our option. When Comte talks of the world passing through the consecutive stages of Fetichism, Polytheism, Monotheism and Positivism, he deceives himself and us. He speaks like one who should describe the progress of an individual from Infant to Boy, and from Boy to Man, and should add as the next stage, "and then he became a Woman." Polytheism was indeed a stage developed out of Fetichism, and Monotheism a stage out of Polytheism. But *Positivism* is no stage beyond Monotheism, for it is not on the same road at all. Instead of a development, it is a solution of continuity; instead of a growth, it is the stroke of the axe at the very root of the tree. What can be more monstrous than to call it the development of belief in God, to arrive at belief in no God? If Comte were right, it would prove that among all the feelings and affections of our humanity, the religious sentiment alone, since the world began, has been false, diseased, distorted and misapplied. While every other feeling corresponded to some reality, the parental, the filial, the conjugal, the patriotic, each to their true and proper objects, this alone, the highest of all, has from first to last been thrown away on an imaginary entity; this alone, the source of holiest joy, truth, and virtue, has been a delusion and a lie.

Perhaps it is a true thought which books like those of M. Pécaut bring before us. In the long pilgrimage of our race we have reached a point where the way to the Celestial City is no longer clear, and where no Angel or Interpreter stands by to direct us. To the right lies the old road which our fathers trod, and where we yet can recognize their venerable footsteps. But that path is a quicksand now, hardly able to bear the weight of a traveller who would plant his feet firmly as he goes. To the left there is another path, but it turns visibly before our eyes away from that City of God which has been hitherto our goal, and passes down fathomless abysses of lonely darkness where our hearts quail to follow. Straight before us lies a field hardly tracked as yet by the few pilgrim feet which have passed over it, a vast field full of flowers and open to the sun. May the "King of that Country" guide us, so that walking thereon we may find a new and straighter road to the Celestial City on high beyond the dark River; and to the "Beulah land" of peaceful faith here upon earth!

ESSAY VI.

THE DEVIL.[1]

An alarming rumour has recently gone forth that in the new Revision of the Bible the Lord's Prayer will be altered, and instead of praying to be delivered from "evil" we shall be called on to pray to be delivered from the "Evil One," *i.e.*, the Devil. It would be hard to say whether such an emendation of the text would be more startling or painful. One thing there has been hitherto left about which Christians of every church were agreed; and wherein even men who could follow no other Christian formula were wont to join. And now that blessed note of harmony in a jarring world threatens to become a discord too! The prayer, merely to pronounce whose exordium was an act of faith, hope, and charity together, is doomed to become a test of orthodoxy, a subject of debate in each congregation and household. Assuredly thousands amongst us who have prayed all their lives to be "delivered from evil" will deem it nothing short of a blasphemy to pray to be delivered from a personal "ghostly enemy" in whose existence they have not the smallest belief.

[1] *Histoire du Diable. Ses Origines, sa Grandeur, et sa Décadence.* Par Albert Réville. Strasburg and Paris, 1870. An excellent translation of this little book, very handsomely got up, and adorned with portraits of the Egyptian and Assyrian Devils, has just been published. 12mo. pp. 72. London: Williams and Norgate. 1871. The present Essay was originally written as now printed, but was curtailed in the first publication by the exigencies of space in the *Fortnightly Review*, and for other reasons.

The mere suggestion of such an unfortunate result of criticism in the case of the Paternoster must, I presume, call forth some debate on the half-obsolete "doctrine of devils," and may very probably afford some startling revelations as to the extent to which the belief in it now prevails in the minds of Englishmen. In the present paper I propose to make some inquiry into the subject; and to follow the brilliant pages of M. Réville in an important branch of the subject, namely, the question, How Christendom came by its Devil? The lower races of mankind, as Sir John Lubbock tells us (*Origin of Civilization*, p. 254), believe in no Satan, for the obvious reason that their gods themselves have no moral character, and where morality is wholly disconnected from religion, a tempter can have no part to play. It is only in the higher forms of human thought that we come to the idea of a devil; and—singular paradox!—it is in the religion of Europe that the hideous chimera has risen to its full height of monstrosity. The How and the Why of such an abnormal growth, and the story of its decline and decay, seem every way worthy of attention.

The Report of the Committee of the House of Commons for inquiring into the Adulteration of Food and Drink must have suggested to many readers the remark: What a wonderful amount of abominable stuff is the human machine capable of absorbing without being altogether clogged and brought to a standstill! But it is by no means only the food of the body which, it appears, may be thus adulterated with at least partial impunity. Mental food seemingly quite as well qualified to poison the intellect, paralyze the will, and stop the action of the heart, is yet every day gulped down by multitudes in the sight of all men; and when we look that they should show signs of its morbific action, lo! we find them going cheerfully about their business as if they had supped full, not of horrors, but of good bread and cheese. If we could have set ourselves, for example, to create a conception which ought (so to speak) to disagree with the human mind, we should unhesitatingly say that such a notion would be the existence of a great Bad God; a being of absolute malignity who ceaselessly employs his stupendous supernatural powers, by inward suggestion and outward temptation, in luring each of us to his subterranean dungeon, where he will preside over our combustion for infinite ages. Certainly such a notion is far from being nourishing, refreshing, or, as we should have supposed, in any way wholesome or digestible. Yet, marvellous to relate! this oil-of-vitriol kind of thing slips down the throats of tens of thousands of honest Britons at least once every week, and they go home afterwards from church and eat their luncheons with admirable appetite, and never, by word or deed, betray that they have drained a cup to which that of Hecate was a mild *tisane*. Sweet and gentle elderly ladies,

> whose eyes
> Grow tender over drowning flies,

and who refuse to believe any harm of the worst scapegrace among their nephews, allow this particular horror to enter their minds unchallenged, and even seem to turn it over under the tongue as if it were a bon-bon, and inquire, plaintively, in the same breath, Does their visitor believe in the eternity of future punishment—and will he not take another lump of sugar in his tea? Between these good folk and their neighbours who refuse to believe in the horrid dogma there is hardly a pin to choose so far as cheerfulness goes, or general easiness of demeanour. One believes he walks on a thin crust of lava over a bottomless crater, and the other thinks he treads on rock; but there is no perceptible difference in the way they put their feet to the ground. One loses his son and believes he may possibly be in Hell; the other loses his daughter and is sure she is gone to a better world. But the tears of the two fathers are much alike; the grief of the first is not more inconsolable than that of the second. Truly the paradox would be inexplicable were it quite clear that those who—so to speak—bite freely at unhealthy ideas, actually masticate them and assimilate them with their mental constitutions. The fact seems rather to be that both clergy and laity are apt to take a great many more such things into their mouths than ever go any farther. Some divines and parents, indeed, obviously are possessed of a natural pouch, similar to that of the pelican, wherein they lodge an astonishing quantity of undigested notions, and whence they distribute them liberally to the young without any necessity for swallowing them on their own account.

With respect to the particular dogma of the existence of a Devil, the attitude of the Christian world at this moment is not a little singular. The idea is ostensibly accepted by the whole mass of members of all the great churches, Greek, Roman, and Protestant, national and dissenting. Only by the small sects of Universalists and Unitarians, and for a few years back has it been officially répudiated. Not one clergyman in a thousand hints at a doubt of Satan's personality, while many insist upon it with as much urgency as if (as Mr. Maurice suggests) the great message of the Gospel had been, "The Kingdom of Hell is at hand." Nine-tenths of the educated men and women in England have duly learned in childhood to "renounce the Devil," as if on the assumption (authorized, indeed, by the formularies of the Church) that we were born his subjects or children. In a word, Christendom at large professedly believes in Satan with as much formality and emphasis as it believes, let us say, in the Third Person of the Trinity.

On the other hand, and as an off-set to this official recognition of the Devil, we have to place his actual status in the minds of men of the present generation; and it appears that if we have in our creed a Devil *de jure*, we are far from having one *de facto*. Theological legitimists, like the old Jacobites, still continue on stated occasions to express their conviction of the rights of the potentate "over the water" —or over another element. But practically, and for all the purposes of common every-day life, they live peaceably under quite another dynasty. Nothing is more notorious than that of the once compact bundle of doctrines which Wycliffe and Luther began to untie, and which each sect and individual has been knotting up into little select *fasces* ever since, the rotten stick, labelled "The Devil," is the one which the fewest persons retain now-a-days in their private collections. At all events, it is always the first thing to drop out when the band of orthodoxy grows a little loose. Great thinkers and small thinkers agree here, if nowhere else. Profane folk laugh whenever the Devil is mentioned, as if there were a hidden joke in the very word; and pious people smile when the parson alludes to him, and say, like La Mothe le Vayer, "Mon ami, j'ai tant de religion que je ne suis point de ta religion."

Of those who remain, and who think that they believe in such a being, M. Albert Réville, in the paper before us, says, very aptly, that "if they only knew how people acted who really believed in a Devil," their delusion would quickly be dispelled. They would then perceive that their conventional adhesion to the dogma is an extremely different thing from the awful soul-prostrating faith in it, such as their fathers entertained two or three centuries ago.

It can hardly be doubted that it would be a benefit to the world if this outworn doctrine were confessedly abandoned. Such decaying *exuviæ* of faith, still clinging about us, are unhealthful and embarrassing things at the best. The proverbial "wisdom of the serpent" is displayed by rubbing off its old skin at the proper time, and allowing the new one, however tender, to shine unincumbered; and not by "stopping its ears to the voice of the charmer," as the Fathers ingeniously explained that difficult feat, by jamming one ear against a stone, and cramming their tails into the other.

In matters however remotely connected with religion, the principle that "lies should be served on one plate and truth on another" is pre-eminently valuable. It would be hard to say how much of the worst form of scepticism of our day is due to nothing else than the pertinacity wherewith the clergy insist on always embarking in one boat to sink or swim together the things of deepest import and simplest evidence, with the things of pettiest consequence and most uncertain proof. At best much inconvenience always comes from maintaining a public creed which is not conterminous with the private creed of its professed adherents; leaving Faith like a Roman noble shivering in one wing of his palace, while vast suites of halls and chambers, once filled with life and animation, are now silent and dark. Perhaps it may seem vain to hope that persons who, in our day, still linger in the old world of thought sufficiently fondly even to suppose that they believe in

"The Chief of many thronèd Powers,
Who lead the embattled Seraphim to war,"

will be in any way affected in their opinions by a mere historical study of the great myth, or of the Rise and Progress, Decline and Fall, of this singular Eidolon of Jewish and Christian imagination. Nevertheless, as Isaiah thought he did something to expose the folly of contemporary paganism when he described how the image to be worshipped was cut out of the trunk of a tree, one part of which was applied to roasting meat and warming mankind, while the other part was fashioned into a god; so M. Réville may hope to achieve a little in the way of discountenancing devil-belief by showing how the ugly idea was manufactured out of notions half of which at least we have long ago consigned to contempt and oblivion.

Are Satan and Ahrimanes merely the Jewish and Persian forms of the same myth? It would seem that they are of wholly different origin, and that the "root-idea" of each is entirely distinct; or, that if they sprang from the same source, it was at the immeasurably remote epoch before the Aryan and Semitic branches of the human family were separated, and when the myth itself had scarcely begun to be developed. The two separately evolved ideas were indeed brought into juxtaposition at the time of the Jewish Captivity, and a singular exchange of costume took place between them, causing the similarity of character thenceforth to appear greater than it actually is. Satan, on his side, assumed a grandeur almost bringing him up to the level of Ahrimanes; and the latter in the more modern portion of the Zend Avesta (the Boundehesch) is made to leap to earth in the shape of an adder, and to tempt Meschia and Meschiane, the parents of mankind, apparently in imitation of the story of Genesis, wherein an actual serpent (not yet identified with any spiritual power) effects the same mischief. But the earlier idea of Ahrimanes differs altogether from the first idea of Satan. The story of the former is briefly this. In the most ancient parts of the Zend Avesta, Evil is not personified at all: it is spoken of as *drucks*, "destruction," "falsehood," against which Ormuzd and good men contend. Goodness is understood as a positive thing, and evil as its negation. In each rational being there is said to exist a good, holy will; and also its shadow or negative. The famous passage supposed to be the inaugural address of Zoroaster himself, at the beginning of his prophetic mission (Gâtha Ahunavaiti, Yasna 30), shows where the doctrine had then advanced. "In the beginning there were twins, the Good and the Base in thought, word, and deed. Choose one of those two spirits. Be good, not base. Ye cannot belong to both of them. Ye must choose one, either the originator of the worst actions, or the true Holy Spirit. Some may choose the hardest lot. Others adore Ahura Mazda (Ormuzd) by means of faithful actions." In later ages Angro Mainyus (Ahrimanes) became a positively Evil Being of almost equal power with Ahura Mazda. To him is attributed the creation of all noxious beasts and insects, the addition of smoke to fire, of thorns to roses, and generally of all evil, falsehood, and pain to the world. He is the chief of the seven arch-demons, just as Ahura Mazda is the chief of the seven Amschaspands or archangels; and is lord also of an infinite train of *devas*, or fiends, beings whom the Yasna says are "nourished by evil-doers," and into whom evil-doers themselves are transformed after death. But, great as Ahrimanes became in the developed Zoroastrian belief, the blessed faith that "somehow, good shall be the final goal of ill," never seems to have deserted the worshippers of Ormuzd. They held that at the end of all things, after the final resurrection, and the three days' penance by the wicked in the rivers of molten metal, Ahrimanes himself, with all his train of demons, would repent and adore Ahura Mazda, and be received into Gorôtman (paradise). Nay, so important was felt to be this doctrine of the final Restoration of all spirits, that the assertion of it forms a part of the morning prayer which every Parsee is bound to use. The charitable hope which Burns was thought to commit a sort of blasphemy in breathing in Christian Scotland, a few years ago,—that the arch-enemy should

     Tak' a thought and men',

has thus, it seems, been a part of the religious duty of "heathens" to entertain for about three thousand years. To the pious Parsee the conception of the final perdition of a single spirit, not the restoration of the worst of them, was the blasphemous idea. He would have said, that it implied the final defeat of the "Great Wise God"; and perhaps would not have greatly erred in that conclusion.

But when the notion of the personality of Ahrimanes had become complete, and his power had been extended to the whole measure of physical and moral evil in the world, it began to be felt by the ancient Zoroastrians that their fundamental dogma of the Unity of God, and his supremacy over all beings, was endangered. To correct this error, at the time of the revival of the faith under the Sassanian kings, there began to be heard of a Zeruane Akerene (Time without Bounds), the First Cause of both Ormuzd and Ahrimanes. But this conception (though still held by a few Parsee teachers) has been shown by recent European students of Zend MSS. to be wholly unsupported by the older sacred writings, which only describe Ormuzd as existing *in* "Boundless Time," by no means as derived *from* it.

In nearly all respects it will be seen presently that the biography of the Jewish Satan contrasts strangely with that of the Persian Ahrimanes as above described. When the former first makes his appearance on the stage of Hebrew thought, it is under the aspect of a talking reptile; or rather the reptile first appears as a *bonâ fide* speaking animal, such as those of which the folk-lore of all nations is full; and not till long ages afterwards was this Serpent of Eden identified with a supposed angel, having an office somewhat analogous to that performed by the malicious snake. There is no trace of a belief in Satan in the patriarchal ages, nor during the period immediately succeeding the Exodus and the conquest of Canaan. Had the compilers of the Pentateuch and of the Books of Joshua and Judges known of the existence of such a being, it is inexplicable why they should have not alluded to him as often as do the Evangelists. "Gods of the nations," evil and "lying spirits" they speak of, and of those who consult them; but of the Arch-Fiend they seem not to have heard a rumour. On the contrary, when we first come on definite traces of Satan in Scripture, he has not yet assumed such a position at all. His "fall like lightning from heaven" no prophet's reverted eye had yet beheld. The great poet of the Book of Job saw Satan, in his sublime vision, not as a rebel and outcast of paradise, but as going in and out of the court of Jehovah with others of the sons of God, coming thither to do homage. Nay, he imagines him to hold there a certain office as Public Prosecutor; and that he is permitted to descend to earth (if we may so speak without irreverence for that glorious book) in the character of an "agent provocatif." How much of this conception, and of all the myths which have been built on it ever since, we owe to the genius of the poet himself — perhaps almost wholly creating the character for his artistic purposes, or else defining and immortalizing a vague and temporary phase of Eastern thought—can never be known. Long after the days of Job, and when the Jews (as Maimonides confesses) had acquired their knowledge of the angels from the Persians in Babylon, Satan became a "Prince of the Powers of the Air," with his train of subordinate archdemons; and the story of his rebellion and fall gradually took shape.

When the first Hebrew conception of the Elohim had settled into the strict monotheism wherein Jehovah alone was adored as the sole God of Israel, the theology of the age attributed to Him the doing of every act and inspiring every thought, both good and bad. Under this *theocratic pragmatism*, as the Germans call it, the Lord "hardens the heart of Pharaoh;" and his "Spirit" comes on Samson, and makes him rise and slay forty men, to pay a wager with their spoil. There is obviously, as yet, no question in the Hebrew mind whether the act so inspired be right or wrong, worthy or unworthy of Divine guidance. Some of the purposes of Jehovah are carried out by angels, obedient, spiritual messengers, who fly about and visit the patriarchs in visible shapes, and drive Saul melancholy mad, and startle the ass of Balaam. One of these fulfils the office of Accuser-General or "adversary" (*Satan*). In the performance of his invidious, but as yet apparently loyal and legitimate service, this angel grows suspicious and malicious; and we can trace, as to him are attributed, a series of acts of enmity to the human race in general, and to the house of Israel in particular (Zechariah iii. 1), the dislike of the Jews to him gradually rising, till he is at last made responsible for all evil under the sun. The turning-point of the national creed in this matter is most acutely fixed by M. Réville between the dates of the Second Book of Samuel and of the First Book of Chronicles. In the former (xxiv. 1) the ill-omened census of David is attributed, according to the old theory, to the inspiration of Jehovah. "The anger of the Lord was kindled against Israel, and *He* moved David against them to say, Go, number Israel and Judah;" after which He punishes the people by a pestilence for David's action. But in the latter book (1 Chronicles xxi. 1), recording the same story, the evil inspiration is laid at the door of the Devil, and we are told "*Satan* stood up against Israel and provoked David to number the people;" after which (verse 7) the sequel, "God was displeased with this thing," follows much more easily.

From the critical moment in which this strange exchange of functions took place between Jehovah and Satan, we can easily understand how the consciences of the pious Jews of the great prophetic age constantly sought refuge from the dread mysteries of the order of Providence, by laying more and more the blame of evil on Satan, and thereby relieving their faith in the goodness of Jehovah from too severe a strain. Just as, in a previous still less reflective epoch, their fathers had not been disturbed by the attribution of evil inspirations to the holy Jehovah, so they, only a little more advanced, were content (as are millions to this hour in Christendom) to attribute such evil to God's creature, Satan, without asking whence this incarnate Evil derived his nature, or obtained his power of access to the soul.

The age of the Apocrypha, with its intermixture of Persian and Alexandrian ideas, saw Satan, or, as the Septuagint call him, DIABOLOS, the *Slanderer*, already robed in some of the borrowed glory of Ahrimanes, and no longer a servant of Jehovah, but a rebel banished from those courts of heaven wherein the poet of Job beheld him freely entering. He now hates God, and labours to injure man, from rebellious spite to the Creator. He is at the head of a grand hierarchy of evil powers; the Asmodeus of the Book of Tobit, the demon of lust (identified by M. Bréal with a similar Persian fiend), being one of the chief. Death itself is discovered to be Satan's work; and every inexplicable disease —blindness, dumbness, madness, epilepsy, and St. Vitus's dance—is traced directly to his malignity. Sometimes one of his minions, sometimes a legion of them, takes possession of a man altogether, and makes him a "demoniac," whose deplorable state only the exorcism of a divinely commissioned apostle, or of Messiah himself, can relieve. At the name of Jehovah, indeed, the devils tremble and retreat, never presuming, like Ahrimanes, to contend face to face with the Power of Good; and their circle of action is always strictly limited by the Divine Will. But the malignity of the Jewish evil spirits is sharpened by despair, for they know that for them await only the eternal fires.

Such was pretty nearly the state of the Hebrew belief regarding devils at the time when Christ was born in Palestine. To his followers, who were anxious to identify him with the Messiah, his relations with persons supposed to bear in their diseased bodies or minds the special mark of Satanic possession, was a matter of paramount importance. The Messiah could in no way, as they imagined, prove his mission so effectually as by constraining the devils to acknowledge his superior power. Incidents which apparently corroborated this supremacy became of more interest as "evidences" than all the divine precepts and affecting parables to which in our day Christians turn to justify their faith; and the road to orthodox belief was diligently paved with histories which have long since become stumbling-blocks in the way. Modern liberal Christians have exhausted themselves in efforts to determine whether Christ did or did not share the common belief of his countrymen in Satanic agency; the conclusion that he did so being only less painful than the opposite horn of the dilemma, that he *knowingly* sanctioned a superstition which he did *not* share. The reader who desires to see the subject candidly discussed will do well to consult the pages of M. Réville. In concluding his remarks he urgently reminds us, that if Christ did believe in the Devil, he never insists on the doctrine; that he tells us that our evil thoughts "proceed" out of our own hearts, and not (as a Rabbin would have taught) from the suggestion of Satan; and that he even calls one of his disciples "Satan" when he makes an immoral suggestion; thus using the term in a merely metaphorical sense as any disbeliever in the doctrine might do now. The same observations apply to St. Paul, who avowedly believes in Satan, but who, in his delineation of the great struggles of the soul, always makes the Flesh, not the Devil, the opponent of the spirit of righteousness. During the whole New Testament period, though the devils occupy quadruple the space they did in the older canon, they are still lingering in the human mind in a half-shadowy condition. They are neither visible nor palpable; and the more grotesque mediæval ideas concerning them were yet unimagined. It needed another atmosphere to develope such monstrous growths out of the spawn as yet hidden.

The primitive Christians used Satan, chiefly it would seem, as a ready-made and easy explanation of everything which thwarted their progress or aided their enemies. The Roman Empire itself was shrewdly suspected of being the kingdom of the Devil. All the oracles and miracles of the heathen gods were believed to be accomplished directly by the help of the evil spirits. In illustration of all this M. Réville might have quoted a passage in Tertullian's "Apology," which, long as it is, I am tempted to introduce, as affording a general view of the part allotted to the devils in that same patristic teaching to which some of our living divines revert as the "pure milk of the Word," which we in our day have only to imbibe and be blessed :—

"But how from certain angels, corrupted of their own will, a more corrupt race of demons proceeded is made known in the Holy Scriptures. Their work is the overthrow of man. Wherefore they inflict upon the body both sickness and many severe accidents, and on the soul perforce sudden strange extravagances. Their own subtle and slight nature furnisheth to them means of approaching either part of man. Much is permitted to the power of spirits, as when some working evil in the air blighteth the fruit or grain, and when the atmosphere, tainted in some secret way, poureth over the earth its pestilential vapours. They commend the gods to the captive understandings of men, that they may procure for themselves the food of sweet savour and of blood offered to images. [This idea, that the devils fed on the idol sacrifices, is upheld by Athenagoras, Justin Martyr, Chrysostom, Gregory Nazianzen, and many others of the Fathers.] Every spirit is winged. Whatever is done anywhere they know. The councils of God they both snatched at in the times when the prophets were proclaiming them, and now also cull in the readings which echo them. And so, taking the allotted courses of the future, they ape the power while they steal the oracles of God. But in the (heathen) oracles, with what cunning do they shape their double meanings to events; witness the Crœsi, witness the Pyrrhi! It was in the manner of which I have before spoken that the Pythian god sent back the message that a tortoise was being stewed with the flesh of a sheep. They had been in a moment to Lydia. . . . . By dwelling in the air and being near the stars, they are able to know the threatening of the skies. They are sorcerers also as regards the cure of sickness. They first inflict the disease, and then prescribe remedies."—*Tertullian, Apol.* i. 23.

Such was the world to the primitive Christians; a place in which devils exercised every imaginable spiritual and physical power, causing at once evil thoughts in the minds of men, diseases in their bodies, and blights on their fields! Within and without, from the height of the stars to the depths of hell, the universe was full of these agents of malignity and deception. Truly the days of the Roman Empire were bad enough, but this view of human existence in them surpasses, for horror, anything that history has told us. Nor was it exclusively among the Christians that a belief in devils at that time prevailed. Polytheism itself, as it became a more moral creed, tended towards a dualism previously unknown, and the Magian religion, which found a welcome in Rome amid the general Maëlstrom of faith, added, doubtless, its part to the popularity of the idea of evil spirits. Apollonius of Tyana was as much the enemy of demons as any Christian saint of them all; and Iamblichus, the lofty-minded pious Egyptian priest, raised—

Eros and Anteros at Gadara;

like a Catholic exorcist. That strange hybrid between the religions of Christ and Zoroaster, Manicheism, became, at a very early period, a faith numbering thousands of adherents, and has left to this day its dregs in the sect of Yezidis in Persia, who offer distinct worship to Shaitan.

Finally, the Talmud, compiled at this time, affords ample evidence that the Jewish mind received in full the fashion of the age. How much the ascetic practices, which now also came into vogue, and drove men by hundreds crazy with fasting and austerities, abetted the growth of a belief in tempting devils, Asmodeus, Belphegor, and Mammon, inspirers of Lust, Gluttony, and Avarice, it is needless to point out. St. Anthony's experience was enough to have originated the nightmare of diabolic agency, had none such ever been heard of before.

But the most important part played by Satan in the religion of the primitive Christians was unquestionably that which they assigned to him in the awful drama of the Atonement. The original conception of the nature of that event, as held by the saints and Fathers of the first centuries, has been too much overlooked by those who in our day discuss its moral character. The "ransom of blood," understood commonly in modern times to have been paid on Calvary to the justice of God, was taken by the Fathers in quite a different sense, namely, as paid in discharge of the claims of the Devil. St. Irenæus distinctly taught that mankind since the Fall had become the property of Satan in the sense in which slaves belonged to their masters; and that it would have been unjust for God to rob him of souls which belonged to him. Christ, as a perfect man, and therefore independent of the Devil's claims, had offered himself as a ransom for the rest of mankind; and the Devil had accepted the bargain. By-and-by it was observed that in this negotiation Satan had made an egregious blunder; and Origen candidly admitted that he had been outwitted, and had been induced to accept the ransom of Christ's life, which the Redeemer had given knowing that he could not retain him in hell. This idea (to our minds so shocking), of the Devil being the deceived party and Christ the deceiver, was accepted almost universally throughout the Church till the scholastic theology discarded it in favour of the scheme, expounded in Anselm's "Cur Deus Homo,"—namely, that it was the Father's justice, and not the Devil's claims, which were satisfied by the sacrifice of Christ.

But even while the Devil was supposed to have relinquished his infernal rights to human souls, in consideration of Christ's blood, he was paradoxically believed to be still tempting, and betraying thousands continually to his prisons below. The time and care of the saints were principally occupied in evading his toils; and as to sinners, they were altogether his servants. The whole *cultus* of Christianity assumed a new aspect from this dread Shadow, always in the background. Baptism became primarily an exorcism. To become a Christian was to "renounce the Devil, his pomps, and his works." To be turned out of the Church was to be "delivered to Satan."

Of course the Natural History of Devils occupied intelligent minds not a little during this first Reign of Terror. The mysterious allusion in Genesis to the "Sons of God" (the *Beni Elohim*), who "saw the daughters of men that they were fair," furnished sufficient data for an entire authoritative Demonogony, to which St. Augustine added the touch that at their fall the devils (whose bodies had been previously aërial) acquired gross animal forms, subject to all carnal passions. This point once established, there followed, in the simple order of development, the invention of *Incubi* and *Succubi*, or devils who haunted sleeping men and women; with other fiends of ill design, like the one who seduced St. Victor under the semblance of a young girl lost in a wood. Decrees of Councils from the fourth century onward begin to notice these perils, and advise bishops to look sharply after women who wander about at night along with heathen goddesses. The Sabbath of the Brocken was already brewing in the mind of terrified Christendom.

As soon as the devils were known to assume visible forms, it became naturally a matter of extreme curiosity to determine what was their proper shape and semblance. The Father of Lies, of course, was understood to practise various deceptions in this as in every other way; and his audacity in the case of St. Martin went so far as to present himself disguised as Christ. But his ordinary working dress, if we may so describe it, was at that time merely a *domino noir*. He was the Angel of Darkness, and as a black figure was often seen to escape when heathen temples were overthrown and idols shattered. It was somewhat later in the course of his career ere he adopted the horns and hoofs of the god Pan; and presented himself to Europe under the familiar guise wherewith he is identified in our imaginations, and wherein the characteristics of the harmless ruminant are so unscientifically combined with the propensities of the "Roaring Lion going about seeking whom he may devour."

The next step, taken in the sixth century, and made by St. Theophilus, was the notable discovery that compacts could be made with the Devil. Documents duly signed by the high contracting parties conveyed on one side the diabolic promise to give the man riches, power, revenge, or whatever else he desired; and on the other the human engagement to submit to the demon's summons of the soul to the regions below at a stipulated period. The interest of the innumerable tales to which this brilliant idea gave birth centred on the acuteness of the man in cheating the Devil at the last moment by some flaw in the contract, or by the interference, on behalf of the sinner, of some benevolent saint or of the Virgin descending to the rescue.

Of course the man who, believing in a Power of Evil, voluntarily accepted such allegiance and bound himself to do his will for the sake of some coveted reward, was guilty of a moral offence tantamount (so far as his poor benighted mind could go) to absolute renunciation of all duty and religion. There *was* such a sin as Demonolatry, although no demon existed to receive the worship. The enormous mischief of the popular delusion lay in the fact that it constantly presented this capital offence of spiritual treason as a temptation to all men spurred by passion to seek any of the prizes supposed to be attainable by its means. Love, jealousy, hate, covetousness, ambition, were naturally excited to madness by the idea that their complete gratification was always possible; and the wretched being who once imagined he had "sold his soul" of course from that hour became desperate and irreclaimable.

In the Middle Ages we find the doctrine of devils assuming a shape altogether in accordance with the spirit of the time. Feudalism, with its accurately ranged orders, was matched by corresponding orders in the diabolic realm. Just as the barons and knights assembled round the king and swore fealty to him, so the sorcerers were believed to assemble at their Sabbath on the Brocken and to swear allegiance to Satan. Even the favourite sport of the time had its parody in the nightly chase of the infernal Wild Huntsman. The ceremonies of the Church were travestied and the Pater Noster repeated backwards to worship the Devil. In a word, day and night did not rule the natural world more completely than the Church and the Devil filled between them the imagination of our fathers. From the thirteenth to the fifteenth century the superstition seems to have been at its height. Satan had reached the zenith of his grandeur. As a specimen of the way in which his doings occupied the minds of men, the reader should consult the *Liber Revela-*

tionum de Insidiis et Versutiis Dæmonum adversus Homines, by the Abbot Richalmus, who flourished in 1270. Everything which happened of a disagreeable sort to this good man, from the distractions of his mind at Mass to the nausea he felt after eating unwholesome food, from the false notes of his choir to the coughing fits which interrupted his sermons, all was the work of a malicious fiend. "For example," says he, "when I sit down to read a pious book, the devils manage to make me immediately feel sleepy. When I try to rouse myself by drawing my hands out of my sleeves they bite me like fleas, and so distract my attention." The business of some devils, he observes, is solely to make men ugly, and he knows a case wherein a little devil-kin has been hanging on a holy man's under lip for twenty years to make it pendent in an unseemly manner. There are as many devils, he assures us, round each of us, as there are drops of water round a drowning man. "The uses of the sign of the cross and of salt are indeed considerable in repelling these enemies. When a devil has taken away a monk's appetite, it is surprising how eating a little salt with his meat will improve it again." Thus, for 130 chapters, continues this remarkable book of Revelations, whose popularity, like that of the *Golden Legend* of Voragine, on the same topic, proves sufficiently how far both works were in harmony with the feelings of their age.

Now at last, then, the world was ripe for the terrible cruelties to which the belief in Satan led up, and which were its logical outcome. Angela de Labaréte, a noble lady, was in 1275 burnt at Toulouse as a sorceress—the first of the long array of victims to the same superstition, who (according to Gibbon's calculation) exceeded in number in one country of Europe alone, and in a single century, all the martyrs of the ten Roman persecutions. The dreadful story of the witch trials needs not to be told again in these pages.

For three centuries they went on, growing more frequent, and shifting their area from one part of Christendom to another, till at last every nation, Catholic and Protestant, had caught the hideous frenzy; and, as we look back over the horrible scene, it would seem as if France, Spain, Italy, Germany, the Netherlands, England, and America were, like the "Black Country" at night, blazing everywhere with lurid fires, whose fuel was the living flesh of men and women and innocent children.

It was when the witch persecutions had only just commenced in Southern France that Dante drew his portrait (dignified in comparison to the demonology of the age) of the great

> Imperator del doloroso regno ;

and from his descriptions it is probable that the Devil of Orcagna and of the few other Italian painters who condescended to touch him, was derived. But it was when the witch mania was in its fury throughout Europe and America that England's great republican poet took on himself the astounding task of rehabilitating the celestial rebel. The grotesque fiend of the popular imagination, transformed into the magnificent Lucifer of Paradise Lost, was a stroke of poetic fancy which perhaps even Milton would scarcely have dared had not St. Avitus of Vienne preceded him on the same track.[1] Be this as it may, his success was equal to his boldness, and it may be fairly said that from his time we have had at least two Devils in English imagination.

[1] The resemblance between this Saint's old Latin poem, *De Initio Mundi* and the *Paradise Lost* of Milton, both as regards plot, characters, and even long parallel passages, has been recently brought to light by an American critic. Todd, in his *Inquiry into the Origin of Paradise Lost*, betrays that he had never read St. Avitus. He says, "Mr. Bowle, in his catalogue of poets who have treated Milton's subject, mentions Alcinus Avitus, Archbishop of Vienna (!), who wrote a poem in Latin hexameters, *De Initio Mundi*, but offers little else respecting it. Possibly some of the sentiments and expressions in this poem might arrest the attention of Milton."—*Todd's Milton*, vol. i. p. 60.

One is the semi-ridiculous Mediæval Devil, the "Old Nick," or "Muckle-horned Clootie," with the aspect of Pan and a disposition which, although malicious and cunning, is yet easily liable to be cheated and outwitted by ordinary mortals. The other is the superb Miltonic Lucifer, whose blasted form of "archangel ruined" the pencil of Ary Scheffer can scarcely render grand enough for our ideal; and who, instead of contending with clowns in ignoble trial of wits, is the very incarnation of giant Pride, the mighty rebellious Will which prefers

"Rather to reign in hell than serve in heaven!"

This latter and nobler Devil has indeed so impressed himself on the minds of all cultivated Englishmen that he is almost universally accepted by us as the true Biblical Satan; and what we have learned from Milton is so jumbled with what we have learned from the Bible, that nine out of ten amongst us would probably, on sudden inquiry, unhesitatingly answer that there exists Scriptural authority for a whole series of myths for which our English poet is alone responsible. As we have now seen, the Old Testament Satan really afforded only a hint of the Miltonic Lucifer; while the New Testament Beelzebub bore scarcely any resemblance to him whatever.

Lastly, as the Devil took his place in the masterpieces of Hebrew, Italian, and English literature, so, in the beginning of our own age, he re-appeared once more in the great poem of Germany. And what a true modern Devil is Mephistopheles! His creator foresaw that, at least for the current century, not Cruelty, not Malice, not Falsehood, not Pride, would be the great evil of the world, but—the Incarnate Sneer.

When the flames of the witch persecutions at length died away (no longer ago than in 1781 in Spain, and in 1783 in

Switzerland), and the world began to breathe again after its dream of terror and cruelty, it became evident that the Devil had lost much of his intimidating power. Rationalism was advancing, not only in the realm of theology, but of medicine, physiology, and psychology. The wild and baseless notions which did duty for science before the age of Bacon faded gradually away, and men began to see things in the light of common day, and not of a hundred will-o'-the-wisps of unreclaimed fancy. The Reformation had laid the train of thought which is even now exploding, one after another, all the strongholds of superstition. The inkstand which Luther threw at the Devil at Wartburg proved to be a true prophetic symbol, for the black fluid has done more to extinguish the powers of darkness than all the holy water of the saints. Experience proves that as religion becomes more spiritual, in the true sense of the word, the belief in "spirits," good, bad, or indifferent, invariably evaporates. Such beings are the creations, not of Faith, not of reliance on the intuitions of conscience and the religious sentiment, but, on the contrary, of a carnal and materialistic mind, which seeks assurance of supernal things through the evidence of the bodily senses, and uses mechanical means for obtaining spiritual ends. In proportion as the priesthood resigns its pretensions to work sacramental miracles, so far prayer and exhortation take the place of exorcisms and incantations. As the Divine Power becomes recognized in the ordinary course of nature, and is no longer sought exclusively in the realm of miracle and prodigy, so the whole world of spirit-marvels is pushed farther back out of the path of thought. Of course the Devil and his doings are the very first to undergo the influence of this silent rising of the intellectual tide. Even for those who still believe in his existence he has dwindled into an invisible and impalpable being, whose suggestions are made only in the heart, and not through external malific artifices; and whose influence must be combated, not by charms and exorcisms, but by moral efforts and prayers. In a word, the Devil is dying out.

Does there remain no lesson to us from all this chain of error after error which for so many centuries has fettered our race? What has been the principle in human nature on which this belief has fastened, and by whose energy it must have been supported so long? Is it the need laid on us to find some explanation of all the evil we behold within and around us in creation? M. Réville thinks this cannot be so, because the myth of Satan offers no logical solution of the problem at all, but rather adds new difficulties thereto. But is he right in arguing that because the story of the Devil *ought* not to satisfy a troubled mind, it is therefore a fact that it has not satisfied thousands for twenty centuries? It is a matter of hourly astonishment to any one who earnestly contemplates the religion of his fellows to observe how small a part logic plays in it, and how readily men are put off with answers to inquiries which are no answers at all. The "schemes of salvation," for example, which are commonly announced as vindications of the Divine justice, and are popularly accepted as such,—what are they but vindications of their authors' incapacity to understand the rudiments even of human equity? It would seem nowise more improbable that our ancestors should have taken the myth of Satan as a satisfactory account of the origin of evil, than that millions in our day should take other parts of the same theology as affording satisfactory views of the goodness of God.

We have seen in this sketch a gradual rising of the moral sense of mankind in reference to the source of evil. In the earliest stage of all, and long before Hebrew thought had reached the level whereon the Book of Genesis was written, there was no connexion between religion and morality; for the gods of savages have no moral attributes, and are merely unseen Powers imbued with all the passions of the savage himself. By degrees, and as soon as the moral law begins to make itself felt in the yet half-brutal human soul, the idea that the higher powers approve such virtues as man yet perceives, and punish his crimes, dawns on the understanding. When he has reached the development of a Greek of the days of Hesiod he has become well assured that—

> "Jove's all-seeing and all-knowing eye
> Beholds at pleasure things that hidden lie,
> Pierces the walls which gird the city in,
> And, on the seat of judgment, blasts the sin."

And this although, at the same moment, this justice-vindicating Zeus is believed to be himself capable of what at a further stage are recognized as atrocious crimes. At the far higher moral stand-point of the author of the Elohistic fragment of Genesis, the Elohim are recognized as holy; but there is no sense yet, or even in the later writers of the Pentateuch, that God may not consistently tempt men to sin or "harden the hearts" of kings, and prompt all manner of injustice. As we have noticed above, this very imperfect conception changes between the dates of the Book of Samuel and of Chronicles. Evil inspirations could no longer be suffered to be attributed directly to Jehovah. His servant Satan must whisper them in the ear of David. Then, as the next step, the Satan who effects such mischief can be no longer recognized as the servant of God. He must be a rebel against Jehovah, and his evil work must be done, not by His behest, but in opposition to Him. At this point of advance, it would seem, the human mind stopped for about twenty-six centuries. It was trapped, in fact, in a sort of theologic *cul de sac;* for, as God was recognized as Creator of all things, He must needs, it was clear, have been Satan's

Creator also. No further separation could be made on the Hebrew basis, between the powers of good and evil, than to allege that the latter, though made originally by God, had in remotest time rebelled against and opposed Him. The questions how and why an All-foreseeing Being created this foe to Himself and his creatures, and an Omnipotent One granted him the necessary powers for carrying on his rebellion, were either never thought of, or they were soon laid aside as unanswerable. Evil existed, and the Devil caused it. That was all that was known on the subject. It was some satisfaction, at least, to be sure that the earth rested on an elephant, and the elephant on a tortoise, even though nobody could conjecture on what the tortoise might stand.

Now, in our day, we have come at last to be forced to look into this tremendous problem a little more deeply. With the disappearance of the Devil, the plain and hideous fact of the existence of evil is left staring us in the face. God help us to make the next great step safely! Is it too presumptuous to surmise that its direction will prove to be that of a retrocession from the arrogant dogmatism which has caused us, first, to give to the Divine Might the name of "Omnipotence," because, forsooth, we know nothing of its bounds or conditions; and then, secondly, to argue back from that purely arbitrary metaphysical term, that He could do this or that, if it so pleased Him, since He is "Omnipotent"? Who has given us to know that God is absolutely able to do *everything*? The simple proposition (which it might seem the blindest could not have overlooked) that no conceivable power, of whatever magnitude, can possibly include contradictions, might have taught us more modesty than we have hitherto shown in scanning the order of providence. When we have thoroughly taken in the idea that God could not make twice two five, nor the three angles of a triangle more than two right angles; then we may begin to ask ourselves, May not contradictions equally great, for all we can know, lie in the way of every removal of evil which we would fain demand at the hands of the Lord? And may not the accomplishment of the highest of all possible good, the training to virtue of finite spirits, be as incompatible with a thornless and sinless world as would be the making of a circle and a triangle having the same mathematical properties?

Philosophically considered, the error on which the doctrine of the existence of a Devil is founded is precisely the same as that into which Aristotle fell when he treated Lightness and Coldness as positives, instead of merely as the negations of weight and heat. We are all prone to make the same mistake, even as regards our own natures, and to talk as if our lower, blind, and animal part were something more than that Negative mind (Akomano) which Zoroaster named it. To call our passions inspirations of devils, and treat our lower nature as the Devil's realm, and our delinquencies as cases of his victory and possession, is, of course, the next error, and the most natural one in the world; just as it is natural to speak of cold "causing" water to freeze, and of night being the "dominion of Darkness." But as physical science repudiates the latter phrases, so must our theology henceforth renounce the former. And in the highest region of our conceptions the same principle must hold. We speak of God as a Person, because we are compelled to believe that, between the only alternatives conceivable to us—personality and impersonality—personality is the highest, and, therefore, that God is personal. But for the very same reason that we attribute to Him positive and personal existence, we are bound to deny the same to His antithesis. Whatever other explanation may or may not be found for the existence of pain and sin, it is impossible that it can be other than impersonal and negative. The Black Sun imagined by the novelist, whose rays were streams of darkness and frost, was not a more unscientific conception than that of a mighty intelligent Will, wholly evil, as God is wholly good.[1]

[1] While the present volume has been passing through the press, Lord Lyttelton has published the second series of his *Ephemera*, in which he does me the honour to devote an article to the refutation of the present Essay. Lord Lyttelton says that the reason why the theory I advocate (that of the non-existence of a Devil) ought to be resisted, is the general one that "forced and peculiar constructions of Scripture are inexpedient." In the same week the Duke of Somerset has published his essay on *Christian Theology and Modern Scepticism*, and therein describes the "first difficulty" in the way of accepting the authority of the Bible to be, the presence therein of the doctrine of devils and diabolic possession. "The educated Protestant," he observes, "no longer believes what the Evangelists believed and affirmed" (p. 17). I can only reply to Lord Lyttelton's courteous criticism by observing that, in writing my Essay, I had much more in my thoughts such a view of the matter as that of the Duke of Somerset, than the remotest intention to introduce "a forced and peculiar construction of Scripture." I rejoice to find that even so decided an adversary as Lord Lyttelton will go with me so far as to treat the eternity of future punishment and the final restoration of the Devil as open questions; while he appears to agree with Mr. Brookfield in denying the materiality, though not the personality, of the being in question. May I venture to remark that there are controversies in which, when our opponent is willing to go with us a mile, we may hope, ere long, to find him contented to go with us twain?

ESSAY VII.

A PRE-HISTORIC RELIGION.[1]

ANCIENT History, it has been well said, tends continually more to become the History, not of Facts, but of Opinions and Sentiments. What actually occurred at any given time and place, what deeds were done, what words were spoken, what were the characters of the actors of each scene, grows ever more doubtful as we are enabled to check one narrative by another; or to apply to the antique chronicle the rules by which we determine the value of modern evidence. But on the other hand, the common Belief of contemporary and succeeding generations concerning those doubtful things said and done, and the feelings, whether of admiration or of contempt, wherewith they regarded the actors and speakers, are matters very plainly revealed to us, and afford to the student of human nature his best and safest materials.

In proportion as such a view of the proper scope of ancient history becomes recognized, and books are written more carefully collating and delicately weighing the indices of opinion and feeling, and expending less time in disquisitions over irrecoverable details of facts, it may be hoped that there will arise for us quite a new aspect of the old world. We shall live again—not with the few who acted its great dramas of war and conquest, but with the many

[1] *Tree and Serpent Worship.* By James Fergusson, F.R.S. London: India Museum. 4to. pp. 247.

who looked on at them at lesser or further distance, and felt their hearts beat, like our own, with triumph and regret, love and detestation. We shall learn, not what Theseus and Regulus did, but what were the types of character which the whole Greek and Roman nations set up as their ideals. We shall acquire a true knowledge, not of the History of the Six Days of Creation or of the Exodus, but of what the Hebrews in the time of their kings believed about the origin of the world and the early migrations of their race. We shall be able to satisfy ourselves, not of the incidents of that wondrous story over which Strauss and his critics may wrangle for ever, but of what the writer of each Gospel and each Epistle, the men of the apostolic age, and the men of the patristic ages, successively thought and felt about its great subject.

To this newer form of historical research, the contributions which pour in on all sides, regarding the ancient creeds of the world, are especially valuable. Already the difference between our views and those which even well-informed and liberal men entertained twenty years ago, on the whole subject of comparative theology, is enormous; and as the various pieces of the puzzle are put together, the place for each new acquisition appears easier to find, till by degrees the hope of a not wholly incomplete "Philosophy of All Religions" comes into view. Nor are those grander and more complete systems which may deserve properly to be classed as Religions alone useful for such a purpose. Between a great body, such as the Christian or the Brahminical, with its organized Hierarchy, and Canonical Books, and those minor beliefs and superstitions which have prevailed in less formal shape over the world, there are many degrees of importance, down to the fairy tales and folk-lore which our fathers banished to the nursery, but which the scholars of our generation find nowise unworthy of notice;

and which certainly formed during the Middle Ages a sort of secondary popular religion in Europe. Few problems are more curious than the rise and the distribution of these *invertebrate* creeds (if we may so describe them) over the globe. The short and easy method of our fathers which derived them all out of that very capacious receptacle, Noah's Ark, will hardly serve our turn better now than in the case of the beasts and plants of South America and New Zealand. Perhaps, as our zoologists and botanists have discovered that in geology lies the key to their secrets, and that the distribution of the fauna and flora is everywhere the monument of the changes of land and sea in far off epochs, so the myths and emblems which we likewise find scattered apparently so unaccountably, may finally be all affiliated to the races of men among whom they originally sprung, and who as aborigines or conquerors have dwelt in the localities where they flourish. As Heraldry has been often the clue to Genealogy, so may fables and forms of worship, often of the lightest or the rudest kind, afford hints of incalculable value in aiding the philologist and the ethnologist to track out the various branches of the human family in their wanderings over the globe. How it is that during all their journeyings these heirlooms of fancy never seem to drop; how they endure through successive religious conversions and reformations, springing up like wild flowers after the plough has turned again and again the ground they live in,—is a marvel of psychology. We cannot explain it; we can only note the fact that while "marble may moulder, monuments decay," while some of the noblest works of the human mind have been destroyed in the conflagration of libraries, while poems, pictures, statues, which gold could not purchase now, have disappeared out of the treasure-house of humanity for ever, these mere idle superstitions, these playful fairy legends, these gossamer threads of thought, float on for ever in the very air we breathe. The Jupiter of Phidias has long been dust, but the story of Llewellyn's dog is still told from the Himalayas to Snowdon, and will be told while the Aryan race survives upon the globe.[1]

Obscure forms of religion and crude superstitious beliefs and observances have in them both the general antiquarian interests of this curious order of wild-flower myths, and also the special theological value of disclosing to us the first feeble stirrings of the religious sentiment, the half-blind "feeling after God if haply they might find him," of yet infant nations, conscious of want and dependence, and dimly conscious also of an unseen Power on whom they depend. The instinct which makes the tendril of the vine creep up the stem of the oak, and its roots shoot through the dark soil towards the water,—even so blind and unconscious seem these first religious impulses of man. Among them, therefore, the true principles of science call upon us to look for the simple elements of those sentiments which have long since become complex and conventional. And they afford us more than such a field for study; they give us by their mere existence the reassuring proof that Religion is not a matter primarily of ideas, but of Sentiments; and that Sentiments are permanent in human nature, while the Ideas in which they clothe themselves, the fashions of their intellectual garments, for ever change. The first shape which each sentiment assumes as it passes out of the world of feeling into the world of thought—a shape gross in the lower race, the Scythian, the Negro, the Australian; finer and more delicate in the higher, the Greek, the Persian, or the Jew,—that Idea is by degrees worn out, to be replaced by another. But the feeling which originated it, though constantly developed

---

[1] See the wonderful collection of these tales in Baring-Gould's *Curious Myths of the Middle Ages*.

and exalted, is never lost. The "conservation of force" holds as true of human Sentiment as of any physical agent. The sweeping away of old religious Ideas (which Comte would have us think equivalent to the sweeping away of Religion), is in fact quite an opposite process. It is the periodical clearance of a mass of mental rubbish which has become a burden and a stoppage, and the opening of free space for new development, not of ideas *absolutely* true, yet of ideas relatively nearer to truth than those which preceded them. The cycles of religious revolution, the secular outbursts of apparently the most desolating Doubt, are but the new births of Religion. The serpent casts its outgrown scales, and renews its immortal youth; the phœnix rises fresh-plumed from its pyre.

A large contribution to our knowledge of these cruder religions of the world, these stirrings of the religious sentiment among the inferior races of mankind, has been made in the splendid book which I now purpose to review. Mr. Fergusson is the Murchison of a new Siluria; he has traced out and described a buried world, underlying all the continents of the present globe. The subject is almost new in his hands. The share which the worship of Serpents and Trees has had in universal primeval history has probably attracted the passing thoughts of scarcely a dozen living scholars; and certainly the vast extension of it, which our author exhibits, is altogether a fresh discovery. I think I shall hardly wrong my readers if I assert that even such as have taken interest in comparative mythology will find these researches open to them a flood of new ideas. For the majority of us, were we to follow Gibbon's advice, and before beginning to read, go over in our minds during a country walk all that we have already learned touching the theme of this book, it is to be feared that a very short excursion indeed would suffice for our purpose. "There were the serpents of Eden and of Moses; and Æsculapius' serpents; and there was the sect of Gnostics called Ophites, because they worshipped serpents; and the idols of Vishnu have generally got serpents twisted about them; and in the Norse mythology there was the great Midgard serpent. Then for Tree-worship there was the Norse Yggdrasil; and the Tree of Life and Knowledge in Eden; and Apollo's Laurel, and Minerva's Olive; and the Oaks of Dodona, and the 'groves' mentioned in the Bible; and it is said the Druids worshipped Hesus under the form of an oak, and cut the mistletoe at Yuletide—a practice not yet exploded in England." That is, I venture to think, not a very unfair summary of the amount of knowledge possessed by nine out of ten "general readers" about the matters on which Mr. Fergusson has given us a magnificent quarto volume. Wishing that some hydraulic press could be invented to enable weak reviewers to condense into magazine articles such masses of facts, I shall do my best to present the more salient conclusions of a work whose costliness necessarily limits its circulation, and of which therefore an analysis will be generally more desired than a critique.

My first remark must be that the way in which the book is compiled is itself unusual. Such works mostly seem to have their origin in a theory of some sort which has occurred to a philosopher in his study. Anxious to bring it forth to the world, he makes a nest for it of a reasonable quantity of sticks and straws, collected wherever he can find any suitable to his purpose; and then sits down and broods over it till it comes out full fledged in a goodly octavo. The present tome has apparently taken shape in quite a different manner. Mr. Fergusson having found a quantity of sculptures bearing traces of a curious extinct religion, first set about studying them accurately, drawing from them sundry inferences, and illustrating them by parallels taken from history and archæology; all very much as a geologist who finds the track of a foot in the sandstone, by degress obtains a pretty distinct idea of the long lost beast which left it there uncounted ages ago. As Mr. Fergusson has not had the pretension to start with the statement of any large generalization, the reader—and more especially the reviewer—misses that easy synthesis which at once saves him the labour of careful perusal and enables him to assert, with dogmatism equal to that of the author, that he does, or does not, agree with his conclusions. There is nothing for the student of *Tree and Serpent Worship* to do but to read the book all through carefully; and when he has done so, and perceived all the stores of information which are brought together in its construction, he will probably be more inclined to admire the author's modest way of putting forth the few hypotheses he ventures upon, than to presume hastily to contradict him.

The two idolatries of Trees and of Serpents, seem to have been nearly always allied and co-existent. Sometimes the worship of Trees was most prominent, sometimes that of Serpents, but it is rare to find the one altogether dissevered from the other. In many cases the religion was a well-defined *latria* of living Serpents kept in temples erected for them; and of Trees held as objects of direct worship and laden with gifts. In other cases, the serpents and trees were merely honoured in subsidiary manner, with a sort of *dulia*, while higher gods received more direct and formal worship.

The origin of both Tree and Serpent Worship Mr. Fergusson finds very simply in the natural qualities of both objects. We are not called upon by him either to identify the etymologies of Fire and Serpent; or to look on the latter as the types of the former; nor yet does he ask us to see that the Serpent means the "Sun," and a Tree the "Moon," or *vice versa;* or "Heavens," or the "Dawn," or any other astronomical phenomenon whatever. "With all their poetry and all their usefulness," he says, "we can hardly feel astonished that the primitive races of mankind should have considered Trees as the choicest gift of the gods, or believed that their spirits still delighted to dwell amongst the branches or spoke oracles through the rustling of their leaves. Nor is the worship of the Serpent so strange as it might at first sight appear." As old Sanchoniathon remarked, "The serpent alone of all animals, without legs or arms, or the usual appliances for locomotion, still moves with singular celerity. He periodically casts his skin, and by that process, as the ancients fabled, renews his youth. Thus, too, a serpent can exist for an indefinite time without food or hunger."

Strangely enough to our apprehension this honour of the serpent was not one mainly of fear but of love:

Although fear might seem to account for the prevalence of the worship, on looking closely at it, we are struck with phenomena of a totally different character. When we first meet Serpent worship, either in the wilderness of Sinai, the groves of Epidaurus, or in the Sarmatian huts, the serpent is always the Agathodæmon, the bringer of health and good fortune. He is the teacher of wisdom, the oracle of future events. His worship may have originated in fear, but long before we became acquainted with it, it had passed to the opposite extreme among its votaries. Any evil that ever was spoken of the serpent came from those who were outside the pale, and were trying to depreciate what they considered as an accursed superstition.

May we not add that the idolatry of Trees and Serpents, like other idolatries, must have always involved some vague conception of a beneficent Spirit represented by, or, at most, enshrined in, the idol? The worship of reptiles and vegetables *as such* can never have really occurred among mankind; any more than the worship of a marble statue of Apollo or a wooden one of the Madonna *as* a statue and nothing more.

The races of men among whom Tree and Serpent worship prevailed were not at any time either the Aryans or Semites. The Touranians, undoubtedly, were its great supporters; so much so, that Mr. Fergusson thinks himself justified in arguing backward from any distinct symptom of such worship, to the existence, in the same age and country, of a considerable Touranian or, at all events, inferior population underlying the Aryan or Semitic conquerors. Thus the Serpent *dulia* of the Jews he attributes to the Canaanites; and that of the Greeks to the Pelasgi, whom he considers as Touranians, and imagines to have survived and carried down their traditions after the return to Greece of the descendants of Hercules (the Serpent-slayer, *i.e.*, conqueror of Serpent-worshippers), even to the latest ages of Greek civilization. In any case it appears that new and valuable hints for the historian and ethnologist will hereafter be found in following out this "trail of the serpent" in the literature, the coins, and the sculptures of the ancient world.

A curious circumstance connected with Serpent worship is its apparently arbitrary alliance with the practice of Human Sacrifices. Mr. Fergusson considers it to be established that wherever human sacrifices existed there also was the Serpent an object of worship; and where they have been most frequent and terrible, as in Mexico and Dahomey, there also has serpent worship been the typical form of the popular religion. Nevertheless, no direct connexion between the two things is traceable. "No human sacrifice was anywhere made to propitiate the serpent, nor was it ever pretended that any human victim was ever devoured by the snake-god." And, though the sacrifices are never found without the serpent worship, the serpent worship has often largely prevailed without the sacrifices.

Before commencing the description of Serpent Worship and its monuments in India, which form the great substance of his book, Mr. Fergusson takes a rapid survey of the traces left by the same cultus all over the world. The amount of information condensed into these fifty quarto pages is very remarkable, and it would be vain to attempt to give any fair résumé of it in still smaller compass. Nevertheless, I must endeavour to state the outlines of his conclusions.

Dahomey is the present chief seat of Serpent worship, where it is now practised with more completeness than anywhere else, and where this most ancient of idolatries may probably have remained from the earliest times almost unchanged. And as the student of the new science of Prehistoric Archæology goes to the savages of Polynesia and Greenland to understand the meaning and use of the stone and bronze weapons he finds in the lacustrine dwellings of Switzerland, so the student of the pre-historic religion of Serpent worship will certainly do well to examine in Dahomey its yet surviving barbarities. The chief God of the national triad is the Serpent; the second the Tree-God; and the third the Ocean. " The first, called *Danh gbwe*, is esteemed the Supreme Bliss and General Good." He has a thousand female votaries and is worshipped with all the splendour his savage people can afford. The "customs" of Dahomey with their sacrifices of 500 or 600 victims at the death of a king, or of 30 or 40 as an annual slaughter to the honour of ancestors, are here seen in that unaccountable connexion with a worship of which they form no part, of which I have spoken above.

In *America*, there is a whole world of archæological interest waiting for investigation. The mounds of Ohio and Iowa have been declared to be serpent images 1000 feet long.

The ruined temples of Mexico and the brief mention which the Spanish historians deigned to give of the diabolic religion of their enemies, open out a most curious problem. Was Serpent worship indigenous in the western continent, and did human nature here, as so often elsewhere, seem to reproduce for ever the same ideas? Or, does the legend of Quetzal-coatl,—the *Feathered Serpent* born of a Virgin, the Lycurgus and Bacchus of Central America, who came from some unknown land like Manco Capac of Peru, and returned thither, having civilized Anahuac—point to a connexion in long past years between America and the further India where, at the date assigned to Quetzal-coatl, Serpent worship was in its glory? Mr. Fergusson seems to incline to the last suggestion, yet candidly admits that the fact that all American Serpent worship was that of the native noxious Rattlesnake, argues against the Indian hypothesis.

Returning to the old world, where Mr. Fergusson begins his survey, we find *Egypt* with only a "fractional part" of its great theology occupied by either trees or serpents.[1]

In *Greece*, as already remarked, the frequent traces of both worships, very loosely connected with the Olympian mythology, forces us to suppose that we have here an instance of the religions of two distinct races intermingled; the lower cropping up through the higher like weeds in a cornfield. Not to dwell on the numerous earlier myths regarding Serpents, the Pythons and Hydras, Echidna and the Dragon of the Garden of the Hesperides (the Greek counterpart of the Hebrew Serpent of the Tree of Life in Eden), there appear actually in historic times the Serpent kept in the Erechtheum, whose escape warned the Athenians

[1] A learned friend has favoured me with some notes tending to show that Mr. Fergusson, in this short chapter, has not done justice to the extent of Serpent worship and Serpent honour in Egypt. He seems, especially, to have overlooked the importance of the myths relating to Apoph or Typhon, the Evil Serpent, a personage whose history it is particularly desirable to explore.

to fly from the Persians; and the serpents of Æsculapius at Epidaurus, which the Roman Senate sent an embassy to obtain. The latter incident indeed will form one of the most astonishing in that future History of Opinion of which I have spoken. The facts are stated by Livy (x. 47), Valerius Maximus (i. 8, 2), and Aurelius Victor (xxii. 1); while Ovid devotes a long poem (Met. xv. 5) to their embellishment. A plague, it seems, ravaged Rome, and in the year of the city 462—more than a century, be it remembered, after Socrates, two generations after Plato—a living Serpent was solemnly fetched from Greece to Italy, and received with divine honours on the banks of the Tiber by the Senate and People of Rome! Of course, on the advent of the sacred reptile "the plague was stayed"; and Æsculapius received in Italy the thanksgivings which, according to the Book of Numbers, were offered on a strangely similar occasion in the Arabian Desert to Jehovah. From this time a Serpent, portrayed in a conventional attitude, was in the Roman world the recognized type of a sacred place; and the Epidaurian serpents, as Pausanias tells, held their place among the gods of Greece till long after the age of Christ.

Nor did the twin-idolatry of Trees fail to find its place in the hospitable pantheon of Greece. When Minerva contended with Neptune for the patronage of Athens (an event which Phidias did not disdain to commemorate in the magnificent western pediment of the Parthenon, now in the British Museum) she created the Olive Tree to match Neptune's gift of the Horse, and planted this her Tree of Knowledge on the Acropolis, committing it to the care of the Serpent-god, Erichthonius. The Erechtheum, whose ruins still form the loveliest Ionic temple in the world, was built over the spot, and the Olive stood, as Fergusson believes, in the beautiful portion of the Pandroseum which is supported by Caryatids,—an hypothesis fairly accounting for the hitherto inexplicable form of that gem of architecture. Beneath, in a cell adjoining the well of Neptune, lived the Serpent, whose actual reptilian existence seems proved by the fact mentioned by Herodotus (viii. 41), that when the Persians approached Athens, the Serpent was announced to have refused its food and fled; whereupon the people at length quitted their city in despair, as warned by their tutelary deity.

The Oak, or rather grove of oaks, at Dodona, was always attributed by tradition to the planting of Pelasgi, and existed till the time of Constantine; a period of at least two thousand years. The oracle which spoke therein was said to come from the sacred pigeons rustling among the leaves, and from bells with which the branches were hung. No temple existed there; the grove itself was the sacred place. Again, the laurel of Apollo at Delphi was as sacred as the oak of Dodona. Under its shade the Python took refuge; one combination more of Tree and Serpent.

In ancient *Italy* the Etruscan relics preserve no memorial of the kind we are seeking. But at Lanuvium, sixteen miles from Rome, was a dark grove sacred to Juno; and near it the abode of a great serpent, the oracle of female chastity. In later ages we find Persius speaking of the custom above mentioned of painting certain conventional figures of serpents on walls, to indicate the sanctity of the spot; a practice of which there are several examples at Herculaneum and Pompeii. Most surprising of all, however, are the legends of Romans and Greeks born of serpents. Scipio Africanus is said to have believed himself the son of a snake; and Augustus allowed it to be understood that his mother Atia had received him from a serpent. Alexander the Great before he undertook to prove himself the son of Jupiter Ammon was supposed (apparently by Philip himself) to be the son of a serpent who actually appeared to him in a dream in later years to save the life of his general Ptolemy. To find such fables gravely told by writers like Plutarch and Lucian, and even mentioned by Cicero without any expression of contempt, is truly astonishing. We ask ourselves, Can there be any legends current amongst us which will seem equally absurd to posterity?

Passing from Rome to her barbarian conquerors we find among the *Teutonic* tribes no traces of Serpent worship, but many of the worship of Trees. The last relic of this old creed is probably the *Stock-am-Eisen*, the Apprentice's tree, still standing in the heart of Vienna. In ancient Sarmatia and modern Poland both Trees and Serpents were worshipped by the peasantry even to the limits of the present century.

Scandinavia offers the most complete puzzle to mythologists, and an excellent illustration of the folly of relying on mere philological analogies in such researches. Were Woden, or Boden, and Buddha the same person? Woden came from the East to Europe just when active missionaries were spreading Buddhism on all sides; and the fourth day of the week is Wednesday in the West, and *Budhbar* in the East. But can we leap to the conclusion that the religions were therefore identical? Fergusson says, "There are not, perhaps, two other religions in the world so diametrically opposed to one another, nor two persons so different as the gentle Sakya Muni, who left a kingdom to alleviate the sufferings of mankind, and Odin, 'the terrible and severe God, the Father of slaughter.'" If the two religions came anywhere in contact, it was at their base, for underlying both was a strange substratum of Tree and Serpent worship. The Yggdrasil Ash Tree, in the Norse mythology, with one of its roots over the Well of Knowledge, and with Nidhög gnawing its stem, suggests obvious analogies, not only with the Tree of Knowledge and Serpent of Eden, but with the Bo-Tree of Buddha. Olaus Magnus in the sixteenth century speaks of serpents as still kept as household gods in Sweden: a circumstance which, when we remember the insignificant nature of the northern reptile, seems to point to some Southern or Eastern tradition of its importance.

In *Gaul*, as in Germany, Tree worship seems to have prevailed; but of Serpent worship there is no trace, save one childish legend reported by Pliny as from the Druids.

As to *Great Britain*, Mr. Fergusson's views will probably be more contested than those he has given of any other country. Perhaps most readers, to whom the notion of a connexion between the Druids and Stonehenge and Serpent worship have been more or less vaguely familiar, will be startled to learn that "there are only two very short paragraphs in any classical authors which mention the Druids in connexion with Britain; not one that mentions Serpent worship; and not one English author prior to the thirteenth century who names either the one or the other." Our knowledge on the subject is almost wholly derived from the Welsh Triads; and, even in them, the word Druid occurs but rarely. The relation of Stonehenge and Avebury to either Druidism or Serpent Worship, Mr. Fergusson treats as wholly imaginary. The bare Wiltshire downs were, he thinks, the very last places likely for the grove-loving Celts to choose for their temples, though they might (especially if battle-fields) choose them for the site of tombs.

On the east coast of *Scotland* are many megalithic monuments, several of which bear sculptures of serpents, while others, apparently of almost equal antiquity, bear the Christian cross. To all appearance these serpent monuments mark the furthest wave of the great Woden-movement which spread from the Caucasus to Scandinavia.

After this hasty sweep over Africa, America, and Europe, which I have permitted myself to make in the reverse order of that adopted by Mr. Fergusson; after finding Serpent and Tree Worship alive in Dahomey, and leaving its broad and unmistakable traces in Central America, ancient Greece, Rome, Scandinavia, Germany, Gaul and Britain; we turn with a new comprehension of the universality of these marvellous delusions to the brief hints which the Jewish Scriptures have preserved of their existence, even among the people who had Isaiah for their prophet, and the author of the Book of Job for their great poet.

The Garden of Eden, bounded on one side by the Euphrates, was doubtless conceived of as occupying a position in Mesopotamia. Here, in the earliest record of Semitic thought, we find the two inseparable relics, the Tree and the Serpent; a Tree of Knowledge and a Serpent "more subtle than any beast of the field,"—doubtless the Hea or Hoa, the Serpent God, the third of the Babylonish triad of gods. Very ingenious is Mr. Fergusson's idea that this story, and the curse of the serpent, was introduced by the monotheistic author of the fragment of Genesis in which it is found, for the purpose of teaching the hatred of the early Serpent worship, which in his time and for ages afterwards was doubtless still flourishing. Jehovah cursed the serpent, and "put enmity between his seed (*i.e.* his worshippers) and man of woman born." May I surmise that here also we find the traces of that notion, so prevalent, according to Sir J. Lubbock, in the border land of prehistoric times; that the later race alone is *human*, the progeny of a mortal woman, and the elder primeval race, with its ruder creed and weapons, merely impish, dwarf, and bestial?

Next to the Tree of Eden, a trace of the same worship may be found in Abraham's terebinth at Mamre; worshipped, according to Eusebius, down to the time of

Constantine, and still the same, if we may believe tradition, which spreads its leafy boughs laden with acorns beside the vineyards of Eshkol.

Again, we find in Exodus, Jehovah speaking to Moses in the Burning Bush (or Tree)—a Tree, according to Josephus, hallowed before the event. At the same moment, Moses's Rod was turned into a Serpent; a wonder afterwards repeated by both Moses and Aaron; and imitated by the Egyptian magicians then and ever since, by means of pressure on the back of the serpent's neck productive of temporary catalepsy.

But the most suggestive of all the stories of Serpent *dulia* is that told in Numbers xxi. The Israelites having murmured as usual, "the Lord sent fiery serpents, and they bit the people." On their repentance Moses is directed to "make a fiery serpent and set it on a pole" (the caduceus of the Healing God), "and it shall come to pass that every one that is bitten, when he looketh upon it, shall live." The worship thus inaugurated is no more mentioned in the Pentateuch; but assuming the received chronology to be anything near the truth, it actually survived for more than seven centuries, and in the days of Hezekiah "the children of Israel did burn incense" to the self-same brazen Serpent, actually preserved in the very Temple (2 Kings xviii. 4). The reformer king at the same time "cut down the Groves, and brake in pieces the Serpent," thus combining in common ruin the two ever-parallel idolatries. But no religion was pure enough to destroy altogether the marvellous infatuation. Even after the great Christian Reformation, the Serpent worship cropped up like the hydra itself. The Ophites or Serpentinian Gnostics preferred, as Tertullian tells us, the Serpent to Christ, "inasmuch as the former brought the knowledge of good and evil into the world!" (Tertullian, *De Præscript. Hereticorum*, cxlvii.)

We now pass to Serpent Worship in ancient *Persia*, and here the theory of the author that the Aryan races were never, and the Touranian races always, serpent worshippers, meets with strong confirmation. In the theology of Zoroaster, Dahaka, or Zohak, was an evil being created by Ahrimanes. In Persian mythology he is a king who reigned at Babel for 1000 years, having two serpents growing between his shoulders, and daily devouring men until his own destruction by the "Brilliant Feridoun," the servant of Ormuzd. Here again, the religion of the pre-Aryan, as in Genesis that of the pre-Semitic race, is represented as detestable and accursed.

The Tree worship of ancient Persia and India is even more curious than the passing spurn of Zoroastrianism at Serpent worship. Both Zend Avesta and Vedas are full of mysterious allusions to the Hôm, or Soma tree, and its sacramental juice. In modern times the Brahmins have taken a creeping shrub, the *Asclepias*, to be the Soma; and its sacred juice that profane German Haug has unhesitatingly styled " a nasty drink." But there is reason to believe with Windischmann, that the original Homa was a very different tree, and identical with the Tree Gogard, the "Tree which enlightened the eyes." Suspicions may also exist that it was the *Am*pelus, the Vine of Bacchus. May I add the suggestion (from the audacity of which Mr. Fergusson must be exonerated), that the Homa, the Soma, the Gogard, the Ampelus of Bacchus, and the Tooba tree of Mahomet, were all one with the Vine of Noah; and that all the awful and solemn mysteries connected therewith may be summed up in the Anglo-Saxon tongue as—" getting drunk " ?

Cashmere was a very kingdom of Serpents and their worshippers or *Nagas*, as the Indians call them; namely, human beings with serpents growing between their shoulders, or at least so conventionally depicted. The connexion between the early Buddhists and these Serpentinians of Cashmere, helps our author's further theories considerably; but space fails me to detail particulars.

In *Cambodia*, in the further India, Serpent worship reached its utmost splendour. The great temple of Nakhon-Vat, wholly devoted to this strange cultus, is even in its ruins one of the noblest buildings in the world. First discovered in 1858 and 1860 by M. Mouhot, they have since been photographed by Mr. J. Thomson, and exhibit architecture of the utmost splendour, and of a style curiously resembling the Roman form of Doric. Six hundred feet square at the base, the building rises in the centre to the height of 180 feet, "while every part is covered with carvings in stone, generally beautiful in design and always admirably adapted to their situation." Every angle of the roof, every cornice, every entablature, bears the seven-headed serpent; and instead of the Greek *cella* with the statue of the *genius loci*, there are courts containing tanks, in which (we are compelled to infer) the living Serpents dwelt and were adored. The date of this marvellous structure must be somewhere about the tenth century of our era; at all events before the fourteenth, when the Siamese conquered Cambodia, the cities of the Serpent worshippers were deserted, and Buddhism was established.

In *China* the traces of Serpent worship are obscure; the most notable being the popularity of the emblem of a monstrous heraldic dragon; and a legend of two heaven-sent serpents who attended the first ablutions of Confucius.

Scattered all over *Oceanica* and *Australia* are instances enough to countenance the hypothesis that it was by way of the islands the cultus penetrated to Central America.

All the Cingalese Buddhist histories describe Buddha as himself converting the Nagas of *Ceylon*; but in Mr. Fergusson's opinion, the conversion was far from complete. Tree worship has been more openly adhered to in the island than that of Serpents. King Asoka, the Constantine of Buddhism, B.C. 250, sent a branch of the Bo-tree to the king of Anuradhapura, who received it with the utmost honours and planted it in the centre of his capital. The city is now a desert and its temples in ruins; but the Bo-tree still flourishes, and every year thousands of pilgrims repair to it to offer up prayers which are "more likely to be answered if uttered in its presence."

Reaching *India* at last, the sphere of his principal researches, Mr. Fergusson attempts a preliminary sketch of the very difficult ethnology and religious history of the peninsula. Into this maze I cannot spare space to follow him. His leading idea here, as throughout the book, is that Serpent worship is always the cropping-up of the superstition of an underlying Touranian race, and that to neither of the great Aryan immigrations—called the Solar and the Lunar races—was it due. The Aryan Buddha, however, by falling back on other Touranian ideas, caused its great revival; and the Serpent-emblazoned Topes of Sanchi and Amravati are the existing monuments of the fact. With the disappearance of Buddhism from Hindostan and the rise of modern Brahminism under the leadership of Sankara Acharya about the beginning of the ninth century A.D., the erection of such buildings ceased; but not on that account has the worship of either living or sculptured serpents died out of India. To the description of these two great Topes, and the magnificent collection of photographs and lithographs of their sculptures, the remainder of Mr. Fergusson's book is devoted.[1] As the descriptions are, of course, not

---

[1] A beautiful model of one of the gateways of the Sanchi Tope formed one of the most interesting objects in the Fine Arts Department of the International Exhibition of 1871, in South Kensington.

intelligible without the plates, I can only offer a general account of these very remarkable ruins.

Before doing so, however, I must allow myself to give utterance to an expression of surprise at Mr. Fergusson's doctrine, repeated here from his Architecture, that the Aryan race were never builders, *because* "they always had too firm a conviction of the immortality of the soul, and consequently of the existence of a future state, ever to care much for a brick or stone immortality in this world; and no material art satisfied the cravings of their intellectual powers." (p. 78.) It may be a fact that the Aryan races were not architects. I cannot presume to argue in the face of Mr. Fergusson's vast erudition on the subject; albeit to admit the Aryan origin of the peoples who built the temples of Athens and the churches of Rome, and York, and Strasbourg, and yet maintain that the genius of architecture is foreign to their blood, is, to say the least, a startling paradox. But whatever Mr. Fergusson's *fact* may be, the *reason* he assigns for it is, of course, open to criticism, and against this reason I cannot but vigorously protest. That a vivid belief in a future life would nullify all ambition for a stone immortality, is surely very improbable, in the first place; and in the second, the example of the Egyptians seems to prove precisely the opposite conclusion. If ever there were a race which intensely felt the consciousness of the great truth, "that the soul of a man never dies," it was that same race which so vehemently desired a stone immortality, that it loaded the earth with Pyramids, which are hardly so much works of architectural art, as mere dumb expressions of that longing. It is impossible that Mr. Fergusson can have overlooked this fact. I cannot conjecture how he disregards it.

The ruins of Sanchi in Central India between the towns of Bhilsa and Bhopal, and those of Amravati on the Kistna, are of an age immediately preceding and following the Christian era. Those of Sanchi are the most ancient; the principal Tope, as there is good reason to believe, having been erected by King Asoka, about B.C. 250. Stone building was then evidently in its infancy in India, and only beginning to replace wood, whose forms of construction it is made to imitate. All the details, and especially the forms of the very singular surrounding stone rails and their gateways, are, as Mr. Fergusson says, "very good carpentry, but very poor masonry." Three forms pervade all the monuments of both Sanchi and Amravati:—1. Topes or Stûpas, mound-like buildings erected for the preservation of relics; 2. Chaityas, which, both in form and purpose, resembled early Christian churches; 3. Viharas, residences of priests and monks attached to the Topes and Chaityas. The Topes at Sanchi form part of a great group of such monuments, extending over a district of seventeen miles, and numbering forty or fifty tumuli. The great Tope consists of an enormous mound, built in the following manner. First, a basement 121 feet in diameter, and 14 feet high. On the top of this a terrace or procession path 5 feet 6 inches wide. Within this rises the dome, a truncated hemisphere 39 feet high, originally coated with chunam. On the top of the dome, is a level platform measuring 34 feet across. Within this was a square Tee or relic box, of sixteen square pillars with rails, and, over all, a circular support for the umbrella which always crowned these monuments. But the most remarkable feature of the building is the rail, which surrounds it at the distance of 9 feet 6 inches from the base, and consists of 100 pillars 11 feet high, exclusive of the gigantic gateways. These gateways are covered with the richest and most fantastic sculptures, both in the round, and in bas-relief. About one half of their sculptures represent the worship of Trees or of Dagobas (relic shrines), others represent scenes in the life of Buddha, and others again ordinary events, feasting, concerts, and so on. The merit of these sculptures, Mr. Fergusson considers as "superior to that of Egypt, but inferior to the art as practised in Greece." They are "extremely different to the usual sculptures brought home from India. Neither at Sanchi nor at Amravati are there any of those many-armed or many-headed divinities, who form the staple of the modern Hindoo Pantheon. There are none of those monstrous combinations of men with the heads of elephants, or lions, or boars. All the men and women are represented as acting as men and women have acted in all time." The sculptures at Sanchi are the more rude and vigorous. Those at Amravati are on a scale of excellence, "perhaps nearer to the contemporary art of the Roman Empire under Constantine, than any other that could be named, or of the early Italian Rénaissance."

Two races may be readily distinguished as depicted in the sculptures. First, the Hindoos, originally pure Aryans, though of mixed blood at the age of the sculptures, evidently the dominant race. The men wear the *dhoti* and turban; the women are covered with jewels, but strangely divested of clothing. This last is a feature so remarkable that, being also found elsewhere, Mr. Fergusson concludes that before the Mahometan conquest nudity in India conveyed no sense of indecency. The second race wore kilts and cloaks, and (most marked peculiarity) are represented with beards, which the Aryans never wear. The women wear neat and decent dresses and no ornaments. It would appear that these are the aborigines of the country.[1]

---

[1] A great Oriental scholar, between whose judgment and that of Mr. Fergusson I cannot presume to hold the balance, maintains that our author is wrong in treating any of the sculptures as historical records. They are, he conceives, mere illustrations of the fairy tales popular in the age to which they belong. The distinction between Fairy Tales, Mythology, and Religion, in early epochs, appears by no means easy to define. Whether the works in question may be taken to belong to the same class as the frieze of the Parthenon portraying the actual contemporary Panathenaic Processions; or to that of the metopes of the same

Some obscurity exists as to the precise meaning of the Serpents introduced into these sculptures. Are the Hindoos intended to honour them? Do the serpents (nagas) honour the Hindoos? But no doubt at all exists about the reverence which men are everywhere represented as paying to Trees. Plate xxv. for example represents the Bo-tree of Buddha growing out of a temple. Devas bear offerings to it above and four Hindoos stand before it, below, with closed hands in the attitude of prayer. "Taken altogether," says Mr. Fergusson, "the Tree is the most important object of worship" in the Sanchi Tope. " It is difficult to convey an idea of the extreme frequency of the illustrations of it."

The Amravati Topes are in a much more ruinous state than those of Sanchi. Fortunately Sir Walter Elliot procured a quantity of sculptures from them, and sent them to England in 1856. These—discovered by Mr. Fergusson in 1867 in the coach-house of Fife House—are a perfect treasury of knowledge of ancient Indian religion and manners, as the beautiful photographs of them in this volume amply testify. The great Tope at Amravati was of enormous size. Its dimensions as recorded by Colonel Mackenzie are 195 feet for the inside diameter of the outer circle and 165 feet for that of the inner. On the first of the measurements Mr. Fergusson appends the following note: "By a curious coincidence this is exactly twice the diameter of the outer circle at Stonehenge. The outer rail in the Indian example is 14 feet high; that at Stonehenge is as nearly as can now be measured 15ft. 6in." In Mr. Fergusson's opinion the two buildings were erected much about the same time and for the same purpose, viz., that of cenotaphs or relic-shrines. Each of the four gateways at Amravati projected about 30

temple illustrating the fabulous legend of the wars of the Centaurs and Lapithæ; or, lastly, to that of the colossal group of the pediment representing the great mystery of Athenian religion, the birth of Pallas Athene,—I do not venture to offer an opinion.

feet beyond the outer rail, but they are all so much ruined that the dimensions cannot be exactly ascertained. The sculptures brought away proved on examination to be of three kinds: 1. Large and coarse, belonging to the central building. 2. Carvings so delicate as to seem rather to belong to ivory than to stone belonging to the inner rail. 3. A group belonging to the outer rail. The quantity of these sculptures was amazing. The central discs of the pillars alone contained from 6000 to 7000 figures:

"If we add to these the continuous frieze above, and the sculptures above and below the discs on the pillars, there probably were not less than from 120 to 140 figures for each intercolumniation, say 12,000 to 14,000 in all. The inner rail probably contains even a greater number of figures than this, but they are so small as more to resemble ivory carving, but except perhaps the great frieze at Nakhon Vat (in Cambodia), there is not even in India, and certainly not in any other part of the world, a storied page of sculpture equal in extent to what this must have been when complete. If not quite, it must in all probability have been nearly perfect less than a century ago."

The subjects of these sculptures are of course very various —animals, bulls, elephants, etc., very well depicted, feasts, concerts of instruments, scenes from the life of Buddha, and so on. Most prominent, as well as most interesting as touching on our subject, are the groups of Tree and Serpent worshippers everywhere to be observed.

At Sanchi, the Serpent worship had been in the background, and the Tree worship prominent. At Amravati, in the oldest part, the Tree flourishes as usual, but in the later portion the Serpent appears ten or twelve times as the principal object of worship; twice he shields the head of Buddha, and forty or fifty times he appears spreading his protecting hood of heads over Rajahs and persons of importance.

This may be reckoned the culmination of Buddhistic Serpent worship in India. Four centuries later Brahminism revived, and Buddhism was banished to the Further India, Ceylon, China, and Thibet. But was there then an end of this ever-reviving hydra of idolatry? Not at all! The Serpent still plays an important part in that half of Hindu worship which is addressed to Vishnu, and appears constantly in his images, extending its hood of heads over him, or twisted round his throne. In a letter which Mr. Fergusson has published in his Appendix, dated January, 1869, Dr. Balfour says, "Snake worship is general throughout peninsular India, both of the sculptured form and of the living creature." The vitality of the idolatry is as remarkable as the vitality of the idol. The Serpent and his worship are always "scotched but not killed." [1]

Let me now attempt to sum up some of the results towards which these marshalled facts of Mr. Fergusson most clearly point. In the first place, we find that a certain form of worship has once extended over nearly the whole known world. We find that it lingered long, even amid Greek and Roman civilization; and subsisted side by side with the Monotheism of the Jews so late as the days of Hezekiah. We find that it cropped up through Buddhism and Brahminism as it had done through the Norse and Grecian mythologies, and that it formed a large part of the religion of ancient America. Finally, we find that it still exists in all its horrid glory among the sanguinary savages of Dahomey; and dwells yet unconquered among our own subjects of Hindostan. Here is assuredly food enough for reflection. Let it be remembered that this is a religion without a Book or an organized Church; a religion which never had a Prophet or an Apostle, and which offers, consequently, absolutely no ground on which to exercise

[1] See for both Tree and Serpent Worship a very remarkable article, "The Religion of an Indian Province." *Fortnightly Review*, February, 1872.

historical criticism. It is (as we said at starting) a contribution to the History of Opinion and Sentiment; but no contribution worth naming to the ordinary History of facts and persons. The more we consider it the more mysterious it appears. That a creature like the Serpent, naturally dreadful, should come to be universally beloved, that the owner of the poison-fang should be constantly identified with the Restorer of Health; this is of itself a paradox. Again, the ever-recurring connexion between the Tree and the Serpent, the beautiful and beneficent vegetable and the noxious reptile, is well-nigh incomprehensible. Future thinkers pondering these facts may see light through them, and be enabled to gain new and valuable insight thereby into human nature's strange recesses. For the present, we can but perceive that a fresh demonstration has been given of the Moral Unity of our race; and of the progressive character of Religion from a lower to a higher stage all over the world. Those old Aryans whose sculptured forms we behold upon the ruined mound of Sanchi with their clasped hands praying to the Tree of Life, were but the fathers after the flesh and after the spirit of us who have indeed gained many truths in advance of them, but who still too often

> Lift lame hands of faith, and grope
> And gather dust and chaff, and call
> To what we feel is Lord of all,
> And faintly trust the larger hope.

ESSAY VIII.

THE RELIGIONS OF THE WORLD.[1]

A FIRST glance at Bunsen's Biography and its illustrations suggests the reflection that to the subject thereof, the lot of humanity certainly "fell in pleasant places." A man who has always looked at life out of the windows of such abodes as Palazzo Caffarelli and Villa Piccolomini, Carlton Gardens and Hurstmonceaux, the Hübel at Berne and Charlottenberg on the Neckar, must needs be hard to please if he find it not a pleasant prospect. Assuredly not among such exceptionally dark-souled ones was Karl Christian Bunsen. Only to look at his beaming countenance on the title-page with its broad brow and smiling lips and large blue eyes *à fleur de tête*, suffices to make us recognize him as a perfect type of the sanguine temperament, a born disciple of that school of philosophy which never fails to find

Sermons in stones and good in everything.

Bunsen was a gifted, energetic, successful man, healthy in body, superabundantly healthy (were such a thing possible) in mind and heart, and peculiarly fortunate in the chief relations of life. He was happy; and if piety, earnest-

---

[1] *A Memoir of Baron Bunsen*, by Baroness Bunsen. London: Longmans, 1868. 2 vols. 8vo.

God in History, by C. C. J. Baron Bunsen. Translated from the German by Susanna Winkworth. London: Longmans, 1868.

ness, and warmth of human kindness merit happiness, he deserved his pleasant lot. It is good to come close to such a life now and then, to be *frotté de bonté et de bonheur*, and to warm ourselves for a few moments at such a hearth of kindly affections and fervid enthusiasms. We shall think none the less but rather the more of his last great book, which it is the main purpose of this paper to review, if we pause for a few moments over these tomes of loving recollections. Not for us be the criticism which prejudges that *because* a man was unusually sound in heart and head, unusually full of faith in God and in the Good which is to be "the final goal of ill," therefore his judgments ought to be suspected, and his conclusions set down to the score of unreasoning optimism. If we find what we deem errors in Bunsen's book, we shall not lay them at the door of his happy temperament, but account for them (as we most justly may) as the result of the hurried labour of a life rapidly drawing to its term. Is there cause to marvel if the reaper on whom the night is closing fast, eagerly panting to fulfil his task, should fill his bosom, not only with much ripe corn, but also with a few idle flowers and weeds?

Bunsen was born in 1791 at Corbach in Waldeck; his father a soldier, his grandfather an advocate. Having completed his studies at Göttingen, he travelled to Paris, and thence migrated to Florence and Rome, where his early friend Brandis was secretary to the Prussian Legation, then headed by Niebühr. Bunsen's talents were almost immediately recognized by the great critic, and ere long, through a series of well-merited promotions, he passed from the rank of an attaché to that of a secretary and finally himself became Minister; a position he held with honour for many years. A visit of the King of Prussia, then Crown Prince, to Rome originated a friendship almost romantic, which the sovereign afterwards testified by the highest possible honours offered to Bunsen on the occasion of a journey to Berlin in 1827. Meanwhile Bunsen had married an English lady of birth and fortune (Miss Waddington), whose pen now records in widowhood the unbroken happiness of their union. Their residence in the beautiful Palazzo Caffarelli in Rome with its splendid view over the Forum, the Coliseum, and the long stretches of the Appian Way, was soon brightened by the presence of a numerous family and by the frequent visits of that choicest tribe of European Bedouins who find their way each year to the City—Eternal, at all events, in its attractiveness.

Difficulties, arising out of the question of civil marriages, having occurred between Prussia and the Papal court, Bunsen's mission terminated in 1838, and he visited England, to find all her doors open to him, and soon to form for the country of his wife an attachment only second to that which he bore to that of his fathers. On the next change at the embassy, the wishes of the English court aided the king's desire to pass over Bunsen's lack of the usual rank for so high a mission. He represented Prussia thenceforth in London for a long series of years, beloved and honoured as, perhaps, no other foreigner has ever been amongst us. To the social world, he was the amiable and courteous gentleman, over-flowing with a kindliness all the more delightful, inasmuch as it surpassed by several degrees the warmth of manner which would have been expected, or perhaps admired, in an English statesman. To his diplomatic brethren, he was an able and honourable *confrère*. To the orthodox Protestant camp he was the champion who had withstood the Pope on the question of the concordat with Prussia, and had negotiated the establishment of the Anglo-Prussian Bishopric of Jerusalem. Lastly, to the Liberal party in the English Church, the Broad Church of Arnold, Maurice, and Hare, he was the beloved friend and associate who united the learning of a recluse scholar with the practical power of a man of the world, and a freedom of critical judgment equalled only by the enthusiasm of his Christian piety.

At last, his public career brought to an honourable close, Bunsen retired to spend his last years in study at Heidelberg and at Bonn, with occasional visits to the shores of the Mediterranean. In the society of his wife, family, and friends (among whom the gifted translatress of his chief works, Miss Winkworth, was among the most welcome), this good and happy man passed his elder life, neither deeming that few nor evil had been the days of his pilgrimage. Just ere completing his three score years and ten, after a decline marked by little suffering, he died surrounded by his children, and with his last strength reiterating the expression of his fervent faith in God, and Christ, and immortality.

Of Bunsen's chief legacies to the world, his *Description of Rome*, his *Hippolytus and his Times*, his *Egypt's Place in Universal History*, his *Signs of the Times*, his *Church of the Future*, and his *God in History*, I can only here speak of the last, which the affectionate labours of his friend Miss Winkworth have now given to the English public in a very perfect translation. To this work, then, I devote the remainder of my space.

When Bunsen was a young man of twenty-six, he wrote in his journal a prayer, of which the substance lies in these words:

What in childhood I yearned after, what throughout the years of youth grew clearer before my soul, I will now venture to examine. The revelation of Thee in man's energies and efforts, Thy firm path through the stream of ages, I long to trace as far as may be permitted to me even in this body of earth. The song of praise to Thee from the whole of humanity in times far and near, the pains and lamentations of earth and their consolation in Thee, I wish to take in clear and unhindered. Preserve me in strength and truth of spirit to the end of my earthly existence if Thou seest good, and should I not finish what I shall have begun, let me find peace in the conviction that nothing shall perish which is done in Thee and with Thee; and that what I have imperfectly, however imperfectly conceived and indistinctly expressed, I shall yet hereafter behold in completeness, while here some other man shall perfect what I have endeavoured to do.[1]

It would truly seem as if the holy desire of his youth had remained the aim of his life, and that before he left the world he was permitted in great measure to fulfil it, and to leave behind him the record of the "Song of Humanity," such as his ear had caught it echoing across the wide plains of history. Of the four last years of his life, three were spent in the composition of this book. If in our examination of it, along with much that is of great and durable value, we find what seem in our eyes blemishes and shortcomings, at least we may have faith that as the former part of his youthful prayer has been accomplished, so has also the latter; and that "what on earth he imperfectly conceived and indistinctly expressed, he now beholds in completeness," looking over all from those higher ranges of thought, those clearer heights of contemplation where the Immortals dwell.

God in History has a magnificent idea for its theme. It aims to survey the whole field of human religious consciousness for the purpose of proving the unity of the Divine plan in the moral order of the world. In reading it we seem to see the writer wearied with the cares of statecraft, quitting in his honoured age the camp of contending parties, and climbing up in solitary study to a Pisgah height, whence he could look down, not indeed on the Promised Land of the Future, but back over the long desert of the Past, through which the cloudy Pillar of Providence has led our race by many a devious road. Then, as if in haste lest his days on earth should be too short for the work, with the eagerness of one

[1] *Life*, vol. i. p. 120.

who felt the importance of that which he had to tell, and with somewhat also of the authority of one who had beheld a vision and only announced what he had seen and heard, he dictated this book, through long successive hours, like another Milton, to his daughters. A book produced under such circumstances has a peculiar and exceptional value. It is *not* the value of a Critical History of Religion: that greatest of histories must wait yet many a day for a pen able to trace even its outlines. But in a true and important sense Bunsen's work has a merit beyond that of even a perfect cyclopædia of theologic history: it is in itself a Lesson of Theology. Let me explain my meaning, as near as may be, in his own phrases.

The question may be treated as an open one: is there, or is there not, a moral unity in the history of humanity? Has there been a development of the higher elements of our nature under any law of progress? Bunsen maintains there is such a moral unity, and that there has been such a development; and writes his book to demonstrate the thesis. In doing this he assumes a position towards Christian and heathen religions which in some respects is peculiar to himself. On the one hand, he allots to Christ the place of "the uniting bond of two worlds;" "no *product* of the ancient world, yet its *consummation*; no mere *herald* of the new world, but its abiding Archetype, the perennial well-spring of life to humanity through the Spirit." The Bible is, he thinks, the "Book of Humanity." Christ is set "between the two halves" of history, and the Hebrew religious consciousness as traced in the Bible is made by him the keynote and standard of all that follows. On the other hand, Bunsen is far indeed from denying that it was the same divine inspiration which spake through the poets and philosophers of Greece, and the prophets of Eastern heathendom, as in the seers and apostles of Palestine.

The second, third, and fourth books of *God in History* are devoted to a most candid and sympathizing study of the religious development of the Gentile races of Asia and Europe; and had the work no other merit, it would deserve our gratitude for the noble extracts which it contains from the best literature of the ancient pagan world, and the striking observations of the author upon them. Nor let it be forgotten, that fifteen years ago, when Bunsen's task was undertaken, such true liberalism was far less common than now. Men still thought, then, that they went very far on the road of toleration if they admitted that human reason, "*unassisted* reason," (that singular invention of Protestant piety), had taught to heathens the existence of God and the ruder elements of morality. The idea that God *inspired* heathens had as yet hardly been whispered in the churches, nor the doctrine that in any sense He "led" Greeks and Hindoos as well as "Israel" like sheep. The whole history of opinion in this matter, in truth, is most curious, and worthy of a moment's recall, if we would understand how large was the heart of Bunsen, which, already brimming over with Christian enthusiasm, had room also for warm recognition of the Divine, wherever he found it outside Christianity.

In old classic days the polytheistic nations were always ready to admit that other races besides themselves were Divine favourites. The Greeks looked with respect on the Thracian Xamolxis, the Assyrian Bel, and the Egytian Isis and Osiris. The Romans were only too enthusiastic in welcoming to their Pantheon the gods of conquered nations; Mithras of Persia and Serapis of Egypt; and when they thought they had identified their own gods with the local deities of other lands—Jupiter with the Druids' Hesus, or Mercury with the Egyptian Thoth—no sort of jealousy seems to have disturbed them. The Gods were good to all.

Higher minds among them reached to the faith in One equal and omnipresent Benevolence. Lucan makes Cato ask while passing by, unconsulted, the oracle of Ammon:

> Canst thou conceive the vast Eternal Mind
> To rock and cave and Libyan waste confined ?
> Is there a place which God would call His own
> Before a virtuous mind, His spirit's noblest throne ?
> Why seek we further ? Lo ! above, around,
> Where'er thou wanderest, there may God be found,
> And prayer from every land is by His blessing crowned.[1]

But it has been the opinion of modern Christendom that between the fortunate souls born on the hither side of the pale, and the hapless spirits outside it, a great gulf is already fixed. The Divine Light has been constantly described by our divines as if it fell upon the earth, not through the open blue expanse, with nothing hid from the heat thereof, but through some chink or cranny of a subterranean cave, lighting up the small round spot of Europe and Palestine, and leaving all the rest of the planet in Egyptian night. God has been habitually magnified from our pulpits, and infant lips taught to praise Him, *not* because his mercies are over all his works, but precisely on the contrary, because we enjoy a monopoly of the best of them, and because each babe among us may boast:

> I was not born, as thousands are,
>   Where God was never known,
> And taught to pray a useless prayer,
>   To blocks of wood and stone.

But better thoughts of the Divine Father have come to us at last. A century ago men misdoubted Pope's Christianity, because he prayed to the "Father of All, in every age and every clime adored." But in our day, such an invocation would merely imply that the speaker had es-

[1] *Pharsalia*, b. 9.

caped beyond the doors of the very narrowest conventicle of obsolete orthodoxy. Thousands of Englishmen have dwelt in heathen and Moslem lands; England's empire includes a hundred millions of Brahminists and Buddhists; and English scholars, with their French and German allies, have opened to us the marvellous tomes of Eastern literature, till we have been driven to feel, as never before, that these "heathens" were indeed "men of like passions with ourselves"; men who joyed and sorrowed, and struggled and aspired, and prayed and wrestled with the dread mysteries of life and death and sin and suffering, even as we have done. Then we have seemed to hear a voice from those tens of millions of our brother-men; a cry like that of Esau of old, a remonstrance with God: *Hast thou but one blessing, O my Father?* And our hearts have answered, "Not so! For them also the Father, from the depths of forgotten time, ere yet the earliest Vedic hymn invoked His light—for them also He has had a blessing."

And as the modern natural philosopher with his spectrum proves to us that in sun and planet and star there exist the same elementary substances we have known upon our world, so does the new theologian, like Bunsen, from the refracted lights of truth and love shining from the poetry and the prayers of men of far-off lands and distant centuries, demonstrate to us beyond all doubt or cavil, that in their souls existed the self-same elements as in our own. We recognize at last that we have no more monopoly of God's love than of the sunlight; of His spirit than of the winds of heaven.

The work which Bunsen undertook, I think, he has in a great measure accomplished. He has shown that there is a moral unity in history; that there exists a Continuity of Forces in the spiritual world; that the same

Divine light has been more or less shining, the same Divine work more or less rapidly going forward, in all lands and centuries. He has shown that "through the ages one increasing purpose runs," and that history, fairly consulted, justifies the oracle in our souls which bade us believe

> One God who ever lives and loves,
> One God, one Law, one Element,
> And one far-off Divine event,
> Towards which the whole creation moves.

This is the work Bunsen has done. His book is one long cumulative argument to the reality of the human consciousness of Divine things; an argument so vast and multifarious that even should many of its minor propositions provoke criticism and fail to stand the test of candid examination, there will yet remain overwhelming weight to enforce its grand conclusion.

The book is this; and it is also one of the most kindling and living works in recent literature, illuminating with gleams of poetical insight many an obscure valley in the landscape of history, bridging across many a chasm, and lighting up like a setting sun the flaming summits of human glory and genius. It is a book to inspire the coldest nature with somewhat of the "enthusiasm of humanity."

Such are (in my humble estimation) the merits of *God in History*. Justice compels me to add what I deem its chief defects. It fails where it was almost impossible it should not fail. The scheme was too vast to be brought within the limits of one book, or even of one author's life. Probably the present age is that of all others in which it is most completely impracticable for one man, however gifted and laborious, to master all the materials for such a work. Two hundred and fifty years ago, when Raleigh wrote his *History of the World;* or one hundred years ago, when the seven folios of *Universal History* pretty well exhausted the known, and (as it was thought) the knowable concerning the ancient world, it was comparatively practicable for an industrious student in a lifetime to gather up the facts for his philosophy of history. But those old materials are but as a single camel's load compared with the mounds of long buried knowledge which must now be ransacked—the monumental records of Egypt; Assyria risen from the ashes which consumed Sardanapalus and Belshazzar; the dim vestiges by lake and shore of the childhood of the western world ascending back to the times when the mammoth and the rhinoceros roamed the forests of Europe; chief above all the stupendous stores of Oriental thought, the Vedas and their commentaries, the Zend Avesta, the Chinese sacred books, and that measureless bulk of Buddhist literature of which one section alone (the *Tanjur*) fills 225 folios. To build all this into a complete system, first exercising the rigorous criticism required to divide the trustworthy from the doubtful, and this again from the utterly fallacious, would be the work, not of one scholar, but of a generation of scholars. Our fire is darkened for the moment by the very mass of new materials heaped upon it. It is no disrespect to Bunsen to say that, while he has displayed truly enormous learning in these volumes, I think the critical part of his work has been but imperfectly accomplished. I do not suppose that he, or those who most loved him, would claim for him the almost miraculous power attributed to him by one of his reviewers:

"All languages, both dead and living, were as familiar to him as his own; and all history, from the mystic annals of the Shepherd Kings of Egypt to the diplomatic transactions of his own day, lay spread out like a map before him."[1]

But without such powers his scheme was well-nigh impracticable. To that majority of readers who are neither so

[1] *Edinburgh Review*, April, 1868, p. 469.

ignorant as to be unaware of existing controversies nor so learned as to be able to decide them for themselves, there is much that is tantalizing in Bunsen's frequent practice of making dogmatic assertions on doubtful matters without giving us even a clue to his reasons for accepting one theory and rejecting another. We inevitably ask ourselves, Does not Lepsius, or Champollion, or Haug, or Burnouf (some scholar who has devoted his entire life to this one department of history), give us a different chronology or ethnology, or a different exegesis of this passage, or a different value of that manuscript? As Bunsen rarely cites his authorities, we are left too often with suspended judgment, till a sense of distrust, perhaps greater than the occasion needs, creeps on our minds. In a word, in these days of criticism we can accept no history as satisfactory which does not lay bare its critical basis. Before the pyramid can be built, the stone causeway must be firmly laid.

In particular, I protest against Bunsen's neglect of criticism, or at least of explaining his principles of criticism, in his dealings with Jewish history. He approached this part of his task in the most liberal spirit, and was the last of all men to place himself in the attitude of those who cut the knot of all difficulties by an appeal to authority. In asserting, then, one fact to be true and discarding another recorded in the same book as false, he was surely bound to give us his reasons for such a course. But this is what he fails to do altogether. For example, he quotes at great length, and with some curious German subtleties of explanation, the strange story (Exod. xxxiii.) of Moses being permitted to see the "back parts" of Jehovah. To this he prefixes the observation that the phrase of having "seen God" is never used elsewhere in Scripture except with reference to Elijah; and that the conception of an actual sight of the back of a god-man was "as foreign to the Bible as repugnant to reason and good taste," the "purely spiritual interpretation of the Divine name" proving it so (vol. i. pp. 88–90). But on what authority, I ask, can Bunsen reject the detailed account in the 34th chapter of the same Book of Exodus, wherein it is described how the seventy elders "*saw the God of Israel*"; and again, "saw God, and did eat and drink"; and yet again, how Ezekiel minutely describes, as Swedenborg might have done, "the likeness of the Man upon the throne" of the colour of amber, and with the likeness of fire, from his loins upwards and downwards? (Ezek. i. 26, and viii.) Are we to take it for granted that Exodus xxxiii. is history, and Exodus xxiv. and Ezekiel i. and viii. fables? In another place we are told, with a little more display of criticism, that the story of Abram (Gen. xv.) is no doubt mythical; but that the story of Abraham is true; and that the document, Genesis xiv., "added by an editor of the eighth century B.C., alone would suffice to prove that Abraham had a real historical existence, and was therefore (!) the great-grandfather of Joseph" (i. p. 83). After this, we are not surprised to hear that Moses is "an unquestionably historical personage, both as regards the account of his origin and the events of his life." Both the origin and events of Moses' life have, I think, been "questioned" pretty freely of late! Again, as another example of dogmatism, I must cite Bunsen's assertion (p. 101) that "nothing can be more groundless" than the notion that the Jews derived their ideas of Satan, etc., from the Chaldees; and his unbounded contempt for the supposition that the Jews would have accepted such doctrines from the heathen. But Maimonides himself avows they did so, and the Mischna says the same.[1]

Finally, to give entire utterance to my feelings, I must confess that although the style of writing in *God in History*

---

[1] "Dixit Rabbi Simeon Ben Lakis, 'Nomina angelorum ascenderunt in domum Israelis ex Babylone.'"—Rosch Haschanah (Tract of the Mischna).

is by no means specially bad among German histories, and although Miss Winkworth has shown herself as usual one of the very few who really possess the art of translation, yet I find the inevitable difficulties of dealing with such thoughts as constitute the substance of the book not a little enhanced by the mode of their expression. At the best, it must be owned, every German Tree of Knowledge bristles with a frightful array of thorns!

I shall now proceed to attempt a very brief sketch of the contents of these remarkable volumes. The two now translated[1] bring the subject up to the birth of Christ, and are divided into four books. The first book expounds the purpose of the whole and discusses the theories of the moral order of the world. The second book treats of the religious Consciousness of the Hebrews. The third is devoted to that of the Aryan race in Eastern Asia (the Zoroastrian, Vedic, Brahmin and Buddhist faiths), but includes preliminary chapters on the religion of the non-Aryan races, the Egyptians, Turanians and Chinese. The fourth book discusses the Aryans of Europe, the Greeks, Romans, and Teutons.

After a very remarkable and freely handled, but, in my judgment, unsatisfactory sketch of the history of the religious consciousness of the Hebrews, Bunsen proceeds to treat of that creed which the Jews consider as the second great heretical offshoot of their faith,—Islam. When the old heathenisms of Arabia and Phœnicia had sunk under the influence of tyranny and of the sensuality which always follows tyranny, to the lowest corruption, and when Byzantine Christendom, with its formalism and miserable hair-

---

[1] A third has been published since this Review was written. It is concerned with the "Religious Consciousness of the Christian Aryans," and a Summary of Results.

splitting theologic disputes, had failed utterly to convert the races of the south, then, says Bunsen, Mahomet stepped forth, "his whole soul glowing with the consciousness of God's revelation of himself in the heart, and uttering the prophetic words while he shattered the idols of Mecca:

>The light of Truth is come;
>Vain lies are quenched.

That sense of the Unity of God and of the bond existing between him and the individual human mind which Mahomet found in his own soul and recognized in Judaism and Christianity, is the basis of that universal empire of Islam which appeared to him to be the realization of God's kingdom upon earth." But "he who takes the sword shall perish by the sword." Islam stiffened and hardened into formalism; the wrathful spirit of vengeance and the degradation of marriage destroyed its vigour. The "wings of man's upward flight were paralyzed."

There is doubtless justice in this brief sketch of the story of Mahomet's religion, yet like nearly all others that I have seen (save a few of monstrous over-estimate), the justice seems but scantily meted out. No one disputes the immeasurable superiority of Christianity, *such as we have it*, to Islam. But inasmuch as Christianity itself has failed to make the Greek, the Levantine, the Neapolitan, other than the spiritually barren people we find them, it may not unfairly be argued that had Islam fallen on the richer ground of the North, it would have borne better fruit than it has done, planted in Egyptian sands. We can easily see the defect of Mahomet's creed, and the indescribable spiritual poverty of the Koran as compared with other Eastern sacred books, not to speak of the Gospels. But had we lived in the ninth or tenth century it may be doubted whether English Protestant sympathies, such as they commonly exist amongst us, would not have turned far more to the reverent and tender piety and manly morality of the Saracens and Sicilian Arabs, than to the ascetic formalism, the idolatrous usages, and well-nigh polytheistic belief, of the monks and saints of Christendom.

A striking remark, however, is made by Bunsen, ere he dismisses the subject of Mahometanism, to the purport that on coming in contact with the Iranian race in Persia the combination gave birth to Sufiism ; a philosophy deeply tinged with a pantheism altogether foreign to the sharply-cut monotheism of the Semites.

The third book of *God in History* is devoted to a sketch of the religious consciousness of the Aryans of Eastern Asia prior to Christianity. Educated readers are aware that these Aryans of Eastern Asia are divided into the three great religions of Brahminism, Buddhism, and Zoroastrianism. Brahminism is usually understood by modern scholars to be the later development and corruption of the ancient Vedic faith. Baron Bunsen, however, insists that the distinction is rather a geographical than a chronological one, and that the region of the Indus still retains the nature-worship of Vedism, while Southern India and the banks of the Ganges have long fallen into Brahminism, " the offspring partly of the egotism of the priestly and regal castes, and partly of the enervating influences of the sensuality encouraged by the climate." Before engaging, however, in the analysis of the great creeds of the Aryans, Bunsen undertakes a sketch of what he calls, in German phrase, " The vestibule of the Aryan religious consciousness ; " in plain English the religions which bordered on the Aryan countries, namely, those of Egypt, China, and the tribes of Tartary. Here, again, we are met by that dogmatism whose use by Bunsen I have already lamented. I cannot think that any scholar has a right in the present stage of critical and philological research to make the dogmatic assertion, that "Zoroaster entered on his career about B.C. 3000" (p. 206); that "with the character of Abraham we step at once into the full day-light of the more recent history of the human mind" (p. 221), and that "in Egypt alone has a branch of the West Asiatic stock, viz., the historical Semites, taken root in very early times and put forth an immortal growth of mixed Asiatic and African origin. . . . . The Egyptians are the Hamites of the Bible, and they alone." (p. 223.) The tone of true scholarship regarding points so disputed and so disputable, is surely very different from this. Fortunately, the observations which follow on Egyptian religion do not much depend for value on either chronology or ethnology, but are drawn chiefly from the monuments whose *relative* age is tolerably certain.

"The centre," says Bunsen, "of the consciousness which the Egyptians possessed of God's agency in our history, is the Osiris-worship, the oldest and most sacred portion of their religion. Osiris is the Lord, the judge of men after death." Bunsen does not add what strikes me as the most interesting point, that Osiris was the essential personification of Divine *goodness*. The familiar porcelain images of him found in every tomb, and the amulets representing his all-seeing beneficent eye, are, to my thinking, very touching relics of human love and trust.

Next in importance to the belief in Osiris stands the Egyptian doctrine of metempsychosis, of which Bunsen beautifully says:

> It involves the recognition that there is a solution of the enigma of existence, which is not to be found in the term of a single life on earth, and yet which we are impelled to seek after in order to explain this life. All guilt must be expiated; but the final issue, though reached only after the lapse of unnumbered ages, will be the triumph of the Good, the general reconciliation, and a life in God will be the eternal heritage of the soul.

Grotesque as may seem to us the form such a faith has

taken in the notion of the transmigration of souls into animal forms, it may be questioned whether, on the whole, Christendom has gained much by substituting the terrors of an eternity of torture in a fiery cave, for a term of expiation in the body of a beast. Who can even say that we are right in reading the hieroglyph of the soul of a sensualist turned into the shape of a swine (to be seen on the splendid Soane sarcophagus, and on many other monuments), as anything *beside* a hieroglyph or mere emblem of a retribution which may have been understood in a purely spiritual sense? If we wished to express the truth that by indulging in bestial vice man becomes bestial, how better could we express it in a picture than by drawing a man turned into a disgusting brute?

The religious history of Egypt is full both of encouragement and of warning. The earnestness, nay, rather the vehemence of the national faith in Immortality, several thousand years before Christianity is supposed to have afforded the first certainty thereof, is one of the most important facts of history. The presence of such faith in three civilizations divided so widely as those of the Egyptians, the Brahmins, and the Druids, is the strongest testimony conceivable to the universality of the intuition written on the heart of man by that Hand which writes no falsehoods. Further, the ethical form so clearly assumed by this belief among the Egyptians, is also a testimony to the depth of the human consciousness of moral good and ill-desert. But again, on the other hand, while the religion of Egypt teaches us lessons so encouraging (on which I observe with some surprise that our author has not insisted), it also bears fearful testimony to the possibility of petrifying a creed, till it becomes a stone closing the door of a nation's sepulchre. With such noble beliefs as those in Osiris and in immortal life, with the enormous power which must have been needed to build the temples and pyramids of Egypt, the established religion of the land yet sanctioned such miserable idolatries as the worship of animals; and while its "Prayer Book of the Dead" held up a noble code of morals for long succeeding generations, it can hardly be doubted that it supported and consolidated a tyranny, lay and ecclesiastic, of unsurpassed severity. The pyramids are said to have been erected by the despotic kings, for the purpose of safely preserving their own corpses from the just indignation of their subjects, by whom the sentence of the official Judges of the Dead might be reversed, and the mummies so far destroyed as (according to the Egyptian creed) to prevent their sharing the resurrection. If this be so, the greatest monuments of oppression which burden the earth, have owed their existence to the double influence of a religious dogma, and to the fear of the tyrant for the very victims of his tyranny." [1]

It has been held by some Egyptologers, of whose theory Bunsen makes no mention, that the numerous deities of the Egyptian pantheon were only deified attributes of the One God; and that while the ignorant populace were left to believe that they were separate beings, the priesthood and educated classes perfectly well understood that *Amun*, the King, and *Neph*, the Divine Spirit, and *Phthah*, the Creative Power, and *Khem*, the Reproductive Power, and *Thoth*, the Divine Intellect, and *Osiris*, the Goodness of God, were all one and the same Being; the powers of nature, the Sun, Day and Night, Matter, the maternal principle, and also Moral Ideas, like Truth and Justice, having also male and female personifications. The tutelary triads of the various Nomes of Egypt seem to lend some countenance to this theory, in so far that we can explain them easily as selected attri-

[1] The care taken to make the approach to the sepulchral chambers as difficult and obscure as possible of course countenances this theory. Yet a secret known to the thousands who built the pyramids must have been a very open secret indeed.

butes, united at will as objects of special worship, and understood to form in each case a Unity; whereas, on the hypothesis of their being separate independent personalities such arbitrary conjunctions are inexplicable.[1] If, in the opinion of competent judges, the theory above mentioned should hereafter be accepted, should we not obtain a singular glimpse into the mystery of the connexion between Mosaism and the Egyptian creed? May it not be believed that Moses, "learned in all the wisdom of the Egyptians," and fired at once with loyalty to the God whose unity he had been taught, and with indignation for the oppression of the masses of his countrymen, resolved to break both the chains of priestly and political tyranny, and by boldly preaching to the populace the secret of the hierarchy, to found a commonwealth on the sublime lesson, "Hear, O Israel, the Lord your God is one Lord"? Might not this have been the "Thus saith the Lord," which he heard in his heart in his desert musings, and by whose brave announcement he became one of the arch-prophets of the world?

Passing from Egypt, Bunsen bestows a short chapter on the religious consciousness of the Turanian race; that is, of those vast tribes which occupy Central and Northern Asia, and include, according to modern ethnology, the Tartars, Finns, Turks, and Magyars. The prevailing characteristic of this race, according to Bunsen, is the propensity to magic or Shamanism. The meaning of this phrase needs explanation.

Religion in its noblest form belongs to the noblest parts of our nature. It is ethical, as the outcome and crown of our moral nature. It is intellectual, as the highest result

[1] Sir G. Wilkinson (*Egypt*, 2nd series) describes and copies a stone on which is inscribed, "One Bait, one Athor, and one Akori. Hail, Father of the World. Hail, triformous God." On the obverse are two seated Egyptian figures with something like a dove above them.

of our reason. It is affectional, as the last great aim and perfecting of love. But beside these noble inlets of religion to the soul, there are—as the Revivalists have taught us even in our own land too well—hideous possibilities of attaching religious ideas and sentiments in most unhallowed connexion with lower and more material parts of our complex frame, with the mere nervous system and such brain excitement as may be created by sounds, intoxicating fumes or drinks, or, yet more effectually, by that concentration of the mind on one idea which produces hypnotism and hysteria. He who has seen the dancing dervishes performing their frantic rites, rotating (as the writer has beheld one of them) for twenty consecutive minutes without pause, till he falls pale and giddy to the ground, while his companions bow and shout in chorus, with wild eyes and dishevelled hair, like hungry wild beasts in a cage;—he only who has seen this deplorable sight, or that of the Jumpers of Wales, or Peculiar People of England, leaping and screaming "Glory!" can realize the degradation to which worship can fall when the excitement, which ought to descend from above, is obtained from stimulants from below. The Turanian race, according to Bunsen, have for their peculiar character a propensity to the use of all such spiritual trickeries. Perhaps the case might be more hopefully described by saying that in the simple pastoral and secluded life common to most of these tribes, the vividness of religious faith has the tendency, common among mountaineers, to reverie and to visionary absorption. In the ignorance of a Tartar tent, a resort to magic arts to produce ecstatic raptures would seem easily explicable. The main point of interest is the strength of belief in an invisible world, and the yearning for more intimate connexion with it, thus manifested in races whose lives might have seemed a mere process of browsing and ruminating, like those of their own flocks and herds.

Chinese religion has long been the despair of theologians. A child begins by loving and obeying its human parents, and proceeds in healthy growth of heart and soul to the love of the Father of All. But the Chinese, like stunted children, or human beings destined to eternal infancy, glued in the bud in piteous failure of natural blossoming, have stopped at the point of filial love and piety. Their morality is summed up in obedience to their parents while living :[1] their religion, in the worship of them when dead.

Yet the Chinese have not been without a few great souls who have seen a glimmering, through the gloom, of rays of pure light. Last and greatest, but least familiarly known to us in Europe, was Tshu-hi, whose works, written in the thirteenth century of our era, have recently been translated. From among them, Bunsen has quoted these marvellous passages:

There is an Essence indeterminate, which existed before heaven and earth. Oh, how silent is it! It alone subsists without changes; it is everywhere. Thou mayst call it the Mother of the Universe. I know not how to name it. I call it *Tao* (the Way). I call it the *Great*, the *Vanishing*, the *Distant*, and yet again the *Approaching*. Man copies the Earth, Earth Heaven, Heaven Tao, and Tao its own nature. . . . Tao loves and nourishes all beings, and does not consider himself as their Lord; he is always without desire, wherefore he may be called Little. All beings owe subjection to him, and he does not consider himself as their Lord, wherefore he may be called Great.

Is not this last mysterious doctrine of the *self-abnegation* of God akin to the noble thought that God's whole life of ineffable beatitude is a Giving-forth, a bestowal of good, without one personal desire; an absolute Love in which selfishness has no place; and that all the god-like in man is thus to live outside of himself in love, and all the devil-

---

[1] Mencius (Meng-Zö), author of the 4th canonical book of the Chinese, very neatly resolves all duty into filial piety, by laying it down that children show want of duty to their parents by the five capital sins of Sloth, Gambling, Selfishness, Sensuality, and Quarrelling.

like to live in himself in selfishness? Eternal life is the life of love. Eternal death (were it possible for God's child) would be the final extinction of love, in absolute selfishness.

And again Tshu-hi says:

> No one has lent to Tao his dignity, nor to Virtue its nobleness; these qualities they possess eternally in themselves. The Way produces beings, sustains and preserves them. He brings them forth and does not make them his own; he governs them and suffers them to be free. That is the depth of Virtue.

Bunsen's hopes expressed at the close of this chapter that the rebellion of the Tae-pings was a real great Christian reformation, have, alas, proved delusive, and only show the warmth of enthusiasm with which he greeted all that bore semblance of progress in the world.

After this brief survey of Egypt, Turan, and China, Bunsen proceeds to consider the main stream of human thought; the religious consciousness of the great Aryan race, of which Indians, Persians, Greeks, Romans, Teutons, and Celts are the branches. First among these, he considers the Zoroastrian Bactrians, and gives to Zoroaster, with absolute decision, an antiquity "certainly not later than towards B.C. 2500"—a date which no other scholar would, I believe, be inclined to state equally dogmatically. The great work of Zoroaster in giving to the Vedic nature-worship a distinctly ethical character, Bunsen thoroughly believes, and considers the famous Inaugural Speech of Zoroaster (*Gâtha Ahunavaiti, Yasna* 30, already quoted, *ante*, p. 153) as the record of it:

> The remaining Gâthas, whether they proceed from Zoroaster himself, or only bear the mint mark of his mind, all exhibit similar characteristics. We do not discover Zoroaster to be a man exercising magical powers or exalting himself above humanity. On the contrary he is a seer who announces the Divine will as unmistakably authenticated by the voice within him.

Zoroastrianism, according to Bunsen, spread from Bactria to Media, and from Media to Persia, where its peculiar insistance on the virtue of Truth (Ahriman being always identified as the Lying Spirit) gave to the whole Persian people the character for veracity, so much marvelled at by the mendacious Greeks. The withering tyranny of the successors of Cyrus and the admixture of the Chaldee philosophy in Babylon were the causes, as Bunsen supposes, of such corruption as Zoroastrianism underwent. "Under such a despotism," he says, "how is it possible for a nation really to believe that the good, the wise, the true, does ultimately triumph upon earth?" This is a frequently recurring idea throughout the pages of *God in History*, that political freedom, or at the least, a government free from gross injustice, is indispensable to the maintenance of wide-spread faith in the eternal justice above, Nevertheless, the creed of Zoroaster is to this hour a nobly moral faith, and one by no means intellectually despicable.

From the Iranian branch of the great Aryan family, by whom the religion of Zoroaster was adopted, our author turns to the emigrants who before Zoroaster's age had wandered to the banks of the Indus, and there formed the most ancient detachment (so to speak) of the race, the Indian Aryans. Here was the land of the Vedas, the oldest of human books, in whose Sanskrit words we still trace the brotherhood which unites us Anglo-Saxons with that remotest household of our common Aryan race. Well may Bunsen say:

> The sacred books of the Indian Aryans touch us much more nearly in many respects than the records of the primeval epoch of the Hebrews, for in the former we see and feel the brotherhood of race; but on the other hand they are incomparably more a sealed book to

us than the sacred scriptures of the Jews. We stand in presence of a veiled life; in a similar position to that which we should occupy with regard to the unfolding of the Hebrew mind from the age of Abraham to that of Jeremiah, if we possessed nothing but the Book of Psalms.[1]

Having discussed the topic of Vedic literature elsewhere, I shall here pass over the further observations of Bunsen regarding it.

After a portion of the Aryan race had migrated from the Indus to the Ganges, the Vedic religion, according to Bunsen, transformed itself into Brahminism, "rather the contrary than the continuation of the Vedic religious consciousness." Here the old nature-gods Varuna (*Ouranos*, the sky), Agni (*Ignis*, fire), and the rest, sunk into insignificance before metaphysical conceptions of a different order. The Trimurti of Brahma, Vishnu, and Seeva (Creator, Restorer, and Destroyer)—about whom, as Bunsen says, "so many fantastical, not to say nonsensical, systems have been built up"—now first appeared, and received in time the highest rank among the deities. The poets and singers who had celebrated the Vedic sacrifices became an hereditary caste of priests; the whole cruel and monstrous system of Brahminism followed; and, meanwhile, the keen Aryan intellect occupied itself in the construction of such mental air-castles as the Sankhya and Vedanta philosophies. Thus, while the Iranian branch of the race, guided by the strong spirit of Zoroaster, seized, once for all, on the ethical side of religion, and developed a faith which, after three millenniums, is still the rational and moral creed of the Parsees, the Indian branch, following the intellectual rather than the ethical track, lost itself in a double ruin. On one side was a sacerdotal tyranny and a miserable idolatry. On the other were two systems of philosophy, the one trembling between

[1] Page 298.

pantheism and atheism, the other a nihilism, which left its disciples for consolation such thoughts as these:

> A drop that trembles on the lotus-leaf,
> Such is this life, so soon dispelled, so brief;
> The eight great mountains, and the seven seas,
> The sun, the gods who sit and rule o'er these,
> Thou, I, the universe, must pass away:
> Time conquers all; why care for what must pass away?

Of course, it is not to be imagined that Brahminism, during its long growth of three millenniums, has produced no better fruit than these apples of Sodom. The great Brahmin poems of the Mahabharata and the Ramayana, above all the code of Menu, which has been the Leviticus and the Deuteronomy of the Hindoo nation for so many ages, all testify to a religious and still more clearly to a moral consciousness, never lost in the sands of polytheism, nor absorbed in the formalism and asceticism of the priestly system.

I cannot quit this portion of my subject without expressing my regret that Bunsen should have died before the great reformation of the Brahmo Somaj assumed noticeable proportions in India. With how much pleasure would he, who was hopeful even of the results of the fanatical Tae-ping insurrection, have heralded the rise of a truly pure Theism, whose watchwords are the absolute unity and spirituality of God, the abolition of caste, and the elevation and instruction of woman! The religious consciousness of the Indian Aryans has indeed vindicated itself at last; and when Rammohun Roy published his book of extracts from the Vedas as the text-book of his infant church, he reunited the threads of three thousand years of spiritual history. The Vedic hymn has passed naturally into the Brahmo's prayer, as the worship of the fathers into that of the children.

What is Buddhism? The researches of a dozen great scholars have yet left us very little able to decide the question. Bunsen says frankly:

Our own conception of Buddha is diametrically opposed to that of Burnouf and all his successors (with the exception of Mohl, Obry, and Dancker) in so far that according to them the founder of the most widely diffused creed on the face of the earth, a creed which has introduced or revived civilization amongst all these millions, was a teacher of atheism and materialism. For so we must denominate a system which should teach that there is absolutely nothing but non-existence, therefore in no sense a God; that annihilation is the highest happiness the soul can strive after, and that it is the highest glory of the great saint to have taught the way thereunto. If this were so, then Buddha would at least lie beyond the scope of our present survey. *For there is no more utter denial of a Divine order of the world than the asssumption that existence is nothing but a curse.* (vol. i. p. 345).[1]

The fourth book of *God in History* is devoted to a study of the religious consciousness of the Aryan race in Europe, namely, the Greeks, the Romans, and the Teutons. The elaborate sketches of Greek religious life, including the earlier nature-worship, and that more ethical type which ever succeeds it; the Greek epos and drama; Greek architecture[2] and sculpture; fill some of the best chapters in the work, and are among the finest in recent criticism. Drawing to his conclusion, after setting forth how much of the truly moral, the truly religious, abode ever in the Greek consciousness, he says:

The Pantheon of the Greeks consisted exclusively of divinities of the mind, of Ideals of Humanity, and had its unity in Zeus, a conception which, through Homer and the other Hellenic poets, exerted a guiding influence, of which even the masses were sensible. For Zeus was not a national god, but was designated even so early as the age of Homer,

[1] The correctness of this view of Buddhism is discussed in the next Essay.

[2] Is it a slip of the pen by which, p. 262, vol. ix., he speaks of Phidias as *architect* as well as sculptor of the Parthenon? Is there any doubt of the work of Ictinus?

the "Father of gods and men." It now no longer occurs to any one to deny the mischief of that splitting-up of the consciousness of God, which was caused by a plurality of gods, but we must not forget that this polytheism had grown up out of the commingling of the tribes. As little will any one who has a voice in the European commonwealth of mind be disposed to deny the weakening of the ethical religious consciousness that resulted from the overweening concentration of the mind upon knowledge, or from the idolatry of beauty, involving as it did, a severance of the beautiful and the true from the good. But those alone have a right to cast their stone at the Greeks who know how to appreciate the divinity residing in beauty, and who do not refuse to see the godlike in knowledge. . . . It is very customary to place the distinguishing characteristic of Hellenism in an absence of all earnest worship of God and of religious life in general. We are prepared to maintain, on the contrary, that the whole life of classical antiquity, especially that of the Hellenes, shows itself far more inter-penetrated with prayer and religious feeling than does that of the modern Christian world.[1]

My readers will probably be a little startled at the last challenge, but the whole chapter deserves careful consideration ere we fall back on our accustomed commonplaces about Greek irreligion. Among other remarks, and as an instance of the curious side lights with which the book abounds, I may quote the observation in the preceding volume, that while with the Hebrews the "soul" was synonymous with "self," with the Greeks the body was the "self," and the soul a separate entity. The Hebrew patriarch could talk even of savoury meat as a thing his "soul" loved. The Greek poet (Iliad i.) spoke of the wrath of Achilles—

> Which many thousand *souls* of the sons of the heroes
> Sent down to hell; but stretched *themselves* on the earth
> A prey to the ravening dogs.

Bunsen might have added, that such an identification of "soul" and "self" has never yet taken place amongst ourselves. After so many centuries of Christianity we yet

[1] Vol. ii. p. 347.

habitually say, when a ship has foundered with her crew, that "every *soul* on board perished"; albeit, according to our professed belief, and even the belief of our Viking forefathers, the souls of the drowned were the only things which did *not* "perish" in the wreck.

The Romans, in the opinion of Bunsen, as of other scholars, had for the leading ideas of their national life the notion of Law, and of their own rightful sway over all nations. Sacrifices and prayer were to them the business of the small order of priests; forms highly to be respected and in no wise to be trangressed by a worthy citizen, but yet having nothing to do with a man's heart or inner life. Virgil summed up the Roman ideal when he wrote:

> Others, belike with happier grace,
> From bronze or stone shall call the face,
> Plead doubtful causes, map the skies,
> And tell when planets set or rise ;
> But ROMAN ! thou, do thou control
> The nations far and wide ;
> Be this thy genius—to impose
> The rule of peace on vanquished foes,
> Show pity to the humblest soul,
> And crush the sons of pride.—*Æneid,* vi.

The unity of civilized nations in one empire, the supremacy of Justice and of that Jurisprudence which Bunsen calls the Prose of Justice ; such was the great Roman Thought bequeathed to the world.

Finally we reach the Teuton and Gothic race, the furthest offshoot of the Aryan family, the very antitypes and yet the brothers in blood and language of the Aryans who, on the banks of the Ganges, transformed into Brahminism the old Vedic faith whose relics are imbedded in the wild mythology of Scandinavia. Fidelity, conjugal love, loyalty, courage, reverence for the nobler attributes of women, belief in eternal justice, in expiation and restoration; these were the characteristics which, following Tacitus, and wringing out the spirit of Eddas and Sagas, may be attributed to the great northern race even from heathen times. Have we here the secret why the religious consciousness of the Teuton— less intellectually subtle than the Brahmin, less beautiful in its forms than the Greek—is yet the one which has carried farthest in advance the torch of Divine light in the progress of mankind? Is not, after all, *loyalty*, the free Allegiance of the soul to its rightful LORD, the very highest type of religion? Awe, reverence, intellectual contemplation, sympathy with the beautiful, submission to irresistible decrees, stern adherence to external law—all these sides of religious consciousness, the inheritance of Egyptian, Persian, Hindoo, Greek, Moslem, and Roman, are good and true in their degree. But the highest Consciousness of all is not these, but the inward moral Allegiance of Love.

Marcus Aurelius began his Meditations by thankfully attributing his acquirements and advantages each to his parents or his tutors; his placid temper to his grandsire Verus, his piety to his mother Lucilla, his love of justice to Severus. And thus, perhaps, may mankind hereafter trace back each gift to one of its ancestry of nations, or to one of its great teachers. To the cradle of the future Lord of the world, the Kings both of the East and of the West will bring their gold, their frankincense, and myrrh. From the Jew he will inherit his Faith, from the Roman his Law, from the Greek his Art. Nay, many another heirloom will descend to him, its origin perchance forgotten in the night of time; many a thought and many a sentiment from far-off ancestors in the old Aryan Home, and Semite brothers under Chaldæan skies, and Norsemen from their icy seas storming forth to conquer the world. In the great family of nations perchance, when we come to know it better, we shall find there has been no insignificant or ungifted one; nay, that as in the fairy lore of our Teuton fathers, it is often the humblest, the dwarf, the disinherited, who has been chief of all and the saviour of his brethren. When Cherillus, describing the muster-roll of the vast army of Xerxes, named as last and meanest, "a people who dwelt in the Solymean mountains, with sooty heads and faces like horse-heads smoke-dried,"[1] how little he could foresee that from that despicable race and those barren Solymean hills should come a Conqueror to whose Army of Martyrs the mighty host of Xerxes should be an insignificant troop! "What perishes," says Bunsen, "in the great struggle which throbs through all history is the *limitation* of the individual and the *limitation* of the nation." The positive survives, the negation ceases. The tide of religious consciousness perpetually rises, not indeed by one continuous stream of equal advance, but in successive waves, each of which having contributed to the flow, subsides again and is lost. We need not despair, although again and again we read of one faith after another—"As time went on, it lost its early strength and became blended with errors." The procession of the ages by which our race approaches the altar of Divine wisdom is like no Phidian dream of stately forms of light-bearers and flower-bearers marching calmly in the long line of Time. Rather is it like the passage of some royal summons in feudal days of old, when each messenger bore it on as fast and far as life and strength allowed, then gave it to another's hands, and himself laid down to die. Are not the days of a nation numbered, is not its true life over, when it learns no new truth and turns the truth it has once learned to error?

[1] Josephus, *Contra Apion.* i. 22.

ESSAY IX.

THE RELIGIONS OF THE EAST.[1]

IN the preface to this book the author makes the following observation:

There is to my mind no subject more absorbing than the tracing the origin and first growth of human thought; not theoretically or in accordance with the Hegelian laws of thought, or the Comtian epochs, but historically and like an Indian trapper, spying for every footprint, every layer, every broken blade that might tell and testify of the former presence of man in his early wanderings and searchings after light and truth.

Few readers, I apprehend, possessed of the genuine historic spirit, will hesitate to agree cordially with this sentiment, and to rank the religious development of nations in which such "searchings after light and truth" result, as the most noteworthy element of their civilization. Nor is the interest of the subject exhausted when we have made it a foremost branch of historical inquiry. The science of Comparative Theology, to be built up at last of the materials furnished by such researches will, we are assured, prove as valuable in elucidating the dark problems of the human mind as the science of Comparative Physiology has been in throwing light on those of the body. And as out of the study of the lower animals the physiologist ascends step by step from simpler to more complex forms of life, and traces

[1] *Chips from a German Workshop.* By Max Müller. Two vols., 8vo. 1868.

his way from organs rudimentary in beast and insect up to the human hand and brain; so the theologian may hereafter trace through the humbler forms of fetichism and polytheism, and the imperfections of Vedic and Judaic religions, the prophecy and embryo of that more perfect faith, in whose symmetric development all the incomplete and rudimentary types of the past will become explicable. Professor Müller's delightful volumes treat of many subjects beside those immediately connected with theology, his own special science of Language having of course a prominent place. The interest of the work centres, however, so much in the dissertations on the various sacred books and on mythology in general, that I shall be doing it little injustice in confining my review to the subjects so suggested. The philology of the learned Professor is entirely beyond my criticism, and the minor topics dealt with in his second volume would occupy too much space if even very briefly noticed.

The value of comparative theology becomes constantly more apparent as we descend from a mere superficial view of the various religions of the world, to a deeper analysis of the nature of human faith and worship. Religious ideas (it is often forgotten) are not simple, but complex. Each has two factors; first, the feelings of dependence, allegiance, love, to some dimly discerned Power above, which we sum up under the name of the "Religious Sentiment"; second, the intellectual work which happens to have been done at any given time or place, in transmuting these Sentiments into Thoughts; or, in other words, in constructing a theology. No religious Ideas could exist were there no religious Sentiments behind them, and no religious ideas do practically exist till a certain process of crystallization has been applied to such sentiments.

The first factor is constant so far as that what ever has been the sentiment of one age is not lost, but developed and ennobled in subsequent generations. As the Moral Sense first dimly dawns in the mind of the savage, and then grows into a definite, though imperfect, sense of Justice; and later on slowly extends, step by step, to the sense of Truth, Purity, and Love; so the Religious Sentiment, which is in a measure the reflex of the Moral Sense, developes slowly also.

The second factor of religious ideas is, from the nature of the case, variable and incessantly changing with every advance of knowledge and every process of reflection. It is itself compounded of two variable elements; namely, first, the original thought of the individual, which may be almost nil, or may be vast enough to create a whole new creed; secondly, of the traditional thought which he has derived from teachers and books, and this, again, of course may be great or small—a mental ancestry stretching through a princely line of saints and sages, or the low brief pedigree of a barbarian's legends. Here the study of comparative theology is of incalculable value, enabling the student to inherit, not only the traditions of his direct line of teachers, but of all past generations. The different Ideas into which the same Sentiment has been translated in varied lands and ages are to the last degree instructive, and corrective of our haste and dogmatism; nor can a man fairly estimate the worth of any familiar notion till he has seen and weighed its antagonist idea. Nay, not only in an intellectual, but a moral sense, the knowledge of such various creeds is valuable. Religion never comes to us in greater majesty than when "a cloud of witnesses" proclaims its truth. Never do moral lessons touch us more nearly, never do expressions of trust in God, or hope of immortality, carry with them such fresh strength as when they are borne to us from far-off ages and distant lands, and we know they have come from the lips of men who never spoke our speech nor learned our lessons, and whose whole lives were passed under conditions utterly foreign to all our traditions. To hold by the full cord of all the faith of all the ages, is assuredly far more secure than to cling by a single thread, even if that thread be the golden strand of Christianity.

Each man's religion, observes Professor Müller, is to him unique. It is his native language, the mother-tongue of his soul; none other may bear any comparison with it so far as he is concerned. We might carry the simile further, and say that, like the old pedants who held that the languages of barbarians were not proper languages at all, but had only the sense of the lowings and bleatings of kine and sheep, so bigots even now talk as if the vast religions of the ancient world and of the East were not worthy to be called religions, and had in them no meaning and no sanctity. The thesis of half the later apologists of Christianity (down to the author of *Christ and other Masters*, well reviewed in these volumes[1]) might be described somewhat in this wise: "Given, a multitude of creeds having innumerable parallels, in doctrine, myth, rite and precept, with our own. Prove that everything in them is absurd and wicked, and everything in our own faith credible and holy."

It was not so in earlier times. The Apostles and Fathers were ready to acknowledge the "light which lighteth every man that cometh into the world," wherever they beheld a scintillation of it, whether in poems like that of Aratus, or in that philosophy "by which," as Clemens Alexandrinus said, "the Almighty is glorified among the Greeks." St. Chrysostom's argument (Homil. 12) for the divine inspiration of conscience as the source from whence heathen legislators drew their laws, reads like a piece of modern free-thinking:

<blockquote>For it cannot be said they held communication with Moses, or that</blockquote>

[1] Vol. i. p. 50.

they heard the prophets. How could they when they were Gentiles? It is evident it was from the very law which God placed in man when he formed him.

But as the Church lost its primitive vigour of faith, which sufficed to itself without requiring the denial of all divine element in other creeds, the narrower, poorer faith of later ages needed to put forth a different claim: Christianity was declared to be not only the best, but the only religion; all others were devil-worship and delusion. No modern Paul would have preached from the text of the altar of the Unknown God. He would have called it an altar of Satan. One faith only could be admitted to be unmingled truth, and for its sake, and expressly to distinguish it from all others, it was affirmed that the long cycle of Biblical miracles had been wrought. All other creeds were mere jumbles of unredeemable error, and their pretended wonders mere delusions and impostures. Penetrated with notions like these, our missionaries went forth to attack the giant religions of the East with the courage of David against the Philistine. But their Bibles, flung fearlessly at those massive fronts, have somehow hitherto failed to slay the enemy, or even to stun him; and we must wait for his overthrow till a different order of attack be inaugurated.

In just the opposite spirit from this narrow and bigoted one does Professor Müller address himself to the task of examining the religions of the heathen world. Had his book no other merit, the preface alone, in which the true method of such inquiry is vindicated, possesses a value we shall not readily over-estimate. "Every religion," he says, "even the most imperfect and degraded, has something that ought to be sacred to us, for there is in all religions a secret yearning after the true though unknown God." Truly this is the spirit, not only of a philosopher, but of a pious man. Strange is it, as all who have travelled beyond the precincts of Christendom can tell, to note with what scorn, surpassing mere irreverence, Christians commonly enter the mosques and temples of other creeds, and standing among crowds of prostrate worshippers move and speak, as if purposely to display their contempt. Nay, in Christendom itself to watch a Protestant in a Romish church, or an Anglican in a Dissenting chapel, is often to see embodied in looks and manner the feelings *not* of sympathy or community in the eternal human sentiments of religious love and hope, not even of pity for supposed fatal and soul-destroying error; but of inhuman ridicule and disgust. Not one man in a thousand enters the temple of a creed in which he does not believe, with any reverence or even any interest beyond vulgar curiosity. But *that* man sees what others wholly miss; even the essential meaning of the cultus. Just so will those few who, like Müller, enter the vast fane of Vedic or Zoroastrian faith, not rudely or contemptuously, but with respectful sympathy, find therein a purpose which for ever escapes the mere profane inquirer.

The sources of knowledge concerning existing heathen religions are of very various value. The obvious results of a creed on the character and manners of the nation which adopts it have always afforded a favourite "short method with the Pagans," whereby it was easy to demonstrate that all such creeds *could* contain nothing good since so little good came from them. But to argue back from the practice to the theory of any religion would, I fear, prove an unsatisfactory mode of procedure, even if applied to our own. The "intelligent foreigner," after perusing our police reports, examining the processes of our traffic, or merely perambulating the streets of London or Paris, before or after dark, would hardly construct the Sermon on the Mount as the source to which all he beheld plainly pointed as authority. Professor Müller himself mentions the despair of a poor Hindoo convert, who somehow managed to reach England still possessed of the simple faith, that Evangelical piety filled all our hearts and Evangelical morality guided the greater part of our actions. To expect that far *less* pure and noble creeds should exercise more perfect influence, and that Confucian wisdom should reign in Pekin, Brahmin devotion at Benares, and Zoroastrian morality among the Parsees at Bombay, is paying, to say the least, a bad compliment to Christianity.

A second source of knowledge of heathen creeds is derived from the oral teaching of living priests; the doctrines they promulgate concerning God and other beings of the invisible world; their cosmogony, ethics and ceremonial laws, and their lessons concerning a future state. This oral teaching is of course a most important element in forming our estimate of each creed, and has hitherto been almost our sole guide to the great religions of the East. It is, however, obviously liable to lead us into many mistakes. In the first place we derive from it at best only an idea of the religion in its present shape, which often (as in the case of Brahminism) is one of great degeneracy. Secondly, such teachings as Eastern priesthoods now afford shade off always into mythologies, more or less puerile, and bearing to religion no more relation than the Legends of the Saints do to Christianity. To say what is the creed itself and what is mere hagiology and fable is impossible, unless we go beyond the living priests to some higher authority. Again, each great creed has undergone enormous modifications. Even what must be termed its theology has changed in the course of ages, and differs, altogether, in different parts of the wide empire over which it stretches. The Trimurti, for instance, of Brahma, Vishnu, and Seeva, with all their myths of avatars, and the pantheon of subordinate gods, is a comparatively modern phase of Brahminism. Among the elemental deities of the Vedas these things are not to be found. Buddhism is almost a different creed in China, in Thibet and in Ceylon, and what the priesthood of one country teaches as its doctrines, that of the others denies or modifies. Lastly, all mythologies vary, not only in different places but at different times; being in a constant state of flux and change; sometimes of alternate solidification into fable, and rarefaction into metaphor. We continually think of heathen religions as if each had its compact Body of divinity or its Thirty-Nine Articles; and, moreover, as if it possessed (what our churches have never achieved) a priesthood teaching precisely the same doctrines at all times and everywhere, neither more spiritual nor more carnal, more philosophic nor more stupid the one than the other. As things actually are, we may fairly rate the judgment of an Eastern creed derivable from its living priests at the value which would pertain to a summary of Christianity obtained by going about Europe asking questions of an Anglican bishop, an Italian capuchin, a Scotch presbyter, and a Greek papas; and digesting their answers, as best we might, into a system of theology, omitting whatever might seem merely sensible and common-place, and carefully noting everything grotesque and surprising which came in our way.

Take it as we may, the creation of the theology and mythology of each religion is a process more remarkable and more interesting the more we endeavour to get near to it and realize how it can have been accomplished. I know of few better attempts to deal with its mystery than in the essay on *Semitic Monotheism* in these volumes:

> The primitive intuition of God, and the ineradicable feeling of dependence on God, could only have been the result of a primitive revelation in the truest sense of the word. Man, who owed his existence to God and whose being centred and rested in God, saw and felt God as the only sense of his own and of all other existence. By

the very act of creation God had revealed himself. This primitive intuition of God, however, was in itself neither monotheistic nor polytheistic, though it might become either. It is too often forgotten by those who believe that a polytheistic worship was the most natural unfolding of religious life, that polytheism must everywhere have been preceded by a more or less conscious theism. In no language does the plural exist before the singular. No human mind could have conceived the idea of Gods without having previously conceived the idea of a God. The primitive intuition of Godhead is neither monotheistic nor polytheistic, and it finds its expression in the simplest and yet the most important article of faith—that God is God. This must have been the faith of the ancestors of mankind before any division of race, . . . but it was not yet secured against the illusions of a double vision. Its expression would have been "there is a God," but not yet "there is but one God."

In all heathen nations, and even partially among the Jews, the various aspects of nature, and names given to different attributes of God, led to the multiplication of deities, and thence by rapid degrees to the formation of myths and legends, and endless genealogies." How all those arose, which we find were actually believed, it is hard indeed to imagine. A certain large number may be set down at once as not so much Myths as Metaphors; the inevitable shape into which expression of natural phenomena fell when language was yet all alive with imagery, and possessed no abstract nouns, no auxiliary verbs; no terms, in short, which did not draw a picture instead of narrating a fact. "Words," says Müller, "were then heavy and unwieldy. They said more than they ought to say." Thus, what is poetry now was common prose then, or rather there was no distinction between prose and poetry, and men said that "Night was the mother of sleep and dreams," just as simply as we say, "Sleep and dreams come at night time." Innumerable other myths are traced by modern scholars (I confess, as it seems to my ignorance, with tedious iteration and much coercion of fancy) to descriptions of solar phenomena. Every hero, according to these critics, is the Sun, every heroine the Moon; and every event is affirmed to represent the Sun rising or the Sun setting, the Sun among clouds or the Sun at dawn, the Sun at the solstice or the Sun at the equinox, the Sun entering the Bull or the Sun quitting the ram—till the unlearned mind marvels whether the ancient heathens were born and died, married, reigned, fought, or had any real existence other than as types of the Sun; or whether they attended at all to their own affairs and not exclusively to those of the Solar System. But when we have done our best to understand all these myths, whether mere metaphors or elaborate allegories, we are still perplexed to conceive the mental conditions of what Professor Müller calls the *mythopœic* age, in which they originated, and of the next, when they passed into the minds of subsequent generations as accredited facts. One thing alone is clear, that the mass of such myths have little or nothing in common with the *religion* of the race among whom they were current; and that we may as well study the Protestantism of Elizabeth's reign in the *Midsummer Night's Dream* as the real faith of a Roman of the Augustan age in Ovid's *Metamorphoses*.

The one satisfactory source of knowledge concerning all religions, is neither the moral state of the people who hold them, nor their current myths, but their *Sacred Literature*. This alone supplies us at first hand with the fountain from which all that is really characteristic and important in each creed has been derived. Here we get at the thoughts about God and duty and immortality of real men whose spiritual experience (to use Rowland Williams' great phrase) generated the religious atmosphere in which their disciples ever since have breathed. Here we are face to face with the prophets of old, no longer transfigured and seen through a halo of adoring fable, but as they were in the flesh, writing as best they could, the burning thoughts of their souls. Here then, if anywhere, lies the mine of wealth out of which we must dig our knowledge of the great creeds of the world.

But in such literature there are always varied stages. The earliest books (invariably accounted most sacred) indicate the first vague shape which the creed assumed. The books of the second period, and of lesser sanctity, present the creed in more definite form, and are also, nearly always, of a more distinctly ethical character. Lastly, after every Bible there comes a Talmud, the commentaries and ceremonial regulations by which the earlier prophetic utterances and the secondary ethical precepts are in time overlaid. Usually it happens that during the long interval between the beginning and end of such a cycle of literature in any country, the creed itself has undergone essential modifications, whether, as in Judaism, by rising into a higher spirituality, and incorporating the doctrine of immortality; or, as in Brahminism, by declension into the worship of material idols.

Before endeavouring to recapitulate Professor Müller's conclusions regarding some of these great works, a few reflections on the extraordinary nature of Sacred Books may well be bestowed.

Looking back from the rich garden of literature which human genius and industry (and we may add human vanity and folly) have created for us, "the heirs of all the ages," it is almost touching to learn how the first few books of the world, the wild flowers which sprang up spontaneously in all their glory and freshness in that yet unbroken soil, were cherished and well-nigh adored. A book, strange is it to remember, was once, *per se*, a sacred thing. And as a young writer even now looks on his first printed work with a curious sort of parental sense, beholding the child of his mind standing before him, the mysterious *logos* embodied in tangible shape, no longer a part of himself, but having as it were independent life, so, in those far-off ages, mankind looked on the first books with awe and wonder as Incarnate Thoughts. Beneath a synagogue in Jerusalem there is a vault where, even yet, old worn-out books and manuscripts are piously buried, a memorial of the time when every written law was believed to have had, not only a human scribe, but an inspiring deity to direct the legislator, and every poem was understood to have had a Muse, by whose aid so wondrous an achievement was brought about. By degrees the best of the old, and the oldest of the best books, through all the pious Eastern lands, became hallowed and set apart, to be confounded no more with merely mortal works. They were canonized as saintly Christian men were afterwards canonized, first by the common voice, then perhaps, as in the case of the Buddhist scriptures, by decrees of councils, and, at last, by universal consent and tradition. Is this very marvellous? Have we any difficulty in conceiving how it happened? Nay, but was it not rather the most natural thing in the world? Who can estimate the mysterious enchantment which belongs to the words of a great book, when generations have passed away uttering them in every hour of joy and agony, and finding expression in them for all their hope and all their penitence? The cathedral roof, which has bent over the prayers of a thousand years, seems redolent of their incense; the altar where our fathers have knelt becomes for us a shrine. So it is with books also, with the very words and phrases which have been as silver trumpets through which men's voices have gone upward to heaven for millenniums. Does any one believe that the outbursts of faith and grief in the Psalms or the old prayers of Basil and Chrysostom, are just the same now, no richer or fuller of meaning than when they were first written? Had they been buried then in that

Syrian vault and exhumed for some antiquary to decipher to-day, would they be for us what they now are when for ages human hearts have embalmed them? Not so. Words whose sound has gone out into all lands, awakening, consoling, purifying the souls of men age after age, cannot be for us like other words. They come to us breathing memories of childhood and of our mother's prayers, and through them we seem to hear a murmur as of the voices of all the holy dead. Such sanctity as this depends little upon theories of "inspiration," or arguments concerning the authority of a canon or the authenticity of a codex; but nothing is more natural than that a devout mind should attribute directly to God's dictation what seems at once so sacred and so beautiful.

It is not hard to recognize these truths applied to our own scriptures and liturgies. Can we not discern also that, in a great measure, the same principle must hold good for nations whose sacred books have far less beauty and meaning *for us*, and far less absolutely, by any standard we can admit for a moment; but which may very possibly have a certain habitual fitness and home sentiment, for the nations to whom they belong, which even greater books may lack? Doubtless, Arab and Indian melodies are immeasurably inferior to German and Italian airs, yet we should not marvel, but take it as a trait of human nature, if an Arab or Indian listened delighted to the monotonous jangle of his native instruments, and shed tears over tunes which rather inclined us to laughter. The fact that a Brahmin can find in the Vedas, or an Arab in the Koran, much more than we can find in either of beauty and sublimity, should cause us no surprise. The wonder is rather, how we western Europeans, we of Aryan race, feel such intense sympathy with the literature of a Semitic people, and are far more at home in Genesis than in the *Iliad*, in the speculations of Job than in those of

Plato. The explanation is to be found, perhaps, first in the marvellous greatness of the Hebrew literature; and in its intensely human character which ever recalls to each of us the freshness of youth, and gives it a claim to be the literature not of one people but of humanity. Secondly, we English and Germans, who of European nations most prize the Bible, have been for a thousand years fed upon it, till Jewish and Syrian ideas come to us far more naturally than those of our own Odin-worshipping ancestors. To *them*, indeed, it may well be doubted whether the Hebrew Scriptures (could they have read them) would have seemed half so fine as Beowulf or the elder Nibelungen-Lied. But on the strong wild stems of Norse and Teuton races the graft of Judaic thought has flourished vigorously, and we, the fruit thereof, show more mental likeness, perchance, to the graft than to our original stem.

It is easy to turn the Sacred Books of the heathens into ridicule, by quoting from them monstrous myths, childish precepts, and especially that almost universal perversion of morals whereby ceremonies are exalted to the level of the most imperative duties. As the Institutes of Menu speak of "killing the inhabitants of three worlds and eating with unwashed hands" as of crimes of parallel magnitude, so nearly every ancient law-book places things *mala in se* and things *mala prohibita* (such as gathering sticks on the Sabbath) in most unfit equality. The error obviously arises from the notion that ceremonial observances are duties directly owed to *God*, and therefore of infinite obligation, while other duties, it is imagined, are only indirectly divine, and are owed to man, and therefore of minor sanctity. Though if there be one point more clear than another in the teaching of Christ, it is his denunciation of such pharisaism, and of the giving of tithes of mint, anise, and cummin, to the neglect of justice and truth, yet from his age to ours

Christendom has never shaken itself wholly free thereof. It is idle then to point to these puerile precepts, and the endless commentaries upon them, as proving the worthlessness of heathen books.

Modern philology and ethnology have grouped the languages and nations of Europe and Asia in wholly different classification from the purely geographical order formerly used; and this new classification Professor Müller conceives to be applicable no less to the religions than the tongues of the various races. The order he adopts may be briefly thus described:

1. The Aryan or Indo-European race, branching into the northern Indian, Persian, Greek, Roman, Sclavonic, Teuton, and Celtic races, with all their languages: Sanscrit (the elder sister), Zend, Persian, Greek, Latin, German, Celtic, French, English, etc.

2. The Semitic race, branching into Assyrians, Jews, Phœnicians, Carthaginians, Arabs, etc.; with their languages, of which Hebrew and Arabic are the most important.

3. The Turanian race, comprising Mongols, Turks, Malays, Siamese, and many of the Indian nations, with their respective languages.

4. The Chinese, with their unique monosyllabic language.

After these, between whom all history, all religion, all literature, and all art are well-nigh divided, there are the African, American, and Polynesian races (variously arranged by ethnologists), with whose languages and religions we have here no concern. The ethnology of the great Egyptian race in the world's pedigree seems to be still a matter of doubt. Their language is said by scholars to have some singular affinities with that of the Hottentots.

By the Aryan and Semitic races has the progress of the world been carried on, and in them our interest, both hereditary and historical, necessarily centres. Now, a very singular parallel, which so far as I am aware has not been hitherto remarked, may be traced between the religious history of these two great tribes. I venture to suggest it as one of the most curious parallels in history.

In both Aryan and Semitic races there have existed several minor creeds which, in process of ages, have disappeared. In the Aryan race, for example, there have been the religions of Greece and Rome, Odin-worship and Druidism. In the Semitic race there have been the Assyrian, Phœnician and sundry other idolatries. But in each race there has also been one great religion which, beginning at the very dawn of history, has lasted to the present hour, namely, Vedic-Brahminism among the Aryans, and Judaism in the Semitic race. And each of these great religions has had two vast offshoots, or schisms, which, also, still survive; namely, Zoroastrianism and Buddhism from Brahminism; and Christianity and Islam from Judaism. Further. All six of these religions are possessed of a Sacred Literature, to which divine authority is attributed by their adherents; namely, among the Aryans:

> The Vedas of the Brahmans;
> The Zend-Avesta of the Zoroastrians;
> The Tripitaka of the Buddhists;

and among the Semitic race:

> The Old Testament of the Jews;
> The New Testament of the Christians;
> The Koran of the Moslems.

Beside these Aryan and Semitic Scriptures, there only exist in the world two other ancient sacred books of any value, namely the Kings of the Confucian Chinese, and the Taote-king of the Taoists of China; the Grunth of the Sikhs being a comparatively modern work.

Lastly, as if to perfect the parallel, recent calculations tend to show that at the present hour, after four thousand years of development, the great religions of the Semitic and Aryan races are almost on an equality in point of numbers; Brahminism and Buddhism, with the small remnant of Zoroastrians, counting together (according to an authority accepted by Professor Müller) about 44 per cent. of the human race; and Judaism, Islam, and Christianity numbering nearly 45 per cent. on the same calculation.

It would be impossible to heighten the effect of so amazing a coincidence by any reflections. One fact, however, must not be forgotten. Among all these creeds, Christianity alone is extending itself; all the rest, without exception, are dying out. Whether the extension of Christianity have any considerable motive force beside the superior energies, the conquests and colonizings of the Anglo-Saxon race, and whether a collapse of the British Empire would leave the progress of Christianity undisturbed, we need not inquire. The prior question would need to be settled before any conclusion could be drawn from such premisses: What share has Christianity, and especially free and moral Protestant Christianity, had in making the Englishman what he is, and giving to Queen Victoria those realms on which the sun never sets?

I propose briefly to follow Professor Müller, not into all the varied woods and groves of literature wherein he has cut his "Chips," but through his more weighty discussions on the Sacred Books of the East. Of these, those of the Aryan race have chiefly occupied him, leaving room for one essay only on the Confucian books, and one on Semitic Monotheism. To begin, then, with the oldest and most interesting of all.

"In the Aryan world," says Professor Müller, "the Veda is certainly the oldest book." And it is emphatically a *book*, not a mere monument or record of conquests and successive dynasties. Here lies its immense interest, for, "poets are better than kings, and guesses at truth are more valuable than unmeaning titles of Egyptian or Babylonian despots." The word Veda means "knowledge," being, in fact, the same word as "wit" or "wise." There are four books known as Vedas, and commonly represented in the four hands of Brahma the Creator, namely, the Rig Veda, the Yagur Veda, the Sama Veda, and Atharva Veda. But the three last, says Professor Müller, no more deserve the name of Vedas than the Talmud deserves the name of Bible. The Yagur Veda is, in fact, a prayer-book; the Sama Veda, a hymn-book; and the Atharva Veda, a sort of rubric; each for the use of a different order of priests at the sacrifices. The Rig Veda, containing the most ancient hymn of praise, is *the* Veda par excellence. It consists of two parts, the oldest hymns or Mantras, called Sanhitâ, and a number of prose comments called Brâhmanas and Sûtras. The Rig Veda Sanhitâ consists of ten books containing 1028 hymns; and 600 years before Christ the scholars of India had counted these 1028 hymns, and found they contained 10,402 verses, and 432,000 *syllables*, a number approximately verified in existing MSS. The date of these hymns must be somewhere between 1200 and 1500 B.C., albeit no MS. exists of much more than five centuries old. This high antiquity, demonstrated by various arguments, is corroborated by a curious observation. In modern literature one epoch, nay one single author, often uses the most varied styles of composition, poetry, history, criticism, science. But in ancient times, says Müller, "the individual is much less prominent, and the poet's character disappears in the general character of the *layer of literature* to which he belongs. It is the discovery of such large strata of literature following each other in regular succession, which inspires the critical historian with confidence in the truly historical character of the successive literary productions of ancient India," where "an age of poets was followed by an age of collectors and imitators; then by an age of theological prose writers, and finally by an age of writers of scientific manuals."

Of the sanctity of the Rig Veda, in the opinion of Brahmins, nothing too much can possibly be said. "The Veda is *sruti*, or Hearing; all other books, even the great code of Menu, is *smriti*, or Recollection." "The views entertained of revelation, by the orthodox theologians of India," says Müller, "are far more minute and elaborate than those of the most extreme advocates of verbal inspiration in Europe." The whole Veda is the work of deity, and even the men who received it were raised above common fallible mortality. The human element is utterly denied a place. "The Veda existed before all time in the mind of God." As the institutes of Menu say, "To deities and to men, the Scripture is an eye of light; nor could the Veda Shastras have been made by human faculties, nor can they be measured by human reason unassisted by revealed glosses and commentaries. Such codes of laws as are not founded on the Veda produce no good fruit after death. All systems which are repugnant to the Veda must have been composed by mortals and shall soon perish. Their modern date proves them vain and false."[1] The real writers of the Veda however, like those of other books, for which similar claims have been advanced, make no pretension to write by divine dictation, but implore the Deity to inspire them. One of them cries, "O Indra! Whatever I now may utter, longing for thee, do thou accept it. Make me possessed of God!" (Rig Veda, vi. 47, 10.) Another "utters for the first time the Gâyatrî, which now for more

[1] Institutes of Menu, c. 12, v. 94, 95.

than three thousand years has been the daily prayer of every Brahman, and is still repeated every morning by millions of pious worshippers." "Let us meditate on the adorable light of the Divine Creator! May He rouse our minds!"

Very various degrees of merit are displayed by the different poems of the Vedas. Some of them are tedious and childish. The gods are invoked, with endless repetitions, to protect their worshippers, and to grant them all sorts of terrestrial blessings. Yet interesting in many ways are even these more puerile hymns. They reveal that mental condition in the writers, of which we have already spoken as a theism which is not yet properly either monotheism or polytheism. Each god, when worshipped, is successively thought of as *the* God, and invested with supreme attributes; and here and there may be traced a dim recognition that the Many are but One; as it is said (Rig Veda, i. 164, 46), "They call Him Indra, Mitra, Varuna, Agni. .... That which is One, the wise call in divers manners." Some of these gods, like Agni (Fire), seem to be merely elementary; others, like Varuna, are already defined personages; but in no case is there any trace of their worship having taken the form of idolatry. The worship of idols in India is a degradation of the Vedic worship of ideal gods.

The Trimurti of Brahma, Seeva, and Vishnu, as already stated, is altogether the product of a later age. In the Atharva Veda occurs the first mention of "BRAHMAN" (used originally in the neuter, and eventually changed into a masculine noun), translated by Professor Müller to signify "Force" or "Will," and said to be the "First-born, the Self-existing, the best of the Gods, by whom heaven and earth were established." Very marvellously, surely, does this name for God, signifying ambiguously both Will and Force, correspond to the latest theories which the modern doctrine of correlated forces has suggested to men of science, even within the last few years, in England. If it become the accepted belief amongst us that the forces of nature hold to God's will the direct relation which man's nervous force does to his will, or in other words, that the dynamic power of the universe is the vital force of God, we shall hardly find in relation to such a doctrine a better name for the great MOVER of all things than "Brahman."

Here and there through the Veda break out expressions of wonder respecting the physical mysteries of the universe, betraying already the deep thoughtfulness and speculative tendencies of that Aryan intellect of which Plato and Aristotle, Kant and Hegel, were inheritors. Listen to the following from the Rig Veda (x. 81-4): "What was the forest, what was the tree, out of which they shaped heaven and earth? Wise men ask this: on what He stood when He held the worlds?" Or to the still more remarkable 129th hymn of the 10th book, of which Professor Müller has given a full translation ending in the lines of which he may well observe; "At this period no poet in any other nation could have conceived them."

> Who knows from whence this great creation sprung?
> He from whom all this great creation came,
> Whether His will created or was mute?
> The Most High Seer that is in highest heaven,
> He knows it—*or perchance even He knows not!*

A matter of still greater interest is the moral life which may be traced through these oldest of human compositions. The Brahmin mind, from the first, was of a highly intellectual cast, while in the Iranian race the moral element visibly predominated. Yet it is evident that, in the age of the Vedas, religion and morality were already linked with that closeness which we discover in the Hebrew writings, and so often miss in those of the Greeks. Many a Christian reader might take unawares for one of the Psalms of Israel some of the hymns quoted by Professor Müller, merely changing the name Varuna (*Ouranos*, Heaven) for Jehovah. Witness the following (Rig Veda, vii. 89):

Let me not yet, O Varuna, enter into the house of clay. Have mercy, Almighty, have mercy!

Through want of strength have I done wrong. Have mercy, Almighty, have mercy!

Whenever we men, O Varuna, commit an offence before the heavenly host, whenever we break the law through thoughtlessness, have mercy, Almighty, have mercy!

How wonderful is it here to find the LAW—that great

> Unwritten law divine,
> Immutable, eternal, not like those of yesterday,
> But made ere time began—

of which Sophocles wrote, here spoken of already in the first dawn of the world, perchance ere yet Moses was born, as "*the Law*"—the law of God, for whose neglect man prays to be forgiven!

And again (Rig Veda, vii. 86):

Wide and mighty are the works of Him who stemmed asunder the wide firmaments and lifted on high the bright and glorious heaven. He stretched out apart the starry sky and the earth. . . .

How can I approach unto Varuna? Will he accept my offering without displeasure? . . . Absolve us from the sins of our fathers, and from those which we have committed with our own bodies. . . .

It was not our own doing, O Varuna! It was temptation, an intoxicating draught, passion and thoughtlessness. Even sleep brings unrighteousness.

The Lord God enlighteneth the foolish. . . O Lord Varuna, may this song go to thine heart.

The likeness of the following (Atharva Veda, iv. 6) to Psalm 139 is remarkable:

The great Lord of the worlds sees as if he were near. If a man stands, or walks, or hides, if he lies down or rises up, King Varuna knows it. He is there as the third. He who should flee far beyond the sky, even he would not be rid of Varuna... King Varuna sees all that is between heaven and earth. He has counted the twinklings of the eyes of men.

In conclusion, Professor Müller tells us there is no trace of the doctrine of metempsychosis in the Veda, but, on the contrary, many references to personal immortality as an accepted fact. A few vague threats of a "pit," and of the "dogs of Yama" (death), hint at punishment for the wicked, and the good man expects a felicity thus conceived of (Rig Veda, ix. 113, 7):

Where there is eternal light, in the world where the sun is placed, in that immortal imperishable world, . . .
Where life is free, in the third heaven of heavens, where the worlds are radiant, where there is happiness and delight, where joy and pleasure reside, where the desires of our desire are attained,—there make me immortal!

Next in age and importance to the Vedas in the Aryan world are the Zoroastrian sacred books; the scriptures of the Parsees, commonly comprised under the name of the Zend-Avesta. Of these books an account was given by the present writer (compiled from the translations of Haug, Spiegel, Westergaard, etc.) in *Fraser's Magazine* three years ago.[1] So far as he has traversed the same ground, Professor Müller, I am happy to find, seems to sanction all the statements of that paper. To those who have not read the article in question, it may be briefly told that the conclusions of recent Zend scholarship are these:—In the beginning of history the Aryan race, a small tribe, perhaps only a family, having one language and one faith, dwelt in a certain spot called Aryana Vaêyo, (the old Aryan Home) believed to have been on the banks of the Araxes, near where the city of Atropatene afterwards stood. It was at all events a region far north of

[1] Reprinted in *Studies Ethical and Social*. 1 vol., 8vo. Williams & Norgate.

India, where winter reigned for ten months of the year.[1] After the lapse of years or centuries—who can tell how many?—the race parted into two great branches: the Iranians, who were agriculturists, labouring in Bactria; and the Brahmins, penetrating into India, where their nomad habits ended. This eventful severance was not effected without some bitter strife and religious dissension. Nay, it was perhaps primarily rather a religious schism than a national disruption. In the rich fossil-beds of Language, where science is daily instructing us more and more to seek for relics of the earlier world which no false dealings with history can have distorted, there appears unmistakable evidence that the Zoroastrian and Vedic creeds bore to each other the inimical attitude of reformed and unreformed churches, of a great Catholicity and a great Protestantism. It was something more than the rancour wherewith, in modern times,

> Some have learned to curse the shrine
> Where others kneel to heaven,

for gods and devils were actually made to exchange places. The Deva in Brahminism are gods. In the Zend-Avesta they are demons. The Asura are the evil spirits of the later Brahminism; and Ahura-Mazda is Zoroaster's name for the Supreme God himself. Indra, god of the sky, chief god of one Vedic period, is the second of the devils in the Zend-Avesta. And so on through a bewildering dance of heaven's and hell's inhabitants. The rites of the two creeds also show intimate connexion, and are visibly only variations of the same original cultus, but here again are traces of the same fierce strife. The sacred Soma, which in the Brahminical religion holds a place analogous to the sacramental Host of Catholicism, is spoken of in one of the most ancient fragments of the Zend-Avesta with extremest horror and

[1] First *Fargard* of the *Vendidad*.

contempt. "Who will pollute," it asks, "that intoxicating liquor which makes proud the priests of the idols?" (Yasna 47.) Here then took place the earliest schism of the world; a schism unhealed after three thousand years. Asia at that hour fell morally asunder. The Brahmin race went on,—to pass through intellectual processes of amazing depth and complexity, and to arrive at last at the miserable result of modern Hindooism. The Iranian race, on the contrary, made a vigorous and healthful Morality the heart of their religion, and after having largely influenced western thought through Jews and Greeks, have left to this hour in the remnant of Parsees no unworthy representatives of Zoroaster's disciples, uncorrupted by either polytheism or idolatry, the impure rites or the cruel laws of the nation amid which they dwell. "A Parsee," says Professor Müller, "believes in one God, to whom he addresses his prayers." According to his catechism he is taught that: "This God has neither face nor form, colour nor shape, nor fixed place. He is Himself alone, and of such glory that we cannot praise or describe Him, nor our minds comprehend Him." "Whoever believes in any other god but this is an infidel." Believing in the punishment of vice and the reward of virtue, the Parsee trusts for pardon in the mercy of God. "If any one commit sin," (says the Zarthosti Catechism), "under the belief that he shall be saved by somebody; both the deceiver as well as the deceived shall be damned to the day of Rastâ Khez" (the final restoration-day of all men and all spirits). "Your Saviour is your deeds and God Himself. He is the Pardoner and the Giver." (Müller, vol. i. p. 176.)

Midway through the millennium which separated the ages of Zoroaster and Christ, there was born in India the second great teacher who rent Brahminism in twain, and founded the religion which even now counts 450,000,000 disciples.

Buddha (the *Enlightened*) was the Auguste Comte of the East. He taught a noble morality,—without a God to command, or a heaven to reward it. He cut away the roots of all authority;—and immediately himself became a supreme and unquestionable authority, so that a few years after his death his followers held, "That which Buddha said, that alone was well said." He proposed[1] the idea of Humanity at large as the object of benevolence—and formed a scheme of politics subversive of the whole order of society. He taught his disciples to spend several hours a day in the repetition of prayers—and forbade them to suppose that any being in the universe paid them the slightest attention. Finally, he instructed mankind that after this life there is nothing to be hoped for—and that the highest virtue leads soonest to the state wherein virtue is at an end for ever.

Such are the original and still orthodox doctrines of Buddhism according to Professor Müller, M. de Saint-Hilaire, and Eugène Burnouf. Some doubt exists whether the book containing the metaphysics of Buddhism be really the record of his teachings or the original speculations of his pupil Kâsyapa; but, however this point may be settled, ancient and modern Buddhist literature bears too many testimonies to the atheism of the system, and too often defines the future Nirvana as empty nothingness, to permit us to deny that philosophic Buddhism is a religion without a God and without a heaven.[2]

A religion like this is an amazing portent in the history of human development. But does its appearance prove that the Religious Sentiment in man is a weak and variable impulse, the result of early impressions and to be swept

[1] Professor Müller says he originated this idea of Humanity. The above parallel between Buddha and Comte, however, is no way sanctioned by Professor Müller.

[2] See a very interesting little work, *The Modern Buddhist*, by a Siamese Minister of State. Translated by Henry Alabaster. One vol. 12mo. 1870.

away by the first strong hand which touches it? Has man indeed no sense of immortality which makes him start and shudder at the endless destruction of Nirvana?

Nay, but it seems to me that the very opposite lesson is taught by the story of Buddhism. The *truth* that was in the teaching of Buddha, even a beautiful, unselfish morality, the millions of the further East seized upon and spread from land to land with a missionary zeal never displayed before or since, save by the disciples of him who preached the Sermon on the Mount. But the dead, cold, hopeless theology linked with that living morality of Buddhism, those nations never truly accepted; and, ere long, he who had taught atheism was himself worshipped as an incarnate God (a god before he descended to earth, a god hearing prayers since he has ascended to heaven), and his Nirvana of nothingness and destruction has turned into a paradise where the blessed "hunger no more, neither thirst any more," for all holy desires have there their fruition. When Buddhism became the creed of millions, the Religious Sentiment of those millions remodelled their creed, and transformed an atheistic philosophy into a devout and hopeful religion.[1]

---

[1] On the subject of the above-assumed Atheism of Buddhism I am indebted to a friend for the following observations:—" It is no wise my wish to deny that large schools of the Buddhists in Ceylon, Thibet, China, and Siam, have in all ages been, and now are, Athiests. Only let it be remembered that from the first have existed other schools of Buddhists who were, and are, Theists. Be it also distinctly remembered that in each of these schools *Worship* has been inculcated,— the worship of Pragna (Nature), of the Buddhas (the Great Company of Saints), of Dharma (or the Law of Life), and, finally, the worship of Adi Buddha. . . . Of this Adi Buddha, take the following account from the ' Aiswarika System,'— the doctrine of 'Iswara,' or God, as opposed to the ' Swabhava,' or Nature-System :—' Know that when in the beginning all was perfect void and the five elements were not, then Adi Buddha, the Stainless, was revealed in the form of fire or light. He who is the form of all things became manifest. He is the Self-existent Great Buddha. He is the cause of all existences in the Three Worlds, and the cause of their well being also. From his profound meditation the universe was produced. He is the Iswara, the sum of perfections, the Infinite, void of members and passions. All things are types of him, and yet he

A most instructive picture of a religious Buddhist, when Buddhism was in its prime a thousand years ago, is given in these volumes in the sketch of the life of Hiouen Thsang, a Chinese whose warm devotion prompted him to travel to India to obtain the sacred books and visit the shrine of his faith. His journal, still existing, has been translated by M. Stanislas Julien, and reveals a character brave, pious, and humane, like a knight errant of chivalry. He lived praying perpetually to Buddha, endeavouring, like a Christian pilgrim, to behold visions and identify the scenes of Buddha's life. Finally he died with the prayer on his lips: "that in every future birth he might fulfil his duties towards Buddha, and arrive at last at the highest and most perfect intelligence."[1] Müller says: "Of selfishness we find no trace in him. His whole life belonged to the faith in which he was born, and the object of his labours was not so much to perfect himself as to benefit others." Such then is the religion of a good Buddhist. It does not much militate assuredly against the belief that man's Religious

was no type. Adi Buddha is without beginning. He is the essence of wisdom (or Absolute Truth). He knows all the past. He is without a second. He is omnipresent. As in a mirror we mortals see our forms reflected, so Adi Buddha is known in Creation. Adi Buddha has delight in making happy every sentient being. He tenderly loves those who serve him. He is the assuager of pain and grief. He is the giver of the ten virtues; the Creator of all the Buddhas, the Lord of the Universe.' How far do these passages, translated by B. H. Hodgson (to whom Eugène Burnouf owns his obligations), from the original Sanskrit works, disclose the primary form of Buddhism? The reply is, that these works are from Nepaul, in the vicinity of the birthplace of Buddhism, where we might expect to find the purest and oldest traditions. The original Sanskrit works must surely be at least as trustworthy as the Cingalese, Thibetan, and Chinese translations? . . . From these Nepaul works, then, it would appear that Sakya Muni Gautama was a heroic reformer who sought to redeem his people from their servitude to the Brahmanic hierarchy, metaphysics, and caste system, by teaching, and in his life illustrating, the True 'Way of Deliverance' from 'The Circle of Change.' He was an Atheist and an annihilationist in much the same sense as J. G. Fichte was when he taught that the Way towards the Blessed Life was by forsaking the transitory and perishable, and being one with the Eternal."

[1] *Chips*, vol. i. p. 276.

Sentiment is essentially the same, whether in the breast of an old Chinese, who probably never heard of Europe or Europe's faith, or in that of an Englishman of to-day; whether developed into the ecstatic piety of a Tauler, or with infantile weakness beginning (as men are said to have done in the American-Indian history quoted in these volumes) "not yet to worship the gods, *but only to turn their face up to heaven.*"[1]

The sacred canon of Buddhism was settled at the first synod, the Nicæan Council, of the new religion. The whole collection is called the *Tripitaka*, a word signifying Three Baskets. The first basket contains the *Sûtras* or discoveries of Buddha, compiled by his pupil Ananda. The second, the *Vinaya*, contains the code of morality, noted down by another pupil, Upâli. The third, the *Abhidharma*, contains the Buddhist system of metaphysics, arranged by a third pupil, Kâsyapa. Again there is a sacred canon of the Thibetan Buddhists, consisting of two immense collections called the *Kanjur* and *Tanjur*. The first consists of 108 folio volumes, comprising 1083 distinct works, and has been bartered for 7000 oxen. The Tanjur consists of 225 folios. Both have been printed by the Buddhists at Lhassa and at Pekin. The whole sacred literature of the Buddhists, including the *Lotus de la bonne Loi*, translated by M. Eugène Burnouf, the *Lalita Vistara*, or biography of Buddha, and the *Dhamma Padam*, or "Footsteps of the Law," is of such magnitude that though of late years innumerable MSS. have been discovered and many scholars engaged in their examination, a complete view of the subject is yet unattainable. Professor Müller has not (I regret to say) given us in these volumes any extracts from the Buddhist canon similar to those he has taken from the Vedas. A few pas-

---

[1] Popul Vuh—a supposed relic of the legendary history of Guatemala. *Chips*, vol. i. p. 337.

sages from the *Dhamma Padam* may give the reader an idea of the character of these books:

> Conquer anger by mildness, evil by good, falsehood by truth... Be not desirous of discovering the faults of others, but zealously guard against your own... Abstain from foolish conversation and from betraying the secrets of others. Abstain from coveting, from all evil wishes to others, from all unjust suspicion. To be free from sin, be contented, be grateful, subject to reproof, having a mind unshaken by prosperity and adversity. He is a more noble warrior who subdues himself than he who in battle conquers thousands... As the mighty rock Maha-meru-parvati remains unshaken by the storm, so is the wise unmoved by praise or disapprobation. All the religion of Buddha is contained in these three precepts: purify thy mind; abstain from vice; practise virtue. To the virtuous all is pure. Therefore think not that going unclothed, fasting or lying on the ground, can make the impure pure, for the mind will still remain the same.

Another precept commands every Buddhist before he sleeps to *wish well* to all mankind. Should there be a person towards whom he finds he cannot perform such an act of mental benevolence, he is further counselled to *resolve on doing that person some kindness*, when, it is added, he will find no further difficulty in wishing him well.

All virtues, says Professor Müller, in the Buddhist religion are said to spring from *maitrî*, and this *maitrî* can only be translated (Eugène Burnouf affirms) by the word "charity." "It does not express friendship," he says, "but that universal feeling which inspires us with good-will to all men, and constant willingness to help them."

Such are the precepts of Buddhism; precepts which many who have dwelt in Buddhist countries affirm to have a real practical influence on the lives of the millions by whom they are revered as divine revelation. Let us rejoice that so it should be, and that almost the largest of existing creeds— assuredly the largest of all, if we count the numbers of past generations—is not a mere mass of idle fable and corrupt rites, and that God has by no means "left himself without a witness" among these thronging myriads of His children. It is a strange reflection that among the departed whom we look to meet hereafter in the Land of Souls, the followers of Buddha must outnumber all the rest of that Company of Heaven to which we shall be admitted by

> The shadow cloaked from head to foot,
> Who keeps the keys of all the creeds.

Before quitting these interesting volumes, I must beg to question one remark of the author. His fact is no doubt correct, but the inference he draws from it seems to me seriously erroneous. The modern doctrine of the slow development of humanity through tens of thousands of years from lower types of animal life, is affirmed by Professor Müller to be exploded by the discovery of philologists, that language, so far as it can be traced back, is always human and rational, and always in a state of development. "The idea," he says (vol. ii. p. 8), "of a humanity emerging slowly from the depths of an animal brutality can never be maintained again." And why? Because "the earliest work of art wrought by the human mind, more ancient than any literary document, and prior to the first whisperings of tradition—the human language—forms an uninterrupted chain from the first dawn of history down to our own times." First, the Professor asserts, there was a period (to which he gives the name of *Rhematic*) when a language was spoken containing the germs of Turanian, Semitic, and Aryan speech. Then, in successive periods, these three divided and subdivided into all the languages of Europe and Asia: a Confusion of Tongues occupying some five thousand years, and going on at the present time.

But this slow evolution, and multiplication of species of language, is, if I mistake not, precisely analogous to that very development of *animal* species which the geologist traces in the successive strata of the earth's crust, and on which he founds his theory of progressive life. He, also, finds at the earlier periods, simpler forms; but forms even then beautiful and appropriate; and as he advances, he finds these forms of animal and vegetable life multiply in number and increase in complexity of organization. The very ground of his argument is, that such appears to have been the order of succession, and not the reverse process. That the first discovered relics of *language* are not senseless, but rational, and grammatically organized, is no more against the theory of human development than that the earliest known fossils are not chaotic lumps, but remains of organisms obviously well adapted to the conditions under which they once had life. In neither case have we reached the bottom of the strata. There may well have been a long succession of ages (on Darwin's hypothesis there was an immensely extended succession of ages) between the first existence of man and Professor Müller's Rhematic period of languages, or before any period of which, from the nature of the case, we can recover a trace. According to Professor Müller's own account, in another essay,[1] the first development of monotheism took place "when together with the awakening of ideas, the first attempts only were being made at expressing the simplest conceptions, by means of a language *most simple, most sensuous, and most unwieldy* "—a Saurian or Megatherium sort of language, in short, compared to agile Greek and stalwart English. We cannot possibly get below this to the very earliest formations or *azoic* rocks of language (if such there ever were), for the period to which they should belong could leave no relics behind, save such as we believe we have actually found, namely, bones and stone weapons. Surely the fair conclusion to be drawn from the facts is

[1] On Semitic Monotheism.

precisely the converse of that which the Professor has stated, namely, that in human Language, as in all other fields of inquiry, the evidence in favour of a slow progress from simple to complex, from the lower forms of life to the higher, is altogether complete and overwhelming?

Three modes of creation alone are imaginable:

A Retrograde Creation, ever falling back, like the works of human hands, from cosmos to chaos—the Creation of a Toy.

A Stagnant Creation, finished from the first and unchangeable—the Creation of a Stone.

A Progressive Creation, ever unfolding in beauty and joy —the Creation of a Flower.

Of these three, God has chosen that His world should be of the third order. Who is it that will say, He has not chosen well?

ESSAY X.

THE RELIGION AND LITERATURE OF INDIA.[1]

THE peculiar pleasure taken by Americans, like Washington Irving and Hawthorne, in exploring the nooks and corners of England and re-attaching the threads of tradition which connect their new country with the old home in Europe, might not inaptly be paralleled for us Englishmen, by the interest of researches concerning the progenitors of our whole Aryan stock in Persia and India. While antiquarians of the earlier school have been disputing what proportions of our language, laws, religion, and social customs are derived respectively from Saxons, Normans, Danes, Romans, and Celts, the students of Zend and Sanscrit literature have been occupied in revealing to us an ancestry, behind all the ancestries of which we had hitherto taken count; a primeval Home whence have come even the names of our closest relationships, and the fables and fairy-tales of our nurseries. Who would have dreamed heretofore that when an English parent spoke of his "daughter," he recalled, in that familiar word, the days, millenniums past, when the young maiden of the old Bactrian dwelling was "*she-who-milks-the-cows*," even as our legal term "spinster" reverts to the comparatively recent time when it was her task to "*spin*"? Who that told a child the heart-breaking tale

[1] *Ancient and Mediæval India.* By Mrs. Manning. Allen & Co., London, 1869. 2 vols. 8vo., pp. 435 and 380.

of Llewellyn's Dog, supposed that he was repeating a legend familiar to men of our blood who dwelt under the shadow of the Himalayas when busy England was a forest?

As yet the bearings of the great discoveries of Orientalists have been little apprehended. The innumerable points at which they must eventually impinge on our opinions yet wait to be marked. Even their most obvious theological consequences have been but casually noticed in any work of importance. But the time has nearly arrived when such a mass of new truths cannot lie inactive in the minds of the cultivated classes, but must begin to leaven all our views on etymology, history, philology, art, literature, and comparative theology. The share which the revived study of Greek at the Renaissance had in directing the movements of that great age, must in a certain partial degree have its parallel in the results of the modern acquisition of Sanskrit in our own. As one realm of Heathendom was rehabilitated then, and the devils with which mediæval imagination had peopled it vanished in the sunrise, so now another and yet wider field is conquered back from the kingdom of darkness to partake of our sympathies and widen our comprehension of human nature itself. A new world is given to the scholars of the day, and it will be hard if it does not in many ways "redress the balance" of the old.

A singular contrast may be traced between the new science of Indo-Persian antiquity and that which a little preceded it, of Egyptology. In opening up Egypt to us, Belzoni, Champollion, Wilkinson, and Lepsius gave us the material portion of a nation's life. In expounding the Vedas and the Zend-Avesta, Jones and Wilson and Max Müller and Haug and Burnouf have admitted us to the inner and spiritual part. The buildings and sculptures, the dress, utensils, toys, nay, the very bodies of the departed Egyptian race, all these the sands of the Nile have given back. But except the enigmatical, half-comprehensible "Book of the Dead," and a few fragments from papyri, all the scholars who have used Champollion's key to hieroglyphics have failed to present us with anything to be called even a specimen of Egyptian literature. Not merely is there no Iliad, no Ramayana of Africa, but not a single counterpart to a Pindaric Ode, or Vedic Hymn. Thus we know the Egyptians, even while their embalmed forms stand beside us in our studies, only as it were at second hand. We see what they *did*, and we infer what they *were*. But their hearts have never spoken to ours save in the touching cry of bereaved affection from a coffin-lid; or in the awful symbols on some grand sarcophagus, pointing like a dumb Job to death and judgment, and the faith that, over them both, Osiris the Redeemer liveth.

In India all this is reversed. We have recovered the inner life of the nation, but not the outward. Here, in the real *Juventus Mundi*—that youth which had already waned, ere Homer sang or David prayed—here dwelt the poet-prophets of the Vedas, in whose hymns we may read to-day of hopes and fears and doubts and speculations which once filled the hearts and stirred the brains, whose dust has been scattered for ages to the four winds. Here we have no mummies with their parody of immortality; no tombs stored with food and furniture and trinkets; no mural pictures showing us every detail of the battles and the agriculture and the trades of the dead nation. But though we have not one tangible object belonging to them, we have learned the very words of the men who wandered by the banks of Indus three thousand years ago, and possessing those words we are truly nearer to them as intelligent beings than we can ever hope to be to Egyptian or Ninevite.

India then, that same India over which our flag is flying from the Himalayas to Cape Comorin, is the field for literary research which offers the richest treasures yet to be explored. The Morning Land still keeps its dew, and it may yet be gathered fresh and sweet before the army of critics and commentators have marched over it and left us but dust.

A better devised book than the one I now purpose to notice it would not be easy to name. It aims to bring together within the compass of two goodly volumes a general bird's-eye view of all that has been yet disinterred of Indian literature, with the revelations thereby afforded of life in the Peninsula from the earliest Vedic ages onwards. The incomparable industry of the authoress in collecting and sifting the materials for so great a work, is fully equalled by the judgment shown in their selection. There is for the reader no wading through tedious or half-comprehensible passages, such as abound in the original Eastern books. The interesting and remarkable points in each old poem or story have been picked out, and the passages from remote works bearing on the same point collated; insomuch that the reader can enjoy in a few hours the fruits which it would have cost him a dozen years of study to gather for himself. As to the original matter carrying on the thread of the work, I can only regret that the writer did not give us much more of it; for the observations are always instructive, and often most suggestive and original. Great taste has also been shown in the selection of translations from various scholars, Wilson, Max Müller, Goldstücker, Muir, and others; sometimes affording us fragments of really harmonious poetry, and again, when accuracy of interpretation is more to the purpose, giving us quaint little bits of obvious literalism. In a word the book affords for Indian literature precisely the sort of museum which Dr. Gray desires the public collections to supply for Natural History. Instead of crowded ranges of objects good bad and indifferent over which the eye wanders idly and the mind wearies, we have a reasonable quantity of specimens carefully selected as the most characteristic and remarkable, some of them in the fullest glory which the taxidermist-translator can preserve; and others, perhaps still more instructively, prepared as skeletons. The review of a book which is itself a vast Review must of necessity be the briefest epitome. My object will be to afford some general idea of the sort of treasures to be found in this cabinet of "curiosities of literature."

Twelve centuries before the Christian era is the latest date to which competent scholars assign the final compilation of the Rig-Veda Hymns in the shape wherein they now stand. During all the intervening ages the absolutely divine honours paid to the book throughout India—honours even exceeding those which Jews, Moslems or Puritan Christians have paid to their scriptures—have probably secured for us the well-nigh unchanged transmission of each venerable verse. Of course the age of the Rishis, or sacred poets, who were the authors of the hymns, must ascend considerably higher in point of antiquity than the recension of their poems. To draw from their fragmentary allusions a picture of life as it then existed, is a task of great interest.

In the first place, it seems the Vedic Aryans had long migrated from the northern cradle of their race, and were settled in the part of India which lies between the Indus and the Saraswati. M. de Saint-Martin has identified most of the seven rivers mentioned in the Vedas as those of the Punjaub. Their enemies the Dasyus (literally "Robbers," a dark race, and probably the aborigines of the country, still infested their borders. They were given to agriculture, and used ploughs and carts drawn by oxen. They had roads, and caravanserais at distances along the roads. Metals were in common use, and gold coins called Nishkas were circulated. Gambling was a prevailing vice; several hymns alluding to it and deploring its results with those of intoxication. Women were not shut up in Zenanas, but appeared in public drawn in chariots, and are spoken of with tender affection. There is no evidence of the existence of castes at this earliest period, but they appear in the time of the Yajur-Veda. Trade was already flourishing. In the Rig-Veda it is said that "Merchants desirous of gain crowd the great waters with their ships." Kings, and wealthy men, were splendid in their habits, and the natural treasures of India were all discovered and used. Gold and gems were plentiful. Swift horses were highly estimated; the most precious of all sacrifices to the gods being the Aswamedha, or sacrifice of a horse. Elephants were tamed and greatly cherished; the God Indra being described in the Rig-Veda as invoked for their protection.

The religion of these Aryans of the Vedic times is a subject far too large and complicated to be here properly treated. Some of the passages of the sacred hymns throwing light upon it have been quoted in this volume in the preceding Essays. Our present author has drawn together a number of extracts from various translations, enabling the reader to form considerable acquaintance with the curious variety of incipient theologies and nascent philosophies which are bound up together even in the first and oldest Veda. The prevailing principle seems to be, that while the Nature-gods, the Sky, Heaven, Fire, the Sun, the Dawn, etc., are all separately adored, the particular god who is invoked in any hymn is, for the time being, nearly always identified as supreme and universal. One god has many names, and sometimes bears the name of another god; metaphysical ideas are deified; and, in a very prominent manner, Agni (or common domestic fire) is treated as the earthly representative of the Sun. Noble psalms of praise, and touching entreaties for the forgiveness of sins, are made to these beings when contemplated as supreme; but the whole system is evidently as yet inchoate and in a fluid state. We cannot but surmise that, if at that period a Zoroaster or Moses or Buddha had been born in the Punjaub, he would have seized on the yet vague aspirations of his countrymen, and moulded them into a defined creed. But Brahminism was then, and has ever since been, a religion (perhaps the only religion in the world), not tracing its origin to one mediatorial prophet-soul. Everywhere else in East and West we find faith clinging to some one great name, some man or demi-god to whom weaker mortals look and cry, "Thy God shall be our God: what thou hast seen, that can we take on thy assurance;" some Moses who has seen Jehovah on the mount of vision, and the reflected glory of whose face suffices to convince the herd. Brahminism has had a host of major and minor prophets, during its five and thirty centuries of sway, from the old Rishis who wrote the Rig-Veda to their followers who added the Upanishads and Dharma Sastras, and the modern Brahmins who write nothing at all. But it has had no Zoroaster, no Moses, no Mahomet.

The modifications which the early Vedic faith underwent in the course of ages offers a study no less difficult than its original form; or rather formlessness. Not a trace of the *Trimurti* of Brahma, Seeva, and Vishnu, which now occupies the summit of the Hindoo pantheon, can be found for ages after the Vedic period, and the whole gross and hideous mythology of later times was then unborn.

Taking these slight clues in hand the reader cannot fail to be interested in the passages selected by Mrs. Manning, as displaying the moral and philosophic feelings and thoughts of the authors of the most ancient Vedas. These authors, it appears, were seven, or (on better authority, according to

Max Müller) eight poets, called *Rishis*. The families of these poets were in after-times all registered, and became the depositaries of the eight *Mandalas* or books, into which the collection of hymns was divided. The most interesting of these Rishis were two, to whose lives and doings constant reference in after-times was made, namely Vasishta and Viswâmitra. Strange to say, here almost in the earliest glimpse of human religion we find the representatives of the Priest and of the Prophet. Vasishta is the author of the most touching hymns in the Vedas; or as the Hindoos would express it he is the Seer to whom they were divinely communicated. "They are," says Mrs. Manning, "simple genuine utterances, confessing sin, and yearning after an unknown God." Viswâmitra, on the other hand, was a powerful soldier, the originator of the great religious ceremonies and the composer of psalms of the cursing order: "May the vile wretch who hates us fall! May his breath of life depart! As the tree suffers from the axe, as the flower is cut off, as the cauldron, leaking, scatters foam, so may mine enemy perish!"[1]

So important were these two Rishis that their names became typical in Hindoo story, and re-appear as living personages long ages after the date of the Vedas. In the Ramayana each of them plays an important and characteristic part, much as the names of Isaiah and Daniel were revived in writings supposed to carry on their ideas and sentiments.

In reviewing Mrs. Manning's quotations, the difficulty must not be forgotten of obtaining anything like a veritable translation of a single sentence of an ancient book. Two errors constantly beset all efforts to attain such an end. One is the production of a mere cloud of words, each having perhaps some pretension to be the best known rendering of the original, but forming altogether in their syntax

[1] Muir, *Original Sanskrit Texts*, vol. i. p. 372.

something extremely like nonsense. Such translations the English reader very properly declines to accept as the pregnant sentences which have held their place as inspired oracles among civilized nations for thousands of years. The other error is the rendering of the ancient book, not only into the words, but into the thoughts of modern Europe, so that we possess in the supposed translation, not what an Eastern poet said thirty centuries ago, but what an Englishman would say for him if set down with the heads of his subject dictated. This last error was more common among the older generation of scholars than the present, and few things are more mortifying to the humble student who has built up his theories of ancient religion and morality on the supposed fidelity of their translations than to find the ground taken from under him by a new translator who assures him that the text in question is a mere Christian paraphrase of the original, and that there is nothing in the Sanskrit or Zend to warrant his deductions. For an example of this sort of thing we have no need to go beyond the famous Gâyatri, or holiest text of the Vedas, in the third Mandala of the Rig-Veda, a verse specially interesting, as it has been repeated by millions of pious Hindoos every morning for at least three thousand years. It was translated by Sir William Jones thus: "Let us adore the supremacy of that Divine Sun, the Godhead, who illuminates all, who recreates all, from whom all proceed, to whom all must return; whom we invoke to direct our understandings aright in our progress towards His holy seat."[1] Our present authoress, following (doubtless correctly) the greater accuracy of Professor Wilson,[2] gives us this magnificent prayer reduced to the following distressing dimensions: "We meditate on that desirable light of the divine Savitri (the Sun-God), who influences our pious rites"!

[1] *Works*, vol. xiii. p. 367. [2] *Works*, vol. xiii. p. 367.

The secret of the rise and progress of the priesthood in India, till it culminated in the monstrous usurpation of the Brahmins of recent ages, is a problem full of interest, and not devoid of instruction even for us in England in the nineteenth century. Nothing can be more antihistorical than the notion of Voltaire and his compeers that the various priesthoods of Heathendom, the bonzes, talapoins, and Druids, whom he so delighted to ridicule and abuse, were thoroughly wide-awake sceptics, wholly free from the superstitions of their flocks and playing upon them with conscious hypocrisy. Common sense shows us that even the foremost men of each age and country have their minds so imbued and dyed with the belief and sentiments among which they have been brought up that it is at most only a question of a few shades lighter or darker between them and their contemporaries and compatriots. The exercise of the priestly office tends probably in a greater degree than that of any other profession to impress the character, and create a new type for itself. But the priestly mind so moulded, is the reverse of a sceptical one. It was because the French abbés were so little like priests, and so much like men of the world, that they shrugged their shoulders at the Mass. Human nature, ecclesiastical or otherwise, leads men to magnify, not to disparage, their own functions. "Nothing like leather," cries the shoemaker; and it would be marvellous indeed if the individual who is recognized by others as exercising the highest of all possible offices, even that of an Ambassador of Heaven, should make light of his mission. St. Paul thought it was actually a logical argument to prove immortality, that "if the dead rise not, then are we of all men the most miserable." Every minister of religion must similarly feel driven to believe that the faith to which his whole life is devoted is true, or else he is of all men most silly;—

instead of (as he constantly affirms) all men the only one truly wise.

The Brahmins were then undoubtedly men who believed in themselves, their gods, and their office. But such genuine faith by no means excluded an equally clear confidence in the utility of judicious appeals to the hopes and fears of their disciples, entailing the usual amount of impudent assertion of special Divine favour, and superstitious reliance on magical ceremonies. Here in the very dawn of the world we find the two leading features of priestcraft fully marked already. The priest places himself as the indispensable mediator between the layman and the Deity; and his power to influence the gods is exercised through the medium of sacramental rites, to which he affirms that he alone can give efficacy.

Among the earliest functions of the Indian priestly tribe was that of *Purohita* or house-priest attached to a princely household. An old Aryan, like an old Israelite, thought that good fortune would surely befall him if he could but have "a Levite to be his priest"; and the Hindoo Levite was in no way slow to impress on him the truth of such a conviction. Accordingly the Rishi Vamadeva says (p. 70):

The king before whom there walks a priest lives well established in his own house; to him the earth yields for ever, and before him the people bow of their own accord. Unopposed he conquers treasures. The gods protect him.

Threats against recalcitrants who would not pay priestly dues were of corresponding strength. In the Rig-Veda, x. 160, a wealthy man who offers no libation is "grasped in the fist by Indra and slain." Complaints of "niggards" and "men who give nothing" are as common as in the addresses of Irish parish priests from their altars. If a wicked king eat a Brahmin's cow he is assured he will find the beef poisonous. "The priest's tongue is a bow-string, his voice is a barb, and his wind-pipe is an arrow-point smeared with fire." In the Atharva-Veda (v. 18), it is declared that, "Whenever a king fancying himself mighty seeks to devour a Brahmin, his kingdom is broken up. Ruin overflows it as water swamps a leaky boat." Highly edifying tales of kings who gave their priests fabulous bribes of thousands of girls and tens of thousands of elephants, and were divinely rewarded accordingly, are likewise plentiful. The last chapter of the Aitareya Brahmana tells us that, "The gods do not eat the food of a king who keeps no house-priest. Even when not intending to make a sacrifice, a king should appoint a house-priest." Nor is it only in purse that the king has to pay for the spiritual advantages, but also in person. One part of the ceremony of appointing a house-priest requires that the king wash the holy man's feet: doubtless a wholesome exercise of humility wherewith to commence future relations.

But the Brahmins evidently placed their grand reliance, beyond what threats and promises could afford them, on the influence to be obtained through the use of an elaborate and splendid *cultus*. The principle in human nature which leads us to feel attachment for whatever costs us much, has been doubtless understood by the founders of all religions. How much of the Jews' devotion to their faith has been due, not only to its purity and grandeur, but also to the sharpness of the impression ploughed into their minds during thirty centuries by the perpetual repetition of the Mosaic feasts and ceremonies, it would be impossible to say. As one of the ablest living Jews, Philipssohn, has remarked, these rites built up the nation into a citadel, wherein the truth of the Divine Unity was lodged, to be preserved for ever as in the fortress of the human race.

And to the natural influence of ceremonies on the minds

of the men who share in their performance, the Brahmins added the wildest belief in their efficacy as celestial machinery capable of compelling the Deity. Few weaknesses of human nature afford a more curious study than this, the all but ubiquitous belief in the efficacy of magic ceremonies, as contradistinguished from spiritual prayer. That a man, himself capable of being moved by the entreaty of his children, should believe that his Creator may be touched by his own imploring cry is natural and obvious. But that the same man, who would only be vexed by the performance before him of unmeaning and wearisome ceremonial antics, should suppose that a higher being than himself takes especial delight in them, and becomes through their means favourable to the antic-maker's wishes, this is truly paradoxical. Yet the belief seems almost ineradicable! In vain for three thousand years have the world's greatest prophets denounced it. Isaiah and Micah might as well have held their peace for all the attention which Europe or Asia have paid to their arguments. At this very hour, a not inconsiderable section of the national church of this Protestant country labours with might and main to revive the faith in the magical efficacy of one class of such observances; and to send us back from beautiful symbols of self-abnegation and self-consecration to the heathenism of "feeding on a sacrifice," precisely as if no one had ever asked, "Of what avail your sacrifices? Cease to do evil. Learn to do well."

In no religion does the notion of formal sacrifice seem to have reached a greater height of absurdity than in Brahminism. Southey's "Curse of Kehama" has rendered some notion of it familiar to us. "He who knows the proper application of sacrifice," says Haug, "is in fact considered as the real master of the world, for any desire he can entertain may be thus gratified. The Yajna (sacrifice) taken as a whole is looked on as a machine every piece of which must tally with another; or as a staircase by which one may ascend to heaven. It exists from eternity. The creation of the world is the fruit of sacrifice." This wonder-working sacrifice is, alas! all the time, *not* a grand act of devotion or self-immolation, but simply the accurate performance of a complicated ritual observance involving in one case the slaughter of a horse, and in another the preparation and drinking of the juice of a particular herb. In the fifth chapter of her book, Mrs. Manning has given us very curious details of the forms belonging to the most interesting of these rites, the Soma-sacrifice, accompanied by a plan of the hall or inclosure prepared for its celebration. Her information is derived from Dr. Haug, who actually induced a Srotriya Brahmin, properly qualified by "Apostolic succession," to rehearse the whole ceremony for his edification in a secluded corner of his own premises—of course not without a suitable "consideration," though we presume a lesser one than in the good old time when, we are told, the *honoraire* of the Hotri, or celebrant, was a fee of one hundred and twelve cows. Nothing was ever devised more intricate than these rites with their innumerable little fires and seats and posts, and processions up and down and round about. The shortest period expended in their performance is five days, and we are informed that they *may* last a thousand years. The most curious point about the whole ceremony however is one which I wish that Mrs. Manning had brought out with greater distinctness. It is that it includes both a Baptism and a Eucharist; a rite intended to signify Regeneration, and a rite consisting in "feeding on a sacrifice"; and drinking a liquid which is itself frequently described as a god, and which receives adoration.

The baptismal part of the ceremony, Mrs. Manning says,

was apparently suggested by "a feeling nearly akin to belief in original sin":—

The gods, and especially Vishnu and Agni (fire), are invoked to come to the offering with the Dikshâ. Dikshâ, we are told, means "a new birth." Agni as fire, and Vishnu as the sun, are invoked to cleanse the sacrificer. The worshipper is then covered up in a cloth, on the outside of which is placed the skin of a black antelope; and after a certain time has elapsed and specified prayers have been recited, the New Birth is considered to have been accomplished, and the regenerated man descends to bathe.

As the proper nourishment of a new-born child is milk, the regenerated sacrificer is, after baptism, made to drink milk by the aid of a special spoon. After many more tedious operations, he is prepared for the great ceremony of the fifth day, when the Soma is consecrated by the seven assistant priests, and drunk by them and the sacrificer at morning, midday and evening. Our authoress has given us a drawing of the plant from which the Soma juice is crushed, and we are informed in a note, that it is the *Asclepias Acida* of Roxburgh, now more commonly called the Sarcostema Viminalis, or Sarcostema Brevistigma. It has hardly perceptible leaves, small sweet white flowers, and yields a pure milky juice of an acid flavour in great abundance. It grows on the hills of the Punjaub and the Coromandel coast; but to make it sacrificially efficacious, it must, like the mandrake, be "plucked by night," by moonlight, and torn up by the roots, not cut down. When so gathered it must be carried on a cart drawn by two he-goats. The Soma thus obtained is much more in the Brahmin theology than a mere object of sacrifice or symbol. All other things connected with sacrifice, the horn, the post, the kettle, and even the ladle, are all praised in extravagant terms as sacred; but the Soma alone, "becomes an independent deity. The beverage is divine; it purifies, it is a water of life, it gives health and immortality." Muir has translated a hymn concerning it from the Rig-Veda, viii. 88:—

> We've quaffed the Soma bright,
>   And are immortal grown ;
> We've entered into light,
>   And all the gods have known.
> What mortal now can harm,
>   Or foeman vex us more ?
> Through thee beyond alarm,
>   Immortal God ! we soar.

I have discussed in a preceding essay the obscure question of the nature of the original sacred plant for which the Brahmins seem to have substituted the Asclepias. The juice of the latter does not appear to be intoxicating, as the true Soma must undoubtedly have been.

The third means by which the Brahmins assured their power was also not without significance. They did not approve of "secular education." Like M. Dupanloup, they desired that the young should be brought up very literally "aux genoux de l'église." "Godless Colleges" were unheard of in Ancient India. The laborious care with which all students were affiliated to "spiritual fathers," and instructed by them in the duty of ordering themselves lowly and reverently to pastors and masters, is extremely clear. There never was, and never could be, a "Young India," till English rule had left space for the growth of so portentous a plant. Every youthful Brahmin was required to live twelve years with his Brahmin tutor, called his Guroo, and was *permitted* to spend forty-eight years, if he pleased, as a student. The lessons consisted mainly in the acquirement of the holy verses orally and by heart. There were also "Parishads" or universities for older students; institutions whose fame still lingers in the north-west of India.

I now proceed to offer, following our authoress's guidance, a brief synopsis of Sanskrit literature.

At the head of all, and always assigned by far the highest honours, are the Four Vedas.

1. The *Rig-Veda*, the most ancient and sacred of all Sanskrit books. It consists of all the oldest hymns.

2. The *Sama-Veda*. This book consists of hymns, nearly all of which are also to be found in the Rig-Veda, but are here arranged in order to be chaunted by the priests.

3. The *Yajur-Veda* consists of various rituals and liturgies. The whole of this Veda is considerably more recent than the two former. As already remarked, the institution of caste first appears in it. The Yajur-Veda is itself of two distinct epochs—the older portion is called the Black, and the latter the White Yajur-Veda. As *the* sacrificial Veda (as its name imports), it obtains great respect, and is spoken of by some of the commentators as superior to all the other Vedas; just as the Book of Leviticus might have been perhaps regarded by a Rabbin as more important than the Psalms.

4. The *Atharva-Veda*, consisting of both hymns and prose pieces, belonging to a later age and marked by a peculiarly servile and cringing spirit.

Added to the Sanhita or hymns which it contains, each Veda has a portion called its *Brahmana*.

The *Aitareya Brahmana*, belonging to the Rig-Veda, consists of eight books of prayers, proper for the Soma sacrifice; and narrations connected with it and other sacrifices.

The Sama-Veda has eight Brahmanas attached to it; but their contents are not fully known. They appear to refer to various incantations.

The Satapatha Brahmana belongs to the White or later Yajur-Veda. It describes sundry pastoral festivals and ceremonies, especially those of the full moon. The most important portion, however, consists of strange speculations on the origin of things. Some of these are wild in the extreme. "Prajapati," for instance, the source of all created things, is himself described as the seven Rishis in one person; while other notions about sin, death, and immortality, are to us quite inexplicable. In this Brahmana we find many allusions to *Manu*, the originator of all worship; the ancestor of the Aryan Hindoos; the original MAN, from whom the Sanskrit, and our own word for a human being, is derived. The German *Mannus*, the ancestor of the Teutons, can hardly fail to be identified with this mythological patriarch of the whole Aryan family.

Again, beyond the four Vedas and their Brahmanas, the next order of compositions are mystic writings called *Aranyakas* and *Upanishads*, supposed to be supplementary to the former scriptures. One of these, the *Brihad Aranyaka*, contains a passage so curious that I cannot pass it over. It is in the form of a dialogue between a Brahmin and his wife. The wife asks:—

"What my lord knoweth of immortality may he tell me?"

Yajnavalkya replied: "Thou, who art truly dear to me, thou speakest dear words. Sit down. I will explain it to thee. . . . A husband is loved, not because we love the husband, but because we love in him the Divine Spirit. A wife is loved, not because we love her, but because we love in her the Divine Spirit. . . . It is with us when we enter the Divine Spirit, as if a lump of salt was thrown into the sea. It cannot be taken out again. The water becomes salt, but the salt disappears. When we have passed away, there is no longer any name. This I tell thee, my wife."

Maitriyi said: "My lord, thou hast bewildered me, saying that there is no longer any name, when we have passed away."

The philosophic husband replies to this feminine "longing after immortality" by observing that what he has told her is "sufficient to the highest knowledge," and that as the Divine Self is all in all, there cannot be any other immortality for man than that of the lump of salt. "Having said this,

Yajnavalkya left his wife for ever and went into the solitude of the forests." A very logical conclusion! Other people beside the poor puzzled wife (our authoress observes) were dissatisfied as time went on with the salt theory of existence, and the doctrine of transmigration was projected out of their aspirations, till it became at last a portion of the national creed, in whose earlier form it had no place. "A living dog," said the Jew, "is better than a dead lion." "It is better to live an individual existence," said the heart of Hindoo humanity, "even as a snake or a rat, than to be absorbed and lost in Deity like the lump of salt in the sea."

Beside the *Aranyakas*, and of the same character with them, are the *Upanishads*, which are the portion of Sanskrit literature chiefly studied by modern Hindoos, and possessed of the greatest philosophical interest. The word Upanishad is supposed to mean "secret," and the books bearing that name are treatises attempting to solve the great secrets of the universe; the nature of God, and of the soul, and the history of creation. They are somewhat numerous, and were composed by various independent thinkers at different times. The writers' names are never mentioned. "They appear," says Mrs. Manning, "to have been possessed by an ardent spirit of aspiration of which Sanskrit religious literature is the result and the exponent."

Many of the Upanishads have been translated into English, and contain some of the best known expressions of Hindoo piety. In one of them, the *Talavakara Upanishad*, the following fine thoughts concerning the nature of God are to be found :—

Know that that which does not see by the eye, but by which the eyes see—is Brahma.

Know that that which does not hear by the ear, but by which the ears hear—is Brahma.

Know that that which does not breathe by breath, but that by which breath is breathed—is Brahma.

.... By him who thinks that Brahma is not comprehended, by him He is comprehended.

He who thinks that Brahma is comprehended, he does not know Him.

Another Upanishad has the acute observation: "He who has reverence acquires faith. The reverent alone possesses faith. He who can control his passions possesses reverence."

After giving us a sketch of the Vedas, the Aranyakas, and Upanishads, of which the above is an epitome, Mrs. Manning proceeds with great clearness and ability to draw the outlines of the Hindoo systems of philosophy. Into the rarefied air of these acute speculations we need not ascend very far. The underlying conception of all was the existence of a Supreme Soul (variously called Brahma, Brihaspati, Viswakarman, Atman, Parabrahm, and Iswara), and that He is the only reality, all else being perishable and delusive. More or less personality is attributed to this Supreme Soul in different systems. The metempsychosis, which was unknown to the Rishis of the Vedas, here occupies a prominent place in all speculations, and the means of escape from perpetual transformation by absorption in the Supreme Soul is the practical aim of every philosophy.

There are six recognized systems, or Darsanas, of Hindoo philosophy. The first is the *Sankhya* system, taught by Kapila. Its principal doctrine is, that rest from transmigration is to be obtained by true knowledge, and that true knowledge consists in regarding man and the world as altogether worthless and perishable. Kapila added little or nothing about the eternal Reality behind these transitory things, and this (not unimportant!) portion of the scheme was completed by Patanjali, forming the second or *Yoga* system of philosophy. Patanjali's four chapters are appended in the best manuscripts to the Sutras (or leaves) of

Kapila; and form together the work called *Sankhyapravachana*.

The third philosophic system is the *Nyayi* of Gotama, which again was supplemented by the *Vaiseshika* or fourth system of Kanada. These two Darsanas both occupy themselves with elaborate investigations into the mental constitution of man and the laws of logic, as means for the attainment of true knowledge. Lastly, the fifth and sixth systems are called the *Purva Mimansa* and the *Uttara Mimansa*; the first originated by Jaimini, and the second by the eminent sage Vyasa, whose name we find Indian Brahmos of the present day associating with the Western prophets and teachers, for whom they desire to express the greatest respect. It is this last system, the Uttara Mimansa of Vyasa, to which the title of *Vedanta*, familiar to English ears, is applied; the word meaning "the ultimate aim of the Vedas." All the other systems of philosophy recognize the Vedas as sacred, but the two Mimansas treat them as absolute revelation, and are in fact commentaries and interpretations of their earlier and later portions. "The Vedanta," says our authoress, "simply teaches that the universe emanates in successive developments from Brahma or Paramatman, the Supreme Soul; that man's soul is identical in origin with the Supreme Soul; and that liberation from transmigration will be obtained so soon as man *knows* his soul to be one with the Supreme Soul." The Vedanta system represents the religion of Hindoo philosophy, or rather the religion of philosophers. "To suppose that men who accepted the Sankhya or Nyaya systems would therefore take no interest in the Vedanta would be somewhat like supposing that if a man studied Aristotle he would necessarily despise the Psalms." The great Hindoo theologian Sankara Acharya, of whose poem, the *Atma-Bodha*, Mrs. Manning proceeds to give an account, was an enthusiastic Vedantist. As a glimpse of the ocean of uncertain chronology on which we are sailing, we may remark that the age of this teacher is placed by tradition at about 200 B.C., and that H. H. Wilson brings him down to the eighth or ninth century A.D.

Before quitting the subject of Hindoo religious philosophy, our authoress is obliged to interpolate a notice of a most remarkable work—the *Bhagavad Gita*—whose assigned place is an episode of the great epic poem, the *Mahabharata*; but whose purport is wholly religious and philosophical. The effect of the interpolation of such a treatise into the middle of the heroic tale is, to our western feeling, not a little grotesque; and much as if a chapter of Thomas Aquinas had got itself wedged into the "Nibelungen Lied," or the opening of Hooker's "Ecclesiastical Polity" were to be found in the middle of the "Faerie Queen." The story of the Mahabharata has conducted us to the eve of a tremendous battle. Two armies are drawn up in array, the trumpet sounds for the charge, and the combatants rush half-way to meet each other. At this appropriate moment Arjuna, the hero, bids Krishna, his divine charioteer, stop and discuss with him the mysteries of the universe, through eighteen chapters, terminating in a grand solution of the—to us—all too familiar controversy of Faith *versus* Works!

Absurd as is this *mise en scène*, the poem in question contains some of the noblest thoughts to be found in any language. It has long been known by means of Wilkins' translation to that rather small section of "general readers" who peruse Eastern books. There are to be found in it such passages as the following:

> A man attains perfection by being satisfied with his own office, and worshipping Him from whom all things have their origin. Better to perform one's own duty, though it be devoid of excellence, than to do well the duty of another. Krishna says: "This is a kingly

science and a kingly mystery. All this universe has been created by me. All things exist in me. I am the father, mother, sustainer of this universe. Even those who worship other gods worship me. . . . I am the same to all beings. Even those who are born in sin, even women and Sudras take the highest path if they come to me.

The eleventh chapter contains a very remarkable scene, in which Krishna, at Arjuna's entreaty, shows himself in his proper form:

Gifted with many mouths and eyes, with many wonderful appearances, with many divine ornaments, holding many celestial weapons, wearing celestial wreaths and robes, anointed with celestial perfumes, the all-miraculous infinite Deity with his face turned in all directions! If the light of a thousand suns were to break forth in the sky at the same time, it would be similar to the brilliance of that mighty One.

Those amongst us who feel disposed to despise such a vision as evidence of heathenish conceptions of Deity may perhaps do well to remember that the Hebrews, even while they asserted that "no man could see God and live," yet believed that the Seventy Elders on the Mount had "seen the God of Israel," "as it were a jasper and a sardine stone," and with "the appearance of fire."

The main drift of the whole Bhagavad Gita is to show that the philosophy which taught that liberation comes from knowledge, must yet be supplemented by obedience and virtue.

Passing from both Vedas and philosophical Darsanas, we arrive at the *Puranas*, which belong to a still later age—probably about the ninth century A.D. They were eighteen in number, and are, says Wilson, among the most popular works in the Sanskrit language. Feasts are regulated by them, and texts quoted from them have validity in civil as well as religious law. Vishnu, often identified with Brahma, is here the ruling god; and the means of propitiating him, or becoming united with him, occupy a large portion of the contents of the Puranas.

Next below the Puranas come the *Tantras*, which appear to concern themselves with mystical and debasing rites. While the Puranas are used by the educated classes, the Tantras are "patronized by the less respectable members of Hindoo society."

A very important class of books now comes into view, the *Dharma Sastras* or law-books of India. The first and chief of these is the celebrated *Institutes of Menu*, translated by Sir William Jones, and formerly assigned by Orientalists an antiquity of B.C. 1200, but now brought down to a much more recent date. The name of the book, says Mrs. Manning, is itself a kind of pious fraud, for the "laws" are merely the laws or customs of a school or association of Hindoos called the Manavas, who lived on the banks of the Saraswati, and were an energetic and prosperous people. Their system seems to have worked so well that it was adopted by other communities, and then the organizers announced it as a code given to men by their divine progenitor Manu, or Menu. They added also passages which assert the *quasi* divine claims of Brahmins, but a great deal of this portion of the Code seems to have existed only in theory, and never to have had practical validity. In Sanskrit plays and poems, where the real state of things is betrayed, weak and indigent Brahmins are not infrequent; and Sudras are found to have political rights. The whole of the authoress's synopsis of this most curious work amply deserves study. Space can only be spared here to remark on one of its topics; the regulations of domestic life.

The condition of women in India seems to have constantly deteriorated since the Vedic ages. At the time of the Institutes of Menu it had reached a stage of absolute *subjection*, but had yet something worse to fall to, the *abjection* of the modern practice of incarceration for life, and death by suttee. "Day and night," say the *Institutes* (chap. ix.

vv. 2, 3, etc.), "must women be held by their protectors in a state of dependence. Their fathers protect them in childhood, their husbands in youth, their sons in age. A woman is never fit for independence. . . . Women have no business with the texts of the Vedas. Having therefore no evidence of law and no knowledge of expiating tests, sinful women must be as foul as falsehood itself. . . . She who keeps in subjection to her lord her heart, her speech and her body shall attain his mansion in heaven. . . Even if a husband be devoid of good qualities or enamoured of another woman, yet must he be constantly revered as a god by a virtuous wife." The Code does not hint at the practice of widow-burning; but by making the position of single women and widows absolutely unbearable, the ground was laid for the two great crimes of later ages against women, viz., infanticide and suttee. The stupendous selfishness of men, who were not content with reducing a woman, body and soul, to the adoring and unreasoning dependence of a dog during the life of her husband, but required her, after his death, to "emaciate her body, live on flowers, and perform harsh duties, till death," led to these not unnatural results. They were the most merciful mothers who put their female children out of a world which offered them no mercy; and perhaps not the most unmerciful Brahmins who urged the widows to terminate their miseries on the funeral pile. The way in which, while all this was going on, the great poets of the Ramayana and Mahabharata, and the dramatists of later days, continued to idealize women, and represent them as perfect angels of heroism and devotion, would be astonishing did we not remember that the same thing happened in Greece; and that Sophocles drew Antigone, and Euripides, Alcestis, when the real "woman of the period" was either shut up in her *gynækonitis*, or came out of it only as one of the *hetæræ*. The man, as a poet, liked to imagine woman free and noble. The man, as a husband and citizen, was perfectly content to keep her a prisoner for life and to leave her to be burned to death with his corpse as her final reward and glorification.

At the present day in India it is an ordinary thing for a lady to be born in the upstairs zenana, and never once to have trodden the earth, even of the most confined garden, before she is borne to her grave. What misery existence must be among a knot of women thus immured together with nothing but their loves and hatreds and jealousies to brood upon, is awful and piteous to think of. Every house in India, belonging to the higher classes, must be a convent peopled with Starrs and Saurins. That the whole population, male and female, should be physically and morally weak when their mothers have undergone for centuries such a *régime*, is inevitable. The Hindoos have spoiled the lives of their wives and daughters, and Nemesis has spoiled theirs, and made them the easy prey of their Saxon conquerors, whose ancestors were naked savages when they were a splendid and cultured race, but whose women, even in those old days of Tacitus, were " thought to have in them somewhat of the Divinity." The marvel is not that Hindoos are what we find them, but that any race can have survived so long such a monstrous infraction of natural laws. Most marvellous of all is it, that Hindoo women with the "set of their brains," as we should think, turned to idiotcy through centuries of caged-up mothers, yet display, when rare occasions offer, no mean share of some of the higher forms of human intelligence. At this moment the Brahmos are congratulating themselves on the appearance of a Bengalee poetess who composes beautiful hymns suitable for theistic worship; and Mr. Mill has borne testimony to his official experience in India of the extraordinary aptitude for government of such Hindoo princesses as have ruled as regents for their sons. "If," he says, "a Hindoo principality is strongly, vigilantly, and economically governed, if order is preserved without oppression, if cultivation is extending and the people prosperous, in three cases out of four that principality is under a woman's rule. This fact—to me," he adds, "an entirely unexpected one—I have collected from a long official knowledge of Hindoo governments."

After the Institutes of Menu come the Codes of *Yajnavalkya* and *Parasara*. To all these are attributed the rank of *Smriti* or Divine Revelation. But (as has happened elsewhere) infallible books were found ere long to need infallible interpretations; and commentaries and digests of these inspired codes soon multiplied, and became almost as important as the codes themselves. Mrs. Manning gives some account of these, and then proceeds to write some singularly interesting chapters on Hindoo Medicine, Astronomy, Grammar, and Architecture. With regret I must leave this part of her work aside as incapable of compression, and turn to her second volume, which is devoted to what may be called the secular literature of India, with a supplementary chapter on Commerce and Manufacture.

The traveller who has familiarized himself with the streets of beautiful Florence and proceeds from thence to Pisa, is apt to feel somewhat confused as to identity of place. There is the same Arno, and a very similar Lung-Arno with rows of palaces. But the one city is lonely and strange and the other bright and full of vigorous life; and between the two he feels as we do in a dream when we imagine we see a place or person and yet find them altogether other than we know them to be. Very similar sensations must surely have been experienced by the European scholars who discovered the great Hindoo poems, and, like the Ancient Mariner, were the first

> that ever burst
> Into that silent sea.

Here were all the forms of art to which they had been accustomed, and of which Greece was deemed the very creatrix. Here were long grand Epics, and here were noble dramas, and lyrics, and tales, and even fables, from which those of Æsop seemed borrowed. It was another and a complete cycle of literature; yet, in each case, the resemblance was incomplete, the forms less perfect, the legends more wild and seemingly often unmeaning; the unities more neglected. That one great miracle-age of Grecian art had not indeed repeated itself in India. Kalidasa could not take rank beside Sophocles any more than the Rishis of the Vedas could rank beside the Psalmists of Israel. But yet there was power, beauty, originality in the Sanskrit poems, such as almost constituted an equal wonder, falling, as they did spontaneously, into such closely corresponding forms.

The reader who will give the volume before us a perusal cannot, we think, fail to be amazed at the richness of imagination and the delicacy of natural sentiment displayed in the Hindoo poems. Unfortunately, the limited space of a review necessarily forbids even an attempt to convey those qualities, and the most which can be done here is to give a bare *résumé* of the character of the work whose choice flowers Mrs. Manning has gathered into a splendid bouquet.

The two poems which bear to Hindoo literature the relation which the Odyssey and the Iliad do to that of Greece, and which have been almost equally prized by the nation to which they belong, are the *Ramayana* and the *Mahabharata*. The age of both is presumed to be considerably anterior to the Christian era; and at all events to be earlier than that of the great Codes of Hindoo law. The Ramayana is a complete poem, composed by the poet Valmiki. The Mahabharata is a vast piece composed at different times and by different authors, some before and some after the age of the Ramayana. The story narrated in the Ramayana, is that of the hero Rama, now worshipped in India as a god, and represented as one of the incarnations of Vishnu. He is described as the son of the King of Ayodya (the modern Oude), and is born, like most other heroes of fable, semi-miraculously. The adventures of Rama and his faithful wife Sita, are some of them touching, some absurd; the chief being the carrying off of Sita by Ravana, the demon-King of Lanka, or Ceylon. To recover her, Rama enters into an alliance with the king of the monkeys and invades Ceylon. A bridge is formed of rocks (of course still *in situ*) over which Rama and his quadrumanous friends make their way and recover the dame, whose story has combined the mishaps of Proserpine with the destiny of Helen. Many parts of this poem, even in translation, are full of grace; and the tenderness of parental and filial affection has hardly ever been more beautifully described.

The Mahabharata is still larger than the Ramayana, containing in its present form 100,000 stanzas. Its authorship is attributed to Vyasa, but, as mentioned above, it is undoubtedly the work of many hands. The quarrels of two great allied families form the staple of the story; its name signifying "the great history of the descendants of Bharata." The heroes are the five brothers, Pandavas; and the heroine is Drapaudi, a woman who is strangely represented as the wife of all five. This trait of manners is the more remarkable as modern Brahminical law is entirely opposed to polyandry, and the Indian commentators are exceedingly troubled at the incident in their great national epic. The custom, however, still exists among the Buddhists of Thibet, and the tribe of Nairs in Southern India; and its appearance in the Mahabharata proves the age of that great poem to have been prior to that of the Institutes of Menu and the other codes of Hindoo law.

After a series of wars whose narrative is interrupted by many episodes (in one of which is the legend of a deluge), the Mahabharata closes in a peculiarly striking manner. The brothers Pandavas remain masters of the field, and kings of their native country, all the rival race being slain. But "leanness enters into their souls," and they set off, accompanied by Drapaudi and their dog, to walk to Mount Meru, where Indra's heaven rises among the summits of the Himalayas. They walk on in single file, till after long years Drapaudi sinks down and dies; and then each brother in succession falls, till the eldest remains alone; the mysterious dog still following him. Indra now appears and offers to bear the hero in his chariot to heaven. He asks that his brothers and his wife may be taken there also. Indra tells him they have already reached heaven through the portals of the grave, and that he alone has been privileged to enter it wearing his fleshly form. Then Yudhishthira asks that his dog may accompany him. But Indra scornfully observes, "My heaven hath no place for dogs;" whereupon the hero says that "to abandon the faithful and devoted is an endless crime."

> Yon poor creature, in fear and distress, hath trusted in my power to save it;
> Not therefore for e'en life itself will I break my plighted word.

Fortunately the dog turns out to be Yama, the god of Death, who has ever followed his steps hitherto (an allegory in the vein of Bunyan), and marvellously sets the hero free to accept Indra's invitation. But not even here do his trials end. He enters heaven, and seeks instantly for his wife and his brothers; but he is told they are in hell! "Then to hell will I go also," cries the hero,—like Mr. Mill,—and thither he actually descends. But hell to the righteous is only Maya (delusion). He and his beloved ones are in paradise for ever.

There is something to my thinking so perfectly Teutonic in all this, that I can hardly express my surprise at finding it in an Eastern book. The distinct ideas of heaven and hell, the nature of the trials offered to the hero, and his sense of duty to his dog, would all seem natural in a German story; but how strange a testimony do they bring to the essential unity of the Aryan mind, occurring, as they do, in a Sanskrit poem, to which we can attribute no later age than the Christian era!

The story of Rama and Sita is again treated in a third and minor poem of later date called the *Raghuvansa*, attributed to Kalidasa, the great dramatic poet; and besides this there are many other *Kavyas* or epics of less and lesser importance. The subjects of most of them appear constantly to hover round one or other episode of the Ramayana or Mahabharata.

The Hindoo Drama was opened to Europeans nearly a century ago by Sir William Jones's translation of its masterpiece, "*Sakuntala*," of which Goethe expressed the highest admiration. In 1827 Professor Wilson published "Select Specimens of the Theatre of the Hindoos," whose first play, the celebrated "Toy-Cart," affords some indications whereby to estimate the date of the golden age of the Indian drama. Buddhism still exists among the characters of the piece, but has lost its ascendancy, and Siva is the chief object of worship. These and other signs are believed to point to the fourth century of our era for the date of the dramas in question; while Kalidasa, the greatest of the succeeding Sanskrit dramatic poets, is held to have flourished about A.D. 500.

Hindoo dramas are neither tragedies nor comedies. The grave and gay mingle in turn, but none of them end in death, either on the stage or behind the scenes; and Eastern decorum shows itself in the prohibition of eating, kissing, or sleeping before the public. They are, in short, very much what they call themselves, "poems which can be seen." Stage scenery there seems to be none. The acts of the drama might not be less than five nor more than ten. Intervals too long to be imagined in the acts were understood to take place between them. Men and gods were made to speak Sanskrit; women and slaves spoke Prakrit, a language bearing to Sanskrit the relation of Italian to Latin. Married women having passed the age of beauty being in Hindoo imagination mere cumberers of the ground, cultivated *hetæræ* appeared in India as in Greece, and the "Toy-Cart" presents us with its Aspasia. There are certain conventional characters on the Hindoo as on the classic and romantic stage; among them the *Vita* or parasite and the *Vidushaka* or buffoon. The number of existing Hindoo dramas is now small; whether many have perished or few were ever composed is unknown. The "Toy-Cart" is by an unknown author. Three dramas are attributed to Kalidasa, and three more to another admired poet, Bhavabhuti. "Sakuntala" appears to be recognized as the most beautiful; but in it, as in all the rest, the use of supernatural machinery is so exorbitant that it is hard for the slow British imagination to keep sufficient pace with its transitions to permit of much interest in its plot. Southey seems to have wonderfully realized this element of wild Hindoo fancy when he composed the "Curse of Kehama." Miracles, however, like the "Curse," or even the gigantic conception of Kehama multiplying himself into eight Kehamas and driving "self-multiplied"

At once down all the roads of Padalon,

may be conceived; and the apparition in a fiery chariot which carries off Sakuntala admitted as legitimate stage practice. But when we are called on further to believe that the desperately enamoured king Dushyanta, almost immediately after his marriage, miraculously forgets Sakuntala altogether, and snubs her when she presents herself at court, our sympathy in the subsequent adventures of the heroine becomes languid, if not extinct.

Several centuries later than the age of Kalidasa was written another Indian drama of an entirely different description. Its author was a poet named Krishna Misra, supposed to have lived in the twelfth century A.D., and the object of this work was the establishment of Vedanta doctrine. It is in fact a religious allegory, like the Holy War or Pilgrim's Progress; its name signifies "The Rising of the Moon of Awakened Intellect," and the *dramatis personæ* are Delusion, the king, with his subjects Love, Anger, Avarice, etc., and his allies Hypocrisy, Self-Importance and Materialism, and on the opposite side Reason with an army of Virtues. The struggle between the rival forces is sharp, but finally Tranquility enables Reason to harmonize with Revelation (consummation sought in other places besides India!), and thereupon the Moon of Awakened Intellect arises and shines. Our authoress has given a full and most curious account of this very remarkable piece, to which we recommend every admirer of glorious old Bunyan to refer. There is real wit in the Hindoo poet as in the Puritan tinker. Hypocrisy is represented as a Brahmin, and receives a message from his king as follows:—

> Beloved Hypocrisy! King Reason and his advisers have determined to revive Awakened Intellect, and are for this purpose sending Tranquility into holy places. This threatens destruction to all our kind, and it behoves you to be specially active and zealous. You are aware that no holy place on earth is equal to the city of Benares. Go then to

Benares, and exert yourself to frustrate the devotions of the pious people there assembled.

To this address Hypocrisy replies that he has done what is wanted at Benares so effectively already, that those who by day attend the holy rites are by night the greatest of sinners.

Besides its Epics and its Dramas, Sanskrit literature boasts also of its Lyric poetry. One poem of this class called the "Messenger Church," attributed to Kalidasa, is greatly praised by Mrs. Manning. Another, also by Kalidasa, "The Seasons," is spoken of in rapturous terms by Sir William Jones, and by its English and German translators.

A more remarkable class of books, however, than the last is that of Hindoo Fables. India is indeed the proper home of the Fable. Between A.D. 531 and 599, the great collection called the *Panchatantra* was translated into Pehlevi at the command of Nushirvan, King of Persia, under the name of Fables of Bidpai or Pilpay; and it is chiefly to these that the common tales of our nurseries are traceable. What may have been the real age of the Panchatantra (or Five Sections) is uncertain; it preceded at all events the collection of the *Hitopadesa* (Good Advice). Both sets of fables are much alike, and arranged in a similar framework; namely, the instruction of a Brahmin to the sons of a king, who are entrusted to him for six months' education in *niti* (politics). The lessons so bestowed, it must be owned, are somewhat Macchiavellian, and may be summarized, Mrs. Manning says, in the following simple doctrine: "Rogues, if cunning, succeed. Simpletons, though good and learned, fail. Good morals are allowed, however, to be good in themselves, and are to be preferred where no failure is risked."

Lastly, there exists in India a mass of fictions of the class of the Arabian Nights, the most popular being "The Ocean of the Streams of Narrative," "Twenty-five Stories told by a Vetala," "Thirty-two Tales told by Images," and "Seventy-two Tales of a Parrot." So concludes the vast cycle of Sanskrit literature, having contributed to the library of mankind nearly every known form of composition, saving only a History. Neither ancient nor mediæval India, so far as we know, ever had an Historian or even an Annalist; and in the enormous mass of their relics we are left to pick out as best we may from internal evidence the chronology even of their greatest works. We know almost everything about their minds, their opinions, their laws, even their lightest fancies. We can reconstruct their whole existence probably with greater accuracy than we can picture the lives of our own ancestors in our own land a thousand years ago. But the sequence of events, the wars and conquests, the dynasties and revolutions which ordinarily fill for us the pages of the past are, in the case of India, almost a total blank.

It must be confessed that the story of the Hindoo mind as revealed in Sanskrit literature, cannot be contemplated even in such a hasty review as the present, without a sense of sadness and regret. That early dawn of religion which breaks in the Vedas, instead of shining to the perfect day of rational faith, was followed only by fitful gleams of sunshine and cloud, and sank at last, as the ages went by, into the thick darkness of unredeemed idolatry. The one great reformation which alone ever broke the continuity of Brahmin ecclesiastical history, the rise and supremacy of Buddhism for a thousand years, passed away from India like a breeze over a field of corn; and no record save a few old ruined topes remain to tell thereof. If we could conceive of Protestantism flourishing for yet twenty generations in England, and then being utterly swept off and forgotten, and Catholicism reinstated over the land, with only the mouldering dome of St. Paul's left to recall to the antiquary the schism of the past, then we should have an analogue of the marvellous story of the two great rival creeds of the East.

But is there no lesson for us—even if we cannot stretch imagination to such a catastrophe—in the example of India's religious history? What were the causes which led to the deterioration of that vast Established Church, which in the days of the Bhagavad Gita had teachers with the spirit of prophets and the piety of saints? The answer seems unmistakable. Religion fell wholly out of secular hands into that of a priesthood, of the most powerful priesthood in the world; and what did it do with it? It accomplished precisely the end for which all priesthoods are for ever striving. It turned religion into a matter of rites and sacraments. Then symbols became idols, and formal observances were exalted above moral virtues; and the India of to-day, with its three million gods, its hideous idols, and its gross and cruel rites, displays the outcome of the three millenniums of priestly rule.

It is indeed time that a new reformation should arise in India, capable of taking deeper root in human nature than Buddhism, with its sleeping deity and Nirvana paradise, was ever qualified to do. I rejoice to believe that we see the beginning of such a reformation in the noble work of Keshub Chunder Sen and the Brahmos of India.

ESSAY XI.

UNCONSCIOUS CEREBRATION.

A PSYCHOLOGICAL STUDY.

THE old Hebrew necromancers were said to obtain oracles by means of Teraphim. A Teraph was the decapitated head of a child, placed on a pillar and compelled by magic to reply to the questions of the sorcerer. Let us suppose, for the sake of illustration, that the legends of such enchantments rest on some groundwork of fact; and that it might be possible, by galvanism or similar agency, to make a human corpse speak, as a dead sheep may be made to bleat. Further, let us suppose that the Teraph only responded to inquiries regarding facts known to the owner of the head while living, and therefore (it may be imagined) impressed in some manner upon the brain to be operated on.

In such a Teraph we should, I conceive, possess a fair representation of the mental part of human nature, as it is understood by a school of thinkers, considerable in all ages, but especially so at present. "The brain itself," according to this doctrine, "the white and grey matter, such as we see and touch it, irrespective of any imaginary entity beside, performs the functions of Thought and Memory. To go beyond this all-sufficient brain, and assume that our conscious selves are distinct from it, and somewhat else beside the sum-total of its action, is to indulge an hypothesis unsupported by a tittle of scientific evidence. Needless to add, the still further assumption, that the conscious self may possibly survive the dissolution of the brain, is absolutely unwarrantable."

It is my very ambitious hope to show, in the following pages, that, should physiology establish the fact that the brain performs all the functions which we have been wont to attribute to "Mind," that great discovery will stand alone, and will not determine, as supposed, the further steps of the argument; namely, that our conscious selves are nothing more than the sum of the action of our brains during life, and that there is no room to hope that they may survive their dissolution.

I hope to show, not only that these conclusions do not necessarily flow from the premisses, but that, accepting the premisses, we may logically arrive at opposite conclusions. I hope to deduce, from the study of one class of cerebral phenomena, a presumption of the *separability* of the conscious Self from the thinking brain; and thus, while admitting that "Thought may be a function of Matter," demonstrate that the Self in each of us is not identifiable with that which, for want of a better word, we call "Matter." The immeasurable difference between such a remembering, lip-moving Teraph as we have supposed and a conscious Man indicates, as I conceive, the gulf leaped over by those who conclude that, *if* the brain can be proved to think, the case is closed against believers in the spirituality and immortality of our race.

In brief, it is my aim to draw from such an easy and every-day psychological study as may be verified by every reader for himself, an argument for belief in the entire *separability* of the conscious self from its thinking organ, the physical brain. Whether we choose still to call the one "Spirit" and the other "Matter," or to confess that the definitions which our fathers gave to those terms have ceased to be valid in the light of modern science—that "Matter" means only "a form of Force," and that "Spirit" is merely "an unmeaning term for an unknown thing"— this verbal controversy will not in any way affect the drift of our argument. What we *need* to know is this: Can we face the real or supposed tendency of science to prove that "Thought is a Function of Matter," and yet logically retain faith in personal Immortality? I maintain that we may accept that doctrine and draw from it an indirect presumption of immortality, afforded by the proof that the conscious self is not identifiable with that Matter which performs the function of Thought, and of whose dissolution alone we have cognizance.

My first task must be to describe the psychological facts from which our conclusions are to be drawn, and which seem in themselves sufficiently curious and interesting to deserve more study on their own account than they have yet received. Secondly, I shall simply quote Dr. Carpenter's physiological explanation of these facts. Lastly, I shall, as shortly as possible, endeavour to deduce from them that which appears to me to be their logical inference.

The phenomena with which we are concerned have been often referred to by metaphysicians,—Leibnitz and Sir W. Hamilton amongst others,—under the names of "Latent Thought," and "Preconscious Activity of the Soul." Dr. Carpenter, who has discovered the physiological explanation of them, and reduced them to harmony with other phenomena of the nervous system, has given to them the title of "Unconscious Cerebration"; and to this name, as following in his steps, I shall in these pages adhere. It will probably serve our purpose best, in a popular paper like the present, to begin, not with any large generalizations of the subject, but with a few familiar and unmistakable instances of mental work performed unconsciously.

For example; it is an every-day occurrence to most of us to forget a particular word, or a line of poetry, and to remember it some minutes or hours later, when we have ceased consciously to seek for it. We try, perhaps anxiously, at first to recover it, well aware that it lies somewhere hidden in our memory, but unable to seize it. As the saying is, we "ransack our brains for it," but failing to find it, we at last turn our attention to other matters. By and by, when, so far as consciousness goes, our whole minds are absorbed in a different topic, we exclaim, "Eureka! The word, or verse, is—So and so." So familiar is this phenomenon that we are accustomed in similar straits to say, "Never mind; I shall remember the missing word by and by, when I am not thinking of it;" and we deliberately turn away, not intending finally to abandon the pursuit, but precisely as if we were possessed of an obedient secretary or librarian, whom we could order to hunt up a missing document, or turn out a word in a dictionary, while we amused ourselves with something else. The more this very common phenomenon is studied, the more I think the observer of his own mental processes will be obliged to concede, that, so far as his own conscious Self is concerned, the research is made absolutely without him. He has neither pain nor pleasure, nor sense of labour in the task, any more than if it were performed by another person; and his conscious Self is all the time suffering, enjoying, or labouring on totally different ground.

Another and more important phase of unconscious cerebration, is that wherein we find our mental work of any kind, a calculation, an essay, a tale, a composition of music, painting, or sculpture, arrange itself in order during an interval either of sleep or wakefulness, during which we had not consciously thought of it at all. Probably no one has ever written on a subject a little complicated, or otherwise endeavoured to think out a matter any way obscure, without perceiving next day that the thing has somehow taken a new form in his mind since he laid down his pen or his pencil after his first effort. It is as if a "Fairy Order" had come in the night and unravelled the tangled skeins of thought and laid them all neatly out on his table. I have said that this work is done for us either asleep or awake, but it seems to be accomplished most perfectly in the former state, when our unconsciousness of it is most complete. I am not now referring to the facts of somnambulism, of which I must speak hereafter, but of the regular "setting to rights" which happens normally to the healthiest brains, and with as much regularity as, in a well-appointed household, the chairs and tables are put in their places before the family come down to breakfast.

Again there is the ordinary but most mysterious faculty possessed by most persons, of setting over-night a mental alarum-clock, and awaking, at will, at any unaccustomed hour out of dreamless sleep. Were we up and about our usual business all night without seeing or hearing a timepiece, or looking out at the stars or the dawn, few of us could guess within two or three hours of the time. Or again, if we were asleep and dreaming with no intention of rising at a particular time, the lapse of hours would be unknown to us. The count of time in dreams is altogether different from that of our waking life, and we dream in a few seconds what seem to be the events of years. Nevertheless, under the conditions mentioned, of a sleep prefaced by a resolution to waken at a specified hour, we arrive at a knowledge of time unattainable to us either when awake or when sleeping without such prior resolution.

Such are some of the more striking instances of unconscious cerebration. But the same power is obviously at work during at least half our lives in a way which attracts no attention only because it is so common. If we divide our actions into classes with reference to the Will, we discover that they are of three kinds—the Involuntary (such as the beating of the heart, digestion, etc.), the Voluntary, and the Volitional. The difference between the two latter classes of actions is, that *Voluntary* motions are made by permission of the Will and can be immediately stopped by its exertion, but do not require its conscious activity. *Volitional* motions, on the contrary, require the direct exertion of Will.

Now of these three classes of action it would appear that all Voluntary acts, as we have defined them, are accomplished by Unconscious Cerebration. Let us analyze the act of Walking, for example. We intend to go here or there; and in such matters "he who wills the end wills the means." But we do not deliberately think, "Now I shall move my right foot, now I shall put my left on such a spot." Some unseen guardian of our muscles manages all such details, and we go on our way, serenely unconscious (unless we chance to have the gout, or an ill-fitting boot) that we have any legs at all to be directed in the way they should go. If we chance to be tolerably familiar with the road, we take each turning instinctively, thinking all the time of something else, and carefully avoid puddles or collisions with fellow-passengers, without bestowing a thought on the subject. Similarly, as soon as we have acquired other arts beside walking,—reading, sewing, writing, playing on an instrument,—we soon learn to carry on the mechanical part of our tasks with no conscious exertion. We read aloud, taking in the appearance and proper sound of each word and the punctuation of each sentence, and all the time we are not thinking of these matters, but of the argument of the author; or picturing the scene he describes; or, possibly, following a wholly different train of thought. Similarly in writing with "the pen of a ready writer" it would almost seem as if the pen itself took the business of forming the letters and dipping itself in the ink at proper intervals, so engrossed are we in the thoughts which we are trying to express. We unconsciously cerebrate that it will not answer to begin two consecutive sentences in the same way; that we must introduce a query here or an ejaculation there, and close our paragraphs with a sonorous word and not with a preposition. All this we do not do of *malice prepense*, but because the well-tutored sprite whose business it is to look after our p's and q's, settles it for us as a clerk does the formal part of a merchant's correspondence.

Music-playing, however, is of all others the most extraordinary manifestation of the powers of unconscious cerebration. Here we seem not to have one slave but a dozen. Two different lines of hieroglyphics have to be read at once, and the right hand is to be guided to attend to one of them, the left to another. All the ten fingers have their work assigned as quickly as they can move. The mind (or something which does duty as mind) interprets scores of A sharps and B flats and C naturals, into black ivory keys and white ones, crotchets and quavers and demi-semi-quavers, rests, and all the other mysteries of music. The feet are not idle, but have something to do with the pedals; and, if the instrument be a double-actioned harp, they have a task of pushings and pullings more difficult than that of the hands. And all this time the performer, the *conscious* performer, is in a seventh heaven of artistic rapture at the results of all this tremendous business; or perchance lost in a flirtation with the individual who turns the leaves of the music-book, and is justly persuaded she is giving him the whole of her soul.

Hitherto we have noticed the brain engaged in its more

servile tasks of hunting up lost words, waking us at the proper hour, and carrying on the mechanical part of all our acts. But our Familiar is a great deal more than a walking dictionary, a housemaid, a *valet de place*, or a barrel-organ man. He is a novelist who can spin more romances than Dumas, a dramatist who composes more plays than ever did Lope de Vega, a painter who excels equally well in figures, landscapes, cattle, sea-pieces, smiling bits of *genre* and the most terrific conceptions of horror and torture. Of course, like other artists, he can only reproduce, develope, combine what he has actually experienced, or read, or heard of. But the enormous versatility and inexhaustible profusion with which he furnishes us with fresh pictures for our galleries, and new stories every night from his lending library, would be deemed the greatest of miracles, were it not the commonest of facts. A dull clod of a man, without an ounce of fancy in his conscious hours, lies down like a log at night, and lo! he has got before him the village green where he played as a boy, and the apple-tree blossoms in his father's orchard, and his long-dead and half-forgotten mother smiles at him, and he hears her call him "her own little lad," and then he has a vague sense that this is strange, and a whole marvellous story is revealed to him of how his mother has been only supposed to be dead, but has been living in a distant country, and he feels happy and comforted. And then he wakes and wonders how he came to have such a dream! Is he not right to wonder? What is it—*who* is it that wove the tapestry of such thoughts on the walls of his dark soul? Addison says, "There is not a more painful act of the mind than that of invention. Yet in dreams it works with that care and activity that we are not sensible when the faculty is employed."[1] Such are the nightly miracles of Unconscious Cerebration.

[1] *Spectator*, 487.

The laws which govern dreams are more than half unexplained, but the most obvious of them singularly illustrate the nature of the processes of the unconscious brain-work which causes them. Much of the labour of our minds, both conscious and unconscious, consists in transmuting Sentiments into Ideas. Possessing a certain feeling, we render it into some intellectual shape more or less suitable. Loving a person we endow him with all lovable qualities; hating him, we attribute to him all hateful ones. Out of the Sentiment of the Justice of God men first created the Ideas of a great Final Assize and a Day of Judgment. Out of the Sentiments of His originating power they constructed a Six Days Cosmogony. In the case of Insanity, when the power of judgment is lost, the disordered Sentiment almost invariably precedes the distracted Thought, and may be traced back to it beyond mistake; as for example in the common delusion of maniacs that they have been injured or plotted against by those persons for whom they happen to feel a morbid dislike. As our conscious brains are for ever at work of the kind, "giving to airy nothing" (or at least to what is merely subjective feeling) "a local habitation and a name," so our unconscious brains, after their wont, proceed on the same track during sleep. Our sentiments of love, hate, fear, anxiety, are each one of them the fertile source of whole series of illustrative dreams. Our bodily sensations of heat, cold, hunger, and suffocation, supply another series often full of the quaintest suggestions,—such as those of the poor gentleman who slept over a cheesemonger's shop, and dreamt he was shut up in a cheese to be eaten by rats; and that of the lady whose hot bottle scorched her feet, and who imagined she was walking into Vesuvius. In all such dreams we find our brains with infinite play of fancy merely adding illustrations, like those of M. Doré, to the page of life which we have turned the day before, or to that which lies upon our beds as we sleep.

Again, the small share occupied by the Moral Law in the dream world is a significant fact. So far as I have been able to learn, it is the rarest thing possible for any check of conscience to be felt in a dream, even by persons whose waking hours are profoundly imbued with moral feeling. We commit in dreams acts for which we should weep tears of blood were they real, and yet never feel the slightest remorse. On the most trifling provocation we cram an offending urchin into a lion's cage (if we happen to have recently visited the Zoological Gardens), or we set fire to a house merely to warm ourselves with the blaze, and all the time feel no pang of compunction. The familiar check of waking hours, "I must not do it, because it would be unjust or unkind," never once seems to arrest us in the satisfaction of any whim which may blow about our wayward fancies in sleep. Nay, I think that if ever we do feel a sentiment like Repentance in dreams, it is not the legitimate sequel to the crime we have previously imagined, but a wave of feeling rolled on from the real sentiment experienced in former hours of consciousness. Our dreamselves, like the Undines of German folk-lore, have no Souls, no Responsibility and no Hereafter. Of course this observation does not touch the fact that a person who in his conscious life has committed a great crime may be haunted with its hideous shadow in his sleep, and that Lady Macbeth may in vain try and wash the stain from her "little hand." It is the imaginary acts of sleeping fancy which are devoid of moral character. Now this immoral character of unconscious cerebration precisely tallies with the Kantian doctrine, that the moral will is the true *Homo Noumenon*, the Self of man. The conscious Self being dormant in dreams, it is obvious that the true phenomena of Conscience cannot be developed in them. Plutarch says that Zeno ordered his followers to regard dreams as a test of virtue, and to note it as a dangerous sign if they did not recoil, even in their sleep, from vice; and Sir Thomas Browne talks solemnly of "Sinful Dreams," which, as their biographies abundantly show, have proved terrible stumbling-blocks to the saints. But the doctrine of Unconscious Cerebration explains clearly enough how, in the absence of the controlling Will, the animal elements of our nature assert themselves—generally in the ratio of their unnatural suppression at other times—and abstinence is made up for by hungry Fancy spreading a glutton's feast. The *want* of sense of sin in such dreams is, I think, the most natural and most healthful symptom about them.

But if moral Repentance rarely or never follow the imaginary transgressions of dreams, another sense, the Saxon sense of Dissatisfaction in unfinished work, is not only often present, but sometimes exceedingly harassing. The late eminent physician, Professor John Thompson, of Edinburgh, quitted his father's cottage in early manhood, leaving half woven a web of cloth on which he had been engaged as a weaver's apprentice. Half a century afterwards, the then prosperous and celebrated gentleman still found his slumbers disturbed by the apparition of his old loom and the sense of the imperative duty of finishing the never-completed web. The tale is like a parable of what all this life's neglected duties may be to us, perchance in an absolved and glorified Hereafter, wherein, nevertheless, *that* web which we have left undone will have passed from our hands for ever. Of course, as it is the proper task of the unconscious brain to direct voluntary labours started by the will, it is easily explicable why it should be tormented by the sense of their incompletion.

But leaving the vast half-studied subject of dreams,

which belongs rather to the class of involuntary than of unconscious cerebration, we must turn to consider the surprising phenomena of true Unconscious Cerebration, developed under conditions of abnormal excitement. Among these I class those mysterious Voices, issuing we know not whence, in which some strong fear, doubt, or hope finds utterance. The part played by these Voices in the history both of religion and of fanaticism it is needless to describe. So far as I can judge, they are of two kinds. One is a sort of lightning-burst suddenly giving intensely vivid expression to a whole set of feelings or ideas which have been lying latent in the brain, and which are in opposition to the feelings and ideas of our conscious selves at the moment. Thus the man ready to commit a crime hears a voice appealing to him to stop; while the man praying ardently for faith hears another voice say, "There is no God." Of course the good suggestion is credited to heaven, and the other to the powers of the Pit, but the source of both is, I apprehend, the same, namely, Unconscious Cerebration. The second class of Voices are the result, not of unconscious Reasoning but of unconscious Memory. Under some special excitement, and perhaps inexplicably remote association of ideas, some words which once made a violent impression on us are remembered from the inner depths. Chance may make these either awfully solemn, or as ludicrous as that of a gentleman, shipwrecked off South America, who, as he was sinking and almost drowning, distinctly heard his mother's voice say, "Tom! did you take Jane's cake?" The portentous inquiry had been addressed to him forty years previously, and (as might have been expected) had been wholly forgotten. In fever, in a similar way, ideas and words long consigned to oblivion are constantly reproduced; nay, what is most curious of all, long trains of phrases which the individual has indeed heard, but which could hardly have become a possession of the memory in its natural state, are then brought out in entire unconsciousness. My readers will recall the often-quoted and well-authenticated story of the peasant girl in the Hôtel Dieu in Paris, who in her delirium frequently "spouted" Hebrew. After much inquiry it was found she had been cook to a learned priest who had been in the habit of reading aloud his Hebrew books in the room adjoining her kitchen. A similar anecdote is told of another servant girl who in abnormal sleep imitated some beautiful violin playing which she had heard many years previously.

From Sounds to Sights the transition is obvious. An Apparition is to the optical sense what such a Voice as I have spoken of above is to the hearing. At a certain point of intensity the latent idea in the unconscious brain reveals itself and produces an impression on the sensory; sometimes affecting one sense, sometimes another, sometimes perhaps two senses at a time.

Hibbert's well-known explanation of the philosophy of apparitions is this. We are, he says, in our waking hours, fully aware that what we really see and hear are actual sights and sounds; and what we only conjure up by fancy are delusions. In our sleeping hours this sense is not only lost, but the opposite conviction fully possesses us; namely, that what we conjure up by fancy in our dreams is true, while the real sights and sounds around us are unperceived. These two states are exchanged for each other at least twice in every twenty-four hours of our lives, and generally much oftener; in fact every time we doze or take a nap. Very often such slumbers begin and end before we have become aware of them; or have lost consciousness of the room and its furniture surrounding us. If at such times a peculiarly vivid dream takes the form of an apparition of a dead friend, there is nothing to rectify the delusion that what we have fancied is real, nay even a background of positive truth is apparently supplied by the bedstead, curtains, etc., etc., of whose presence we have not lost consciousness for more than the fraction of time needful for a dream.

It would, I think, be easy to apply this reasoning with great advantage, taking into view the phenomena of Unconscious Cerebration. The intersection of the states wherein consciousness yields to unconsciousness, and *vice versâ*, is obviously always difficult of sharp appreciation, and leaves wide margin for self-deception; and a ghost is of all creations of fancy the one which bears most unmistakable internal evidence of being *home-made*. The poor unconscious brain goes on upon the track of the lost friend, on which the conscious soul, ere it fell asleep, had started it. But with all its wealth of fancy it never succeeds in picturing a *new* ghost, a fresh idea of the departed, whom yet by every principle of reason we know is *not* (whatever else he or she may have become) a white-faced figure in coat and trowsers, or in a silk dress and gold ornaments. All the familiar arguments proving the purely subjective nature of apparitions of the dead, or of supernatural beings, point exactly to Unconscious Cerebration as the teeming source wherein they have been engendered. In some instances, as in the famous ones quoted by Abercrombie, the brain was sufficiently distempered to call up such phantoms even while the conscious self was in full activity. "Mrs. A." saw all her visions calmly, and knew that they were visions; thus bringing the conscious and unconscious workings of her brain into an awful sort of face-to-face recognition; like the sight of a *Doppel-gänger*. But such experience is the exceptional one. The ordinary case is, that the unconscious cerebration supplies the apparition; and the conscious self accepts it *de bonne foi*, having no means of distinguishing it from the impressions derived from the real objects of sense.

The famous story in my own family, of the Beresford ghost, is, I think, an excellent illustration of the relation of unconscious cerebration to dreams of apparitions. Lady Beresford, as I conjecture, in her sleep hit her wrist violently against some part of her bedstead so as to hurt it severely. According to the law of dreams, already referred to, her unconscious brain set about accounting for the pain, transmitting the Sensation into an Idea. An instant's sensation (as Mr. Babbage, Sir Benjamin Brodie, and Lord Brougham have all illustrated) is enough to call up a long vision. Lady Beresford fancied accordingly that her dead cousin, Lord Tyrone, had come to fulfil his promise of revisiting her from the tomb. He twisted her curtains and left a mark on her wardrobe (probably an old stain she had remarked on the wood), and then touched her wrist with his terrible finger. The dreamer awoke with a black and blue wrist; and the story took its place in the annals of ghost-craft for ever..

Somnambulism is an unmistakable form of unconscious cerebration. Here, while consciousness is wholly dormant, the brain performs occasionally the most brilliant operations. Coleridge's poem of Kubla Khan, composed in opiate sleep, is an instance of its achievements in the realm of pure imagination. Many cases are recorded of students rising at night, seeking their desks, and there writing down whole columns of algebraic calculations; solutions of geometric problems, and opinions on difficult cases of law. Cabanis says that Condillac brought continually to a conclusion at night in his sleep the reasonings of the day. In all such cases the work done asleep seems better than that done in waking hours; nay there is no lack of anecdotes which would point to the possibility of persons in an unconscious state accomplishing things beyond their ordinary powers altogether. The muscular strength of men in somnambulism and delirium, their power of balancing themselves on roofs, and of finding their way in the dark, are physical advantages reserved for such conditions. Abnormal acuteness of hearing is also a well-known accompaniment of them, and in this relation we must, I conclude, understand the marvellous story vouched for by the late Sir Edward Codrington. The captain in command of a man-of-war was one night sleeping in his cabin, with a sentinel as usual posted at his door. In the middle of the night the captain rang his bell, called suddenly to the sentinel, and sharply desired him to tell the lieutenant of the watch to alter the ship's course by so many points. Next morning the officer, on greeting the captain, observed that it was most fortunate he had been aware of their position and had given such an order, as there had been a mistake in the reckoning, and the ship was in shoal water, on the point of striking a reef. "I!" said the astonished captain, "I gave no order; I slept soundly all night." The sentinel was summoned, and of course testified that the experienced commander had in some unknown way learned the peril of his ship, and saved it, even while in a state of absolute unconsciousness.

Whatever residue of truth may be found hereafter in the crucible wherein spirit-rapping, *planchette*, mesmerism, and hypnotism shall have been tried; whatever revelation of forgotten facts or successful hits at secrets, will, I believe, be found to be unquestionably due to the action of Unconscious Cerebration. The person reduced to a state of coma is liable to receive suggestions from without, and these suggestions and queries are answered by his unconscious brain out of whatever stores of memory it may retain. What a man *never* knew, *that* no magic has ever yet enabled him to tell; but what he has once known, and in his conscious hours has forgotten, *that*, on the contrary, is often recalled by the suggestive queries of the operator when he is in a state of hypnotism.

A natural dream sometimes does as much, as witness all the discoveries of hidden treasures, corpses, etc., made through dreams; and generally with the aid of the obvious machinery of a ghost. General Sleeman mentions that, being in pursuit of Thugs up the country, his wife one morning urgently entreated him to move their tents from the spot—a lovely opening in the jungle—where they had been pitched the previous evening. She said she had been haunted all night by the sight of dead men. Information received during the day induced the General to order an examination of the ground whereon they had camped; and beneath Mrs. Sleeman's tent were found fourteen corpses, victims of the Thugs. It is easily conceivable that the foul odour of death suggested to the lady, in the unconscious cerebration of her dream, her horrible vision. Had she been in a state of mesmeric trance, the same occurrence would have formed a splendid instance of supernatural revelation.

Drunkenness is a condition in which the conscious self is more or less completely obfuscated, but in which unconscious cerebration goes on for a long time. The proverbial impunity with which drunken men fall without hurting themselves can only be attributed to the fact that the conscious will does not interfere with the unconscious instinct of falling on the parts of the body least liable to injury. The same impunity is enjoyed by persons not intoxicated, who at the moment of an accident do not exert any volition in determining which way they shall strike the ground. All the ludicrous stories of the absence of mind of tipsy men may obviously be explained by supposing that their unconscious cerebration is blindly fumbling to perform tasks needing conscious direction. And be it remembered that the proverb "*in vino ceritas*" is here in exact harmony with our theory. The drunken man unconsciously blurts out the truth, his muddled brain being unequal to the task of inventing a plausible falsehood. The delicious fun of Sheridan, found tipsy under a tree and telling the policeman that he was "Wil-Wil-Wilberforce," reveals at once that the wag, if a little exalted, was by no means really drunk. Such a joke could hardly have occurred to an unconscious brain, even one so well accustomed to the production of humour. Like dreams, intoxication never brings new elements of nature into play, but only abnormally excites latent ones. It is only a Porson who when drunk solemnly curses the "aggravating properties of inanimate matter," or, when he cannot fit his latch-key, is heard muttering, "D——n the *nature of things!*" A noble miser of the last century revealed his true character, and also the state of his purse, whenever he was fuddled, by murmuring softly to himself, "I'm very rich! I'm very rich!" In sober moments he complained continually of his limited means. In the same way it is the brutal labourer who in his besotted state thrashes his horse and kicks his wife. A drunken woman, on the contrary, unless an habitual virago, rarely strikes anybody. The accustomed vehicle for her emotions—her tongue—is the organ of whose services her unconscious cerebration avails itself.

Finally, the condition of perfect anæsthesia appears to be one in which unconscious cerebration is perfectly exemplified. The conscious Self is then so absolutely dormant that it is not only unaware of the most frightful laceration of the nerves, but has no conception of the interval of time in which an operation takes place; usually awakening to inquire, "When do the surgeons intend to begin?" Meanwhile unconscious cerebration has been busy composing a pretty little picture of green fields and skipping lambs, or something equally remote from the terrible reality.

There are many other obscure mental phenomena which I believe might be explained by the theory of unconscious cerebration, even if the grand mystery of insanity does not receive (as I apprehend it must do) some elucidation from it. Presentiments and dreams of the individual's own death may certainly be explicable as the dumb revelations of the diseased frame to its own nervous centre. The strange and painful, but very common, sense of having seen and heard at some previous time what is passing at the moment, appears to arise from some abnormal irritation of the memory (if I may so express it), evidently connected with the unconscious action of the brain. Still more "uncanny" and mysterious is the impression (to me almost amounting to torture) that we have never for years quitted the spot to which in truth we have only that instant returned after a long interval. Under this hateful spell we say to ourselves that we have been weeks, months, ages, studying the ornaments of the cornice opposite our seat in church, or following the outline of the gnarled old trees, black against the evening sky. This delusion, I think, only arises when we have undergone strong mental tension at the haunted spot. While our conscious selves have been absorbed in speculative thought or strong emotion, our unconscious cerebration has photographed the scene on our optic nerves *pour passer le temps !*

The limitations of unconscious cerebration are as noticeable as its marvellous powers and achievements. It is obvious at first sight, that, though in the unconscious state mental work is sometimes *better* done than in the conscious (*e.g.* the finding missing names awake, or performing abstruse calculations in somnambulism), yet that the unconscious work is never more than the *continuation* of something which has been begun in the conscious condition. We recall the name which we have known and forgotten, but we do not discover what we never knew. The man who does not understand algebra never performs algebraic calculations in his sleep. No problem in Euclid has been solved in dreams except by students who have studied Euclid awake. The mere voluntary and unconscious movements of our legs in walking, and our hands in writing and playing music, were at first in infancy, or when we began to learn each art, actions purely volitional, which often required a strong effort of the conscious will for their accomplishment.

Again, the failures of unconscious cerebration are as easily traced as its limitations. The most familiar of them may be observed in the phenomena which we call Absence of Mind, and which seems to consist in a disturbance of the proper balance between conscious and unconscious cerebration, leaving the latter to perform tasks of which it is incapable. An absent man walks, as we say, in a dream. All men indeed, as before remarked, ˙perform the mechanical act of walking merely voluntarily and not volitionally, but their consciousness is not so far off but that it can be recalled at a moment's notice. The porter at the door of the senses can summons the master of the house the instant he is wanted about business. But the absent man does not answer such calls. A friend addresses him, and his unconscious brain instead of his conscious self answers the question *à tort et à travers*. He boils his watch for breakfast and puts his egg in his pocket; his unconscious brain merely concerning itself that something is to be boiled and something else put in the pocket. He searches up and down for the spectacles which are on his nose; he forgets to eat his dinner and wonders why he feels hungry. His social existence is poisoned by his unconquerable propensity to say the wrong thing to the wrong person. Meeting Mrs. Bombazine in deep widow's weeds, he cheerfully inquires, " Well, and what is Mr. Bombazine doing now?" albeit he has received formal notice that Mr. Bombazine departed a month ago to that world of whose doings no information is received. He tells Mr. Parvenu, whose father is strongly suspected of having been a shoemaker, that "for his part he does not like new-made men at the head of affairs, and holds to the good old motto, 'Ne sutor ultra crepidam;'" and this brilliant observation he delivers with a pleasant laugh, giving it all possible point and pungency. If he have an acquaintance whose brother was hanged or drowned, or scraped to death with oyster-shells, then to a moral certainty the subjects of capital punishment, the perils of the deep, and the proper season for eating oysters, will be the topics selected by him for conversation during the awkward ten minutes before dinner. Of course the injured friend believes he is intentionally insulted; but he is quite mistaken. The absent man had merely a vague recollection of his trouble, which unfortunately proved a stumbling-block against which his unconscious cerebration was certain to bring him into collision.

As a general rule, the unconscious brain, like an *enfant terrible*, is extremely veracious. The "Palace of Truth" is nothing but a house full of absent-minded people who unconsciously say what they think of each other, when they consciously intend to be extremely flattering. But it also sometimes happens that falsehood has so far become second nature that a man's very interjections, unconscious answers, and soliloquies may all be lies. Nothing can be more remote from nature than the dramas and novels wherein astute scoundrels, in the privacy of an evening walk beside a hedge, unveil their secret plots in an address to Fate or the Moon; or fall into a well-timed brain fever, and babble out exactly the truth which the reader needs to be told. Your real villain never tells truth even to himself, much less to Fate or the Moon; and it is to be doubted whether, even in delirium, his unconscious cerebration would not run in the accustomed ruts of fable rather than along the unwonted paths of veracity.

Another failure of unconscious cerebration is seen in the

continuance of habitual actions when the motive for them has ceased. A change in attire, altering the position of our pockets, never fails to cause us a dozen fruitless struggles to find our handkerchief, or replace our purse. In returning to an old abode we are sure, sooner or later, to blunder into our former sleeping-room, and to be much startled to find in it another occupant. It happened to me once, after an interval of eight years, to find myself again in the chamber, at the table, and seated on the chair where my little studies had gone on for half a lifetime. I had business to occupy my thoughts, and was soon (so far as consciousness went) buried in my task of writing. But all the time while I wrote my feet moved restlessly in a most unaccustomed way under the table. "What is the matter with me?" I paused at last to ask myself, and then remembered that when I had written at this table in long past days, I had had a stool under it. It was that particular stool my unconscious cerebration was seeking. During all the interval I had perhaps not once used a similar support, but the moment I sat in the same spot, the trifling habit vindicated itself afresh; the brain acted on its old impression.

Of course it is as easy as it is common to dismiss all such fantastic tricks with the single word "Habit." But the word "Habit," like the word "Law," has no positive sense as if it were itself an originating cause. It implies a persistent mode of action, but affords no clue to the force which initiates and maintains that action. All that we can say, in the case of the phenomena of unconscious cerebration, is, that when volitional actions have been often repeated, they sink into the class of voluntary ones, and are performed unconsciously. We may define the moment when a Habit is established as that wherein the Volitional act becomes Voluntary.

It will be observed by the reader that all the phenomena

of Unconscious Cerebration now indicated belong to different orders as related to the Conscious Self. In one order (*e.g.*, that of Delirium, Somnambulism, and Anæsthesia) the Conscious Self has no appreciable concern whatever. The action of the brain has not been originated or controlled by the will; there is no sense of it either painful or pleasurable, while it proceeds; and no memory of it when it is over.

In the second order (*e.g.*, that of rediscovered words, and waking at a given hour), the Conscious Self has so far a concern, that it originally *set the task* to the brain. This done, it remains in entire ignorance of how the brain performs it, nor does Memory afterwards retain the faintest trace of the labours, however arduous, of word-seeking and time-marking.

Lastly, in the third class, more strictly to be defined as that of *Involuntary* Cerebration, (*e.g.*, that of natural dreams), the share taken by the Conscious Self is the reverse of that which it assumes in the case of word-seeking and time-marking. In dreams we do not, and cannot with our utmost effort, direct our unconscious brains into the trains of thought and fancy wherein we desire them to go. Obedient as they are in the former case, where work was to be done, here, in the land of fancy, they seem to mock our futile attempts to guide them. Nevertheless, strange to say, the Conscious Self—which knew nothing of what was going on while its leg was being amputated under chloroform, and nothing of what its brain was doing, while finding out what o'clock it was with closed eyes in the dark—is here cognizant of all the proceedings, and able in great measure to recall them afterwards. We receive intense pain or pleasure from our dreams, though we have actually less to do in concocting them than in dozens of mental processes which go on wholly unperceived in our brains.[1]

[1] Reid boasted he had learned to control his dreams, and there is a story of a

Thus it would seem that neither Memory nor Volition have any constant relation to unconscious cerebration. We sometimes remember, and sometimes wholly forget its action; and sometimes it fulfils our wishes, and sometimes wholly disregards them. The one constant fact is, that *while the actions are being performed*, the Conscious Self is either wholly uncognizant of them or unable to control them. It is either in a state of high activity about other and irrelevant matters; or it is entirely passive. In every case the line between the Conscious Self, and the unconsciously working brain is clearly defined.

Having now faintly traced the outline of the psychological facts illustrative of unconscious cerebration, it is time to turn to the brilliant physiological explanation of them afforded by Dr. Carpenter. We have seen what our brains can do without our consciousness. The way they do it is on this wise (I quote, slightly abridged, from Dr. Carpenter).

All parts of the Nervous system appear to possess certain powers of automatic action. The *Spinal cord* has for primary functions the performance of the motions of respiration and swallowing. The automatic action of the *Sensory ganglia* seems to be connected with movements of protection— such as the closing the eyes to a flash of light—and their secondary use enables a man to shrink from dangers of collisions, etc., before he has time for conscious escape. Finally, we arrive at the automatic action of the *Cerebrum;* and here Dr. Carpenter reminds us that, instead of being (as formerly supposed) the centre of the whole system, in direct connexion with the organs of sense and the mus-

man who always guided his own fancy in sleep. Such dreams, however, would hardly deserve the name.

cular apparatus, the Cerebrum is, according to modern physiology,—

"A superadded organ, the development of which seems to bear a pretty constant relation to the degree in which intelligence supersedes instinct as a spring of action. The ganglionic matter which is spread out upon the surface of the hemispheres, and in which their potentiality resides, is connected with the Sensory Tract at their base (which is the real centre of conveyance for the sensory nerves of the whole body) by commissural fibres, long since termed by Reid, with sagacious foresight, 'nerves of the internal senses,' and its anatomical relation to the sensorium is thus precisely the same as that of the Retina, which is a ganglionic expansion connected with the Sensorium by the optic nerve. Hence it may be fairly surmised—1. That as we only become conscious of visual impressions on the retina when their influence has been transmitted to the central sensorium, so we only become conscious of ideational changes in the cerebral hemispheres when their influence has been transmitted to the same centre; 2. That as visual changes may take place in the retina of which we are unconscious, either through temporary inactivity of the Sensorium (as in sleep), or through the entire occupation of the attention in some other direction, so may ideational changes take place in the Cerebrum, of which we may be unconscious for want of receptivity on the part of the Sensorium, but of which the results may present themselves to the consciousness as ideas elaborated by an automatic process of which we have no cognizance."[1]

Lastly, we come to the conclusions to be deduced from the above investigations. We have credited to the Unconscious Brain the following powers and faculties:—

1. It not only *remembers* as much as the Conscious Self can recall, but often much more. It is even doubtful whether it may not be capable, under certain conditions, of reproducing every impression ever made upon the senses during life.

2. It can *understand* what words or things are sought to be remembered, and hunt them up through some recondite

[1] Report of Meeting of Royal Institution. Dr. Carpenter's Lecture, March 1, 1868, pp. 4, 5.

process known only to itself, till it discovers and pounces on them.

3. It can *fancy* the most beautiful pictures and also the most terrible ones, and weave ten thousand fables with inexhaustible invention.

4. It can perform the exceedingly difficult task of mental arrangement and logical division of subjects.

5. It can transact all the mechanical business of walking, reading, writing, sewing, playing, etc., etc.

6. It can tell the hour in the middle of the night without a timepiece.

Let us be content with these ordinary and unmistakable exercises of unconscious cerebration, and leave aside all rare or questionable wonders of somnambulism and cognate states. We have got Memory, Fancy, Understanding, at all events, as faculties exercised by the Unconscious Brain. Now it is obvious that it would be an unusual definition of the word "Thought" which should debar us from applying it to the above phenomena; or compel us to say that we can remember, fancy, and understand without "thinking" of the things remembered, fancied, or understood. But Who, or What, then, is it that accomplishes these confessedly mental functions? Two answers are given to the query, each of them, as I venture to think, erroneous. Büchner and his followers say, "It is our physical Brains, and these Brains are ourselves."[1] And non-materialists say, "It is our conscious Selves, which merely use our brains as their instruments." We must go into this matter somewhat carefully.

In a certain loose and popular way of speaking, our brains are "ourselves." So also in the same way of speaking are our hearts, our limbs, and the hairs of our head. But in

---

[1] Büchner's precise doctrine is, "The brain is only the carrier and the source, or rather the *sole cause* of the spirit or thought; but not the organ which secretes it. It produces something which is not materially permanent, but which consumes itself in the moment of its production."—*Kraft und Stoff*, chap. xiii.

more accurate language the use of the pronoun "I" applied to any part of our bodies is obviously incorrect, and even inadmissible. We say, indeed, commonly, "I struck with my hand," when our hand has obeyed our volition. It is, then, in fact, the will of the Self which we are describing. But if our hand has been forcibly compelled to strike by another man seizing it, or if it have shaken by palsy, we only say, "My hand was forced," or "was shaken." The limb's action is not *ours*, unless it has been done by our will. In the case of the heart, the very centre of physical life, we never dream of using such a phrase as "I am beating slowly," or "I am palpitating fast." And why do we not say so? Because, the action of our hearts being involuntary, we are sensible that the conscious "I" is not the agent in question, albeit the mortal life of that "I" is hanging on every pulsation. Now the problem which concerns us is this: Can we, or can we *not*, properly speak of our brains as we do of our hearts? Is it more proper to say, "I invent my dreams," than it is to say, "I am beating slowly"? I venture to think the cases are precisely parallel. When our brains perform acts of unconscious cerebration (such as dreams), they act just as our hearts do, *i.e.* involuntarily; and we ought to speak of them as we always do of our hearts, as of organs of our frame, but not our Selves. When our brains obey our wills, then they act as our hands do when we voluntarily strike a blow; and then we do right to speak as if "we" performed the act accomplished by their means.

Now to return to our point. Are the anti-Materialists right to say that the agent in unconscious cerebration is, "We, ourselves, who merely use our brains as their instruments;" or are the Materialists right who say, "It is our physical brains alone, and these brains are ourselves"? With regard to the first reply, I think that all the foregoing study has gone to show that "we" are *not* remembering, *not* fancying, *not* understanding, what is being at the moment remembered, fancied, or understood. To say, then, that in such acts "we" are "using our brains as our instruments," appears nothing but a servile and unmeaning adherence to the foregone conclusion that our brains are nothing else than the organs of our will. It is absurd to call them so when we are concerned with phenomena whose speciality is that the will has nothing to do with them. So far, then, as this part of the argument is concerned, I think the answer of the anti-Materialists must be pronounced to be erroneous. The balance of evidence inclines to the Materialists' doctrine that the brain itself performs the mental processes in question, and, to use Vogt's expression, "secretes Thought" automatically and spontaneously.

But if this presumption be accepted provisionally, and the possibility admitted of its future physiological demonstration, have we, with it, accepted also the Materialist's ordinary conclusion that *we* and our automatically thinking brains are one and indivisible? If the brain can work by itself, have we any reason to believe it ever works *also* under the guidance of something external to itself, which we may describe as the Conscious Self? It seems to me that this is precisely what the preceding facts have likewise gone to prove—namely, that there are two kinds of action of the brain, the one Automatic, and the other subject to the will of the Conscious Self; just as the actions of a horse are some of them spontaneous and some done under the compulsion of his rider. The first order of actions tend to indicate that the brain "secretes thought;" the second order (strongly contrasting with the first) show that, beside that automatically working brain, there is another agency in the field under whose control the brain performs a wholly different class of labours. Everywhere in the preceding pages we have traced the extraordinary *separation* which continually takes place between our Conscious Selves and the automatic action of the organ, which serves as our medium of communication with the outward world. We have seen, in a word, that we are not Centaurs, steed and rider in one, but horsemen, astride on roadsters which obey us when we guide them, and when we drop the reins, trot a little way of their own accord or canter off without our permission.

When we place the phenomena of Unconscious Thought on one side, and over against them our Conscious Selves, we obtain, I think, a new and vivid sense of the separation, not to say the antithesis, which exists between the two; close as is their mutual interdependence. Not to talk about the distinction between object and subject, or dwell on the absurdity (as it seems to me) of the proposition that we ourselves are only the sum-total of a series of cerebrations— the recognition of the fact *that our brains sometimes think without us,* seems to enable us to view our connexion with them in quite a new light. So long as all our attention was given to Conscious Thought, and philosophers eagerly argued the question, whether the Soul did or did not ever sleep or cease to think, it was easy to confound the organ of thought with the Conscious Self who was supposed alone to set it in action. But the moment we marshal together for review the long array of the phenomena of Unconscious Cerebration, the case is altered; the severance becomes not only cogitable, but manifest.

Let us then accept cheerfully the possibility, perhaps the probability, that science ere long will proclaim the dogma, "Matter can think." Having humbly bowed to the decree, we shall find ourselves none the worse. Admitting that our brains accomplish much without our conscious guidance, will help us to realize that our relation to them is of a variable—

an intermittent—and (we may therefore venture to hope) of a *terminable* kind.

That such a conclusion, if reached, will have afforded us any *direct* argument for human immortality, cannot be pretended. Though we may succeed in proving "that the Brain can think without the Conscious Man," the great converse theorem, "that the Conscious Man can think without a Brain," has as yet received no jot of direct evidence; nor ever will do so, I hold, while we walk by faith and not by sight, and Heaven remains "a part of our religion, and not a branch of our geography."

But it is something, nay it is surely much, if, by groping among the obscurer facts of consciousness, we may attain the certainty that whatever be the final conclusions of science regarding our mental nature, the one which we have most dreaded, if reached at last, will militate not at all against the hope, written on the heart of the nations, by that Hand which writes no falsehoods; that "when the dust returns to the dust whence it was taken, the Spirit"—the Conscious Self of Man—"shall return to God who gave it."

ESSAY XII.

DREAMS,

AS ILLUSTRATIONS OF INVOLUNTARY CEREBRATION.

In the preceding Essay I have endeavoured to range together a considerable number of facts illustrative of the automatic action of the brain. My purpose in the present article is to treat more at length one class of such phenomena to which I could not afford space proportionate to their interest, in the wide survey required by the design of the former paper. I shall seek to obtain from some familiar and some more rare examples of dreams, such light as they may be calculated to throw on the nature of brain-work, unregulated by the will. Perhaps I may be allowed to add, as an apology for once more venturing into this field of inquiry, that the large number of letters and friendly criticisms which my first paper called forth have both encouraged me to pursue the subject by showing how much interest is felt in its popular treatment, and have also afforded me the advantage of the experience of many other minds regarding some of the obscure mental phenomena in question. In the present case I shall feel grateful to any reader who will correct from personal knowledge any statement I may make which he finds erroneous.

Dreams are to our waking thoughts much like echoes to music; but their reverberations are so partial, so varied, so complex, that it is almost in vain we seek among the notes of consciousness for the echoes of the dream. If we could by any means ascertain on what principle our dreams for a given night are arranged, and why one idea more than another furnishes their cue, it would be comparatively easy to follow out the chain of associations by which they unroll themselves afterwards; and to note the singular ease and delicacy whereby subordinate topics, recently wafted across our minds, are seized and woven into the network of the dream. But the reason why from among the five thousand thoughts of the day, we revert at night especially to thoughts number 2, and 4, instead of to thoughts number 3, and 6, or any other in the list, is obviously impossible to conjecture. We can but observe that the echo of the one note has been caught, and of the others lost amid the obscure caverns of the memory. Certain broad rules, however, may be remarked as obtaining generally regarding the topics of dreams. In the first place, if we have any present considerable *physical* sensation or pain, such as may be produced by a wound, or a fit of indigestion, or hunger, or an unaccustomed sound, we are pretty sure to dream of it in preference to any subject of *mental* interest only. Again, if we have merely a slight sensation of uneasiness, insufficient to cause a dream, it will yet be enough to colour a dream, otherwise suggested, with a disagreeable hue. Failing to have a dream suggested to it by present physical sensation, the brain seems to revert to the subjects of thought of the previous day, or of some former period of life, and to take up one or other of them as a theme on which to play variations. As before remarked, the grounds of choice among all such subjects cannot be ascertained, but the predilection of Morpheus for those which we have *not* in our waking hours thought most interesting, is very noticeable. Very rarely indeed do our dreams take up the matter which has most engrossed us for hours before we sleep. A wholesome law of variety comes into play, and the brain seems to decide, "I have had enough of politics, or Greek, or fox-hunting, for this time. Now I will amuse myself quite differently." Very often, perhaps we may say generally, it pounces on some transient thought which has flown like a swallow across it by daylight, and insists on holding it fast through the night. Only when our attention has more or less transgressed the bounds of health, and we have been morbidly excited about it, does the main topic of the day's interest recur to us in dreaming at night; and that it should do so, ought, I imagine, always to serve as a warning that we have strained our mental powers a little too far.[1] Lastly, there are dreams whose origin is not in any past *thought*, but in some *sentiment* vivid and pervading enough to make itself dumbly felt even in sleep. Of the nature of the dreams so caused I shall speak presently.

The subject of a dream being, as we must now suppose, suggested to the brain on some such principles as the above, the next thing to be noted is, How does the brain treat its theme when it has got it? Does it drily reflect upon it, as we are wont to do awake? Or does it pursue a course wholly foreign to the laws of waking thoughts? It does, I conceive, neither one nor the other, but treats its theme, whenever it is possible to do so, according to a certain very important, though obscure, law of thought, whose action we are too apt to ignore. We have been accustomed to consider the myth-creating power of the human mind as one specially belonging to the earlier stages of growth of society

---

[1] A distinguished man of science has told me that he finds the dreams of the first part of the night to be usually connected with the events of the past day, while those of the morning revert to long past scenes and interests.

and of the individual. It will throw, I think, a rather curious light on the subject if we discover that this instinct exists in every one of us, and exerts itself with more or less energy through the whole of our lives. In hours of waking consciousness, indeed, it is suppressed, or has only the narrowest range of exercise, as in the tendency, noticeable in all persons not of the very strictest veracity, to supplement an incomplete anecdote with explanatory incidents, or to throw a slightly known story into the dramatic form, with dialogues constructed out of their own consciousness. But such small play of the myth-making faculty is nothing compared to its achievements during sleep. The instant that daylight and common sense are excluded, the fairy-work begins. At the very least half our dreams (unless I greatly err) are nothing else than myths formed by unconscious cerebration on the same approved principles, whereby Greece and India and Scandinavia gave to us the stories which we were once pleased to set apart as "mythology" proper. Have we not here, then, evidence that there is a real law of the human mind causing us constantly to compose ingenious fables explanatory of the phenomena around us,—a law which only sinks into abeyance in the waking hours of persons in whom the reason has been highly cultivated, but which resumes its sway even over their well-tutored brains when they sleep? [1]

[1] A correspondent has kindly sent me the following interesting remarks on the above:—"When dropping asleep some nights ago I suddenly started awake with the thought on my mind, 'Why I was *making* a dream!' I had detected myself in the act of inventing a dream. Three or four impressions of scenes and events which had passed across my mind during the day were present together in my mind, and the effort was certainly being made, but not by my fully conscious will, to arrange them so as to form a continuous story. They had actually not the slightest connexion, but a process was evidently going on in my brain by which they were being united into one scheme or plot. Had I remained asleep until the plot had been matured, I presume my waking sensation would have been that I had had an ordinary dream. But perhaps through the partial failure of the unconscious effort at a plan, I woke up just in time to catch a

Most dreams lend themselves easily to the myth-making process; but pre-eminently dreams originating in Sensation or in Sentiment do so. Of those which arise from memory of Ideas only, I shall speak by and by.

Nothing can better illustrate the Sensation myth than the well-known story recorded of himself by Reid. "The only distinct dream I had ever since I was about sixteen, as far as I remember, was two years ago. I had got my head blistered for a fall. A plaster which was put on it after the blister pained me excessively for the whole night. In the morning I slept a little, and dreamed very distinctly that I had fallen into the hands of a party of Indians and was scalped." [1]

The number of mental operations needful for the transmutation of the sensation of a blistered head into a dream of Red Indians, is very worthy of remark. First, Perception of pain, and allotment of it to its true place in the body. Secondly, Reason seeking the cause of the phenomenon. Thirdly, Memory failing to supply the real cause, but offering from its stores of acquired knowledge an hypothesis of one suited to produce the phenomenon. Lastly, Imagination stepping in precisely at this juncture, fastening on this suggestion of memory, and instantly presenting it as a *tableau vivant*, with proper decorations and *couleur locale*. The only intellectual faculty which remains dormant seems to be the Judgment, which has allowed memory and imagination to work regardless of those limits of probability which she would have set to them awake. If, when awake, we feel

trace of the 'unconscious cerebration' as it was vanishing before the full light of conscious life. I accordingly propounded a tentative theory to my friends, that the brain uniting upon one thread the fancies and memories present at the same time in the mind, is really what takes place in dreams—a sort of faint shadow of the mind's natural craving for and effort after system and unity. Your explanation of dreams, by reference to the 'myth-making tendency,' seems to be so nearly in accord with mine that I venture to write on the subject."

[1] Works of Dugald Stewart. Edited by Sir W. Hamilton. Vol. x. p. 321.

a pain which we do not wholly understand, say a twinge in the foot, we speculate upon its cause only within the very narrow series of actual probabilities. It may be a nail in our boot, a chilblain, a wasp, or so on. It does not even cross our minds that it may be a sworn tormentor with red-hot pincers; but the same sensation experienced asleep will very probably be explained by a dream of the sworn tormentor or some other cause which the relations of time and space render equally inapplicable.[1] Let it be noted, however, that even in the waking brain a great deal of myth-making goes on after the formation of the most rational hypothesis. If we imagine that a pain is caused by any serious disease, we almost inevitably fancy we experience all the other symptoms of the malady, of which we happen to have heard — symptoms which disappear, as if by magic, when the physician laughs at our fears, and tells us our pain is caused by some trifling local affection.

Each of my readers could doubtless supply illustrations

[1] The analogy between insanity and a state of prolonged dream is too striking to be overlooked by any student of the latter subject. The delusions of insanity seem in fact little else but a series of such myths accounting for either sensations or sentiments like those above ascribed to dreaming. The maniac sees and hears more than a man asleep, and his sensations consequently give rise to numberless delusions. He is also usually possessed by some morbid moral sentiment, such as suspicion, hatred, avarice, or extravagant self-esteem (held by Dr. Carpenter nearly always to precede any intellectual failure), and these sentiments similarly give rise to their appropriate delusions. In the first case we have maniacs like the poor lady who wrote her confessions to Dr. Forbes Winslow ("Obscure Diseases of the Brain," p. 79), and who describes how, on being taken to an asylum, the pillars before the door, the ploughed field in front, and other details, successively suggested to her the belief that she was in a Romish convent where she would be "scourged and taken to purgatory," and in a medical college where the inmates were undergoing a process preparatory to dissection! In the second case, that of morbid Sentiments, we have insane delusions like those which prompted the suspicious Rousseau to accuse Hume of poisoning him, and all the mournfully grotesque train of the victims of pride who fill our pauper hospitals with kings, queens, and prophets. Merely suppose these poor maniacs are recounting dreams, and there would be little to remark about them except their persistent character.

of myth-making as good as that of Dr. Reid. It happened to me once to visit a friend delirious from fever, who lay in a bed facing a large old mirror, whose gilt wood-frame, of Chinese design, presented a series of innumerable spikes, pinnacles, and pagodas. On being asked how she was feeling, my poor friend complained of much internal dolour, but added with touching simplicity: "And it is no great wonder, I am sure! (whisper) I've swallowed that looking-glass!" Again. A young lady painted her thumb one night with extract of aloes to cure herself of the habit of sucking. In the morning she woke with her thumb in her mouth and the aloes all sucked off. She had dreamed she was sailing in a ship of wormwood; that she drank extract of wormwood; that a doctor ordered her to eat ox-gall, and then advised her to consult the Pope, who sent her on pilgrimage to Zoar, where she ate the thumb of Lot's wife.

Again, as regards Sentiments. If we have seen a forbidding-looking beggar in the streets in the morning, nothing is more probable than that our vague and transient sense of distrust will be justified by ingenious fancy taking up the theme at night, and representing a burglar bursting into our bedroom, presenting a pistol to our temples, and at the supreme moment disclosing the features of the objectionable mendicant. Hope, of course when vividly excited, represents for us scores of sweet scenes in which our desire is fulfilled with every pleasing variation; and Care and Fear have, alas! even more powerful machinery for the realization of their terrors. The longing of affection for the return of the dead has, perhaps more than any other sentiment, the power of creating myths of reunion, whose dissipation on awakening are amongst the keenest agonies of bereavement. By a singular semi-survival of memory through such dreams we seem always to be dimly aware that the person whose return we greet so rapturously *has been dead;* and the obvious incongruity of our circumstances, our dress, and the very sorrow we confide at once to their tenderness, with the sight of them again in their familiar places, drives our imagination to fresh shifts to explain it. Sometimes the beloved one has been abroad, and is come home; sometimes the death was a mistake, and some one else was buried in that grave wherein we saw the coffin lowered; sometimes a friendly physician has carried away the patient to his own home, and brought us there after long months to find him recovered.

One of the most affecting mythical dreams which have come to my knowledge, remarkable also as an instance of dream-poetry, is that of a lady who confessed to have been pondering on the day before her dream on the many duties which " bound her to life." The phrase which I have used as a familiar metaphor became to her a visible allegory. She dreamed that Life—a strong, calm, cruel woman—was binding her limbs with steel fetters, which she felt as well as saw; and Death, as an angel of mercy, hung hovering in the distance, unable to approach or deliver her. In this most singular dream her feelings found expression in the following touching verses, which she remembered on waking, and which she has permitted me to quote precisely in the fragmentary state in which they remained on her memory.

> " Then I cried with weary breath,
> Oh be merciful, great Death!
> Take me to thy kingdom deep,
> Where grief is stilled in sleep,
> Where the weary hearts find rest.
>
> * * * *
>
> Ah, kind Death, it cannot be
> That there is no room for me
> In all thy chambers vast . . . .
> See, strong Life has bound me fast:
> Break her chains, and set me free.

> But cold Death makes no reply,
> Will not hear my bitter cry;
> Cruel Life still holds me fast;
> Yet true Death must come at last,
> Conquer Life and set me free.

A dream once occurred to me wherein the mythical character almost assumed the dimensions of the sublime, insomuch that I can scarcely recall it without awe. I dreamed that I was standing on a certain broad grassy space in the park of my old home. It was totally dark, but I was aware that I was in the midst of an immense crowd. We were all gazing upward into the murky sky, and a sense of some fearful calamity was over us, so that no one spoke aloud. Suddenly overhead appeared, through a rift in the black heavens, a branch of stars which I recognized as the belt and sword of Orion. Then went forth a cry of despair from all our hearts! We knew, though no one said it, that these stars proved it was not a cloud or mist, which, as we had somehow believed, was causing the darkness. No; the air was clear; it was high noon, and the *sun had not risen!* That was the tremendous reason why we beheld the stars. The sun would never rise again!

In this dream, as it seems to me, a very complicated myth was created by my unconscious brain, which having first by some chance stumbled on the picture of a crowd in the dark, and a bit of starry sky over them, elaborated, to account for such facts, the bold theory of the sun not having risen at noon; or (if we like to take it the other way) having hit on the idea of the sun's disappearance, invented the appropriate scenery of the breathless expectant crowd, and the apparition of the stars.

Next to the myth-creating faculty in dreams, perhaps the most remarkable circumstance about them is that which has given rise to the world-old notion that dreams are frequently predictions. At the outset of an examination of this matter, we are struck by the familiar fact that our most common dreams are continually recalled to us within a few hours by some insignificant circumstance bringing up again the name of the person or place about which we had dreamed. On such occasions, as the vulgar say, "My dream is out." Nothing was actually predicted, and nothing has occurred of the smallest consequence, or ever entailing any consequence, but yet, by some concatenation of events, we dreamed of the man from whom we received a letter in the morning; or we saw in our sleep a house on fire, and before the next night we pass a street where there is a crowd, and behold! a dwelling in flames. Nay, much more special and out-of-the-way dreams than these come "out" very often. If we dream of Nebuchadnezzar on Saturday night, it is to be expected that on Sunday (unless the new lectionary have dispensed with his history) the lesson of the day will present us with the ill-fated monarch and his golden image. Dreams of some almost unheard-of spot, or beast, or dead-and-gone old worthy, which by wild vagary have entered our brain, are perpetually followed by a reference to the same spot, or beast, or personage, in the first book or newspaper we open afterwards. To account for such coincidences on any rational principle is, of course, difficult. But it is at least useful to attempt to do so, seeing that here, at all events, the supernatural hypothesis is too obviously absurd to be entertained by anybody; and if we can substitute for it a plausible theory in these cases, the same theory may serve equally well for problems a little more dignified, and therefore more liable to be treated superstitiously.

In the first place, a moment's reflection will show that the same sort of odd coincidences take place continually among the trivial events of waking life. "Sitting in my office," writes a correspondent, "with the Post Office Directory open before me, my eye happened to glance casually on the name of a firm whose place of business was a considerable distance away. At that identical moment the door opened and a lady entered inquiring the address of the firm in question." It has chanced to myself within the last few hours to remark to a friend how the word "subtle," applied to the serpent in Genesis, is always spelled "subtil," and within a few minutes to take up *The Index*, of Toledo, Ohio, and read the following anecdote: "A poor negro preacher was much troubled by the cheating of the sutlers of the army which he followed. He chose accordingly for the text of his sermon, 'Now the serpent was more *sutler* than any beast of the field,' etc." It will be owned that this is precisely the kind of chance coincidence which occurs in dreams, and which, when it happens to concern any solemn theme, is apt to seem portentous.

But ascending beyond these trivial coincidences, we arrive at a mass of dream-literature tending to show that revelations of all sorts of secrets and predictions of future events are made in dreams. Taking them in order, we have, first, discoveries of where money, wills, and all sorts of lost valuables are to be found, and such dreams have long been rightly explained as having their origin in some nearly effaced remembrance of information leading naturally to the discovery. In sleep the lost clue is recovered by some association of thought, and the revelation is made with sufficient distinctness to insure attention. A story of the sort is told by Macnish about a Scotch gentleman who recovered in a dream the address of a solicitor with whom his father on one single occasion deposited an important document on which the family fortunes ultimately depended. A singular occurrence which took place some years ago at the house of the late Earl of Minto in Scotland can only be explained in a similar way. An eminent lawyer went to pay a few days' visit at Minto immediately before the hearing of an important case in which he was engaged as counsel. Naturally he brought with him the bundle of papers connected with the case, intending to study them in the interval; but on the morning after his arrival the packet could nowhere be found. Careful search of course was made for it, but quite in vain, and eventually the lawyer was obliged to go into court without his papers. Years passed without any tidings of the mysterious packet, till the same gentleman found himself again a guest at Minto, and, as it happened, occupying the same bedroom. His surprise may be imagined when on waking in the morning he found his long-lost bundle lying on his dressing-table. The presumption of course is, that on the first occasion he hid them in his sleep, and on the second visit he found them in his sleep; but where he hid and found them has never been discovered.

An instance of the renewal in sleep of an impression of memory calling up an apparition to enforce it (it is the impression which causes the apparition, not the apparition which conveys the impression) occurred near Bath half a century ago. Sir John Miller, a very wealthy gentleman, died leaving no children. His widow had always understood that she was to have the use of his house for her life with a very large jointure; but no will making such provision could be found after his death. The heir-at-law, a distant connexion, naturally claimed his rights, but kindly allowed Lady Miller to remain for six months in the house to complete her search for the missing papers. The six months drew at last to a close, and the poor widow had spent fruitless days and weeks in examining every possible place of deposit for the lost document, till at last she came to the conclusion that her memory must have deceived her, and that her husband could have made no such promise as she supposed, or have neglected to fulfil it had he made one. The very last day of her tenure of the house had just dawned, when in the grey of the morning Lady Miller drove up to the door of her man of business in Bath, and rushed excitedly to his bed-room door, calling out, "Come to me! I have seen Sir John! There is a will!" The lawyer hastened to accompany her back to her house. All she could tell him was that her deceased husband had appeared to her in the night, standing by her bedside, and had said solemnly, "There *is* a will!" *Where* it was, remained as uncertain as before. Once more the house was searched in vain from cellar to loft, till finally wearied and in despair the lady and her friend found themselves in a garret at the top of the house. "It is all over," Lady Miller said; "I give it up; my husband deceived me, and I am ruined!" At that moment she looked at the table over which she was leaning weeping. "This table was in his study once! Let us examine it!" They looked, and the missing will, duly signed and sealed, was within it, and the widow made rich to the end of her days. It needs no conjuror to explain how her anxiety called up the myth of Sir John Miller's apparition, and made him say precisely what he had once before really said to her, but of which the memory had waxed faint.

A more difficult class of stories to account for is that of tales like the following:

A lady left her old country house in England and went to Australia with her husband, Colonel H. In the house she had quitted there was a room in which one of her sisters had died, and which the bereaved mother kept constantly shut up. Mrs. H., after some years' residence in Australia, dreamed that she saw her mother lying dead on the bed in this particular room, with certain members of the family around her. Noting the dream with some anxiety, she received in due time the news that her mother had

had a fit in which she died, and that the body had been carried into the long-deserted room, and was at one time surrounded by the relatives in question. Here of course the coincidences were most remarkable and impressive, if the story have come to us with any exactitude—a matter, I must remark, of which the fallacies of memory, the inaccuracy of oral transmission, and the unconquerable propensity of all men to "make things fit" always leaves open to doubt. Taking it, as it stands, however, we may notice that the removal of her mother's corpse to the deserted chamber was not a very singular circumstance in itself, while the daughter's dream of her early home was entirely in accordance with the common rules of dreams. As a sad and mournful feeling suggested the dream (probably some reasonable anxiety for her mother's health), it was very natural that any analogous solemn or dismal circumstances connected with her mother should be woven into it. If she dreamed of her mother's death, nothing was more dream-like than that she should associate with it the previous death of her sister, whom they had mourned together, and see her mother's corpse upon the bed where she had once actually seen that of her sister. Nay, according to the laws of dreaming, I conceive that, given the case of Mrs. H., it could hardly happen that she should have a sad or anxious dream, of which her old home afforded the stage, without making the deserted chamber, which must have been the very centre of all solemn thoughts in the house, its peculiar scene.

There appeared some months ago in *Cassell's Magazine* a ghost story narrated by Miss Felicia Skene, which from every point of view is probably one of the best instances of the kind ever published. A husband, dubious of another existence, promised, if possible, to appear to his wife after death. His widow went on a visit to some friends, and their little girl slept in her bed. In the night the child thought she saw the husband (of whose death she had no knowledge) standing by the bedside and looking at his wife sorrowfully. The child, who was much attached to him, spoke to him, and asked him what present he had brought to her, and tried, though unavailingly, to waken the widow sleeping beside her. Presently the figure passed into an adjoining dressing-room, and the child slept till morning, when she instantly ran into the dressing-room, expecting to find her old friend. Failing to do so, she followed the widow, and asked her eagerly where Mr. —— had gone. An explanation followed. The widow conceived that this revelation *through the mind of a child* was much more satisfactory than any which her own senses, excited by anticipation, could have brought her, and unhesitatingly accepted it as a fact that her husband had come to keep his promise. Now, without denying the possibility of such spirit visitations, it must, I think, be owned that the easier solution even of this story (wherein the circumstances are unusually worthy and befitting) is to be found in the dream of the child. The widow's presence beside her most naturally suggested that of her husband whom she had always previously associated with her. That, thinking she saw him, she should have asked him for his wonted gift, and then have thought he went into the next room, were simple incidents of the dream, which was just sufficiently vivid to make so young a child confuse it with waking fact first at the moment, and much more afterwards, when she found great importance attached to it by her elders.

In these and hundreds of cases of supposed revelations and predictions, both given in normal dreams and in various states of trance, I conceive that a careful reference to the laws of unconscious cerebration will rarely fail, if not to explain, at least to elucidate, in a manner, the *modus operandi* of the mystery. Let it be remembered that we have got to do with a power which (under conditions imperfectly known to us) obtains access to the entire treasury of memory, to the stores of facts, words, and transient impressions accumulated during our whole lives, and to which in our ordinary consciousness we have no means of approach. Those states of abnormal remembrance so often described as experienced by drowning persons, would, if prolonged through our waking hours, very obviously put us in possession of means of judging, balancing, and even of foretelling events of which our normal dim and disconnected vision of the past affords no parallel. A similar faculty, not taking in so vast a sweep, but fastening on some special point to which attention is directed, obviously comes into play in many states, both of "clairvoyance" and (in a lesser degree) in natural dreaming. The very least we can do before deciding that any revelation, past, present, or future, comes from any other sources than such *hyper-æsthetic* memory and judgment founded on it, is to examine carefully whether those faculties must be absolutely insufficient to account for it. The notorious fact that such revelations are always conterminous with *somebody's* possible knowledge, gives us, of course, the best warrant for doubting that they come from any ultra-mundane sphere.

The only class of dream, I imagine, which escapes the myth-making faculty, is the purely intellectual dream, which takes place when we have no sensation or sentiment sufficiently vivid to make itself felt in sleep, and the brain merely continues to work on at some one of the subjects suggested by the calm studies of the previous hours. Such dreams, as Dr. Carpenter remarks, have a more uniform and coherent order than is common to others; and it may even happen in time that, in consequence of the freedom from distraction resulting from the suspension of external influences, the reasoning processes may be carried on with unusual vigour and success, and the imagination may develope new and harmonious forms of beauty. (*Physiology*, 5th edit. p. 643.) Under this head, then, come all the remarkable cases of dreams, of the problems solved by Condorcet, and many others. Nearly every one who has been much interested in mathematical studies has done something of the kind in his sleep, and the stories are numerous of persons rising in sleep and writing out lucid legal opinions.

On the other hand, the absurdities of which the mind is capable when dealing with an idea in sleep are beyond measure ludicrous. A correspondent, to whom I am indebted for many valuable suggestions, sends me the following delicious story: "At a time when I was unmarried, I dreamed that I returned home in expectation of meeting my wife. To my consternation and grief she was transformed into a small piece of bread. I was greatly distressed, thinking that by some neglect of mine I had brought about the sad result. However, I lost no time in endeavouring to restore her if possible, and for this purpose I got a small basin of water, and held the piece of bread, which I knew to be my wife in a transformed state, therein. To my dismay I felt the bread gradually melting in my hand, and then awoke, greatly distressed in mind at my approaching bereavement." At a period of my own life, when my attention was divided between reading Leibnitz and providing soup for the poor in a hard winter, I dreamed that my dog had been cruelly boiled down in the soup. Happily recollecting, however, that her soul was an "indestructible monad," I proceeded to search for it diligently with a ladle in the kettle, and discovered it in the shape of a *pasta*.

But it is when the sleep is not wholly natural, but stimulated by narcotics, that these mental feats assume their most prodigious dimensions. The difference between normal dreams and those produced by opiates, so far as I can learn, is mainly this, that in the former we seem always more or less active, and, in the latter, passive. Whatever strange sights we behold in the natural dream, our own share in what is going on is prominent. In the abnormal dream the marvellous scenery is by far the most important part of the vision. In a word, we are *on the stage* in the first case, and *in the stalls* in the second. The cause of this singular distinction must needs be that the action of morphia, haschish, etc., paralyzes more completely the voluntary and active powers than in natural sleep, wherein, indeed, the true conscious will is dormant, but a certain echo of it still survives, leaving us the semblance of choice and energy. On the other hand, while the opiate obscures even such moonlight of volition, it excites the fancy and myth-creating powers of the brain to supernatural vigour, causing to pass before the eyes of the dreamer whole panoramas of beauty or horror. The descriptions of such miseries in the "Confessions of an English Opium Eater," and many other books, afford amazing evidence of what leaps the Pegasus of fancy is capable of taking under the spur of such stimuli on the brain. Here also the singular facility in adopting suggestions and impressions which distinguishes hypnotism from natural dreaming, seems similarly to prevail. All opium-eaters speak of the fearful degree in which every painful idea presented to them before sleeping becomes magnified into portentous visions of terror. A scent suggesting blood, caused one gentleman to dream of an army of skinless men and headless horses defiling for hours before his eyes; and the "Old Man of the Mountain" no doubt contrived to suggest to his assassins, before they ate the haschish, those ideas which resulted in their dreams of houris and paradise.

Besides the picturing of marvellous scenes, passively beheld, it seems that narcotics can stimulate the unconscious brain to the production of poetic or musical descriptions of them; the two actions being simultaneous. Here we have surely the most astonishing of all the feats of this mysterious power within us; and whether we choose to regard it as a part of our true selves, or as the play of certain portions of nerve-matter, in either case the contemplation of it is very bewildering. What truth there may be in the well-known stories of the composition of "Rousseau's Dream" or of Tartini's "Devil Sonata," I cannot pretend to decide. In any case it is admitted that several musical productions have been composed in sleep. But take the poem of "Kubla Khan." Remember that the man who wrote it only rose, in a very few of his multitudinous waking productions, into the same region of high poetical fancy or inspiration of verse. Then see him merely reading, half asleep, the tolerably prosaic sentence out of Purchas' "Pilgrimage:" "Here the Khan Kubla commanded a palace to be built, and a stately garden thereunto, and thus ten miles of fertile ground were inclosed in a wall." And, dropping his book, from this mere bit of green sod of thought he suddenly springs up like a lark into the very heaven of fancy, with the vision of a paradise of woods and waters before his eyes and such sweet singing breaking from his lips as,

"The shadow of the dome of pleasure
  Floated midway o'er the waves,"

interspersed with weird changes and outbursts such as only music knows:—

"It was an Abyssinian maid,
  And on her dulcimer she played,
  Singing of Mount Abora!"

Consider all this, and that the poem of which this is the fragment reached at least the length of three hundred lines,

—and then say what limits shall be placed on the powers which lie hidden within our mortal coil!

This poem of "Kubla Khan" has long stood, though not quite alone as a dream poem, yet as far the largest and most singular piece so composed on record. A friend has permitted me now to publish another dream poem, not, indeed, of similar æsthetic merit, but in a psychological point of view perhaps even more curious, seeing that the dreamer in her waking hours is not a poet, and that the poem she dreamed is in French, in which language she can speak fluently, but in which she believes herself utterly unable to compose a verse. It has been suggested that in this case the act of unconscious cerebration may be one of memory rather than of creative fancy, and that the lady may, at some time of her life, have read the poem thus reproduced in sleep. Such a feat would of itself be sufficiently curious, seeing that she has not the smallest waking recollection of having ever seen the lines; and they occurred to her (just as "Kubla Khan" did to Coleridge) not as a piece of literature, but as the description of a scene she actually beheld simultaneously with the occurrence to her mind of its poetical narrative. But I conceive that the great inaccuracies of rhyme in the poem render it more than doubtful whether it can ever have been published as a French composition. "Espoir," made to correspond with "effroi," and "vert" with "guerre," are the sort of false rhymes which an English ear (especially in sleep) might easily disregard, but which no French poet, accustomed to the strict rules of his own language, could overlook. If I err in this conclusion, and any reader of this little paper can recall having already seen the lines elsewhere, I shall be extremely obliged for the correction.

Let it be borne in mind that the dreamer saw all she describes as in a vision, and that in the middle of the dream, between the morning and evening visions, there intervened a blank and pause, as if a cloud filled the scene. As in the case of Coleridge, the lady had taken morphia in moderate quantity before her dream.

    Ce matin du haut de l'ancienne tourelle
    J'écoutais la voix de la sentinelle,
    Qui criait à ceux qui passent là-bas
    A travers le pont—*Dis !*   *Qui va là ?*

    Et toutes les réponses si pleines d'espoir
    Remplirent mon cœur d'un vague effroi ;
    Car le chagrin est de l'espoir le fruit,
    Et le suit, comme au jour suit la sombre nuit.

        Qui va là ?
    Un beau jeune homme sur un coursier fier,
    A l'épée luisante, au drapeau vert,
    S'en va tout joyeux rejoindre la guerre ;
    Il chante, "Je reviens glorieux !"

        Qui va là ?
    Une blonde jeune fille sur un palefroi gris,
    En habit de page, vert et cramoisi ;
    Elle murmure, "Je veille sur mon bien chéri,"
    Et le suit en souriant doucement.

        Qui va là ?
    Un bon vieillard, ses cheveux sont blancs,
    Il porte un sac, comme l'or brille dedans !
    Il le cache bien de ses doigts tremblants
    Et grommèle, "Je me ferai riche !"

        Qui va là ?
    Un joli enfant conduit sa sœur
    A travers les champs cueillir des fleurs :
    "Nous t'en donnerons à notre retour,"
    Ils disent en riant follement.

      (Here occurred a long pause.)

La nuit s'abaisse sur l'ancienne tourelle,
Écoute encore à la sentinelle,
Qui crie à ceux qui passent là-bas
A travers le pont—*Dis ! Qui va là ?*

Il vient, tout sanglant, un coursier fier,
La selle est vide, mais il traine par terre
Un mourant, qui serre un drapeau vert :
Bientôt il ne gémira plus.

Qui va là ?
Une blonde jeune fille sur un palefroi gris,
En habit de page, vert et cramoisi,
Qui suit tout éperdue son bien chéri,
Et qui prie d'une voix déchirante.

Qui va là ?
Un triste vieillard, ses cheveux sont blancs,
Il porte un sac, il n'y a rien dedans !
Et dit, en tordant ses doigts tremblants,
"Ah c'est dur de perdre *tout !*"

Qui va là ?
Un joli enfant qui porte sa sœur :
"Un serpent glissant parmi les fleurs
L'a piqué. Mais vois ! Elle dort sans pleurs ?"
Cher petit ! Elle n'en versera plus !

Another dream poem, which a correspondent has been so good as to send to me, is interesting in a different way. It was composed in a dream on the night of August 23, 1866, by the Rev. W. H. Taylor, Principal of the Grammar School of Houghton-le-Spring; and the author died of fever about a week afterwards.

HYMN.

Lord! my weary soul is yearning,
  Yearning for its home of rest ;
Anxious eyes for ever turning
  Towards the mansions of the blest.

But the warfare is not over;
  Foes without, and foes within,
Fiercely o'er my path assail me,
  Tempt me with the bait of sin.

Faint and stricken in the battle,
  I raise my feeble hands and cry,
Save me, save me, Abba, Father!
  Save me, save me, or I die.

Then a voice comes softly, sweetly,
  Bringing peace, expelling fear,
Cheers my drooping spirit, saying,
  Courage, Christian! God is near.

Then revived, encouraged, strengthened,
  Onward I my steps pursue,
Looking upward, looking homeward,
  Keep the golden gates in view.

Then, oh then, dear Lord, receive me,
  Ope the gates, and let me in,
To thy loving bosom take me,
  Ransomed, pardoned, freed from sin.

Lastly, we come to the point wherein I conceive that dreams throw most light on the separability of the self from the automatically-working brain. The absence of the Moral Sense in dreams is a matter touched upon in my former essay, on which I have received the most varied communications. On one hand two esteemed friends have assured me that their consciences are occasionally awake in sleep; on the other, a great many more tell me that their experience entirely corroborates my somewhat hazarded observations. For example, an admirable and most kind-hearted lady palmed off a bad sixpence on a beggar, and chuckled at the notion of his disappointment when he should discover her deception. A distinguished philanthropist, exercising for many years high judicial functions, continually commits forgery, and only regrets the act when he learns that he is to be hanged. A woman, whose life at the time of her dream was devoted to the instruction of pauper children, seeing one of them make a face at her, doubled him up into the smallest compass, and poked him through the bars of a lion's cage. One of the most benevolent of men, who shared not at all in the military enthusiasm of his warlike brothers (the late Mr. Richard Napier), ran his best friend through the body, and ever after recalled the extreme gratification he had experienced on seeing the point of his sword come out through the shoulders of his beloved companion. Other crimes committed in dreams need not be here recorded; but I am persuaded that if we could but know all the improper things done by the most proper people in their sleep with the utmost *sangfroid* and completely unblushing effrontery, the picture would present a diverting contrast to our knowledge of them in their conscious hours.

If the moral sense be not wholly suppressed in sleep, there is certainly enough evidence to conclude that it is only exceptionally active, and chiefly, if not solely so, in the case of dreams assuming the character of nightmares, in which the consciousness is far less perfectly dormant than in others. Let it be understood that I do not deny the presence of the peculiar dread and horror of remorse in sleep. As it is undoubtedly the worst torture of which the mind is susceptible, so it is the form of mental suffering which continually presents itself in the crisis and climax of imaginary woe in a nightmare or in insanity. But this has nothing to do with the normal consciousness of right and wrong, the sense that what we are *actually doing* is morally good or bad; a sense which is never wholly absent in our waking hours, and which (as I conceive) is never present in a perfectly natural dream. If the experience of my readers do not lead them to correct this opinion, then I must be permitted to urge that the discovery of such a law as that which excludes the moral sense from dreams must needs point to some important conclusion concerning the nature of unconscious cerebration. If such cerebration be in any way to be described as our *own* work, how is it possible that so intimate, so indissoluble a part of ourselves as our sense of the moral character of actions should be regularly absent? To divide the idea of a cruel deed from a sense of loathing, or a base one from a sense of contempt, would be an impossible feat for us to accomplish awake. Our perception of such acts is simultaneously a perception of their moral hideousness; yet we do this in dreams, not merely occasionally, but, as I conceive, as a rule of which the exceptions, if any, are extremely rare.

Nay, further. A great proportion of the passions of our dreams seem often *not* reflexes of those experienced in former hours of consciousness, but altogether foreign to our natures, past and present. Passions which never for a moment sullied our consciousness, sentiments the very antitheses of those belonging to our idiosyncrasies, present themselves in sleep, and are followed out by their appropriate actions, just as if we were not ourselves at all, but, in one case, a Jack Shepherd, or in another a Caligula. The man who would go to the stake rather than do a dishonourable act, imagines himself cheating at cards; the woman who never voluntarily hurt a fly, chops a baby into mincemeat.

The theory of Dugald Stewart, that the Will is not dormant in dreams, but has merely lost the power of controlling the muscles,[1] seems to me entirely inadequate to fit cases like these. If the will were awake, it must inevitably rebel against acts so repugnant to it, even if it were powerless

[1] Dugald Stewart's Works, vol. ii. p. 292.

to prevent the brain from inventing them. A sense of discord and trouble would reign in our dreams as of "a house divided against itself." The fact that nothing of the kind is experienced, and that we have, notoriously, not even a sense of surprise in dreams when we find ourselves committing the most atrocious outrages, is surely sufficient to prove that the true self is not merely impotent but dormant.

Finally, not only the absence of the moral sense in dreams, but also the absence of all sense of mental fatigue in them, appears to point to the same conclusion. In dreams we never experience that weariness which invariably in waking hours follows all sustained volition. Wide and wild as may be our flights of fancy, no feather of our wings seems to droop after them. But exertion of will is the most laborious of all things, whether it be employed to attend to a subject of study, to create a fanciful story, or to direct our limbs in unwonted actions. It has been truly remarked, that if the laws of our constitution required us to perform a separate act of volition for every muscular motion we make in the course of twenty-four hours,—in other words, if there were no such power as that of automatic action,—we should expire of the fatigue of a single day's exertion; nay, of the mere rising up and sitting down, and washing and brushing and buttoning, and moving our legs down stairs, and cutting and buttering and chewing and swallowing, and all the numberless little proceedings which must be gone through before even breakfast is accomplished. Nature has so arranged it that we learn the various arts of walking, eating, dressing, etc., etc., one by one, and at an age when we have nothing else to do; so that when the further lessons of how to read, to write, and so on, have to be learned, the rudiments of life's business have long before passed into the class of voluntary acts over which unconscious cerebration is quite sufficiently sensible to preside. And this unconscious brain-work never seems to tire us at all; whether it consists in setting our feet and eyes going in the proper direction for walking or riding, or in painting for us the choicest galleries of pictures in dreamland, or composing for us as many novels as taxed the imagination of Alexandre Dumas. It is the conscious Self alone whose exertions ever flag, and for whose repose merciful Nature has deserved the blessing of Sancho Panza on "the man who invented sleep."

Take it how we will, I think it remains evident that in dreams (except those belonging to the class of nightmare wherein the will is partially awakened) we are in a condition of entire passivity; receiving impressions indeed from the work which is going on in our brains, but incurring no fatigue thereby, and exempted from all sense of moral responsibility as regards it. The instrument on which we are wont to play has slipped from our loosened grasp, and its secondary and almost equally wondrous powers have become manifest. It is not only a finger-organ, but a *self-acting* one; which, while we lie still and listen, goes over, more or less perfectly, and with many a quaint wrong note and variation, the airs which we performed on it yesterday, or long ago.

Is this instrument *ourselves?* Are *we* quite inseparable from this manufactory of thoughts? If it never worked except by our volition and under our control, then, indeed, it might be difficult to conceive of our consciousness apart from it. But every night a different lesson is taught us. The brain, released from its bit and rein, plays like a colt turned to pasture, or, like the horse of the miller, goes round from left to right to relieve itself from having gone round from right to left all the day before. Watching these instinctive sports and relaxations by which we benefit, but in whose direction we have no part, do we not acquire the conviction that the dreaming brain-self is not the true self for whose moral worthiness we strive, and for whose existence after death alone we care? "We are of the stuff which dreams are made of." Not wholly so, O mighty poet-philosopher! In that "stuff" there enters not the noblest element of our nature; that Moral Will which allies us, not to the world of passing shadows, but to the great Eternal Will, in whose Life it is our hope that we shall live for ever.

ESSAY XIII.

AURICULAR CONFESSION

IN THE

CHURCH OF ENGLAND.[1]

CERTAIN well-known coarse attempts to "unmask" the Confessional seem to have effected a purpose very remote from that which their originators designed. By fixing the public mind on gross abuses, which no one seriously apprehends to see revived in the hands of English clergymen, attention has been diverted from the real point at issue, namely, the moral or immoral, spiritual or unspiritual, tendency of the practice of Auricular Confession under ordinary and favourable circumstances. In the following pages, I propose to leave aside altogether any consideration of the evils *accidental* to the practice, and to pass no judgment on

---

[1] *Tracts for the Day.* 1 vol. 8vo. London: Longmans. 1868.
  A Help to Repentance. By the Rev. Vernon Hutton. 4th thousand. London: Longmans.
  Pardon through the Precious Blood, or the Benefit of Absolution. Edited by a Committee of Clergy. 22nd thousand. London: Palmer. 1870.
  The Ordinance of Confession. By William Gresley. 2nd edition. Masters. 1852.
  The Church and the World. Edited by the Rev. Orby Shipley. Article, "Thirty Years in the English Church." 1st series. Longmans. 1866.
  The Church and the World. Article, "Private Confession and Absolution." 2nd series. Longmans. 1867.

the narratives rife through Southern Europe, concerning "Priests, Women and families." I shall attempt to study as candidly as possible the *inherent* moral character of such an act as regular confession to a priest, and draw such conclusions as may seem warranted regarding the attitude to be observed towards the present revival of the practice. That the inquiry is not untimely may be judged by any one who will take the trouble to inform himself of what the whole High-Church party are now doing in this matter, and to what extent all over the country they are raising a claim to receive the confessions of their flocks as a regular portion of their office.

In a world in which Sin occupies the place it holds to-day on our planet, it would seem almost superfluous to protest against the use of any method which aims at its repression. The evils within and around us may well be thought great enough to occupy all our energies, without turning our hand against those who are honestly contending against them also, even if they employ tactics which we deem ill advised and indiscreet. "Let us leave these High-Churchmen," we are inclined to say, "to make what efforts they please to stem the flood of vice in our great cities. If we do not augur much success for their attempt, at least we honour their zeal, and are fully persuaded that to do anything is better than to do nothing." Such first impressions are even in a certain way deepened if we chance to read the manuals of penitence prepared by our English Father-Confessors, such as those quoted at the head of this article. The serious tone of these books, free from taint of cant, and the exalted standard of morality in word and deed obviously accepted by their authors, claim the highest respect; nor can any reader doubt that it is real sin, not mere ecclesiastical error, which is attacked, and real goodness, not mere sheep-like obedience, which is inculcated.

But whatever be the good intentions, the honesty and the zeal, of the modern revivers of the Confessional in our churches, the question is not altered: Is the practice of Auricular Confession to a priest spiritually or morally expedient? Are its natural results strengthening or weakening to the mind? Must it make a man feel more deeply the burden of his sins, or teach him to cast them off on the shoulders of another? Will it (for this is the crucial question of all)—will it bring the sinful soul nearer, in the deep solitudes of the spiritual world, to the One only Source of purity and restoration, and help it to look straight up into the face of God; or will it, on the contrary, thrust a priest always between man and his Maker to intercept even the embrace of the returning Prodigal in his Father's arms?

In the endeavour to find the solution of these questions, it will of course be necessary to leave considerable margin for differences of moral condition such as exist at all times in a given population—a margin which ought to be still further enlarged when we include in our survey a long period of history and the inhabitants of both barbarous and civilized lands. The practice of which the benefits may outweigh its disadvantages, or which may have few disadvantages at all, when applied to a child or a savage, to lawless mediæval barons or brutish serfs, may do indefinitely more harm than good when used by full-grown and educated people in the nineteenth century. Our object in the present paper being a practical one, we shall limit our scope to the class and nation which the revival of Auricular Confession in England alone concerns, and ask: How is it likely to affect English men and women from the age of confirmation to the end of life, and from the highest social and intellectual rank down to that level of poverty and stupidity against which the waves of clerical zeal break for ever in vain? We must assume average intelligence, average religious feeling, and, especially, average moral condition. The old Church of England principle, that men burdened with any "grievous crime" should seek relief from confession to "any discreet and learned minister of God's word," is one whose wisdom we are not at all inclined to dispute; and it is only with the extension of this reasonable rule from the exceptional to the general and universal, that we are now concerned. An elaborate defence of such extension may be seen in one of the books at the head of this article;[1] but, when it was published, twenty years ago, English High-Churchmen had not gone by any means so far in their inculcation of Confession as they do at present; and Mr. Gresley was ready to admit that "in foreign churches where Confession is compulsory and periodical, there is danger of formality" (p. 135); and that women may be led to rely too much on their priests (p. 137), even while he set forth the innumerable reasons why people should renew their confessions and seek "ghostly counsel" again and again. More recent manuals (among which *Pardon through the Precious Blood*, edited by a Committee of Clergymen, appears to be most authoritative) take it seemingly for granted that every one needs Confession as much as he needs the perpetual pardon of God; and the forms recommended for use always refer to the "last Confession," as if the Anglican, like the Romish penitent, made it, as a matter of course, a regular practice. The religious life seems understood by these teachers to commence normally only by a General Confession, just as an Evangelical believes it to commence by "Conversion." The vivid sense of sinfulness (which is the one natural fact of the case) must, as they hold it, rigorously take the shape of Auricular Confession to make it available. "Mere" private contrition

[1] The Ordinance of Confession, by the Rev. William Gresley.

of heart and amendment of life, they treat as wholly unsatisfactory and incomplete, carrying with them no promise of Divine pardon. Not to speak disrespectfully, they practically affirm that a man must repent *en régle*—confess to a priest, do penance, and be absolved—or his repentance will still need to be repented of. Thus Confession has ceased to be an exceptional action, and has become the regular practice of a religious life. It is not to be applied as a specific remedy in cases of acute disease. It is to be used like a daily ablution, as the proper means of purification and health.

Putting aside, then, cases of offenders who have committed heinous offences, we shall suppose the instance of a person of ordinary character and circumstances in the condition of mind desired by the preachers of Confession. He is sensible of his sinfulness, and (a point to which we shall hereafter refer) very much terrified by fear of hell-fire. His pastors instruct him that his private penitence, whatever may be its intensity, affords no sort of security that the benefits of the "Precious Blood" shall be applied to his particular soul, and that to obtain such security he must confess to a priest who has received at his ordination the commission, "Whose sins thou dost forgive, they are forgiven; and whose sins thou dost retain, they are retained." Goaded by remorse and terror, he is taught further to lash his feelings to excitement by such representations as these: "Look at His sacred body nailed to the cross; see His flesh torn and mangled, dripping with blood; this is the work of thy sins. Thy sins have opened His wounds and made them bleed afresh; they have torn wider the rents in His hands and feet."[1] Finally, he makes up his mind to come to confession and (as he is assured) become "clean" and safe. What

[1] The Precious Blood, p. 20.

are the moral and spiritual results likely to follow such an act?

In the first place, the long and close self-examination which is ordered as a preliminary, may, when first practised by a hitherto thoughtless person, very probably open quite a new view to a man of his own character. In some special cases it may perhaps even do the invaluable service of teaching a self-satisfied Pharisee that he ought to put himself in the place of the Publican. Some festering secrets of souls may be healed simply by being brought to light, and spectres dissolved into air by being fairly faced. Long cherished hatred may be tracked to its root, and a selfish life looked at for once as a whole in its proper colours. All these good results, I freely admit, may follow from the self-examination which is required before Confession, and which (it may be added) has formed a recognized portion of all *metanoia*, from the days of Pythagoras and David to our own. But how of the Confession itself? What good or harm is to be done to such a mind as we have supposed, by the process of kneeling down in a vestry before a clergyman, making the sign of the cross, and then for about a quarter of an hour (or, in some cases, for five or six hours) going over the events of life *seriatim:* "I accuse myself of" this falsehood, that unkindness, and so on? If the individual be so ignorant of morals as not to know what is sinful and what is innocent, it must be a great benefit to him to receive instruction from his Confessor, provided always that he is—what priests unfortunately, by some twist of mental conformation, seem very rarely to be—a sound and healthy moralist. In such a case, the Confessional may obviously be a useful school of ethics. But it is surely no small disgrace to our spiritual guides if it should be needed as such, and if their flocks have been so little instructed in the principles of uprightness and charity, as not to know beforehand what is right and what is wrong, and to require to wait till they have sinned, to know what is sinful.

That the fear of having hereafter to confess a sin may sometimes possibly keep a man from committing it, is another argument for the usefulness of the Confessional as a moral agent, on which I need not enlarge. Such a motive would, of course, have no ethical value, and as to its deterrent force, may plausibly be balanced against the encouragement (found undoubtedly by Romish criminals, bandits, etc., and possibly, therefore, also by Anglicans) in the assurance of pardon, obtainable at any moment, by priestly absolution. When we have descended to so low a level of motive in the one case, we are called on to do the like in the other.

Lastly, there is a very great and important result of the practice of Confession, which to some of its upholders doubtless appears among its chief advantages, but which I must be excused for classing altogether in another category, namely, the enormous influence given thereby to the priesthood over the minds of their flocks. To treat fully of this matter, and to trace the share of her confessors in building up the vast edifice of the authority of the Church of Rome, would need, not a few paragraphs in an article, but several volumes. That the influence of the clergy of the Church of England would ever be as evil as that of their brethren of the Church of Rome, I am far from believing; but with the warning of all history before our eyes, I think that he must be a bold man, indeed, who should desire to place in the hands of any priesthood on earth a power whose most partial misuse means ecclesiastical despotism, and the mental and moral slavery of all the weaker minds of the community.

Turning now to the disadvantages of the practice of Confession, we may observe three points in particular:

1. The fostering of a materialistic and mechanical view of religion.

2. The enervation of the moral constitution.

3. The desecration of the inner spiritual life by the exposure to a priest of the most sacred recesses of the penitent soul.

1. In nearly every essay and manual on the subject of Confession, the practice is recommended as indispensable to give *reality* to repentance. So long as a man's feelings of contrition are hid in his own bosom, or only poured out in prayer to God in his chamber, of what avail (it is asked) are they? "To look calmly," says the author of the essay on the *Seven Sacraments* in the *Tracts for the Day* (p. 59), "at the cry, 'Go direct to Christ,' what does it mean? . . . The Protestant directs the penitent to rely wholly and entirely on his own internal feelings; he is not to go out of himself for pardon and grace. From the beginning to the end of the operation, it is something worked out in the mind and heart of the sinner. . . . . . How different is the faith of the Catholic Church and the practice of the Catholic penitent!" Very different indeed, we may truly echo, since this is as good an illustration as could be chosen of the difference between spiritual and sacerdotal religion. An operation, even the blessed operation of penitence and restoration, is of no value, it seems, in Catholic eyes, if it be merely "worked out in the mind and heart of the sinner." A *mere* change of mind and heart, from the love of sin to the love of God,—the alpha and omega of religion,—the change for whose accomplishment in the inner man some sanguine Protestants imagine all Catholic machinery to be honestly, though clumsily, designed,—this greatest of all spiritual events, over which Christ thought that angels rejoice in heaven, is,

after all, we are told, most unsatisfactory and incomplete, if it be not accompanied by spoken confession to a priest, penance of outward act, and the receipt of duly authorized priestly absolution. A man who only prays in the chamber where Christ told him to pray, does not "go out of himself." It is not "going out of" oneself to pray alone. *That*, we presume, is a mere subjective phenomenon, liable, as the author presently points out, to land us in grievous error. To "go out of" oneself, it is necessary to do a great deal more (at least in priestly view) than only to rise up from the swine's husks in the "far country" and return to the Father's feet. It is necessary to speak to a man—a real, tangible, audible man—not merely to the unseen and silent Spirit. Speaking to God is not properly a real act; and as for listening to His whispers in the soul of reproof or pardon, it is the most dangerous thing in the world. We must speak to the priest, and hear from the priest that we are absolved, and then we may *know* we have repented and are "safe." All other knowledge, whether of the sincerity of our contrition or of the renewal of communion which God has granted to us, is to be taken as mere illusion, or at best as wholly untrustworthy. We have not "gone out of ourselves" from first to last.

Is it too much to say that this is the true—if not the only—infidelity, even the distrust of spiritual, and the reliance on physical, facts, displayed in dealing with the very crisis of the soul's history?

The same observations apply to the subjects of Penance and Absolution, in which the sense of Repentance is assumed by the same teachers to be visionary till it has done something else beside undoing as far as may be the evil repented of; and the sense of Restoration is disallowed till a form of words has been pronounced over the penitent by the priest.

Again, the usual practice of allotting for Penance the repetition of certain prayers, in the Anglican as in the Roman Catholic Church, goes a little further in the direction of the mechanical and the profane. Contemplating such a portent as a clergyman ordering, and his penitent performing, such an act as that of prayer to the Father in heaven as a *punishment,* or (as one of our manuals describes it, as an improvement on this notion) as a "token of obedience to the Church," we are tempted to ask, Do either confessor or penitent know what Prayer means? Do they, who use it, as we know, with so much constancy and reverence in their perpetual services, do they understand that it is something more than a *funzione,* as the Italians say—that it may be life's greatest joy, humanity's highest glory? It cannot be but that such devoted men must know it. How, then, can they endure to make of it a "penance"? Are children punished by sending them to their parent's arms, or made to "show obedience" to the nurse by seeking their father's face?

Again, the notion of Sin itself is by these Anglicans strangely materialized. They manifestly hold very high and pure conceptions of right and wrong acts and sentiments; but the reasons why the sinner is to regret and abhor his sins are set forth in a way to lead us to imagine that the hatefulness of bad deeds and feelings, and the loss by the sinful soul of that divine light below whose plane it has fallen, are not by any means the sole or worst evils involved. The two great evils, on the contrary, seem to be, first, that if the soul leaves the body in a state of sin, "it will be driven away from God, and be plunged into a place of darkness and misery for ever;" and, secondly, that the sinner's offences have had a part in causing the sufferings of Christ. "By thine uncleanness," the penitent is advised to say to his soul, "thou hast scourged his body with the most painful stripes. Thou hast had no mercy on his adorable body," etc.[1] Thus, as usual in the orthodox system, a man's mind is forcibly diverted from his own moral guilt to vivid images of Christ's physical sufferings, which (even supposing them to have had a mysterious antedated connexion with his sins) were certainly not *intended* by him to be aggravated, and therefore are not properly the subjects of his genuine contrition. Having really maliciously injured his neighbour A., or been too selfish to help B., he is advised, not to think about his behaviour or feelings towards A. or B., but to goad himself to tortures of remorse for having hurt C., who died long before he was born, and who he believes now reigns the King of Paradise. Instead of writhing under the load of his present shame and guilt, he is urged to ponder on the dangers of exposure at the day of judgment and of the punishment of his sins in eternity. Always, it is the material consequence to himself or to his Saviour, not his actual moral guilt, which is insisted upon.

The conception of Sin as a series of definite wrong acts which can be catalogued and rehearsed, rather than as an evil state of the heart which God alone can fully know, is another instance of materialism. Unless in the case of heinous offences, it would seem as if the idea of a general confession of misdoings and omissions were, to an enlightened conscience, something almost absurd. The thing to be confessed above all—the only thing, in fact, which very much concerns us—is just what such a catalogue must omit. Many a man presenting a long list of actual sins to his confessor might obviously be immeasurably better than one who could hardly tax himself with the omission of a single tithe-giving of mint, anise or cummin, but whose heart and will had swerved from God altogether.

[1] The Precious Blood, p. 20. N.B.—This little book is bound in crimson, and is altogether as sensational as typography and literary dress can make it.

Finally, as regards this department of our subject, it ought to be carefully weighed what meaning is attached to the assurance, tendered to the penitent, that he is "CLEAN NOW." The desire that our sins *should never have been committed*, is of course the very first sentiment of natural repentance; but this being a matter which even God cannot change, no man, it is to be presumed, thinks of asking for it. Again, the desire that God should purify all that is evil in us now, should "give us a clean heart and renew a right spirit within us," is the supreme prayer of every contrite soul; but it is one whose response must come, if it come at all, in a spiritual fact about which we alone may have cognizance, and concerning which a priest's assurance must necessarily go for nothing. If a man find his spirit really "renewed," filled with hatred of the sin he cherished, and of love to God and goodness, it is of the smallest possible consequence to him whether anybody tell him that such is, or is not, the case. On the other hand, if he feel his heart still full of evil passions, it is a ghastly mockery to tell him he is "clean," in any sense such as that which we are now considering. There remains, then, only for the word, as employed in the manuals of confessors, the old sense in which it was used by Hebrews and Brahmins, Romans and Aztecs, the sense of a magical removal of guilt, attainable, as was supposed, by means of a scapegoat, a Soma sacrifice, a Taurobolia, or a human victim. This is not the place to criticize these crude notions of half-civilized races, but it may be remarked that of all the eight different ways in which, as the lamented McLeod Campbell told us, the Christian doctrine of the Atonement may be understood, the lowest possible is that which assimilates it to these heathen rites; first, by representing Christ's sacrifice as a device to save men, *not* from the dominion of sin, but from its punishment; and then by making the application of the benefit depend, *not* on a spiritual identification of the sinful soul by faith and love with its supposed sinless Redeemer, but on a practical transaction between the man and a priest who acts as Christ's delegate, and conveys to him a legal absolution. Throughout the whole treatment of the subject by the Anglican advocates of Confession, it will also be observed that the object professedly sought is "Pardon," in the sense in which that word is distinguished from "Forgiveness"; namely, as representing the Remission of a Penalty, not the Reconciliation of an offended Friend. No priest presumes to tell his penitent that God, through his mouth, assures him of the restoration of His Fatherly love and freedom of communion. *That* fact, like the fact of a renewed spirit, must be felt to be believed; and the voices of all the priests in Christendom could do nothing to make it either more or less certain. But the magical expiation which secures the remission of a remote penalty, is a matter on which sacerdotal authority may successfully pronounce that it has been accurately accomplished.

Whether anxiety for escape from punishment be, or be not, a proper feature of genuine penitence, is a question which has been much obscured by the intrusion of the monstrous doctrine of Eternal Perdition into the natural view of the subject. No amount of religion or virtue could enable a man willingly to renounce religion and virtue to all eternity; and therefore, so long as any one believes that his sins may incur everlasting banishment from God, he is compelled to crave eagerly for the remission of their punishment. But the moment this threat is removed, the case is altered. Genuine contrition occupies itself very little about the suffering which we may have entailed on ourselves by sin; nay, in cases of poignant self-reproach and remorse, the prospect of such suffering is undoubtedly far from unwelcome, but rather a relief. That "justice should be done," even though we lie prostrate beneath it, is the noblest sentiment of the repentant soul; the one by which it most surely re-assumes its filial relationship to the Lord of Justice. To encourage an opposite frame of mind, and inspire urgent desire for escape from punishment, with recourse to such a method as priestly absolution for avoiding it, is assuredly very far from an elevating system of religious training. The slave shrinks from the lash, and appeals to the Overseer to intercede on his behalf. The son cries, "Punish me, for I have deserved punishment, but only receive me again. *That* is all I desire."

A very marked distinction has existed at all times between the two kinds of sacrifices; those which were intended for a propitiation and vicarious satisfaction for sin, and those which were meant as expressions of love and devotion, and of the inner sense of the rightfulness that all which man is and has should be given to God. The High-Church clergy, like the extreme Evangelicals, insist on treating the death of Christ in the former light, and outrun them in making the Eucharist a magical appropriation of that event; a "feeding on a sacrifice." But the Anglicans alone of the two parties in the National Church have attempted to restore, not only the vicarious, but the devotional type of sacrifice, and by their whole scheme of an ornate cultus and perpetual services and ceremonies, to renew in our century the formalism of an earlier age. Not wholly without tenderness can we view this movement, judging it to be in a great measure the result of a fervent longing to retain a grasp of religion amid the gathering clouds of doubt—a grasp unhappily fastened, not on its realities, but on its mere vesture and dress. But it is none the less a sad, a deplorable spectacle. The original idea of such sacrifice of formal devotion as we are speaking of, has been compared to a child's delight in bringing home to his mother the weeds and pebbles with which he has been himself delighted in his daily walk. The mother accepts them lovingly as tokens of her child's love; and the child brings them again and again and soon makes a habit, well nigh sacred, of giving them to her continually. At last it dawns on his mind that she cannot possibly really care for them; that they are of no value to her; and that she has only accepted them because she has understood that he meant them as offerings of affection. What now is he to do? Is he to go on giving his mother the weeds and pebbles still? He has nothing else to give, and his heart yearns to give something, and the habit has become so fixed that there seems a want of filial affection in discontinuing it. Very probably, then, he maintains the practice for a time; but it is obvious that the original purpose is lost, the beauty of the action gone. If he persist long in keeping up the dry and now unmeaning custom, a mechanical spirit inevitably creeps over his performance of it, and all his relations with his parent become falsified and distorted. At last, one day she says to him, "Bring no more vain oblations. My son, give me thine heart. Show thy love to me, not in gifts which I heed not, but in serving my other children, thy brothers." If he hears this warning and still persists in presenting his paltry childish offerings, what hope is there for him? How is he ever to enter into true relations with his mother?

2. The second grave objection to the use of Confession, except in cases of extraordinary guilt, is that it must inevitably tend to enervate the moral constitution. To acquire the habit of running to a priest whenever we feel penitent, or desire to strengthen our good resolutions, or, in fact, are passing through any of the deeper phases of the inner life when God's spirit is striving with ours, can surely have no other

result than to make us weaker and less able to walk alone with God every year of our lives. The conscience which is itself brought to another bar, is no longer the supreme Judge within us. The little seed of good which is fructifying in the depth of our hearts, may only too probably be killed by exposure. The more able and powerful may be our Confessor, the more certain is it that he must shortly assume in our minds a place of authority which will leave us small remnant of self-reliance in matters wherein our judgment may differ from his as to the rectitude of an action; and if we reach the point of blindly accepting his *ipse dixit* in cases of duty, against our own conscience, where are we, but in the net of the Jesuit's "obedience"? Of course, as in every other history of the struggle between Authority and Freedom, there are endless fine things to be said of the invaluable use of authority in keeping foolish and ignorant people straight, and of the terrible consequences of freedom to anybody short of a sage and a saint. Still, if we have read aright the great purpose for which God has made us, and are not mistaken in supposing that He sees it best to permit all the evil and misery which arise from moral freedom, sooner than leave us without it, we may reasonably demur to the stride which priests would take in curtailing that liberty, were we to allow them to be once more the guardians of the consciences of the nations. Even if the ethics taught by any "Catholic" priesthood were uniformly pure and high, if vile casuistry were a thing unknown in their books, if Catholic nations and individuals trained by the Confessional obviously held the clearest ideas of truth and uprightness, if ecclesiastical behaviour never betrayed signs of shuffling or crooked-mindedness, even if all these things were so, we should still gravely object to permitting the Anglican clergy, or any other order of clergy in the world, to assume the sway over men's consciences obtained by the practice of Auricular Confession. As things actually are, it would seem to us one of the most grievous dangers to public morality to entrust them with such power for a generation, even though we fully appreciate the lofty morality of their present instructions.

In this, as in every other of the High-Church restorations of Romish practices, we find ourselves drawn into discussing as a novelty that which in truth has been an experiment tried on an enormous scale for many centuries, and of which there is no real need to speak save by rehearsing the obvious results. Which are the people of Europe whose characters are most straightforward and manly, who care most for public justice, and whose word is most generally accepted by friends and foes as trustworthy? Is it the nations who have enjoyed all the supposed moral benefits of Auricular Confession from the Dark Ages till to-day,—the Spaniards, the Greeks, the Neapolitans, the Irish? Or does it chance that even in those Catholic countries an English or American heretic, the descendant of a dozen generations of unconfessing heretics, is believed on his word and trusted more readily than a native? How is it that every foreigner points with envy and admiration to the public spirit and love of justice which, as M. Taine says, "support England on a million columns"? How is it that we are not learning public and private virtue from the priest-led nations of Europe, if the Confessional be the true school of goodness? How is it that the ages when it reigned supreme and unquestioned, were worse ages than any the world has since beheld? How is it that we are growing a little more humane, a little more truthful, a little more sober, as the generations bear us further from the last days even of Protestant Confession; while the comparison of English domestic morality with that of Southern Europe, and of English charities with those of any other land, show that even as regards the virtues which the Confessional is supposed expressly to guard and to inculcate, we are no whit the worse for its disuse?[1]

3. Lastly, we have to consider among the objections to the revival of the practice of Confession, the desecrating influence on the spiritual life involved in the exposure of the recesses of the soul. The manual already quoted[2] says that penitents have two objections to Confession. One is, that they are afraid the clergyman will betray their secrets —an idle fear. The other is, that they are ashamed—a sentiment which ought to be conquered, because "sin not forgiven now will be proclaimed to our endless shame hereafter, before men and devils, holy angels and God Himself." Our inquiry is whether this latter sentiment be wholly a bad one, which a man will be permanently the better for disregarding and trampling on? This is a very important point in the whole subject we are considering; and to do it justice we must pause an instant to define what is the nature of the shame in question.

There is, first, the kind of shame which consists in the pain of exposure, the sense that we are fallen in the esteem of the person who learns our guilt, and perhaps have become the object of his contempt. To those in whom the sentiment which phrenologists style Love of Approbation is strongly developed, shame of this sort is torture; and to

[1] In connexion with this subject it may be remarked, that the Fathers of the Reformation were all brought up on the Catholic system and never got beyond Catholic ethics. If some of their actions lend a shade of colour to Dr. Littledale's application to them of his term of "scoundrel martyrs," he may look to "the hole of the pit whence they were digged," or rather whence they partially lifted themselves heavenward, for their exculpation.

[2] Pardon through the Precious Blood.

all, save the most hardened, it is probably one of the bitterest drops in the cup of life. Now it is clear that it is this common kind of shame which the advocates of Confession have in their mind as the chief obstacle to the practice, because they constantly insist that the sinner had better make up his mind to compound for the shame of telling his sin to his priest, because "sin not forgiven now will be proclaimed to our endless shame hereafter, before men and devils, holy angels and God Himself."[1] (How anything is to be proclaimed before God hereafter, which, by implication, must be concealed from Him now, we cannot stop to consider.) Thus Confession is represented rather in the light of a security for secrecy, than, as some liberal writers have more charitably supposed it, an outburst of honesty. It is recommended as a wise plan for confining to the ear of a single clergyman secrets which, if not so judiciously guarded, will infallibly be published hereafter to the sound of the Last Trumpet. *Some* shame and exposure the sinner is assured he must needs endure. Who would not seize the opportunity of limiting the disgrace to a single auditor, rather than incur the terrible penalty of being pilloried before the assembled universe—which of course will have nothing better to do than to stand aghast and listen to the long catalogue of our misdemeanours?

Now, putting aside this piece of ecclesiastical bribery, let us hold to the point of the moral advantage or disadvantage of braving the shame of exposure so far as to confess our sins to a priest. Is the process likely to be ethically beneficial or the reverse? It would seem that the pain in question is of very varied influence on the characters of those who endure it. To estimate its results aright, we must distinguish carefully between the effects of being exposed involuntarily and publicly, and to all our little world

[1] Pardon through the Precious Blood, p. 15.

at once; or of being exposed voluntarily only to one person, and under peculiar conditions of penitence pleading on our behalf for a restoration of esteem. And, again, we must distinguish between the exposure of great sins, proving our whole life to have been a hollow pretence, or that of such ordinary weaknesses as do not entirely forfeit our claim to respect. Public involuntary exposure of great sins commonly proves too overwhelming an agony to leave the soul any sufficient balance of self-respect or hope enabling it even to retain such virtues as were previously preserved. The miserable swindler, or fallen woman, under such disgrace, sinks commonly in despair, if not in drunkenness, into complete moral collapse. Only in exceptional cases does public involuntary exposure of either vice or crime, clearing away all fogs of self-deception, leave behind it strength of character and religious or conscientious feeling sufficient to enable the fallen person to start afresh from new ground, and become virtuous in a truer sense than ever. As all who have studied the characters of children, or of persons convicted of crime, are well aware, this shame of exposure is a punishment to be used with extremest caution; very useful as a threat, but nearly always injurious as an actual infliction. It is doubtless most unwholesome for any one to go on bearing an entirely false character with those around him, and to be placed upon a pedestal when he deserves to be on a gibbet; or to be allowed to weave a romance of self-exculpation and glorification when he actually merits nothing but blame and compassion.[1] Even the sudden downfall of absolute disgrace may be less dangerous than this. But, as a rule, public exposure of guilt is a terrible and most perilous trial, to which they who best

---

[1] This is said to be peculiarly the case with inmates of Penitentiaries, who invariably enter them with a rigmarole of a history taken out of a penny novelist, and with whom no real reformation ever begins till they admit this pseudo-biography to be a lie, and tell the plain facts of their lives.

understand human nature are most reluctant to expose any fellow-creature whose reclamation is possible by other means.

Does it follow that private voluntary exposure—a very much milder process, no doubt—is a particularly healthful one? The pang of shame once passed, is passed for ever. No one can ever feel it again in its sharpness. Is it good to have it behind us in our experience, as a thing we have gone through and know the worst of; or to have it always before us as a formless horror of warning? I may be wrong in my conclusion, but it seems to me that the pain we should feel the first time we practised Auricular Confession would leave us harder and more shameless ever after. It might seem to us right to endure it. I can readily imagine a stern sense of self-revenge and thirst for expiation making a man force his lips to utter his own condemnation, as Cranmer held his guilty hand in the fire. But it does not follow that the penance, even if undertaken in the purest spirit of contrition, would leave us any the better for practising it.

This matter, however, is one on which I do not wish to insist. The important point seems to be that of which the advocates of Confession take no notice, namely, that there is another kind of shame beside the shame of exposure There is a shame which is "a glory and grace," and which has nothing to do with the "What will he think of me?" which is all they ever seem to contemplate. It cannot be a dream that there is a spiritual, no less than a physical, modesty implanted in all natures save the very lowest; and if there be such a sentiment, the mode by which it can most grossly be outraged is assuredly by the revelation to a human being of that which passes at the very meeting-place between the repentant soul and God. The shame of such violation of all the sanctities of the spiritual temple as is included in the idea of a "General Confession," or "making a clean breast" to a priest, seems (to one to whom the idea has not been familiarized) something actually portentous; something which must leave the soul which has thus exposed itself no shelter evermore even in the deepest recesses of the spiritual world. To have our whole past laid bare, if only in the crude, imperfect way in which words can describe it; to talk to a man of all that is most awful, most agonizing, and yet (if we have repented and been restored) most inexpressibly tender and sacred in our memories; to uncover every grave of dead sins in our "God's Acre," and exhume the contents for the autopsy of an ecclesiastical coroner,—all this is so purely shocking to the unsophisticated sense, that we feel as if, before it could be done, the soul must be drugged with false excitements. Of course we shall be told that it is to no ordinary human friend that auricular confession is made, but to a priest who stands as the representative of God, and holds the keys of remission from Him. Of the monstrous nature of the last pretension I shall not now speak; but of the fact that it *is* our priest, and not our brother, mother, friend, to whom we are called to make confession, is, I insist, an aggravation of the evil complained of, not a mitigation of it. Love, deep and perfect, the union of two souls filled with the same love to God, and wont to approach Him together, may indeed justify, because it sanctifies, confidences and self-revelations which would be hateful if made to one less near or dear. Though even in the tenderest friendship it is certain that many reservations must be made, yet a great deal which no one else may know, may, without any violation of what I have named spiritual modesty, be confided to the one who is "soul of our soul," the nearest to us of created beings, though yet far less near than our God.[1]

---

[1] It is remarkable that the Mosaic law of Confession says nothing about a priest, but makes the penitent confess to his companion.

But the relation of penitent and confessor, as understood by Christian churches, has nothing whatever to do with this union of hearts. There is nothing reciprocal in it, nor does the penitent suppose the priest has any interest in him beyond one of pure benevolence. For obvious reasons, it becomes especially dangerous and shocking for any such natural human affections to subsist where the sexes of the two are opposite. The confessor is not a friend, and has none of a friend's sacred rights. But he claims, on the other hand, to be just that very thing which it is most mischievous to employ, namely, a human "go-between," standing in the place of God to us, and therefore hindering us from accomplishing that one act wherein lies salvation, namely, looking straight up to God, and enduring as best we may the awful Light of Light shining full on our darkness. The intervention of a priest in such a moment must be tantamount, I conceive, to the nullification of half the purifying power of repentance. And, further, it must establish in our minds a tribunal which is not that of the Holy Spirit within us,—a Pardoner who is not our God. To get behind and beyond this priestly interloper, and once more come directly to the Father, must ever after be tenfold more difficult. In fact, I seriously question whether any man long accustomed to auricular confession can really so break the law of association of ideas as to thrust aside in hours of penitence the thought of his confessor, and think only simply of God against whom he has sinned, and to whom he desires once more to bring his sin-stained heart.

We have now seen reason to doubt that the endurance of the lower form of shame felt by a penitent in confession would be of moral advantage ; and we have seen (I apprehend) excellent reason for believing that the violation of sacred feelings which would form the higher shame, would prove spiritually injurious in an almost indefinite degree.

But it must not be forgotten that there are unhappily many natures to whom these arguments do not apply, for the simple reason that, by an odious inversion of healthy sentiment, they find self-exposure not a pain but a pleasure. Nobody who knows much of the world will be liable to fall into the error of supposing that every one who attends the Confessional does serious violence to himself, or herself, or makes any genuine sacrifice, by such an act. On the contrary, just as fashionable physicians are wearied by the needless pathological disclosures of egotistic patients, so, in all Catholic countries, fashionable confessors have complained of the fatal facility with which their penitents talk of the state of their souls, and detail their spiritual symptoms with as much obvious gratification as others find in describing those of their bodies. *On aime mieux dire du mal de soi-même que de n'en point parler,* says La Rochefoucauld, and the Confessional is often the best evidence of the truth of the remark. Is it needful to observe that to such sickly hysterical natures, whose souls possess no sanctuary which they are not willing at any moment to violate, there cannot be a worse peril than the presentation, in guise of a self-denying duty, of a practice which is really to them one of vicious self-indulgence?

Does any reader ask: Are we, then, never to be absolutely true to any one, never to stand wholly revealed to one single fellow-creature? Goethe says—most falsely as I take it—that we all have that concealed in our hearts which if revealed would make us an object of abhorrence to those who love us. Is this nightmare to haunt us for ever, and are we never to cast it off and feel we are free and honest, and may look the world in the face?

I believe that some feelings like these are at the bottom of a good deal of the favour which the suggestion of a revival of Confession has met with in England, and they have a right, undoubtedly, to be weighed in our estimate of its benefits and ill results. If I am not mistaken, the sentiment in question is essentially one belonging to what may be termed the second period of youth. We are then still in the age of fervent enthusiasms and of very partial self-knowledge. We have violated our early vows of heroic virtue, and are sore with the bruises of our falls. At such an age we naturally feel an intense desire to come into closest communion with the souls we love, and to be utterly and truly known to them, never cheating them of affection which we feel we do not deserve. We are tempted to pour out all the accusations against ourselves which even exaggerated self-reproach can dictate. But in later life and with calmer judgment, we recognize that such "auricular confessions" of love and friendship are in no way needful to place even the tenderest relationships on a footing of absolute candour and veracity. Nay, we learn to know that it is so impossible to see ourselves altogether truthfully (our own breath obscuring the mirror in which we attempt to gaze), and still more impossible to convey to another mind by spoken words what we truly are, that it is, in reality, little or no gain to genuine mutual understanding to interchange such confidences. If we do not add the history of our virtues to those of our faults; describe where we conquered as well as where we fell; how we struggled, no less than when we yielded to temptation; in a word, paint all the lights as well as all the shadows of our lives, we are in fact giving our friend a picture of ourselves as false in its own way as mere self-laudation would be in another. What sincerity really demands in friendship is, that there should be nothing in our outward conduct or inward desires or intentions *now*, which, if our friend should see and understand, would alter his opinion of us for the worse. He has a right to unlock our *hearts*, and see all that is there. God alone has right of entrance into the deep chambers of *memory*.

Thus, then, I apprehend, the thirst for self-revelation, which may lead some young or weak spirits to the Confessional, is one always to be outgrown with advancing wisdom. Still more certainly must it, I apprehend, be outgrown by advancing spiritual life, till a point be reached wherein Divine communion, ever enjoyed in the depths of the soul, would render the suggestion of such an exposure hateful as that of any other sacrilege.

To sum up the argument of the present paper. The advantages to be derived from the practice of Confession,—the benefits of self-knowledge, moral instruction and priestly guardianship,—cannot be weighed against the evils it involves,—the materializing of penitence, the enervation of the moral nature, and the desecration of the spiritual life. A method of combating sin which involves evils of such magnitude, becomes itself an evil. Even supposing that every tale of grossness and misuse be nothing but malignant falsehood, enough, and more than enough, remains in the inherent mischief of the practice of Confession to urge every friend of morality and religion to oppose it to the utmost of his power.

What is the true Confession? The life which shall be open and honest as the day, and yet whose inner springs shall rise pure from hidden depths where no defilement may reach them? It is not very hard to picture what such a life might be. Men go about to urge us to confess our *sins* alone, and to confess them to a single priest, while they are content that we keep closest silence to our nearest and dearest concerning much that we are, and more that we think. Let them extend their notions of honesty a little further.[1] Let them bid us speak out what we think, and live out what we speak; seem what we are, and be what we seem. Let them exhort us to have no secrets, save of sins long since repented and passed into God's keeping; and of generous deeds, in regard to which the left hand may not know what the right has done. Let them bid us strive for that noble state wherein we should feel assured that nothing could ever be discovered concerning us, in word, deed or thought, which would not make those who love us already, love us still more. And then let them add one counsel more concerning a part of life which in old times men heeded most of all should be honest, but which in these days is wrapped by thousands of us in a haze of obscurity, if not of deception. Let them bid us confess before friends and foes, everywhere, and at all times when the avowal may be called for, what we in our inmost hearts believe concerning God and duty and immortality; so that neither the fear of forfeiting the worldly advantages of orthodoxy on one side, or that of meeting the sneer of scepticism on the other, shall drive us one step out of the straight path of absolute sincerity.

In a recent sermon, Mr. Martineau spoke of keeping secrets "not *from* God, but *with* Him;" and advised his hearers to make it a rule "not to speak of everything which passes between the soul and God; not to betray every burden

---

[1] The self-told story of the lady (The World and the Church, p. 225) who went secretly from her father's house to Confession to Mr. Goodwin in a London church, and kept all her doings a mystery till after some interviews, is a very good sample of the way in which Auricular Confession makes a man or woman more honest. To tell our past sins to a stranger who has no natural right to know anything about us, while we hide our whole present course of action and thinking from the parents, brothers and sisters whose love and confidence we continue to accept,—this forsooth is to be specially pious and truthful!

He lays upon us, but to reserve somewhat which shall be His and ours alone." Between such a lesson as this and that of the Anglican Manuals of Confession which we have now reviewed, there seems to lie the whole width of the moral and spiritual horizon.

ESSAY XIV.

THE EVOLUTION OF MORALS AND RELIGION.[1]

[The following brief Essay, written while this book has been in the press, is here reprinted as supplementing the expression of the writer's views on the Development of Morals in Essay I.]

HISTORIES of the progress of the Intellect and of Religious Ideas have occupied the attention of scholars for a considerable time. It may be questioned whether we should not now direct our studies rather to the history of the Religious Sentiment, and to the development through the ages, not of human thoughts about God, but of human feelings towards Him. The furthest insight we are able to obtain into our own nature, seems to show that the share which ideas exercise in the production of feelings is superficial compared to the profound influence of feelings in the formation of opinions; and that the transmission of ideas by means of oral or written language, is, in moral and religious matters, of the smallest possible value, unless, by some extraneous means, the feelings may be brought up to the level whereto the ideas belong. Only in our day have the materials for anything like a sketch of the history of the Religious Sentiment been collected; and much yet remains obscure; but the outline of such a progress begins to be apparent. The Moral

[1] Reprinted from *The Manchester Friend*, January 15th, 1872.

Sense, out of which the higher part of religious feeling (all which distinguishes human piety from a dog's loyalty) must necessarily grow, is itself now recognized as a slowly developed thing, hardly perceptible in the savage, and only through long millenniums acquiring the shape in which we find it within the historic era. The barbaric "ages before morality," of which Mr. Jowett long ago spoke, have, as Mr. Bagehot remarks,[1] been rendered clear to us by the researches of Sir John Lubbock and Mr. Tylor into the state of savages at the present day; and, starting from this earliest period, we may now trace the gradual development together of the Moral Sense and Social Affections; and of the Religious Sentiment which grows with their growth and strengthens with their strength. Without in any way indorsing Mr. Darwin's hypothesis, that the Moral Sense is *nothing more* than the instincts of a social animal developed under the conditions of human life, we may gladly admit that,—even as the immortal part in us seems to be slowly built up within the scaffolding of our animal part, from the first germ of being, through infant and childish life up to manhood,—so the Moral Sense, which is the *sense of the soul*, is developed slowly likewise, not only in the individual, but also in the race, during the millenniums through which it has emerged from the brutal into the human.

1. At the earliest stage of religion, the savage had a vague conception of invisible Powers lurking behind the forces of nature, in sun and moon, star and thundercloud, in the mysterious beasts and serpents, in trees and stones. In other words, at this stage of Fetichism he possessed the Sentiments of awe, fear, and wonder,—but nothing higher. His gods could have no moral attributes, because his own moral nature was as yet too immature and cloudy to project any image of such qualities as Justice or Truth. He recog-

[1] *Fortnightly Review*, December, 1871.

nized neither an Ormuzd nor an Ahrimanes, but only unseen Wills as wayward and passion-led as his own.[1] To take a savage at this stage and endeavour to convey to him a true conception of the goodness of God, is labour thrown away. "Good," as one such barbarian said to a French missionary, "is when I take my enemy's wives. Evil is when he takes mine." The man who has no higher sense of goodness than this, is as incapable of feeling Divine goodness, as a table or a door is incapable of feeling the benevolence of its owner. According to the admirable simile used by a writer on Darwinism in *Macmillan's Magazine*, he is as little conscious of such character in God as a jelly-fish is of the presence of a man, whom a bird or a mouse will perceive and fear; and whom a dog will so far understand as to be able to love. Only through a long upward course, in which intellectual instruction will by no means perform the chief part, can the savage be brought to the level whereon he can have any comprehension of goodness, properly so called.

2. In the second stage, the gods are recognized to be Just, that is, to exercise a certain amount of judicial control over human affairs, precisely corresponding to the point which men's conception of justice has attained. This is the period at which Hesiod warns rapacious kings to fear Zeus, whose all-beholding eye witnesses their tyranny. But at the same epoch this justice-executing Zeus is unhesitatingly credited with horrible personal vices and base deceptions. Even long ages afterwards, when Pindar exhorts his hearers—

> Then, O man with holy fear,
> Touch the character of gods :
> Of their sacred nature say
> Nought irreverent, nought profane.

—he immediately proceeds to glorify in glowing verse one of the worst of the immoralities of Olympos. It is quite obvious

---

[1] See *ante*, p. 171.

that it never so much as crossed the poet's mind that it was "profane" to attribute to Zeus the grossest licentiousness. Such elevation as had taken place in the Moral Sense of the nation was as yet unreflected in the character attributed to the gods; and indeed, in this matter of the virtue of chastity, was probably hardly perceptible at all. It is this second stage of human religion to which poets have always looked back as the Golden Age—

> Quando al piacer nemica
> Non era la virtù;

—when there was no antithesis between pleasure and virtue, for the simple reason that all the virtue then apprehended concerned the externals of justice between man and man, and never touched the inner laws of personal purity, veracity, and sobriety. It is the ideal age of youth which St. Paul describes himself as having passed through: "For I was alive without the law once; but, when the commandment came, sin revived, and I died."

3. The third stage of religion is attained when the Moral Sense and the Affections have both received considerable development. Beyond the earlier vague and imperfect sense of Justice, the moral sense is now so far extended in the directions of Fidelity and Purity, that the conception of Divine Holiness begins to loom on the mental horizon, and the attribution to God of perfidy or licentiousness ceases to be endurable. The Affections, likewise, have grown in the direction of friendship, favouritism, and patriotism, so far, that the notion of God entertaining friendship for particular men, having favourites as a king might have, and loving the particular tribe, country, or town of the worshipper, begins to be a familiar part of the ideal of His character. The limitations in both cases are very obvious. The Holiness of God is not felt to exclude the possibility of His tempting His

creatures to sin, or inspiring immoral actions, even though His own nature is supposed to be pure. And, as the Affections of men, at this stage, are but slightly influenced by the moral qualities of the persons to whom they are directed, so Jehovah may "love Jacob and hate Esau," irrespective of the baseness of the one, and of the honest simplicity of the other. Further, as favouritism has always its counterpart in equally unreasonable dislikes, so the peculiar favour of God shown to certain men or tribes, always implies Divine hatred towards their neighbours and enemies.

This, then, the stage of belief in a partially holy, and partially loving God, is that at which we find nearly all the more religious nations of antiquity when we are first introduced to them; and it is, alas! the stage beyond which the civilized world has hardly advanced a step to this day. The Hebrews had manifestly attained to it in the age in which the Pentateuch was written, when God was in a measure recognized as holy, and yet was supposed to have inspired or rewarded many evil actions; and when He was believed to love "Abraham and his seed," and to hate the Egyptians and Canaanites. Only the later Isaiah, of all the Old Testament writers, soared entirely above this level, and felt that Jehovah loved Edom and Moab as well as Israel, and would reconcile all nations at last. In India, the hymns of the Rig-veda prove that in the very earliest epoch of recorded religious history, the sense of Divine holiness was strong enough to prompt confession of sin, and entreaties for pardon; while the belief in the partiality of the Deity for the Aryans, and his hatred for the Dasyus (their dark-skinned enemies), may be traced as clearly in the maledictory Psalms attributed to the Rishi Viswâmitra as in those of the Bible attributed to David. The Zoroastrians enjoyed, from the first, exceedingly high conceptions of the sanctity and beneficence of Ahura-mazda; but even He was invoked as the enemy of their enemies, albeit, with the blessed underlying faith that in the final day He would pardon Ahriman himself, and restore to His love all the souls in the universe. Practically, as we have said, the civilized world remains at this stage to the present hour. [The Christian, Jewish, and Moslem God, loves the Elect, the Chosen Race, the Faithful, and hates other men; condemning (according to the orthodox Christian creed) a vast number of them to eternal banishment from His presence, in darkness and torture.] He is adored as Holy, and, in a measure, men understand real holiness when they apply the word to Him, but they by no means feel the incongruity from which a thoroughly trained moral sense would revolt, in the attribution to this holy God of many acts recorded in their sacred writings; or of such a system of government as is unfolded in the plan of Atonement as commonly understood. The reason why they do not feel these monstrous derogations from the Divine perfections is obvious. It is because their own Sentiments of love and mercy, truth and justice, are as yet so imperfectly developed that even when accustomed to apply the terms expressive of goodness to God, they simply do not know what they involve. When their hearts are really full of love (as we see in the case of many living saints), their creeds hardly hamper them at all, and their intellectual errors hang so loosely as to be practically harmless. On the other hand, the lessons of Christ, repeated parrot-wise for sixty generations, have failed to bring men, who are *not* loving, to understand anything of the Divine goodness more than in that most imperfect and partial way which we have marked as the third stage of the religious sentiment.

4. Lastly, we may dimly foresee the fourth and final stage of religion, when the sense of what constitutes Holiness will be too lofty to permit of attribution to God of many of the

acts and modes of government which at present are ascribed to Him; and when men will have gained so much of the Divine power of loving and pitying the erring and the unlovely, that they will realize at last, the meaning of calling God the Father of All. No doubt Christ, when he uttered those marvellous sayings about the beatitude of loving our enemies, blessing those who curse us, and praying for those who despitefully use us and persecute us, had attained this exalted stage. He felt the Divine Fatherhood, as none before him, that we know of, had felt it, *because* he had in his own heart a power of pitying the sinful, and pardoning the offending, such as few, if any, had felt before. Even he, however, if we may trust the records, did not see the hideous anomaly involved in his own words, when he represented that same Divine Father as not pardoning all those who "despitefully used" *Him*, but casting them into "outer darkness" for ever. But it remains clear that in this direction must surely lie the path of progress in moral feeling which is to lead us at last to the joy of unbroken sympathy with God. Hitherto, while individual Christians have repeatedly performed heroic acts of forgiveness and kindness to their enemies, and while thousands have devoted their lives to the restoration of the vicious and the criminal, there has been yet hardly an approach to a general sentiment of love for the unlovely; or even a working theory of what that love should be, beyond the Schoolmen's barren distinction, between Love of Benevolence and Love of Complacency. Too many of us, instead of feeling the intense sense of the misery and hatefulness of sin out of which true pity for the sinner can alone arise, are disposed to make light of the evil with mere easy good nature, and so to be really further from the higher charity than those who harshly condemn and righteously abhor it. And, for our personal enemies, the men and women in many ways obnoxious to us, it yet remains almost an insoluble problem how we ought to act towards them. We lack the unselfish, magnanimous, deep-sighted love, for the struggling human spirit beneath its load of passion, meanness, vulgarity, and stupidity, which would inspire us with the right conduct. But only when we have attained this holy love, can our own spiritual progress flow on calmly and surely, and our communion with God cease to be fitful and often interrupted. Only when we ourselves love the unlovely as well as the lovely, shall we attain the goal of the religious life, and "be perfect as our Father in Heaven is perfect, who maketh his sun to rise on the evil and on the good, and sendeth rain on the just and on the unjust." The first stage of religion, when nothing but Power was felt; the second, when men believed God to be Just, but knew not that He was Holy; the third, when they felt Him to be Holy, but conceived of Him still as Partial, will all have been left far behind. We shall then feel and know that He is more than all this—that He is All-loving.

Well says Charles Voysey:—"The greatest reward which a generous, forgiving, loving life, can ever bring, must be to enable us to feel the Goodness of God." There is no use deceiving ourselves with the idea that we can learn His goodness, like an answer in a catechism, by the intellect alone. All that the intellect can help in the matter is but little, and that little chiefly of the negative sort. The sense must grow with our own moral growth. We must scale height after height before we see the heaven-high summit far off in the cloudless blue. Of course, at each step we are aided and cheered onward and upward by the view already attained. Once a man has begun to realize that God is *all which his heart craves to love and adore*, he has gained a level from which he can hardly altogether fall away again. All the disappointed affections of life are calmed, all its terrors of loneliness subdued, all its trials made endurable, by that deep rest of the soul. But there are further and further visions attainable of what His Goodness is, as we grow more good; and of what God's Love may be for us and for all men, as we ourselves love more divinely.

FINIS.

MISS FRANCES POWER COBBE'S WORKS.

1. RELIGIOUS DUTY. 8vo. Cloth. Published at 7s. 6d. 5s.

2. BROKEN LIGHTS. An Inquiry into the Present Condition and Future Prospects of Religious Faith. New Edition. 8vo. Cloth. 5s.

3. DAWNING LIGHTS. An Inquiry concerning the Secular Results of the New Reformation. 8vo. Cloth. 5s.

4. THANKSGIVING. A Chapter of Religious Duty. 12mo. Cloth. 1s.

5. ALONE TO THE ALONE. Prayers for Theists, by several Contributors. Crown 8vo. Cloth, gilt edges. 5s.

6. STUDIES, NEW AND OLD, OF ETHICAL AND SOCIAL SUBJECTS. 8vo. Cloth. Published at 10s. 6d. 5s.

7. ITALICS. Brief Notes on Politics, People, and Places in Italy in 1864. 8vo. Cloth. Published at 12s. 6d. 5s.

8. HOURS OF WORK AND PLAY. 8vo. Cloth. 5s.

May be had from her present Publishers,

WILLIAMS AND NORGATE,

14, HENRIETTA STREET, COVENT GARDEN, LONDON;
AND 20, SOUTH FREDERICK STREET, EDINBURGH.

14, Henrietta Street, Covent Garden, London;
20, South Frederick Street, Edinburgh.

CATALOGUE OF SOME WORKS

PUBLISHED BY

WILLIAMS AND NORGATE.

Beard (Rev. Chas.) Port Royal, a Contribution to the History of Religion and Literature in France. Cheaper Edition. 2 vols. Crown 8vo. 12s

Bopp's Comparative Grammar of the Sanscrit, Zend, Greek, Latin, Lithuanian, Gothic, German, and Slavonic Languages. Translated by E. B. Eastwick. Fourth Edition. 3 vols. 8vo. cloth 31s 6d

Brewster. The Theories of Anarchy and of Law: A Midnight Debate. By H. B. Brewster, Esq. Crown 8vo. parchment 5s

Christ (The) and the Fathers, or the Reformers of the Roman Empire; being a Critical Analysis of the religious thoughts and opinion derived from their lives and letters, as well as from the Latin and Greek Fathers of the Eastern and Western Empires until the Nicene Council, with a Brief Sketch of the Continuation of Christianity until the Present Day in accordance with the Comparative Method of Historical Science. By an Historical Scientist. 8vo. cloth 7s 6d

Cobbe (Miss F. P.) The Hopes of the Human Race, Hereafter and Here. Essays on the Life after Death. With a Preface having special reference to Mr. Mill's Essay on Religion. Second Edition. Crown 8vo. cloth 5s

Cobbe (Miss F. P.) Darwinism in Morals, and (13) other Essays. (Religion in Childhood, Unconscious Cerebration, Dreams, the Devil, Auricular Confession, &c. &c.) 400 pp. 8vo. cloth (pub. at 10s) 5s

Cobbe (Miss F. P.) The Duties of Women. A Course of Lectures delivered in London and Clifton. Second Edition. Crown 8vo. cloth 5s

Cobbe (Miss F. P.) The Peak in Darien, and other Riddles of Life and Death. Crown 8vo. cloth 7s 6d

Cobbe (Miss F. P.) A Faithless World. With Additions and a Preface. 8vo. cloth 2s 6d

Cobbe (Miss F. P.) Broken Lights. An Inquiry into the Present Condition and Future Prospects of Religious Faith. Third Edition. Crown 8vo. cloth 5s

Cobbe (Miss F. P.) Dawning Lights. An Inquiry concerning the Secular Results of the New Reformation. 8vo. cloth 5s

Cobbe (Miss F. P.) Alone to the Alone. Prayers for Theists, by several Contributors. Third Edition. Crown 8vo. cloth, gilt edges 5s

Echoes of Holy Thoughts: arranged as Private Meditations before a First Communion. Second Edition, with a Preface by the Rev. J. HAMILTON THOM, of Liverpool. Printed with red lines. Crown 8vo. cloth 2s 6d

Evolution of Christianity, The. By CHARLES GILL. Second Edition, with Dissertations in answer to Criticism. 8vo. cloth 12s

Gould (S. Baring) Lost and Hostile Gospels. An Account of the Toledoth Jesher, two Hebrew Gospels circulating in the Middle Ages, and extant Fragments of the Gospels of the First Three Centuries of Petrine and Pauline Origin. By the Rev. S. BARING GOULD. Crown 8vo. cloth. 7s 6d

Jones (Rev. R. Crompton) Hymns of Duty and Faith, selected and arranged. Second Edition. 247 pp. Foolscap 8vo. cloth 3s 6d

Mackay (R W.) Sketch of the Rise and Progress of Christianity. 8vo. cloth (pub. at 10s 6d) 6s

Mind: a Quarterly Review of Psychology and Philosophy. Contributions by Mr. Herbert Spencer, Professor Bain, Mr. Henry Sidgwick, Mr. Shadworth H. Hodgson, Professor Flint, Mr. James Sully, the Rev. John Venn, the Editor (Professor Croom Robertson), and others. Vols. I. to XII., 1876-87, each 12s. Cloth, 13s 12s per annum, post free

Oldenberg (Prof. H.) Buddha: his Life, his Doctrine, his Order. Translated by WILLIAM HOEY, M.A., D.LIT., Member of the Royal Asiatic Society, Asiatic Society of Bengal, &c., of Her Majesty's Bengal Civil Service. Cloth, gilt 18s

www.ingramcontent.com/pod-product-compliance
Lightning Source LLC
Chambersburg PA
CBHW022117290426
44112CB00008B/712